China's BRI
in
Different Regions of
the World

Cooperation, Contradictions and Concerns

Sapru House Soundings on Area Studies

China's BRI in Different Regions of the World

Cooperation, Contradictions and Concerns

Edited by

Sanjeev Kumar

KW Publishers Pvt Ltd
New Delhi

Indian Council of World Affairs
New Delhi

First reprint November 2023
Second reprint April 2024

ISBN 978-93-83445-64-6 Hardback

Published in India by Kalpana Shukla

KW Publishers Pvt Ltd
4676/21, First Floor, Ansari Road
Daryaganj, New Delhi 110 002
Phone: +91 11 43528107
Marketing: kw@kwpub.in
Editorial: production@kwpub.in
Website: www.kwpub.in

Contents

Foreword

India and China are two major economies of the world. Both have strategic and economic weight in the emerging global order. The developments in the realm of India's Foreign Policy and China's policies and perspectives are watched with great interest globally by the strategic community, invariably attracting the interest of academicians and scholars.

The Indian Council of World Affairs (ICWA) has been following the developments in China. The Council has been holding conferences, seminars, dialogues, lectures and outreach programmes on different dimensions of China, including its internal and external dynamics.

The Council has several publications focusing on the study of different dimensions of China, including The 18th National Congress of the Communist Party of China: A Major Turing Point for China; India-China Boundary Issues: Quest for Settlement; China: Confucius in the shadow; A China Primer: An Introduction to a Culture and a Neighbour and; China and the Eurasian Region: Geographic and Geopolitical Influences.

The main objective of the current study is to examine the Belt and Road Initiative (BRI) from the viewpoint of individual countries as well as regions across the globe. The implications of BRI in our neighbourhood, in particular, is a subject of interest and enquiry. The edited volume identifies and highlights several broad trends from different regions; and provides valuable insights in terms of analysing BRI and understanding the emerging perceptions and concerns in participating countries.

Indian position on BRI is clear and consistent. Connectivity initiatives must be based on universally recognised international norms. They must respect sovereignty and territorial integrity of nations and follow principles of openness, transparency and financial responsibility.

The ICWA scholars specialising in area studies have made valuable contributions and insights, in particular, Dr. Sanjeev Kumar, Senior Research Fellow, who has edited the volume. I am sure this will further enrich the scholarship and debate on the subject in all the quarters.

7 July 2022

Amb. **Vijay Thakur Singh**
Director-General
ICWA, New Delhi

Contributors

Dr. **Sanjeev Kumar** is a Senior Research Fellow at the Indian Council of World Affairs, New Delhi. He is also the Coordinator of the CSCAP-India National Committee at ICWA. He is a recipient of the ASIA Fellows Award and conducted field research in Shaanxi, Anhui, and Zhejiang provinces of China. He has participated in Track-2 and 1.5 dialogues with Chinese think tanks and multilateral institutions like CSCAP, ARF, SCO and BRICS. He completed related courses in the Visiting Program for Young Sinologists 2016 in Beijing. His research interests lie in the areas of China's foreign and neighbourhood policy, India-China relations, the political economy of China's development, and Chinese politics. Dr. Kumar has published research papers in these areas in reputed journals and contributed chapters in volumes published in India, China, and the US. His recent publication includes *China and the Eurasian Region: Geographic and Geopolitical Influences*, co-editor with Ambassador C V Ranganathan.

Dr. **Pragya Pandey** is a Research Fellow at the Indian Council of World Affairs (ICWA), New Delhi. She specialises in issues related to maritime security, Indian Ocean, Indo-Pacific and regional geopolitics. She has written extensively on these issues. Prior to joining the ICWA, Dr. Pandey was Assistant Professor at the Department of Political Science, Miranda House, University of Delhi. She has received her Ph.D from the Centre for Indo-Pacific Studies, School of International Studies, Jawaharlal Nehru University, New Delhi. She has co-edited volumes titled *Roads, Winds, Spices in the Western Indian Ocean: The Memory and Geopolitics of Maritime Heritage*, *KM Panikkar and the Growth of a Maritime Consciousness in India*, and *1982 UNCLOS Perspectives from the Indian Ocean*. She has presented papers at various national and international conferences and dialogues and has considerable publication to her credit.

Dr. **Rahul Nath Choudhury** is a Research Fellow at the Indian Council of World Affairs, New Delhi. His primary research interest includes foreign direct investments, multilateralism, political economy, geo-economics, and digital trade. He has diverse experience of working in both the public and the private sector in academia and the industry in various capacities. He has contributed to several book chapters and academic journals.

Dr. **Stuti Banerjee** is a Research Fellow engaged in research on North America and Latin America & the Caribbean, the Indo-Pacific, and the Arctic at the Indian Council of World Affairs, New Delhi. This includes producing analytical articles on the politics, economy, and strategic issues of the region. Prior to joining the ICWA, she was an Associate Fellow at the Centre for Air Power Studies (CAPS), New Delhi. She has worked as a Research Intern for the Observer Research Foundation. She has received her Ph.D. from the American, Canadian, and Latin American Studies Division, School of International Studies, Jawaharlal Nehru University, New Delhi.

Dr. **Ankita Dutta** is a Research Fellow at the Indian Council for World Affairs, New Delhi. She has done her Ph.D. in European Studies from the School of International Studies, Jawaharlal Nehru University, New Delhi. Prior to joining ICWA, she was associated with the Foundation for National Security Research, New Delhi as a research assistant and as an assistant editor. Her area of interest includes right-wing politics in Europe, integration policies in Europe, diversity studies, European Union and Politics.

Dr. **Dhrubajyoti Bhattacharjee** is a Research Fellow at the Indian Council of World Affairs, New Delhi. He received his M. Phil and Ph.D. from Jawaharlal Nehru University working extensively on Pakistan's foreign policy decision-making under civilian and military leadership. He has taught as an Assistant Professor in the Department of Political Science, Siliguri College for ten years, after which he has been involved in research with ICWA. His interest also includes India and Vietnam, ASEAN, Israel, terrorism, foreign policy decision making, India and Myanmar, South Asian politics, and political and strategic development in Pakistan and Afghanistan. He has published a book on *Pakistan Foreign Policy Decision Making* along with many research papers and contributed chapters in edited books. *Gandhi and the World* (2022) is his latest publication as co-editor.

Dr. **Teshu Singh** is a Research Fellow at the Indian Council of World Affairs, New Delhi. Earlier, she worked as a Research Fellow at Vivekananda International Foundation, New Delhi, and a Senior Research Officer at the Institute of Peace and Conflict Studies, New Delhi. She holds a Ph.D. in East Asian Studies from the University of Delhi, M.Phil in East Asian Studies from the University of Delhi, and an MA in Political Science from the University of Delhi. She was awarded the Huayu Enrichment scholarship in 2015 from TECC. She has presented papers at several national and international conferences on her subject. She has written extensively on her area of research. Her primary focus areas are China and Taiwan. She focuses on Chinese Foreign Policy, India-China Relations, China and Indo-Pacific, Belt and Road Initiative and Cross-Strait relations.

Dr. **Samatha Mallempati** is a Research Fellow at the Indian Council of World Affairs, New Delhi. She did her M.Phil and Ph.D. from the South Asian Division, School of International Studies, JNU, New Delhi, and Masters in Political Science from JNU. Her research interests include developments in India's neighbourhood, and foreign policy with a specific focus on Sri Lanka, Maldives, and Myanmar. She has published in various journals and regularly contributes to various websites on topics related to internal developments in Sri Lanka, Maldives, and Myanmar. She has edited two volumes, *India-Sri Lanka Relations: Is It Time for Reorientation of Policy?* (ICWA and KW Publishers, 2021) and *Enhancing India-Myanmar Ties: The Way Ahead* (ICWA and KW Publishers, 2021).

Dr. **Naresh Kumar B.K.** is a Research Fellow at the Indian Council of World Affairs, New Delhi. He studied in the South Asian Studies Division, School of International Studies, Jawaharlal Nehru University. Prior to joining ICWA, he worked as Assistant Director in the National Security Council Secretariat. Besides Nepal and Bhutan, his research interests also include foreign policy, national security, geopolitics, South Asia, and global strategic trends.

Dr. **Anwesha Ghosh** is a Research Fellow at the Indian Council of World Affairs, New Delhi. She has taught at the Willy Brandt School of Public

Policy, University of Erfurt, Germany as a Lecturer while conducting Post-doctoral research. She holds a doctoral degree in Peace and Conflict Studies from the University of Erfurt, an MPhil from the Institute of Foreign Policy Studies, Kolkata, and a double master's in History and Development Studies from the University of Calcutta and the University of Rome, La Sapienza respectively. She is the author of *Identity and Marginality in India, Settlement Experience of Afghan Migrants* (Routledge, 2019).

Dr. **Punit Gaur** is a Research Fellow at the Indian Council of World Affairs. He has been associated with Eurasian National University, Nur-Sultan, Kazakhstan as Foreign Expert since 2016. He is also associated with many universities as Visiting Professor such as Bukhara State University, Uzbekistan, Al-Farabi Kazakh National University, Almaty, and Karaganda State University, Kazakhstan. Prior to this, Dr. Gaur was associated with the Centre for Research in Rural and Industrial Development (CRRID), Chandigarh as Associate Fellow and was engaged in a project "Central Asia between many Silk Roads: Indian Policy at the Crossroads" as Project Director, sponsored by ICSSR, India. Earlier, he worked as Assistant Professor (Central Asia) with the same institute CRRID. He has published research papers in books and journals and has presented papers in many national and international seminars in India, Kazakhstan, and other countries.

Dr. **Himani Pant** is a Research Fellow at the Indian Council of World Affairs, New Delhi. She has done her Ph.D. from the Centre for European Studies, School of International Studies, Jawaharlal Nehru University. Her doctoral thesis focused on "The European Union and Russia in their Common Neighbourhood: A Case Study of Georgia and Ukraine, 2004-2016." Prior to joining ICWA, she worked at the Observer Research Foundation and Vivekananda International Foundation. She was also a Visiting Research Scholar at the Katholieke Universiteit Leuven, Belgium in 2018. Her research focuses on developments in Russia, European Union, and Eastern Europe.

Dr. **Jojin V. John** is an Assistant Professor, School of International relations and Politics, Mahatma Gandhi University, Kerala. Previously Dr. John worked at the Indian Council of World Affairs as Research Fellow for East Asia for five years. Before joining ICWA he taught political science in Christ University, Bangalore and held visiting research positions at National Chengchi University, Taipei; Institute of Chinese Studies, Delhi; Seoul National University and Academy of Korean Studies, Korea. Dr. John received Ph.D. from the School of International Studies, Jawaharlal Nehru University. He has several publications to his credit, including book chapters and articles that appeared in academic journals including *Copenhagen Journal of Asian Studies*, *China Report*, *The Journal of International Relations*, *Strategic Analysis*, *India Quarterly* and *Area Studies*.

Dr. **Sudeep Kumar** is a Research Fellow at the Indian Council of World Affairs, New Delhi. His specialisation is in Chinese Politics, Chinese Foreign Policy, and China-India diplomatic relations. He has been awarded his Doctoral degree in "Political Theory" (2015-20) from the Department of Politics at East China Normal University, Shanghai. Earlier, he completed his M.Phil degree in "Chinese Studies" and a Masters degree in "Politics & International Relations" (2010-15) from the School of International Studies, Jawaharlal Nehru University, New Delhi. He has published research papers in peer-reviewed international journals and also made presentations in international seminars and conferences.

Dr. **Temjenmeren Ao** is a Research Fellow on Southeast Asia at the Indian Council of World Affairs, New Delhi. Prior to this he worked as an Associate Fellow at the Centre for Air Power Studies, where he completed a project titled, "China's Aerospace Sector: A Study on its Rise through Transfers of Technology". His area of interest includes the study on the US-China relations, India's relations with the ASEAN states in particular the evolving political, economic, and security engagements. He completed his Masters of Arts in Economics from the Centre for Economic Studies and Planning, School of Social Sciences, Jawaharlal Nehru University (JNU), Delhi, and holds a Ph.D. in International Relations from the School of International Studies, JNU, Delhi.

Dr. **Fazzur Rahman Siddiqui** is a Senior Research Fellow at the Indian Council of World Affairs, New Delhi. He has earned his M.Phil and Ph.D. in West Asian Studies from the School of International Studies, JNU, New Delhi. His area of specialization is Political Islam, Socio-Cultural, Strategic, and Identity Politics in the Arab world. His research area also includes the foreign policy of the WANA region and over the years, he has written extensively on the Arab uprising and emerging geopolitics across the region. He is the author of five books. His most recent book is *Arab World in Transition and the Quest for a New Regional Order* (Macmillan, 2022). His other books include "*The Political Islam and the Arab Uprising: Islamist Politic in Changing Time* (Sage, 2017); *Selected Readings on enduring challenges in West Asia and North Africa* (Meena Book, 2018).

Dr. **Arshad** is a Research Fellow at the Indian Council of World Affairs, New Delhi. He is interested in West Asia and North Africa regions. He has completed his Ph.D. from the Center for the West Asian Studies, Jawaharlal Nehru University. His writings appeared in *Contemporary Review of Middle East, Pan African Journal of Governance and Development, South Asia Monitor,* and *South Asia Democratic Forum.*

Dr. **Sankalp Gurjar** is a Research Fellow with the Indian Council of World Affairs, New Delhi. He has completed his Ph.D. from the Department of International Relations, South Asian University (A university established by SAARC nations), New Delhi. East and Southern Africa, Geopolitics of Horn of Africa, Great Powers and Africa, and the emerging dynamics of the Western Indian Ocean are his areas of interest. His writing has appeared, among others, in *India Quarterly, Strategic Analysis, African Affairs,* and *International Affairs*. He writes regularly for English as well as Marathi publications.

Dr. **Athar Zafar** is a Senior Research Fellow at the Indian Council of World Affairs, New Delhi. He is head of the newly established 'SCO Study Centre' at ICWA. Besides, he is coordinator of CICA Think Tank Forum from ICWA. He is engaged in academic research on Central Asia and the Caucasus regions. His studies also include Afghanistan, Iran, and Russia, especially from a connectivity perspective. Apart from academic activities, at the Council, he coordinates the annual India-Central Asia Dialogue held at Track II as well as participation in the annual SCO Forum meetings. Before joining ICWA he was associated with BBC. He has done his Ph.D. from Jawaharlal Nehru University, New Delhi. He also knows Persian and Tajiki languages.

Introduction

On 29 November 2012, two weeks after his appointment as the General Secretary of the Communist Party of China (CPC), Xi Jinping visited the National Museum in Beijing, accompanied by his colleagues from the Politburo's Standing Committee of the CPC, and for the first time talked about the idea of 'Chinese Dream' and defined it as the 'great rejuvenation of the Chinese nation'. The Party frames the Chinese Dream from the perspective of 'reform, opening up, and socialist modernization'. Further, speaking at the Boao Forum for Asia in March 2015, President Xi Jinping elaborated on his idea of a community of common destiny (CCD). While CCD denotes 'centre of the world' approach, Chinese experts have noted that building CCD faces several challenges, including land and territorial disputes as well as a low level of political trust between China and its some neighbours.

The Belt and Road Initiative (BRI) has been hailed as the 'project of the century', in the Xi Jinping era, also known as 'the third era'. It has been cited by Chinese experts as a 'critical instrument' to realise the CCD and has been directly linked to the Chinese Dream—political and strategic concepts proposed by China in the third era. The Global Development Initiative (GDI) proposed by President Xi Jinping in September 2021 makes the debate interesting as some experts see it as an 'expansion' of BRI.

The BRI has been projected as a 'cornerstone' of China's foreign policy objective. Chinese President Xi Jinping had declared the proposal in his two speeches delivered outside China (in Kazakhstan and in Indonesia) in 2013 taking into account historical narratives about the ancient Silk Road. The declaration of the initiative to the world by China is nearing a decade. This sets the stage for evaluating the implementation and performance, as well as the underlying principles, norms, practice and implications of the initiative from academic perspectives.

The main objective of the study is to examine Chinese policies with regard to BRI from the viewpoint of individual countries as well as regions and continents across the globe. The comprehensive study has been conducted by scholars at the Indian Council of World Affairs specialising in various countries/regions of the world.

An understanding of China's BRI since 2013 must begin with the Chinese domestic context as well as important thematic issues of contemporary times having direct bearing on the subject. Four chapters in Part I of the book aim to fulfil this objective. The first chapter by Dr. Sanjeev Kumar argues that BRI is a result of a convergence of a number of Chinese domestic drivers, such as the timing of strategic opportunities for China and desire to be a dominant power in Asia and the world; to capitalise excess capacity in traditional Chinese industries; to make a positive contribution to the development of it's western region; and secure the requirement of energy for economy. It also examines the domestic conceptual discourse in relation to BRI and spells out contradictions in perspectives. Further, the chapter discusses important policy pronouncements and predicaments over the years.

In his report to the 18th National Congress of the Communist Party of China (in November 2012) Chinese President Hu Jintao highlighted the country's objective to 'build China into a maritime power'. While China is in the process of realising its stated goal, recent literature from China has also referred to the concept of the Free and Open Indo-Pacific (FOIP) as a means to challenge its BRI which is not an objective of the FOIP. The second chapter by Dr. Pragya Pandey focuses on all relevant issues related to the maritime aspects of the initiative. It investigates China's strategic Maritime Silk Road (MSR) initiative by highlighting some of the key projects undertaken so far and evaluates larger implications of MSR for participating countries. The chapter analyses the role of Chinese domestic and strategic factors and their impact on the strategic balance in the India Ocean Region (IOR). It argues that MSR is an ambitious project but its expansive, non-transparent and unsustainable nature under BRI, as well as China's increasing footprint in the Indian Ocean, assertive actions in the South China Sea (SCS) and push in the South Pacific have caused apprehensions among the regional countries.

The third chapter by Dr. Rahul Nath Choudhury examines the economic implications of the BRI in terms of apparent benefits and involved risks. The chapter argues that the participating countries are benefitting to some extent from their increased trade with China and Chinese investment flows. However, along with these benefits, BRI also involves a threat for the participants as BRI projects in many countries have been criticised for their ambiguous bidding process, offering the contract mostly to Chinese companies, inflated costs, and for employing Chinese labourers by depriving the locals.

The fourth chapter jointly written by Dr. Stuti Banerjee and Dr. Ankita Dutta locates BRI in the larger context of strategic competition between the US and China. Studied from the US perspective, the chapter sees a significant challenge to the US economic, political, climate change, security, and global health interests. The chapter argues that the geo-political goals associated with the BRI have significant economic and strategic consequences for the US. It finds a visible shift in the US policy documentation where China has been termed as a strategic competitor, politically, economically, militarily and technologically. Needless to say, the emerging narrative in the US about its relations with China has implications for countries and regions across the world.

Part II of the book consists of chapters on countries of South Asia. In recent times, there has been a rise in China's profile in South Asia. Chinese experts have used terms such as 'new springtime' in China-South Asia relations, 'rediscovery of the strategic status of South Asia' and even 'most relevant region with regard to the rise of China'. It has become a very important region for China as its 'domestic periphery' presents a significant threat to its national security. These peripheral areas are linked to neighbouring countries of South Asia and Central Asia. Hence, the BRI has reinforced the strategic importance of South Asia.

The fifth chapter of the book by Dr. Dhrubajyoti Bhattacharjee analyses the flagship project of BRI, namely the China-Pakistan Economic Corridor (CPEC). Initially, the CPEC was highlighted as a 'game changer' both in China and Pakistan. However, the nature of investment, the controversies associated with the route of the corridor in

Pakistan, conflict in Balochistan, as well as the manner in which Pakistani civilian and military administration have become embroiled in the multi-billion dollar project, has made the CPEC more of a challenge not only to Pakistan but the entire region. It is noteworthy that the strategic agenda has been pursued by China despite large-scale protests against the project in the last few years and sovereignty-related concerns consistently raised by India.

The sixth chapter on Bangladesh by Dr. Teshu Singh explores the status of China's BRI projects in the country. It argues that Bangladesh sees BRI as an opportunity for national development but has 'very cautiously' moved with the BRI as it is aware of the risks involved. The chapter sees BRI as a manifestation of the Chinese Dream and argues that the Chinese concept of "community of common destiny" in Asia runs contradictory to the principle of non-interference in internal affairs.

The next chapter by Dr. Samatha Mallempati on BRI in Sri Lanka and Maldives is understandably a little lengthy, given the recent developments in China-Sri Lanka and China-Maldives relations. The chapter looks at China's relations with the two littoral states in the 21st century, and investments by China, Sri Lankan domestic responses to China's role as well as political and security implications. The issue of 'debt trap' in Sri Lanka has been a matter of intense debate as the country had to hand over its port on a 99-year lease to China. The recent economic crisis in Sri Lanka has intensified debate about China in Sri Lanka. Mainstream discourse in Sri Lanka accepts that loans taken from China to build mega infrastructure projects are difficult to repay due to higher interest rates, it also suggests that there is a lack of transparency in agreements signed and raises questions of the sustainability of some big projects in a small economy like Sri Lanka. The author argues that there are visible differences between China and Sri Lanka as China is determined to engage with Sri Lanka on its own terms. The domestic discourse in the Maldives is critical of the way the FTA has been rushed through the Parliament by President Yameen administration and passed without sufficient consultation in the country. In recent times, China has been asked to restructure the debt by the Maldives, but the request is pending.

The eighth chapter by Dr. Naresh Kumar B. K. analyses the BRI projects in Nepal. His chapter establishes that though the BRI began with much optimism and fanfare in Nepal, the projects remain almost a non-starter. The chapter argues that gradually, buoyancy is replaced by concerns or fear over the Chinese 'debt trap' and Nepal's stated preference for grants over loans. The author notes that these factors would only hinder the progress of the projects in the foreseeable future.

The next chapter by Dr. Anwesha Ghosh examines China-Afghanistan relations, especially after the Taliban seized power in Afghanistan in August 2021. The chapter notes that BRI has not featured in Beijing's list of priorities in Afghanistan so far. Interestingly, the chapter offers some projections about China's Afghanistan policy and observes that China is unlikely to commit itself to any substantial investment or playing any greater role in Afghanistan and it may stick to a wait-and-watch policy.

Part III of the volume consists of six chapters focusing on China's neighbouring regions and countries; such as Central Asia, Russia, East Asia, and Southeast Asia. President Xi had announced the BRI first time in Central Asia and the region is extremely important as it works as a gateway to overland route across Eurasia. China is an immediate neighbour of Central Asia and shares boundaries with three Republics of the region, Kazakhstan, Kyrgyzstan and Tajikistan. China's policy in Central Asia has been primarily aimed at safeguarding its national security interests, resource security and economic development. In this background, the tenth chapter by Dr. Punit Gaur examines China's BRI approach in Central Asia and terms it as neo-mercantilist, which is contradictory to the idea of BRI. One is aware that BRI has not radically changed the Chinese investment profile in Central Asia. The study argues that the primary reasons for this renewed Chinese interest have been attributed to domestic factors such as the need to maintain stability on its borders, especially in the western part of China, secure export markets and energy supplies, and to reduce the gap between the eastern and western parts of China's development. While analysing the issues related to BRI, the author refers to occasional clashes between Chinese migrants and locals, leading to social disruption in the respective countries. Protests have broken out in several China-controlled factories and construction sites against China's attempt to use the Chinese workforce, offering modest wages, working conditions, and against the ecological effect of Chinese enterprises.

The next chapter has been written by Dr. Himani Pant, it is on Russia-China cooperation and the BRI. The author argues that Russia and China are not allies but their relations have prospered at an unprecedented pace since 2014. Unlike Russia, China has the economic might which it has been using towards enhancing its global footprint by means of economic integration projects such as the BRI. The conflict in Ukraine has also highlighted the limitations of their partnership, which can pose obstacles to future engagement. While the two countries increasingly share common interests and their respective antagonisms with the Western economies are likely to have adverse implications on China's integration projects.

The twelfth chapter by Dr. Jojin V. John examines Japan's nuanced approach to BRI. The chapter argues that Japan's response has evolved from an initial balancing approach to complex engagement featuring conditional cooperation and outright competition driven by a complex mix of strategic, economic and normative considerations. The chapter argues that Japan has been treading a middle path between endorsement and containment while enhancing its position as a leading infrastructure development actor by upholding a normative and rules-based order. The competitive dimension of Japan's response involves stepping up Tokyo's infrastructure development commitments and building an international coalition under the Free and Open Indo-Pacific framework. The thirteenth chapter again by Dr. John analyses responses from another East Asian country-South Korea. The country is not directly a part of any designated BRI project, however, South Korea has shown interest since the announcement of the initiative. It viewed BRI as complementing its own efforts to integrate the Korean Peninsula into Eurasia through industrial and multi-modal transport linkages. However, South Korea now undertakes a cautious approach to BRI largely due to the prevalent negative narratives of BRI and the intensification of the US-China strategic competition.

The fourteenth chapter by Dr. Sudeep Kumar analyses China-Mongolia relations in general and China-Mongolia-Russia Economic Corridor (CMREC) in particular. He argues that the rise of China intensified the 'China Threat' debate in Mongolian policy circle. He highlights Mongolia's environmental and ecological stakes in the context of building connectivity and corridor as part of China's BRI. He argues that the primary motive behind China's BRI is domestic such as, closing the developmental gap between coastal and non-coastal regions, utilising excessive manufacturing capacity, putting its foreign currency reserve to use, and securing high-quality development in the manufacturing sector to bolster internal political stability, which has been a crucial aspect in generating political legitimacy for the Communist Party of China (CPC).

The fifteenth chapter on economic statecraft through BRI in Southeast Asia by Dr. Temjenmeren Ao covers all ten countries of the region in a comprehensive manner. The geography, as well as available economic opportunities, makes the region a crucial and strategic for China. He highlights that BRI provides opportunities not only for China but for the countries in Southeast Asia. However, challenges also exist in the implementation of various BRI projects considering the divergence in terms of environmental, social, and security risks. This has resulted in regional pushbacks from some of Southeast Asian countries, such as Malaysia suspending the construction of the East Coast Rail Link (ECRL) and Myanmar downsizing some projects. Further, Vietnam and Thailand have taken a more assertive stance in negotiating the terms of the BRI-related projects; while Malaysia, the Philippines, and Indonesia have been very cautious.

Part IV of the book discusses BRI in the Arab World, situated in the converging area of the Asian and African countries. Chapters 16 and 17 cover the broader region of West Asia and North Africa (WANA) and complement each other in terms of their regional focus. The paper by Dr. Fazzur R. Siddiqui covers mainly the WANA region. The author argues that the WANA region occupies a central place in the vision of BRI because of abundance of hydrocarbon resources in the region. His assessment shows that investment through BRI has largely been welcomed in the region. However, many do not see BRI as an opportunity for their jobless youth as Chinese companies employ both their own money and labour to a large extent. Further, some experts think that the cultural differences between the host and migrants may provoke conflict in future. The other paper by Dr. Arshad focuses on North Africa, the Levant, and Gulf to provide a holistic picture of China's investments in the Arab World. It argues that BRI is a principal policy tool of China to expand its presence in the region. This can be termed as an era of new Arab-China engagement. The study highlights the role of the US and China in the emerging power dynamics in the region, and refers to concerns regarding transparency of projects and the issue of 'debt trap'.

Part V of the book brings experiences and responses from three different continents, i.e. Europe, Africa and Latin America and the Caribbean with regard to China's BRI. In the recent past, China-Europe relationship has become increasingly unstable. The EU and China held their 23rd bilateral Summit in virtual format on 1 April 2022. The Summit could not produce a joint statement or even a list of agreed deliverables, due to differences of opinions on matters of interest and concerns. The chapter by Dr. Ankita Dutta explores China's BRI in terms of narratives and counter-narratives from Europe and highlights the different aspects of debate among the European countries. Through BRI, Beijing aims to connect its hinterland to Europe through Central Asia. The BRI projects in Europe rest on four main pillars—rail, road, maritime and digital routes. The chapter argues that the EU has repeatedly highlighted the issues related to norms and procedures, labour standards, debt sustainability, and transparency of the BRI projects. Other major concerns for the EU remain China gaining control of strategic assets such as ports, airports, etc.; and the risks of weakening environmental, social, or governance standards.

The next chapter on Africa by Dr. Sankalp Gurjar argues that the BRI in Africa has to be understood as part of China's continuing engagement with Africa. It stresses that the Chinese presence in Africa is a structural reality. The study focuses on some of the broad trends and major developments that are clearly discernible in the context of BRI and Africa. It investigates the status of infrastructure projects such as ports, airports, Digital Silk Road, railway and highways and notes that the port projects in East and Southern Africa are yet to take off. Many are mired in the domestic politics of the host countries. The railway projects implemented by China have improved the connectivity. However, these projects are expensive and with the looming economic crisis in Ethiopia and the inability of the Kenyan economy to take off as expected, have turned these projects into white elephants. Uganda has acknowledged that the airport modernisation with investments from China has been an enormously expensive deal. Many other projects that were in the pipeline are now either renegotiated or cancelled altogether. The chapter concludes that it remains to be seen whether the BRI will be successful in Africa or not.

The twentieth chapter by Dr. Stuti Banerjee explores BRI in terms of expectations and challenges it is facing in Latin America and the Caribbean. The region was not part of BRI when the initiative was announced. However, now 21 countries of the region have signed cooperation agreements with China. BRI in Latin America, Central America and the Caribbean has allowed China to strengthen its presence in the region that has been dominated by the US. The chapter argues that some larger economies of the region such as Brazil, Colombia and Mexico have yet to sign cooperation agreements but they are strengthening their relations with China. Even nations, which have not officially joined the BRI due to political or other reasons, can still benefit from China's approach to outward investments. This has blurred the differences between BRI and non-BRI projects in the region. There are concerns in the region about commodity dependence and the unsustainable environmental and social impacts of ties between China and LAC. The cooperation with China is not without its risks, however, the governments and businesses in the region believe the benefits may outweigh the risks.

It is close to a decade since the announcement of the BRI was made; any comprehensive analysis of the subject must include the impact of COVID-pandemic and conflict in Ukraine, which has significantly impacted the prospects of BRI projects. The final section and the chapter by Dr. Athar Zafar investigate BRI in the context of the twin challenges of our recent times, i.e., pandemic and Russia-Ukraine conflict. The chapter highlights the importance of Chinese investment for many recipient countries and notes that the lack of transparency in BRI projects is a major drawback. He also refers to reduction of Chinese investment by 54 per cent in 2020 compared to 2019. This is a significant data to understand the journey and status of BRI as well as its linkages with the Chinese economy. The early enthusiasm about investment in recipient countries seems to have reduced substantially. Significantly, the chapter looks at future scenarios and argues that the COVID-19 pandemic and Russian military operations in Ukraine have created dilemmas over projects' implementation and sustainability in some areas. Finally, the Epilogue covers reflections from various regions and countries.

The factors discussed above in different chapters including problems associated with the BRI bring the issue of multilateralism to the centre stage. China has been experimenting with two parallel but contrasting models for its economic outreach to various regions—the BRI and the Asian Infrastructure and Investment Bank (AIIB). BRI was announced by China without any prior consultation/dialogue with prospective partners and stakeholders. Countries were invited to join the initiative and no serious effort was made to build consensus on the main policies and principles governing the BRI. Some adjustments were announced during the Second Belt and Road Forum in 2019 after the project faced backlash in different regions, including South and Central Asia. The second model of AIIB follows a more consensual approach. The proposal to establish AIIB was put forward in October 2013 by China, the same year that the BRI was launched. A dialogue-driven process was initiated, which took about two years of negotiations with prospective members, and then AIIB was officially launched in January 2016. The process adopted by AIIB was able to build consensus on important principles governing the multilateral institutions such as transparency, accountability and universally recognised norms as well as policymaking and governance. India chose to be a founder member of AIIB as a dialogue-driven consultative process was adopted by China to build consensus on main governing principles. Therefore, it is pertinent to highlight the importance of AIIB model of consensual initiative over the BRI's unilateral initiative. India will certainly continue to engage with consensus-based initiatives since such initiatives allow all members to formulate and shape policy in a consultative process (Raghavan, 2021 and Kumar, 2021).

In his speech at the second Belt and Road Forum held in Beijing (in April 2019) President Xi noted that "We need to act in the spirit of multilateralism, pursue cooperation through consultation and keep all participants motivated" (MFA PRC, 2019). However, in all multilateral endeavours under President Xi Jinping, the BRI remains the 'most contradictory' (Bhalla, 2022). It was announced unilaterally as a 'public good' for the world, yet was posited as a multilateral initiative. The project has been cited as President Xi's biggest contribution to the 'public good' which adds to the "concept of international economic cooperation and the practice of multilateralism". Yet, nine years into its announcement, it remains essentially a set of bilaterally negotiated agreements with over 140 countries, and does not follow the norms of multilateral institutions including transparency, compliance, consensus building and monitoring, norms which are central to other financial multilateral institutions like the AIIB (Bhalla, 2022). This is perhaps the most important contradiction facing BRI.

The BRI was announced as an economic and connectivity initiative, however, significant changes are evident over the years. China's Foreign Minister Wang Yi attended the Third 'China+Central Asia' Foreign Ministers' Meeting on 9 June 2022. In this context, a document released by China's Foreign Ministry noted "We should coordinate efforts to safeguard security in both traditional and non-traditional areas, deepen security cooperation for jointly building the Belt and Road Initiative…" (MFA PRC, 2022). In other words, security issue/cooperation has now become a part of the BRI agenda. It certainly challenges the economic narrative put forward by China since the launch of the project.

Finally, another contradiction facing BRI can be understood from the conceptual discourse highlighted in President Xi Jinping's era. BRI projects have been seen as a 'critical instrument' for realising the goal of 'community of common destiny', which is essentially a political and strategic concept with China at its centre. This aspect has been analysed in detail in the first chapter.

Sanjeev Kumar

References

Bhalla, Madhu (2022). "China's Multilateral Thrust under Xi Jinping: Will it Reshape the Global Order?" Public lecture at NMML, New Delhi on 9 March 2022.

Hillman, Jonathan E. (2021). *The Emperor's New Road: China and the project of the Century* ,Washington DC, CSIS.

Kumar, Sanjeev (2021). "AIIB at Five: India's Engagements" New Delhi, 21 May 2021, at https://www.icwa.in/show_content.php?lang=1&level=3&ls_id=6042&lid=4153. Accessed on 30 May 2022.

Raghavan, TCA (2021). "Preface", in Manish (ed.), *The Belt and Road Initiative: Implications for India*, New Delhi: Pentagon, pp. viii-ix.

MFA, PRC, (2022). "Wang Yi Attends the Third "China+Central Asia" Foreign Ministers' Meeting", 9 June 2022, at https://www.fmprc.gov.cn/mfa_eng/zxxx_662805/202206/t20220609_10700621.html#:~:text=On%20June%208%2C%202022%20local,Prime%20Minister%20and%20Foreign%20Minister

MFA, PRC (2019). "Xi Jinping Attends the Opening Ceremony of the Second Belt and Road Forum for International Cooperation (BRF) and Delivers a Keynote Speech", 26 April 2019, Beijing, at https://www.fmprc.gov.cn/ce/cgmb/eng/zgyw/t1659374.htm

Part I
BRI: Thematic Perspectives

1. China's BRI since 2013: Domestic Drivers, Conceptual Discourse and Policy Pronouncements

Sanjeev Kumar

Abstract

The chapter traces the origin and evolution of China's BRI since 2013. It argues that BRI is the result of a convergence of Chinese domestic drivers such as the time of strategic opportunity and desire to be a dominant power in Asia and the world; excess capacity in traditional industries; regional development strategy; and requirement of energy for sustained economic development. It also examines domestic conceptual discourse and BRI's linkages with the concept of Chinese Dream and the Community of Common Destiny (CCD), a strategic concept for Asia and the world highlighted by President Xi Jinping. Further, it attempts to document and examine important policy pronouncements made by the Chinese government from time to time with regard to the BRI and briefly analyses the challenges and risks involved with the BRI.

I. BRI: A Chinese Move

Chinese President Xi Jinping, in his speech at the Nazarbayev University in Astana (now Nursultan), Kazakhstan, titled "Promote Friendship Between Our People and Work Together to Build a Bright Future" on 7 September 2013, drew inspiration from the ancient Silk Road and noted that "to forge closer economic ties, deepen cooperation and expand development space in the Eurasian region, we should take an innovative approach and jointly build an 'economic belt along the Silk Road'" (MFA PRC, 2013). Later, while speaking at Indonesian Parliament in Jakarta on 2 October 2013, he traced back the history of ancient Maritime Silk Road and stated that China will ... vigorously develop a maritime partnership in a joint effort to build the Maritime Silk Road of the 21st century" (ASEAN China Centre, 2013). This was for the first time President Xi talked about the new initiative of building the Silk Road Economic Belt and the 21st-Century Maritime Silk Road, subsequently known as One Belt One Road (OBOR) and later/now known as Belt and Road Initiative (BRI). The initiative is still known as yi dai yi lu (一带一路) in the Chinese language.

After the announcement of the initiative in September-October 2013, China invited and expected countries of the projected route from Asia, Africa and Europe to endorse and join the initiative. The fact remains that the initiative was announced as a Chinese project in a unilateral fashion, without prior consultations with prospective partner countries. Initially, adequate details about the projects were not available. However, Chinese officials and state media emphasised importance of the project, it was highlighted as a major element of Chinese foreign policy and became a key focus of China's diplomacy in 2014 and 2015 (Swaine, 2015).

In March 2015, National Development and Reform Commission (NDRC), Ministry of Foreign Affairs, and Ministry of Commerce of the PRC, with the State Council's authorisation issued, the document "vision and actions on jointly building Silk Road Economic Belt and 21st-Century Maritime Silk Road" (Vision document hereafter). This was the first major document giving details and sharing the government's vision and objectives of the project. The vision document notes that the Silk Road Economic Belt focuses on bringing together China, Central Asia, Russia and Europe (the Baltic); linking China with the Persian Gulf and the Mediterranean Sea through Central Asia and West Asia; and connecting China with Southeast Asia, South Asia and the Indian Ocean. The 21st-Century Maritime Silk Road is designed to go from China's coast to Europe through the South China Sea and the Indian Ocean in one route, and from China's coast through the South China Sea to the South Pacific, in the other (NDRC, 2015). In 2015, China also launched Digital Silk Road as a part of BRI.

The government maintained that China will actively promote the DSR to construct 'a community of common destiny in cybre space'.

In June 2017, a document titled Vision for Maritime Cooperation under the BRI was jointly released by the NDRC and the State Oceanic Administration of China. The document notes that China will deepen ocean cooperation by fostering closer ties with countries along the Road, supported by the coastal economic belt in China (NDRC, 2017).

The vision document suggests that countries along Belt and Road should strive for following five major goals: they should promote policy coordination; infrastructure connectivity, unimpeded trade, financial integration and people-to-people bonds. These principles were also highlighted in other major documents including joint statements issued during First Belt and Road Forum (2017) as well as Second Belt and Road Forum (2019). Subsequently, industrial cooperation was added as the sixth goal of the initiative in April 2019 (Office of the Leading Group for BRI, 2017).

Further, China announced following six economic corridors as a part of BRI: (i) New Eurasian Land Bridge Economic Corridor, (ii) China-Mongolia-Russia Economic Corridor, (iii) China-Central Asia-West Asia Economic Corridor, (iv) China-Indochina Peninsula Economic Corridor, (v) China-Pakistan Economic Corridor, (vi) Bangladesh-China-India-Myanmar Economic Corridor (Office of the Leading Group for BRI, 2017).

A High-Level Symposium on BRI

A high-level symposium on 'the BRI in the global perspective' was held in Beijing on 10-11 October 2016. The symposium was jointly organised by the National Institute of Global Strategy, Chinese Academy of Social Sciences and Beijing Foreign Studies University with participation from around 40 leading Chinese experts and 30 foreign experts. The experts agreed that BRI is a grand strategy for China to expand its opening-up policy and forge version 2.0 of globalisation (Wang and Zhao, 2017a).

It is noteworthy that a Sri Lankan Scholar brought up the problem of the 'loan standard' for BRI and highlighted that this would affect the progress of BRI in Sri Lanka (ibid.). In other words, the problems associated with the Chinese loan were raised just after the release of the Vision document and implementation of BRI projects in Sri Lanka. Significantly, a Korean scholar emphasised that China should pay attention to the concerns of the countries on its periphery. The construction of Maritime Silk Road might clash with territorial sovereignty and interests of some countries in South China Sea. The experts participating in the symposium also acknowledged the risks and challenges involved with the initiative that included security, political, economic, ecological and social risks (ibid.).

Participating Countries

Initially, a list of China plus 64 countries was publicised as countries along the route or BRI participants (Helen and Winnie, 2016). Details are given below. The list also included name of India, which is not associated with the project.

List of China plus 64

East Asia: China, Mongolia

Southeast Asia: Brunei, Cambodia, Indonesia, Laos, Malaysia, Myanmar, Philippines, Singapore, Thailand, Timor-Leste, Vietnam

Central Asia: Kazakhstan, Kyrgyzstan, Tajikistan, Turkmenistan, Uzbekistan

West Asia and North Africa: Bahrain, Egypt, Iran, Iraq, Israel, Jordan, Kuwait, Lebanon, Oman, Qatar, Saudi Arabia, Palestine, Syria, United Arab Emirates, Yemen

South Asia: Afghanistan, Bangladesh, Bhutan, India, Maldives, Nepal, Pakistan, Sri Lanka

Europe: Albania, Armenia, Azerbaijan, Belarus, Bosnia and Herzegovina, Bulgaria, Croatia, Czech Republic, Estonia, Georgia, Hungary, Latvia, Lithuania, Macedonia, Moldova, Montenegro, Poland, Romania, Russia, Serbia, Slovakia, Slovenia, Turkey, Ukraine

Initially, only countries along the route were referred to as BRI participating countries. However, this criterion was relaxed and cooperation agreements were signed with as many countries as possible. Most recent data suggests that China has signed BRI cooperation agreements/MoUs with 149 countries and 32 international organisations (MFA PRC, 2022). It suggests that the focus is now not limited to the initial 64 countries along the route, rather some kind of cooperation agreement with countries across the globe has become agenda of the initiative.

Figure 1.1: China's Belt and Road Initiative (BRI)

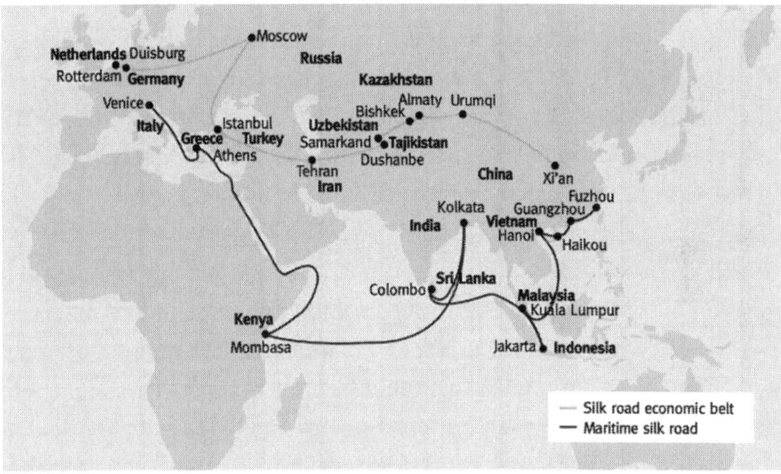

Source: https://news.hkust.edu.hk/news/has-belt-and-road-initiative-become-political-liability-chi

II. Drivers of BRI: Strategic and Economic

BRI is the result of a convergence of a number of Chinese domestic drivers to serve its domestic, economic and strategic interests:

Strategic

Chinese experts have acknowledged that "one of the most remarkable features of Chinese foreign policy since the 18th National Congress of CPC is greater significance attached to the national interest" (Zhang, 2014). Now, it is well documented that Deng Xiaoping's '24 character guidelines' to keep a low profile in international affairs has been sidelined by President Xi Jinping. China's goal is to be a dominant power in Asia as well as the world. In this context, it is pertinent to mention some relevant studies about China's strategic discourse.

Prof. Wang Jishi, a Chinese strategist and former Dean, School of International Studies, Peking University, articulated the strategic idea to Look Westwards and March Westwards in late 2012 (Wang, 2012). He argued that the US rebalancing strategy in Asia is centred on the idea of 'return to Asia' and the US strategy is shifting 'eastwards'. Major global players like India, Russia and the European Union (EU) are beginning to look eastwards. In this context, China should make strategic plans to March Westwards. Wang argued that China should increase economic and trade cooperation with all countries in South Asia, Central Asia, West Asia and the Caspian Sea region. He argued that important interests of the EU, Russia, India, the US, Japan and China converge and compete in these regions. In contrast to Western Europe and East Asia, the countries in South Asia, Central Asia, West Asia and the Caspian Sea region "do not have, nor could they have, a regional military alliance (or opposing alliances) under the leadership of the US" (ibid). March West received serious attention from the top leadership of China as it provided China with an alternative geographical area to expand its influence. Moreover, such policy would accelerate the Western Development Strategy, a national strategy launched in the year 2000 to promote the development of China's western provinces as these provinces are less developed compared to the eastern and coastal provinces. The gradual evolution of BRI is certainly broader than what was suggested by Wang. However, it can be said that Wang Jishi's rationale for March Westwards provided strategic justification for the BRI of China.

Economic

Chinese leader Deng Xiaoping initiated the policy of reforms and opening up in late 1970. China became the second largest economy of the world in 2010. However, the era of double-digit growth was over by 2011 (9.6 per cent). The proceeding years of 2012 and 2013 showed a declining growth rate of 7.9 and 7.8 per cent respectively (World Bank, 2022). Some experts have examined the specific issue of capital return in the Chinese economy. Since the mid-1990s, the rate of capital return in China experienced inconsistency and has dropped with the onset of the Global Financial Crisis since 2008. China was able to avoid the crisis by implementing a US$ 586 billion stimulus package, mostly directed toward local government borrowing to finance infrastructure projects (Wagner, 2020).

By the early 2010s, those stimulus funds had been spent and many local governments faced severe economic problems. Overcapacity exceeded 30 per cent in the iron, steel, glass, cement, aluminium, and power generation industries. The stress on the economy was much evident, domestic construction came under pressure, the number of unused buildings and under-utilised factories were evident for people to observe. There was a risk that the excess capacity in traditional industries would trigger widespread defaults. In this background, the Chinese government decided to launch BRI to make use of its excess capacity in various sectors (Wagner, 2020).

The Chinese model of growth created wealth in China; however, it also resulted in creating developmental and social problems. The reform era saw growth concentrated in eastern or coastal areas in China, the issue of regional disparity and inequalities in individuals' income and wealth suggested that the distribution of growth has not been fair. Some scholars in the past even termed it as a 'crisis' and suggested that if the problem is not solved, the 'middle-income trap' could be a reality.

The vision document noted "In advancing the BRI, China will fully leverage the comparative advantages of its various regions, adopt a proactive strategy of further opening-up, strengthen interaction and cooperation among the eastern, western and central regions, and comprehensively improve the openness of the Chinese economy" (NDRC, 2015). This highlights the significance of BRI from China's domestic economic perspective. In February 2017, China's State Councilor Yang Jiechi confirmed that BRI "adheres closely to China's regional development strategy, new urbanisation strategy and opening up strategy and will provide a strong boost to China's all-dimensional opening up" (*Beijing Review*, 2017). Therefore, benefit to China's domestic economy including positive contribution to regional development strategy remains a major driver for BRI. Further, the initiative offers opportunities for China's economic restructuring, industrial up-gradation as well as 'going global' strategy.

The official designation of target provinces is as follows: (a) Xinjiang as a core area on the Silk Road Economic Belt, (b) Fujian as a core area of the 21st Century Maritime Silk Road, (c) Guanxi as an important gateway connecting the Belt and Road, and (d) Yunnan as a pivot of China's opening– up to South and Southeast Asia (He, 2019).

China released its first big data report 'Belt and Road in big data' in October 2016 in Beijing. As per the report Guangdong, Zhejiang, Shanghai, Tianjin, Fujian, Shandong, Henan, Yunnan and Beijing are the top ten and most active participants in China (*People's Daily*, 2016). It demonstrates that BRI did not impact positively on the regional development strategy of China.

Coastal and eastern regions of China remained the most active participants of BRI. Further, the big data report said that Guangdong province topped all Chinese provincial-level regions in trade volume with relevant countries along the route accounting for 20.9 per cent of the national total. Guangdong is followed by Jiangsu, Zhejiang and Beijing (ibid.).

It can be said that BRI has deviated in practice from the original plan. Among the target provinces (as mentioned earlier) only Fujian rated among the top five in a study that indexed BRI provincial participation rates (He, 2019). The Fujian province's Port of Xiamen and its Port of Fuzhou have 18 sister ports across the world. Studies from China suggest that Fujian province has achieved 'outstanding' results in cooperation with countries along the maritime road (Zhang, 2022).

Energy

The Institute of Quantitative and Technical Economics (IQTE) of the Chinese Academy of Social Sciences (CASS) studied the energy dimension of the BRI. The detailed study suggests how various regions of China will offer themselves as the destination of energy resources and the neighbouring countries to be the 'supplier of energy resources to help China to develop as an industrial power' (CASS, 2016).

On the basis of IQTE study, it is logical to analyse the energy component of China's BRI vis-à-vis various regions: (a) Northeast Asia: Russia and Mongolia are important countries from the perspective of China's energy security. The implementation of BRI has provided more chances for energy supply to China from Russia and Mongolia. The IQTE study on BRI suggests that the "future is likely to witness a new growth pole if power grid inter-connection and oil and gas market integration can be achieved in the Russian Far East, Northeast China and Bohai Sea of China and North Korea". (b) Southeast Asia: the study highlights that Southern China has a good industrial foundation, but poor energy resources. Southwest China, Mekong river valley and Myanmar have abundant water resources, but poor industrial foundations. Malaysia, Indonesia and Brunei have abundant oil-gas resources but do not have matching industrial systems (ibid.). The study also talks about linking energy markets in west China, Central Asia and West Asia. Further, it suggests an energy network, including Iran, Afghanistan, China, India and Pakistan in the future.

In May 2017, China's NDRC and National Energy Administration jointly released a document titled "Vision and Actions on Energy Cooperation in Jointly Building Silk Road Economic Belt and 21st-Century Maritime Silk Road". It aimed to build on the multilateral and bilateral cooperation mechanisms to advance BRI energy cooperation to a higher level (NDRC, 2017a).

Recent studies related to the subject suggest that China's overall approach to the acquisition of overseas energy resources is more coordinated through the BRI. There has also been greater integration of China's energy strategy into the BRI. In the resource-backed mechanism the repayment of loans is converted into securing energy resources of the BRI recipient countries. Now, political support for Chinese companies abroad occurs within this framework of BRI (Taylor, 2021).

III. BRI and Conceptual Discourse in China

The BRI needs to be understood in its proper context as it is not distinct from the conceptual discourse highlighted in the 'new era'. Chinese leadership has emphasised that the world is undergoing 'once a century transformation' and the period of a strategic opportunity no longer exists for China. President Xi Jinping has talked about the idea of 'Chinese dream' and defined it as the 'great rejuvenation of the Chinese nation'The Party frames the Chinese dream from the perspective of reform, opening up and socialist modernisation. For many Chinese observers the concept of BRI "has a very important status in the journey of realising the Chinese dream of the great rejuvenation of the Chinese nation" (as quoted in Swaine, 2015).

President Xi gave a comprehensive speech at the Foreign Affairs Conference in 2018 emphasising on "diplomacy of socialism with Chinese characteristics for a new era". He underscored ten major aspects of thought, which was later highlighted as ten core principles of Xi Jinping's thought on diplomacy. Belt and Road construction was referred to as a principle aimed to achieve shared growth.

Chinese experts have highlighted that BRI is a "critical instrument for realising what the Chinese government calls the Community of Common Destiny" (Wang and Zhao, 2017b). The top leadership of China, especially President Xi has referred to the concept many times. While speaking at the Boao Forum for Asia in March 2015, President Xi elaborated his idea of a community of common destiny.[1] He noted that to build a community of common destiny, we need to make sure that all countries respect one another and treat each other as equals. However, in practice, China has not followed this principle. In January 2017, China issued a White Paper titled "China's Policies on Asia-Pacific Security Cooperation". The white paper clearly warned small and medium-sized countries. It noted that "small and medium-sized countries need not and should not take sides among big countries" (*Xinhua*, 2017). It is evident that China favours a hierarchal approach to international relations and that such a policy has alienated many of its neighbours.

Some Chinese experts see the concept of CCD as a new paradigm for promoting regional collaboration in socio-economic development, and visualise its crucial role in reshaping the international geopolitical landscape (Wang and Zhao, 2017b). China's goal is to "turn China's neighbourhood areas into a community of common destiny" (as quoted in Mardell, 2017). It is pertinent to refer to the international think tank forum on the theme "Building the community of common destiny between China and its neighbours: Challenges and the future" organised by National Institute of Global Strategy, Chinese Academy of Social Sciences on 18-19 November 2016 in Beijing. During the deliberations, Prof. Lin Limin argued that "the biggest challenge facing building the CCD came from trust-building and confidence-building. Historical issues, land and maritime territorial disputes, as well as issues related to civil war all, play a part in that regard" (Wang and Zhao, 2017b). This is an acknowledgement of the contemporary problems faced by China. It should give priority to building trust with its neighbours. Further, Mr. Wang Junsheng, Head, Division of Regional Studies, National Institute for International Strategy, CASS, argued that "the main constrains to building CCD come from several dimensions: historical and territorial disputes, relatively low political trust between China and some neighbouring countries and the challenges of China-US competition" (ibid.). Further, he rightly acknowledged that the concept of CCD carries some ambiguity and needs to be clarified.

The 19th National Congress of the Communist Party of China (CPC) held in 2017 amended the Party's Constitution to include the promotion of the BRI as one of the major future objectives. This was in line with the message coming out from the 19th Party Congress that China has arrived on the world stage and it wants to attach high priority to the BRI. A number of statements by the Chinese leaders after the Party Congress affirmed this trend. State Councilor and Foreign Minister Wang Yi stated that China has "achieved a remarkable transformation—it has stood up, grown rich and is becoming strong. A sea change has taken place in China" (MFA PRC, 2018). Recent Party documents have noted that "Chinese nation has achieved the tremendous transformation from standing up and growing prosperous to becoming strong" (*China Daily*, 2021).

The speech of President Xi Jinping at the Foreign Affairs Conference in 2018 made a clear linkage between China's major-country diplomacy and its ambition to realise the Chinese Dream. It is also important to note that major country diplomacy is poised to get more priority in the coming days, as it is now linked to realising national rejuvenation as well as to build a community of common destiny. BRI is directly linked to China's ambitions to realise its dream and build CCD and hence it will be a priority for the government.

While addressing the UN General Assembly in September 2021, President Xi proposed the Global Development Initiative (GDI). It has been described as another 'global public product' advocated by President Xi following the BRI. He announced the Global Security Initiative at the Boao Forum for Asia in April 2022. The GDI and GSI are new efforts by China to confront and overcome the challenges that the country is facing in the dramatically changed contemporary regional and international environment (Surie, 2022). It extends the debate further as some experts see GDI as an 'expansion' of BRI.

IV. Belt and Road Forums: Policy Announcements and Adjustments

The first Belt and Road Forum (BRF) for International Cooperation was held in May 2017 in Beijing. President Xi Jinping hosted 29 Heads of State and Government at the Forum of countries along the route.[2] While a Joint Communiqué was issued and deliverables were identified, China and the participating countries at the Forum could not sign any specific multilateral agreement on any issue involving all countries of the BRI route. This shows the lack of common consensus among the participating countries. However, it was an event of great importance from China's perspective as it showcased China's ability to organise such a Forum where China tried to build a consensus under its leadership.

Around the same time, BRI faced backlash in parts of the world as it was approaching five years of its announcement (Small, 2018; Deo and Bhandari, 2018). These were related to various concerns, including high costs of the projects, issues related to transparency and fear of 'debt trap'. Subsequently, the government planned to organise Second Belt and Road Forum with a more comprehensive agenda.

The Second Belt and Road Forum

China hosted Second Belt and Road Forum for International Cooperation in Beijing on 25-27 April 2019. The Forum was attended by heads of state/government and other leaders from 37 countries, the UN Secretary-General, the IMF Managing Director and a number of people from institutions across the world.[3] Chinese President Xi Jinping's speech at the Forum targeted the criticisms against the BRI. The Forum highlighted that BRI is the "project of the century that will benefit people across the world" (MFA PRC, 2019). Such statements came as no surprise given the criticism faced by the projects in different parts of the world. Significantly, President Xi stressed on China's commitment to an open economy and economic globalisation and noted that China will take a series of measures to speed up its reform and opening up. He called for intensifying efforts to (a) enhance international cooperation in intellectual property rights (IPR), (b) expand market access for foreign investment in more areas, (c) increase the import of goods and services on a larger scale, (d) jointly promote result oriented 'high-quality Belt and Road cooperation', and (e) promote green development. However, China's commitment will be judged by its actions on the ground.

Outcomes from the second BRF include:

(a) A Joint Communiqué by the head of state/governments who attended the BRI along with an annexure. The joint communiqué highlighted that the major objectives of the forum are: to strengthen development policy synergy; boost infrastructure connectivity; promote sustainable development; strengthen practical cooperation and advance people-to-people exchanges (*Xinhua*, 2019). Notably, the annexure listed projects under the heading "Economic corridors and other projects catalysed and supported by connectivity" did not include BCIM Economic corridor. Further, it included multilateral projects such as International North-South Transport Corridor (INSTC). The inclusion of INSTC opens a new debate about the role of BRI in the context of multilateral connectivity projects of the region which did not involve China earlier.

(b) List of deliverables included 283 results in various categories, such as initiatives proposed or launched by the Chinese side and bilateral and multilateral documents signed during or immediately before the second BRF.

(c) BRI International Green Development Coalition (BRIGC) was launched to provide a platform for policy dialogue and communication as well as sharing of knowledge and data (UNEP, 2019).

(d) China's Ministry of Finance issued Debt Sustainability Framework (DSF). The announcement of such a framework came at a time when many countries criticised China for 'debt-trap diplomacy'. However, the DSF would hold more credibility if it was a multilateral initiative. This also demonstrates the institutional characteristics of BRI, which is essentially a China-led and China-controlled initiative and is primarily based on bilateral cooperation/partnership. Hence, it contradicts the idea of genuine multilateralism.

In the wake of COVID-19, China launched the Silk Road of Health. In June 2020, China hosted a conference of the foreign and other ministers of the BRI partner countries in virtual format on the theme of 'Belt and Road International Cooperation: Combating COVID-19 with Solidarity" and called for investment in building sound and resilient health-related infrastructures, including the development of telemedicine.

Challenges and Risks involved in BRI

Professor Wang Yiwei from the School of International University, Renmin University, Beijing, has underlined the following risks of the BRI. The first problem is political risks, which can be divided into two categories: domestic political risks of various countries and geopolitical risks. The second problem is security risks, which can be further divided in traditional and non-traditional security. It includes: (a) natural risks, (b) environmental risks, (c) threat of extremist forces, (d) threat of non-government organisations, and (e) maritime security risks. The economic risks are demonstrated in the following aspects: (a) macro risks such as possible problems of AIIB and Silk Road Fund, (b) industrial risks- not only problems concerning the overcapacity of China and its industry 'going global', but also that of achieving industrial improvement for countries along the routes, and (c) lack of risk response mechanisms. Legal risks are also important. China has adopted its own socialist legal system, which is different from those countries on the route. Legal risks can occur due to issues related to investment, labour, environmental concerns, poor management, etc. Moreover, this can occur due to different laws in countries along the route. Finally, moral risks faced by BRI at the level of enterprise, individual and national could be also problematic (Wang Yiwei, 2015). Over the years, the risks and challenges outlined by Wang Yiwei has not been proved to be wrong. The maritime aspect of the BRI has faced specific challenges in the field of maritime political security; development of the marine economy; and governance of the marine climate and the marine environment (Zhang, 2022).

While addressing a high-level symposium on the BRI on 19 November 2021, President Xi stressed: "developing an all-weather early-warning and risk assessment platform for China's overseas projects, and coordinating mechanisms for the protection of the country's interests abroad, global counter-terrorism efforts and security control" (Xinhua, 2021). The statement underscores the problems faced by China, especially in dealing with security risks in recent years.

Chinese sources suggest that the country has signed BRI cooperation agreements/MoUs with 149 countries across the globe. However, the journey of BRI has not been smooth. The initiative has invited various controversies and also faced backlash and protests in some countries/regions across the world. China was compelled to announce some adjustments, especially during the second Belt and Road Forum in 2019. However, this has not been considered sufficient enough. The Chinese model of investment requires serious reforms. Moreover, China needs to adhered to universally recognised norms and principles of genuine multilateralism.

Notes

1. The phrase 'community of common destiny' was first used by President Hu Jintao in China. Reference to this term is available in the reports to the 17th Party Congress.
2. Following 29 Heads of State and Government attended the Forum: Argentinean President Mauricio Macri, Belarusian President Alexander Lukashenko, Chilean President Michelle Bachelet, Czech President Milos Zeman, Indonesian President JokoWidodo, Kazakh President Nursultan Nazarbayev,

Kenyan President Uhuru Kenyatta, Kyrgyz President AlmazbekAtambayev, Lao President BounnhangVorachit, Philippine President Rodrigo Duterte, Russian President Vladimir Putin, Swiss President Doris Leuthard, Turkish President RecepTayyipErdogan, Uzbek President Shavkat Mirziyoyev, Vietnamese President Tran Dai Quang, Cambodian Prime Minister Hun Sen, Ethiopian Prime Minister Hailemariam Dessalegn, Fijian Prime Minister Voreqe Bainimarama, Greek Prime Minister Alexis Tsipras, Hungarian Prime Minister Viktor Orban, Italian Prime Minister Paolo Gentiloni, Malaysian Prime Minister NajibRazak, Mongolian Prime Minister Jargaltulga Erdenebat, Myanmar State Counselor Aung San SuuKyi, Pakistani Prime Minister Nawaz Sharif, Polish Prime Minister Beata Szydlo, Serbian Prime Minister Aleksandar Vucic, Spanish Prime Minister Mariano Rajoy and Sri Lankan Prime Minister Ranil Wickremesinghe.

3. Following leaders participated in the second BRF: President Xi Jinping of the PRC, President Ilham Aliyev of the Republic of Azerbaijan, President Alexander Lukashenko of the Republic of Belarus, His Majesty Sultan Haji Hassanal Bolkiah Mu'izzaddinWaddaulah of Brunei Darussalam, President Sebastián Piñera Echenique of the Republic of Chile, President Nicos Anastasiades of the Republic of Cyprus, President Miloš Zeman of the Czech Republic, President Ismail Omar Guelleh of the Republic of Djibouti, President Abdul Fatah Al-Sisi of the Arab Republic of Egypt, the First President of the Republic of Kazakhstan - Elbasy Nursultan Nazarbayev, President Uhuru Kenyatta of the Republic of Kenya, President Sooronbai Zheenbekov of the Kyrgyz Republic, President Bounnhang Vorachith of the Lao People's Democratic Republic, President Khaltmaagiin Battulga of Mongolia, President Filipe Jacinto Nyusi of the Republic of Mozambique, President Bidya Devi Bhandari of Nepal, President Rodrigo Roa Duterte of the Republic of the Philippines, President Marcelo Rebelo de Sousa of the Portuguese Republic, President Vladimir Putin of the Russian Federation, President Aleksandar Vučić of the Republic of Serbia, President Ueli Maurer of the Swiss Confederation, President Emomali Rahmon of the Republic of Tajikistan, President Shavkat Mirziyoyev of the Republic of Uzbekistan, Vice President and Prime Minister H.H. Sheikh Mohammed bin Rashid Al Maktoum of the United Arab Emirates and Ruler of Dubai, Chancellor Sebastian Kurz of the Republic of Austria, Prime Minister Hun Sen of the Kingdom of Cambodia, Prime Minister Abiy Ahmed Ali of the Federal Democratic Republic of Ethiopia, Prime Minister Alexis Tsipras of the Hellenic Republic, Prime Minister Orbán Viktor of Hungary, Prime Minister Giuseppe Conte of the Italian Republic, Prime Minister Mahathir Bin Mohamad of Malaysia, State Counsellor Aung San SuuKyi of the Republic of the Union of Myanmar, Prime Minister Imran Khan of the Islamic Republic of Pakistan, Prime Minister Peter O'Neill of the Independent State of Papua New Guinea, Prime Minister Lee Hsien Loong of the Republic of Singapore, Prime Minister Prayut Chan-o-cha of the Kingdom of Thailand, Prime Minister Nguyen Xuan Phuc of the Socialist Republic of Viet Nam, and Vice President Jusuf Kalla of the Republic of Indonesia.

References

ASEAN China Centre, (2013), "Speech by Chinese President Xi Jinping to Indonesian Parliament, Jakarta," 2 October 2022, at http://www.asean-china-center.org/english/2013-10/03/c_133062675.htm, accessed on 30 May 2022.

Beijing Review (2017), State Councilor Yang Jiechi's interview to the People's Daily and the China Daily, reproduced as: "Welcome to Belt and Road Forum", *Beijing Review*, no. 7, 16 February 2017.

CASS, (2016), *One Belt One Road: Connectivity and Common Development – Energy Infrastructure Development and Energy Market Integration in Asia-Pacific Region*, Beijing, China Social Sciences Press, 2016, pp. 48-107.

China Daily, (2021), "Communiqué of the Sixth Plenary Session of the 19th Central Committee of the Communist Party of China", 12 November 2021, at https://global.chinadaily.com.cn/a/202111/12/WS618da386a310cdd39bc74dcd.html, Accessed on 1 June 2022.

Deo, Neelam and Bhandari, Amit (2018), "The intensifying backlash against BRI, Mumbai, 31 May 2018, at https://www.gatewayhouse.in/bri-debt-backlash/, Accessed on 30 May 2022.

He Baogang (2021), "The Domestic Politics of the Belt and Road Initiative and its Implications", *Journal of Contemporary China*, Vol. 28, No. 116, pp. 180-95.

Helen, Chin and Winnie, He, (2016). "The Belt and Road Initiative: 65 Countries and Beyond", May 2016, at http://www.iberchina.org/files/2016/obor_fung_paises.pdf. Accessed on 31 July 2022.

Kumar, Sanjeev (2017), "Special Report on OBOR: China's Strategic Quest for Market, Energy and Geopolitical Influence: A Status Note on the Eve of the Belt and Road Forum, Beijing, 14-15 May 2017". New Delhi, at https://www.icwa.in/showfile.php?lang=1&level=3&ls_id=538&lid=402, Accessed on 25 May 2022.

MFA, PRC (2013), "Promote Friendship between Our People and Work Together to Build a Bright Future" speech by President Xi Jinping at Nazarbayev University, Astana, 7 September 2013, at https://www.fmprc.gov.cn/ce/cebel/eng/zxxx/t1078088.htm, Accessed on 10 May 2022.

MFA, PRC, (2018), Remarks by Wang Yi, Minister of Foreign Affairs of the People's Republic of China at the 2018 New Year Reception, MOFA, PRC, 30 January 2018, at http://www.fmprc.gov.cn/mfa_eng/zxxx_662805/t15305, Accessed on 30 May 2022.

MFA, PRC, (2019), "Xi Jinping chairs and the leaders' roundtable of the Second Belt and Road Forum for International Cooperation (BRF)", at https://www.fmprc.gov.cn/mfa_eng/zxxx_662805/t1659377.shtml, Accessed on 30 May 2022.

MFA, PRC, (2022). "Swedish expert Stephen Brawer: BRI—A Pathway to a Bright Future For Mankind", at https://www.fmprc.gov.cn/mfa_eng/ddzggcd/gtfy/202208/t20220801_10731428.html. Accessed on 31 July 2022.

Mardell, Jacob, "Building a 'community of common destiny' is the motivating force behind China's future foreign policy", 25 October 2016, at https://thediplomat.

com/2017/10/the-community-of-common-destiny-in-xi-jinpings-new-era/, Accessed on 26 May 2022.

NDRC (2015), "Full Text: Vision and actions on jointly building Belt and Road", 28 March 2015, Beijing, at http://www.china.org.cn/china/Off_the_Wire/2015-03/28/content_35182638.htm, Accessed on 30 May 2022.

NDRC (2017), "Vision for Maritime Cooperation under the Belt and Road Initiative" Beijing, at https://www.yidaiyilu.gov.cn/wcm.files/upload/CMSydylgw/201706/201706200153032.pdf, Accessed on 25 May 2022.

NDRC (2017a), "Vision and Actions on Energy Cooperation in Jointly Building Silk Road Economic Belt and 21st-Century Maritime Silk Road", at https://eng.yidaiyilu.gov.cn/zchj/qwfb/13754.htm, Accessed on 25 May 2022.

Office of the Leading Group for the BRI (2017), "The Belt and Road Initiative: Concept, Practice and China's Contributions Beijing",, May 2017, at, https://eng.yidaiyilu.gov.cn/wcm.files/upload/CMSydylyw/201705/201705110537027.pdf, Accessed on 28 May 2022

Office of the Leading Group for Promoting the BRI (2019), "The Belt and Road Initiative Progress, Contributions and Prospects", Beijing, April 2019, at https://eng.yidaiyilu.gov.cn/zchj/qwfb/86739.htm, Accessed on 28 May 2022.

People's Daily (2016), "China issues first big data report on B&R Initiative", 29 October 2016, Beijing, at http://en.people.cn/n3/2016/1029/c90000-9134303.html, Accessed on 28 May 2022.

Surie, Nalin (2022), "Reflections on China's Drivers, Motivations and Strategic Perceptions", DPG Policy Group, *DPG Policy Brief*, Vol. VII Issue 24, at https://www.delhipolicygroup.org/publication/policy-briefs/reflections-on-chinas-drivers-motivations-and-strategic-perceptions.html, Accessed on 28 May 2022.

Swaine, Michael D. (2015), "Chinese Views and Commentary on the 'One Belt, One Road' Initiative", *China Leadership Monitor*, Summer 2015, at https://www.hoover.org/research/chinese-views-and-commentary-one-belt-one-road, Accessed on 30 May 2022.

Taylor, M. (2021). "China's Evolving Energy Security Strategy", *Asian Affairs,* Vol. 52, No. 4, 2021.

UNEP, (2019), "Belt & Road Initiative International Green Development Coalition (BRIGC)", at https://www.unenvironment.org/regions/asia-and-pacific/regional-initiatives/belt-and-road-initiative-international-green, Accessed on 30 May 2021.

Wang Linggui and Zhao Jianglin (2017a), *The Belt and Road Initiative in Global Context*, International Joint Study Report No.1, Beijing, Social Science Academic Press, 2017.

Wang Linggui and Zhao Jianglin, (2017b), *Building Community of Common Destiny in Neighbouring Areas*, International Joint Study Report No. 2, Beijing, Social Science Academic Press, 2017.

Wang Yiwei, (2016), *The Belt and Road Initiative: What China will Offer the World and its Rise,* Beijing: New World Press, 2016, pp. 80-129.

Wang Jishi (2012), "Marching Westwards: Rebalancing of China's Geostrategy" International and Strategic Studies Report, No. 73 October 2012, at www.ciss.pku.edu.cn/Code/AccessoriesMaker.aspx?id=2270, Accessed on 5 January 2014.

Wagner, Daniel (2020), "The Belt and Road Initiatives: Keeping the Plates Spinning", 21 August 2020, at https://intpolicydigest.org/the-belt-and-road-initiative-keeping-the-plates-spinning/, Accessed on 15 May 2022.

World Bank (2022), data, at https://data.worldbank.org/indicator/NY.GDP.PCAP.KN?end=2019&locations=CN&start=2013&view=chart, Accessed on 15 May 2022.

Xinhua (2021), "Xi urges continuous efforts to promote high-quality BRI development", at http://english.www.gov.cn/news/topnews/202111/20/content_WS6198bcb4c6d0df57f98e53dc.html 2021, Accessed on 20 May 2022.

Xinhua (2017), "Full text: China's Policies on Asia-Pacific Security Cooperation", at http://www.xinhuanet.com//english/china/2017-01/11/c_135973695.htm, Accessed on 28 May 2022.

Xinhua (2019), "Joint Communiqué of the Leaders' Roundtable of the 2nd Belt and Road Forum for International Cooperation", 27 April 2019, Beijing, at http://www.xinhuanet.com/english/2017-05/15/c_136286378.htm, Accessed on 30 May 2022.

Zhang Qingmin (2014), "China's Foreign Policy since 18th National Congress of the CPC", China International Strategy Review 2013, Beijing, Foreign Language Press, 2014, pp. 101-134.

Zhang Yixin (2022), "21st Century Maritime Silk Road makes progress", Chinese Social Sciences Today, 1 July 2022, Beijing, at http://casseng.cssn.cn/news_events/news_events_news_briefing/202207/t20220701_5415151.html, Accessed on 10 July 2022.

2. Beijing's Ambitious 21st Century Maritime Silk Road

Pragya Pandey

Abstract

MSR as an integral part of China's larger BRI initiative is aimed at expanding connectivity infrastructure throughout Southeast Asia, Oceania, the Indian Ocean, and East Africa. The MSR is not only to serve Beijing's economic interests, but also to give it strategic leverage to emerge as a major maritime power in the Indian and the Pacific Oceans. MSR is potentially affecting the balance of power in the region, as China aggressively pursues its maritime strategy across the Indo-Pacific region. Most of these nations participating in the MSR have a huge trade imbalance with China. Beijing's investments are frivolous and inadequately planned in most cases and there is a growing realisation about the broader economic, political and security implications of large-scale Chinese investment under the MSR. The paper aims to analyse China's strategic MSR initiative by highlighting some of the key projects undertaken so far under it and also evaluates larger implications of MSR for participating countries.

In 2013, Chinese President Xi Jinping announced the creation of the 21st Century Maritime Silk Road (MSR) as part of New Silk Road Economic Belt. The project is aimed at expanding connectivity infrastructure throughout Southeast Asia, Oceania, the Indian Ocean, and East Africa. The revival of historical Silk Road is an ambitious and integral part of China's One Belt One Road (OBOR) initiative, rechristened as Belt and Road Initiative (BRI). The BRI has a number of projects in the field of transportation, energy, telecommunication, and infrastructure across the vast network. This chapter will focus on the maritime aspect of the BRI.

The 21st Century MSR is to enhance 'China's maritime connectivity with the larger European market through the South China Sea, the Indian Ocean and the Mediterranean' (Singh, 2017). Highlighting Beijing's vision for maritime cooperation under the MSR, on 20 June 2017, the State Council of People's Republic of China (PRC) released a document titled '*Vision for Maritime Cooperation under the Belt and Road Initiative*' (State Council, PRC, 2017). The document highlights that the overall aim is to "synchronising development plans and promoting joint actions amongst countries along the MSR, setting up the all-dimensional, multi-tiered and broad-scoped Blue Partnership, jointly protecting and sustainably utilising marine resources to achieve harmony between man and the ocean for common development and enhancement of marine welfare" (State Council, PRC, 2017).

Beijing has launched a number of projects under the rubric of MSR in countries including Sri Lanka, Pakistan, Bangladesh, Maldives, Myanmar, Malaysia, Indonesia, Iran, Israel, Oman, Qatar, Saudi Arabia, Egypt, Yemen, Eritrea, Djibouti, Mauritius, Madagascar, Somalia, Kenya, Tanzania, Comoros, Seychelles, Mozambique, South Africa, Ethiopia, Kenya, Morocco, New Zealand, Panama, Solomon Island, Papua New Guinea, and Vanuatu. Since it was launched, there have been concerns about the economic viability and geopolitical implications of BRI. The MSR is not only to serve Beijing's economic interests, but also to give it strategic leverage to emerge as a major maritime power across the Indo-Pacific region. The paper aims to evaluate and assess the MSR as a crucial element of China's ambitious BRI initiative and also analyses major projects under the initiative.

What is MSR?

From time immemorial, the great oceans of the world have played a significant role in the development and sustenance of the human race, facilitating and nurturing civilisational links. Trade between different parts of the world has been carried over the waters of the great oceans. Port cities, therefore, have always acted as nodal points attracting travellers, adventurers and entrepreneurs. History shows us that for pursuing foreign policy goals and promoting the country's national interests and even projecting power, seas and navies of major powers, have played a significant role in determining the global balance of power and redefining world history over the years. Maritime geopolitics is the reality of current times, the Indian Ocean is becoming the centre of economic and strategic attention in global geopolitics with competitive and complex interests of regional and extra-regional powers.

With the MSR, Beijing aims to revive the historical silk route, commonly used for trading activities. Centuries before the Europeans penetrated the region; Chinese had established a comprehensive network of trading relationships with the countries of Asia, the Middle East and to a lesser extent East Africa. The emergence of the maritime power of China goes back to the far-sighted maritime vision of the Song and Ming dynasties, during the period several successful maritime expeditions to Southeast Asia and the Indian Ocean were undertaken. Diplomatic expeditions to the Indian Ocean were sent during the Ming dynasty, led by explorer Admiral Zeng He, who sailed as far as the Persian Gulf, Red Sea, and East Africa.

With the 21st Century MSR, China aims to revive these historical maritime activities and reconnect China with the rest of Asia, Africa and Europe. It envisages a maritime return route to southern Europe through the Suez Canal and back to Asia, with a stopover in East Africa. "The Mediterranean Basin is central in this network, being seen as the "hub-of-hubs", connecting Asia with Europe, Africa and the Americas" (Haralambides and Merk, 2020).

The MSR is an integral and important part of China's BRI, which was summarised by Chinese President Xi, as he said, "China will actively promote international cooperation through the Belt and Road Initiative. In doing so, we hope to achieve policy, infrastructure, trade, financial, and people-to-people connectivity and thus build a new platform for international cooperation to create new drivers of shared development" (National People's Congress of China, 2019, p. 8). However, the whole idea of international cooperation and shared development is clearly a façade behind which China's long term motive is to establish itself as a pre-eminent maritime power in both the Indian and the Pacific Oceans.

The espoused vision of the MSR as mentioned in the document released by the State Council of PRC in 2017 is: "China advocates the Silk Road Spirit - peace and cooperation, openness and inclusiveness, mutual learning and mutual benefit", and exerts efforts to implement the United Nations 2030 Agenda for Sustainable Development in the field of coasts and oceans" (State Council, PRC, 2017). The areas covered in the MSR as described in the Vision document are in line with the priorities of the 21st century Maritime Silk Road. It emphasises that "China will deepen ocean cooperation by fostering closer ties with countries along the Road, supported by the coastal economic belt in China. Ocean cooperation will focus on building the China-Indian Ocean-Africa-Mediterranean Sea Blue Economic Passage, by linking the China-Indochina Peninsula Economic Corridor, running westward from the South China Sea to the Indian Ocean, and connecting the China-Pakistan Economic Corridor (CPEC) and the Bangladesh-China-India-Myanmar Economic Corridor (BCIM-EC). Efforts will also be made to jointly build the blue economic passage of China-Oceania-South Pacific, travelling southward from the South China Sea into the Pacific Ocean. Another blue economic passage is also envisioned leading up to Europe via the Arctic Ocean" (State Council, PRC, 2017). Through the vision documents, China also appeared keen to send a signal that the primary motive of the MSR is not just economic but also to harness the Ocean resources in a cooperative and sustainable manner. However, a few years down the line since the initiative was launched, stated objectives of sustainable and cooperative development are evidently a charade.

At present, the Indian Ocean is increasingly becoming the focus of strategic and economic attention in regional and international affairs and is perceived as the emerging centre of gravity, more so in the context of Indo-Pacific. The Indian Ocean plays an important role in the world energy production and global maritime trade. The Strait of Hormuz and the Strait of Malacca are the world's most important strategic chokepoints by volume of oil transit. At present, about 60 per cent of the global GDP is generated in the Indo-Pacific region. Much of China's MSR is focused on the Indo-Pacific region. The region essentially characterises the vast geography "stretching from the shores of Africa to that of Americas" incorporating maritime sub-regions including the Arabian Sea/Gulf region, the Indian Ocean, the South China Sea and the Pacific Ocean. The region has some of the most critical International Sea Lanes (ISLs) carrying much of the trade between Asian countries, Europe, the Middle East and the Pacific region. Therefore, the safety and security of these ISLs, which is challenged by both traditional and non-traditional threats, is critical not only for the regional countries but also for international economic stability.

There are profound changes taking place as far as the geostrategic environment of the region is concerned with the rise of new power centres. One of the key factors that have been consequential in influencing the recent geopolitical shifts has been China's asymmetric rise and its increasing foothold across the region. China has been strengthening connectivity with the Indo-Pacific sub-regions, including Southeast Asia, South Asia, and South Pacific through its BRI. China's MSR is potentially affecting the balance of power in the region.

Some of the Key projects under the MSR: Problems and Concerns

China has launched and supported a number of infrastructure and connectivity projects under the MSR initiative expanding over a vast maritime geography. One of the most strategic ports is Gwadar in Balochistan province, developed as a part of China-Pakistan Economic Corridor (CPEC) which directly impinges on the issue of sovereignty and territorial integrity of India. Gwadar is a linchpin in China's plan to revive the historical Silk Road linking Asia to Europe and Africa (*The Print*, 2018). Situated near strategic Strait of Hormuz, a US$ 54 billion project (initial figure) launched in 2013 aimed at linking western China to the Indian Ocean via Pakistan. The project includes the country's first deep-water port, a free-trade zone and 50 km (31 miles) of dock space (NDTV, 2017). The real significance of the Gwadar port lies in its strategic location and the role it can play in determining the geopolitics of the region. The port will provide China with an alternate route to Indian Ocean. However, as is the case with most of the projects, there is also a possibility that in case of Pakistan's inability to repay the huge amount of cost to China and therefore forsake the control of the port to China.

In Sri Lanka, China invested huge amounts of money into Hambantota port and airport, the Colombo International Container Terminal (CICT), Colombo port city, and other highways. Sri Lanka's strategic location overlooking the most strategic seas lanes in the Indian Ocean is what makes it a significant part of China's BRI. However, with Sri Lanka's inability to repay the loan, the Hambantota port was handed over to China on a lease for 99 years in 2017. Sri Lanka has a record amount of debt to repay to China, currently, the country is facing its worst economic crisis. Sri Lanka's case is often cited by analysts to warn about China's debt trap diplomacy.

The Maldives is a crucial part of China's maritime silk route vision. Chinese President Xi, visited the Maldives in 2014, same year the country signed up for the BRI. China has financed a number of projects like China-Maldives Friendship Bridge, linking the capital Male to a nearby island of Hulhule. Also, the project of upgradation of Male International airport was awarded to the Chinese company. Maldives has also leased an uninhabited island (Feydhoo Finolhu) to a Chinese enterprise for 50 years at a price of around US$ 4 million, with plans to develop infrastructure for tourism (Roy Chaudhury, 2018). It will allow Beijing to expand its influence in the Arabian Sea region. Another crucial project was, to develop an Ocean Observatory in the Makunudhoo, the westernmost atoll in the north, it will allow the Chinese a vantage point of an important Indian Ocean shipping route. It could serve as a potential intelligence monitoring post (Parashar, 2018). These mega-scale projects already have Chinese debt mounting in the country. According to previous estimates, Maldives' debt to China stood at US$ 3.4 billion raising concerns over its ability to pay it back, especially in the light of economic pressures after two years of COVID-19 pandemic (Press Trust of India, 2021).

Malaysia is strategically located along the Strait of Malacca, one of the world's busiest shipping routes connecting east and west between the Indian Ocean and the Pacific Ocean. This puts the country in an excellent position to capitalise on the expected increase in seaborne trade volume and investment in maritime infrastructure that will arise from the MSR initiative. Malacca also is a focus of China's MSR. China has provided huge loans for mega infrastructure projects including a major rail link, a port at Malacca and a US$ 100 billion megacity named 'Forest City' spearheaded by a Chinese developer, off the country's coast near Singapore, which is expected to be complete by 2035 (Kumar and Kawase, 2022). China is currently the largest investor in Malaysia.

China is building a new industrial city in Duqm near the capital city of Muscat in Oman. This will allow a number of Chinese companies to invest in the country. Oman's strategic location in the Arabian Sea makes it an important link in the maritime silk route. With this project, Oman looks to transform Duqm into an industrial and logistic hub and to diversify its economy beyond oil sector (Jabarkhyl, 2017).

Djibouti in the Horn of Africa is the anchor of China's MSR. China has built its first overseas base at the strategically located island at the junction of the Indian Ocean and Red Sea. China has undertaken a series of construction-related activities including ports, railways, roads and related infrastructure including the Doraleh multipurpose port (Aneja, 2018). Chinese construction activities for support base at Djibouti started in 2017. Over the years, Djibouti's debt to China has reportedly increased to more than 70 per cent of its gross domestic product (Roy Chaudhury, 2021). The small island country hosting multiple foreign military bases, has assumed greater significance in the Indian Ocean geopolitics in recent years.

Kenya in Africa, has also contracted a number of projects for construction of roads, railways and ports with China since it joined the BRI. An important one is building of the Lamu port in Kenya, as part of Lamu Port-South Sudan-Ethiopia Transport Corridor project (LAPSSET) launched in 2012. Lamu Port, which is being built by China Communications Construction Company, is part of Kenya's bid to become the major trade hub in East Africa. Port is designed to have 32 berths and once complete it will be the largest port in Sub-Saharan Africa. Lamu along with the Mombasa, now becomes the two major entry and exit points for Africa's hinterland (*Xinhua*, 2021). There are also concerns about the project turning into another 'white elephants' project along with concerns about environment and coastal communities.

In Madagascar, China is involved in building a deep water port in the Bay of Narinda on Madagascar's North-Western coast. In 2018, the Chinese company signed a 10-year, US$ 2.7 billion fishing deal for fishing rights in Madagascar's EEZ (Carver, 2018). There was widespread protest from the local fishermen against the deal. Also, China has invested in building telecom networks in Madagascar.

In Israel, the Chinese company Shanghai International Port Group (SIPG), in June 2019, signed a 25-year contract with the Israeli city of Haifa. The contract aimed at building and operating of a large shipping seaport in the Mediterranean. The port in Haifa became operational in September 2021. The project aims to make country a regional trading hub (*Xinhua News Twitter*, 2021).

Another region where China's expanding BRI is unnerving the regional countries is the South Pacific. In the South Pacific, Beijing has signed MoUs on BRI with many of the Pacific Island Countries. China has gradually emerged as the biggest bilateral lender in the region. Fijian Prime Minister Josaia Voreqe Bainimarama was one of the Heads of States present at the Belt and Road Forum in May 2017 in Beijing. Papua New Guinea (PNG), Fiji and Niue signed MoU with China on the Belt and Road cooperation in 2018. China's financing infrastructure projects like building of a multi-purpose port in PNG's Manus Island, submarine cable project in PNG, Vanuatu's Luganville Whraf redevelopment and other such initiatives have stoked fear down under of China's strong foothold in the strategically vital neighbourhood. China spent a sum of US$ 80.56 million on Luganville Wharf redevelopment which heightened fears of Chinese naval installation in Vanuatu (Lowy Institute, 2021). Reports were carried by Australian media, that Chinese and Vanuatu officials held preliminary talks concerning a potential Chinese military base at Luganville Wharf, funded by a Chinese state-owned enterprise Shanghai Construction Group (Wroe, 2018). Earlier Australia was prompt in replacing China in construction of high-speed undersea telecommunications cables to and PNG and Solomon Islands. A major recent development in the region has been Kiribati and Solomon Islands switching allegiance from Taiwan to China. Kiribati is particularly important for Beijing as it houses China's satellite tracking station which is China's only offshore satellite facility (Pruett, 2020). China's investment in Solomon Islands has increased substantially since 2019, as the country switched allegiance to Beijing. It has come to light that Chinese Sam Enterprise

Group had struck a deal, securing development rights for the entire Tulagi Island in Solomon and its surroundings, for 75 years initially, which can be renewed further. However, the deal was later scrapped. The island is strategically located and it had served as a deepwater harbour for Allied forces in the Pacific during World War II (*New York Times*, 2019). In April 2022, the two countries concluded a *Framework for Security Cooperation*, which took other regional countries by surprise and is creating anxiety in the region.

China's growing interest in the region has largely been in the context of role of these island nations in China's BRI. Pacific Islands figure prominently in China's initiative as "the 21st-Century Maritime Silk Road is an important maritime passage connecting China's coastal ports to Europe through the South China Sea and the Indian Ocean in one route, and the South China Sea to the South Pacific in the other" (Ping, 2017). In recent years, engagement from China, in the region, has been effective and disruptive.

MSR: An Assessment

Maritime power in its civilian and military importance has been a primary constituent for any rising power in any historical epoch. The Indo-Pacific region is witnessing a new set of power rivalries where naval powers with varying degrees of strength have been competing for influence. Therefore, shifts in the distribution of sea power will largely determine the strategic future of the region.

The MSR is already impacting the strategic balance in the Indian Ocean region. MSR is aimed at allowing China's maritime military power to break free from the geographical constraints of the Western Pacific Island chains. Many countries in the Indian Ocean region endorse the MSR idea because it comes with economic incentives "China has used its full diplomatic abilities to bring together the academia, media, museums and its governmental apparatus to ensure successful implementation of Belt Road and MSR initiatives" (Singh, 2021, p. 17).

The MSR has two major routes, starting from the coastal ports of China and extending up to Europe crossing the South Chain Sea, Malacca Straits, and the Indian Ocean and the second, connecting to the South Pacific. It is to be largely understood as an essential strategic tool to pursue President Xi Jinping's goal of turning China into a major maritime power both in the Indian and in the Pacific region.

There are signs that Beijing plans to use port investments to increase its military and political reach in addition to commercial objectives. Most of the Chinese enterprises driving these infrastructure developments have ties with the Chinese authorities. Many of the ports in Africa being built by China's assistance have also been visited by Chinese naval vessels or are dual-use civilian-military ports (CSIS, 2019).

A number of terms like 'chequebook diplomacy', and 'white elephant projects', have been used to criticise China's strategic ambitions and large-scale investments for mega-scale projects, across the region as part of MSR. China's aid programmes and loans on unfavourable terms in most of the island countries, challenge their economic stability puts them under mounting debt pressure, without a promise of delivering real benefits. In most of the cases Beijing's investments were considered as frivolous and inadequately planned. Many years down the line, the mega infrastructure project, has also had limited impact on employment generation (*South Asia Monitor*, 2020). The pace of investment in the BRI has also slowed compared to what it was initially. The decreased outward investment from China has also to do with domestic economic factors as well.

Most of these nations participating in the MSR have a huge trade imbalance with China. Beijing's willingness to invest had come as an alternative for island nations in the region, which were in need of such assistance. However, with the growing realisation about the broader economic, political and security implications of large-scale Chinese investments, the initial enthusiasm of island countries have gradually turned into concerns about viability and transparency of Beijing's extensive projects in the region. However, at the same time, these islands cannot afford to isolate China given the deeper economic ties they have with the later.

Notwithstanding the actual or stated motive of the BRI, it is quite clear that the scope and scale of the project particularly the maritime dimension could bestow China with powerful long-term strategic influence in the Indian Ocean region, which has regional countries concerned about the project (Upadhyaya, 2021). Beyond the debt-trap issue what also cannot be denied is "the short to medium term economic problems that BRI may create for the host countries, such as acute fiscal issues, balance of payments crises, and a dramatic fall in foreign reserves" (Shukla, 2019).

The expansive, non-transparent and unsustainable nature of Beijing's extensive projects under BRI, its increasing footprint in the Indian Ocean, its assertive actions in the South China Sea and its push in the South Pacific have caused apprehensions among the regional countries.

China has gradually developed a modern and advanced naval force to project power beyond its shores. PLA navy is well equipped with force projection capabilities such as aircraft carriers, attack and conventional submarines, long-range reconnaissance aircraft, and a large number of ocean-going platforms coupled with considerable sea-lift capabilities (Naidu, 2021). Now with the MSR, China is using its financial muscle and economic diplomacy to gain geopolitical clout in the region.

In recent years, there are growing concerns about China's debt trap diplomacy, accompanied by the Covid pandemic and related hurdles in most of the projects and Beijing's economic compulsions have slowed down the progress on many of the projects and highlighted the frailties' of the BRI. As China aggressively pursues its maritime strategy across the Indo-Pacific region, MSR may potentially affect the balance of power in the region.

References

Aneja, Atul (2016), "Djibouti, Myanmar and Sri Lanka anchor China's Maritime Silk Road", *The Hindu* 16 February 2016, at https://www.thehindu.com/news/international/djibouti-myanmar-and-sri-lanka-anchor-chinas-maritime-silk-road/article8240828.ece

Assessing the Risks of Chinese Investments in Sub-Saharan African Ports, Centre for Strategic and International Studies, 4 June 2019, at https://www.csis.org/analysis/assessing-risks-chinese-investments-sub-saharan-african-ports

Carver, Edward (2018), "Local fishers oppose $2.7 billion deal opening Madagascar to Chinese fishing", Place of Publication? 5 November 2018, at https://news.mongabay.com/2018/11/local-fishers-oppose-2-7-billion-deal-opening-madagascar-to-chinese-fishing/

China Xinhua News, Twitter page, 2 September 2021, at https://twitter.com/XHNews https://twitter.com/XHNews/status/1433422350083510285?ref_src=twsrc%5Etfw%7Ctwcamp%5Etweetembed%7Ctwterm%5E1433422350083510285%7Ctwgr%5E%7Ctwcon%5Es1_&ref_url=https%3A%2F%2Feurasiantimes.com

%2Fchinese-investments-in-israels-haifa-port-rattle-the-us-washington-raises-espionage-concerns%2F

"China Is Leasing an Entire Pacific Island, Its Residents Are Shocked", *New York Times*, 16 October 2019, at https://www.nytimes.com/2019/10/16/world/australia/china-tulagi-solomon-islands-pacific.html

"China's BRI promised prosperity, gave debt trap to countries like Pakistan, Sri Lanka, Maldives", *South Asia Monitor*, 10 October 2020, at https://www.southasiamonitor.org/china-watch/chinas-bri-promised-prosperity-gave-debt-trap-countries-pakistan-sri-lanka-maldives

"Chinese Embassy in Fiji, Article by Ambassador ZHANG Ping Entitled "Closer Co-Operation under Belt and Road Win-Win for Fiji, China", 2017, at http://fj.china-embassy.gov.cn/eng/sgxx/dshd/201705/t20170517_1036082.htm

"Chinese-built Lamu Port in Kenya starts operations", *Xinhua*, 21 May 2021, at http://www.xinhuanet.com/english/2021-05/21/c_139959211.htm

Haralambides, Hercules and Merk, Olaf (2020), "The Belt and Road Initiative: Impacts on Global Maritime Trade Flows", International Transport Forum, Discussion Paper, at chrome-extension://efaidnbmnnnibpcajpcglclefindmkaj/viewer.html?pdfurl=https%3A%2F%2Fwww.itf-oecd.org%2Fsites%2Fdefault%2Ffiles%2Fdocs%2Fbelt-road-initiative-maritime-trade-flows_1.pdf&clen=2194542&chunk=true, p. 4.

Jabarkhyl, Nawied (2017), "Oman counts on Chinese billions to build desert boomtown", Reuters, 5 September, at https://www.reuters.com/article/us-oman-china-investment-idUSKCN1BG1WJ

Kumar, P Prem and Kawase, Kenji (2022), "China-backed Malaysia megacity project struggles to gain momentum", 14 March, *Nikkei Asia*, at https://asia.nikkei.com/Business/Markets/Property/China-backed-Malaysia-megacity-project-struggles-to-gain-momentum

Lowy Institute, Pacific Aid map, at https://pacificaidmap.lowyinstitute.org/

Naidu, GVC (2021), "India and Maritime Silk Road", in Manish (ed.), *The Belt and Road Initiative: Implications for India*, Pentagon Press, New Delhi.

National People's Congress of China (2019), "Working Together to Deliver a Brighter Future for BRI", Keynote speech by Xi Jinping, President of the People's Republic of China, at the opening ceremony of the Second Belt and Road Forum for International Cooperation Beijing, 26 April, at chrome-extension://efaidnbmnnnibpcajpcglclefindmkaj/viewer.html?pdfurl=http%3A%2F%2Fwww.npc.gov.cn%2Fnpc%2Fc16175%2F201909%2F58541b5bd2fc416481919ec3d259a1e3%2Ffiles%2F3aa8b87afc19439fb8a0550e50d0cb22.pdf&clen=6496639

NDTV India, 2017, "At a Forgotten Pakistan Port, China Paves A New Silk Road", 26 October 2017, at https://www.ndtv.com/world-news/at-a-forgotten-pakistan-port-china-paves-a-new-silk-road-1767211

Parashar, Sachin (2018), "China's ocean observatory in Maldives sparks fresh security concerns", *Times of India*, 26 February, at http://timesofindia.indiatimes.com/articleshow/63072040.cms?utm_source=contentofinterest&utm_medium=text&utm_campaign=cppst

"Pivot of China's new silk road, Gwadar port has hit a bump in slow internet", *The Print*, 13 January 2018, at https://theprint.in/economy/pivot-of-chinas-new-silk-road-gwadar-port-has-hit-a-bump-in-slow-internet/82426/

Roy Chaudhury, Dipanjan (2018), "President-elect Ibu Solih may look at halting BRI projects in Maldives", *Economic Times*, 19 October, https://economictimes.indiatimes.com/news/international/world-news/president-elect-ibu-solih-may-look-at-halting-bri-projects-in-maldives/articleshow/66278481.cms

Roy Chaudhury, Dipanjan (2021), "China widens presence in Indian Ocean through massive inroads in Djibouti", *Economic Times,* 10 October, at https://economictimes.indiatimes.com/news/defence/china-widens-presence-in-indian-ocean-through-massive-inroads-in-djibouti/articleshow/86676234.cms?utm_source=contentofinterest&utm_medium=text&utm_campaign=cppst

Pruett, Richard K. (2020), "A United States-Kiribati Compact of Free Association Would Yield Mutual Dividend", *Asia Pacific Bulletin,* No. 501, March 2020,at https://www.eastwestcenter.org/publications/united-states-kiribati-compact-free-association-would-yield-mutual-dividends#:~:text=Kiribati%20is%20a%20Pacific%20Micronesian,Micronesia%2C%20and%20the%20Marshall%20Islands.&text=Each%20is%20now%20a%20sovereign,law%20equal%20to%20the%20Constitution.

Singh, Abhay Kumar (2017), "Unpacking China's White Paper on Maritime Cooperation under BRI", IDSA, June 2017, at https://www.idsa.in/issuebrief/chinas-white-paper-on-maritime-cooperation-under-bri_aksingh_280617#footnote1_a663zi2

Singh, Raghvendra (2021), "Remarks", in "Roads Winds, Spices in the Western Indian Ocean: The Memory and Geopolitics of Maritime Heritage", P. Pandey P. and N K. Mahawar N. (eds.), Macmillan Education and ICWA, New Delhi.

Shukla, Srijan (2019), "Two phrases critics of China's BRI must not use – debt trap & threat to sovereignty", *The Print*, at https://theprint.in/opinion/two-phrases-critics-of-chinas-bri-must-not-use-debt-trap-threat-to-sovereignty/229544/

State Council, People's Republic of China (2017), "Full text of the Vision for Maritime Cooperation under the Belt and Road Initiative", at http://english.www.gov.cn/archive/publications/2017/06/20/content_281475691873460.htm

Upadhyaya, Shishir (2021), "The Maritime Dimension of China' BRI: Implications for India", in *The Belt and Road Initiative: Implications for India*Manish (ed.), Pentagon Press, New Delhi.

Wroe, David (2018), "China eyes Vanuatu military base in plan with global ramifications", *Sydney Morning Herald*, 9 April 2018, at https://www.smh.com.au/politics/federal/china-eyes-vanuatu-military-base-in-plan-with-global-ramifications-20180409-p4z8j9.html

3. Economic Implications of BRI

Rahul Nath Choudhury

Abstract

Over the last 9 years since its launch, BRI has expanded to areas such as economic and trade cooperation zones, industrial parks, finance and trade cooperation, innovation and technology, people-to-people and cultural exchange among others. The participants have benefitted to some extent with an increase in percentage of trade with China and direct investment from the country. However, along with these benefits, BRI also involves a potential threat to the participants. BRI projects in many countries have been criticised for their ambiguous bidding process, offering the contract to Chinese companies, skyrocketing costs, and even for employing Chinese labour depriving the locals. In this background, the current chapter aims to explore these two distinct features of BRI viz. the benefits it brings with the expanded volume of trade and the risk associated with it.

The Belt and Road Initiative (BRI), erstwhile known as One Belt One Road (OBOR) is an ambitious plan launched by China in 2013 to develop infrastructure of trade routes connecting China with the rest of the world. Chinese President Xi Jinping announced the BRI plan in two different speeches delivered in Kazakhstan and Indonesia. In Kazakhstan, President Xi explained his plan of restoring land routes from China to Central Asia and Europe which is also known as Silk Route, while in Indonesia, President Xi shared his ambition to connect China to the Middle East and Europe though sea route naming it as Maritime Silk Road. BRI has a component of 6 economic corridors: China-Mongolia-Russia Economic Corridor, the New Eurasian Land Bridge, the China-Central Asia-West Asia Economic Corridor, the China-Indochina Peninsula Economic

Corridor, the China-Pakistan Economic Corridor, and the Bangladesh-China-India-Myanmar Economic Corridor.

The BRI was launched at a time when most of its participants were experiencing an acute deficit in their infrastructure spending. OECD estimated global infrastructure investment needs range annually between US$ 2.9 trillion and US$ 6.3 trillion (OECD, 2018). Asian Development Bank (ADB) reported an investment need of around US$ 26 trillion until 2030 for infrastructure sector in the Asian region only. Globally, by sector, the largest investment needs lie in transport and energy infrastructure (ADB, 2017). They are followed by rail transport, telecommunications and water infrastructure.

Table 3.1: Region-wise Infrastructure Requirement (as % of GDP)

Region	Requirement
Pacific	9.1
South Asia	8.8
Central Asia	7.8
Southeast Asia	5.7
East Asia	5.2

Source: OECD (2018)

The BRI was seen as a means to address these critical needs and thus become attractive to a number of countries around the globe.

Over the years, BRI has been expanded to areas beyond trade routes such as economic and trade cooperation zones, industrial parks, finance and trade cooperation, innovation and technology, people-to-people and cultural exchange among others (BRF, 2019). The economies participating in BRI have benefitted in some ways. One such benefit is their increased trade and investment with China. Along with the benefits, BRI also involves a potential threat to the participants. BRI projects in many countries have been criticised for their ambiguous bidding process, offering contracts to Chinese companies, skyrocketing costs, and even for employing Chinese labour depriving the locals. In 2018, Malaysia cancelled a BRI project worth US$ 22 billion due to alleged inflated costs (Chatzky and McBride, 2020). Another crucial allegation is that, through BRI, China is pushing the participants to huge unsustainable debt (sometimes leading to bankruptcy) making them vulnerable and thus increase its diplomatic and economic influence. Indian political scientist Brahma Chellaney termed it as 'debt trap diplomacy' (Chellaney, 2017). Experts allege BRI of Trojan horse for China-led regional development and military expansion (Chatzky and McBride, 2020). In this background, the current chapter aims to explore these two distinct features of BRI viz. the benefit it brings with the expanded volume of trade and the risk of getting debt trapped by China.

China's Trade and Investment with BRI Participants

As mentioned in its communiqué, trade is a vital part of the BRI. The initiative is also a crucial element of the Chinese trade and investment initiative that seeks to promote regional economic integration and promote greater economic reliance on China and establish Chinese economic influence. China aims to bring synergy between its manufacturing sector and its foreign trade. To bring synergy between its manufacturing sector and its foreign trade, China announced 'Made in China 2025' plan in 2015. Made in China 2025 is a national strategic plan to further develop the manufacturing sector and bring Chinese firms to a higher level of supply chain network (US Chamber of Commerce, 2017). Made in China 2025 naturally fits in the Chinese strategy to transfer lower technology activities toward the BRI countries. Experts view BRI as a crucial tool to support China's 'Made in China 2025' Plan.

The bilateral trade between China and the BRI participants has increased since they have joined the mega plan. The Chinese trade with BRI countries for the period between 2013 and 2021 increased from US$ 1.4 trillion to US$ 1.8 trillion (China.org.cn, 2022). The share of BRI countries in China's total trade increased to 29.7 per cent in 2021 from 25 per cent in 2013. Notably, despite having so much debate on the issue, Chinese trade with BRI partners experienced a merely 4 per cent increase in this period.

Foreign Direct Investment

Over the last decades, foreign direct investment (FDI) in BRI economies has risen significantly. Over the period between 2013 and 2021, China's outward foreign direct investment flows to countries participating in the BRI reached US$ 161.3 billion. Further, Chinese enterprises have invested US$ 43.08 billion in overseas economic and trade cooperation zones established in BRI participating countries. The BRI countries have also made a significant investment in China. The combined investment of BRI countries in China reached US$ 71.2 billion during the period (China.org.cn, 2022).

Among the industries, energy sector received the highest volume of investment of 39 per cent followed by transport (25), real estate (22) and metals (10). The East Asian region received 27 per cent of total BRI investment followed by West Asia (22) Sub-Saharan Africa (21) Arab and Middle East (14) (Nedopil, 2021). These investments are financed through loans provided by Chinese financial institutions and/or contractors with the project often receiving guarantees through the host country's government institution. The prominent companies that executed the BRI construction projects are PowerChina, China Communications Construction and Sinpoec. Notably, all the companies are State-owned Chinese enterprises.

BRI and China's Trade Agreements

Another critical issue around BRI can be analysed from China's engagement in recent trade agreements, especially in light of the Regional Comprehensive Economic Partnership Agreement (RCEP) and Comprehensive and Progressive Trans-Pacific Partnership (CPTPP).

RCEP is a trade agreement covering 15 East Asian and Pacific Nations of different economic sizes and stages of development, representing around 30 per cent of world GDP. The agreement encompasses several areas of cooperation, with tariff concessions as a central principle, which will eliminate 90 per cent of tariffs within the bloc (UNCTAD, 2021).

The CPTPP was originally conceived as Trans-Pacific Partnership or TPP by 12 countries, namely Australia Brunei, Canada, Chile, Japan, Malaysia, Mexico, New Zealand, Peru, Singapore, Vietnam and the United States. TPP was set to become the world's largest free trade deal, covering 40 per cent of the global economy. It is estimated that the CPTPP reduces tariffs by 98 per cent among its members (McBride, et al., 2021). On 16 September 2021, China formally submitted its application to join the CPTPP. China shares strong trade ties with all the members of the CPTPP. It also has preferential or free trade agreements with all the countries except Mexico and Canada. The majority of the members are also connected to China through RCEP. As per the United Nations COMTRADE data, 6 out of the 11 CPTPP countries, China accounts for more than 20 per cent of bilateral merchandise trade. Economies like

Australia, Chile and Peru have above 25 per cent of bilateral merchandise trade with China (Schott, 2021).

Risks Associated with the Investment

Over the last 9 years of BRI, the number of participants in this Chinese initiative has increased continuously. Yet, it raises concern about the sustainability of the projects funded under this plan. Chinese investments have strenuously been criticised for exposing the participating country to huge financial risk. Given their size and scale, the BRI projects inherently carry several risks commonly found in the mega infrastructure development projects. China seems to benefit from such weaknesses of the developing countries.

The Debt Trap

Among many criticisms of the Chinese development model under the BRI scheme, the most common is to push the loan-availing economy to the 'debt trap'. It is referred to a as a method of extending loans to an economy of very high amount which is often not sustainable and also under strict repayment methods. Later, when the debtor country fails to repay the loan, creditor takes control of the property constructed by its loan. There is also concern raised by experts that maintaining debt will create an unfavourable degree of dependency on China as a creditor. Conducting a detailed analysis (Hurley, et al., 2018), identified 8 countries viz. Djibouti, Maldives, Laos, Montenegro, Mongolia, Tajikistan, Kyrgyz Republic, and Pakistan as vulnerable to the Chinese debt trap. As reflected in this list, small and economically weak nations are more vulnerable to the risks of the debt trap.

The implications of Chinese loan were clearly visible in 2018, when China took control of the Hambantota port in Sri Lanka constructed under BRI initiative. *The New York Times* in 2018 highlighted how due to opaque contractual terms and its inability to repay the loans, Sri Lanka had to hand over the control of the Hambantota port for 99-year lease to China (Habib, 2018). China influenced Sri Lanka to construct the port despite several feasibility studies questioning the sustainability of the project. In the same manner, Djibouti in the East African region may lose its control of a container terminal built as part of BRI projects, after it was saddled with debt equivalent to 88 per cent of its GDP of US$ 1.72 billion. Due to the widespread criticism of its policy, a "debt-sustainability framework" was established by China during the Second Belt and Road Forum (WBD, 2019).

Inflated Costs

Alongside, debt trap diplomacy through BRI, China is also accused of inflating the costs of the projects. A few countries such as Uganda, Malaysia have carried out investigations to find out the reasons behind the very high cost of projects. Investigating the construction cost Kampala-Entebbe Highway, in Uganda, built under BRI plan, the auditor general found the cost was highly inflated (Nancy, et al., 2019). This accusation of inflating cost and financing of economically unviable projects, led to cancellation or halt of several projects in various parts of the world. Mass protests have been organised in many countries such as Pakistan, Malaysia, Kazakhstan by the civil society and common citizens against BRI, driven by the concern of rising cost of the projects and their sustainability. After assuming the office in 2018, Malaysian Prime Minister Mahathir Mohammad cancelled a BRI project connecting Malaysia with Singapore through high-speed railway questioning the cost and viability of the project and large-scale corruption allegations. In Africa, Sierra Leone called off a China-funded airport project at the cost of US$ 318 million out of debt-burden concerns in 2018 (Nancy, et al., 2019). In 2018, Myanmar also scaled back a BRI project due to high cost involved in it (Kapoor and Thant, 2018). It is noteworthy to mention that these incidences occurred after China took the control of Sri Lankan port in 2018.

Ambiguous Bidding Process and Widespread Corruption

The BRI has also drawn global attention for its blurred bidding and procurement policy. China maintains a very strict policy against disclosing the contract terms with BRI participants. There is very limited publicly available information about the procedure applied in identifying the firms to execute projects. Any detailed analysis becomes extremely difficult due to lack of comprehensive and cross-country data regarding the bidding process under different BRI projects. Based on the partial information available, it has been found that majority of the BRI projects are awarded to Chinese firms primarily the State Owned Enterprises (SOE) for both construction and supply. Baker McKenzie (2017) reported that Chinese

SOEs have invested or participated in at least 1,700 BRI projects since until 2017. The Center for Strategic and International Studies estimates that around 89 per cent of BRI projects were allocated to Chinese companies in 2018. Ghossein, et al., (2018) in a World Bank working paper suggest that China Communications Construction Company and China Railway Construction Corporation were among the major firms who have won the bid for BRI projects so far. Similar to the bidding process the source of financing organisation for the BRI projects are also concentrated in four Chinese state-owned commercial banks. These are China Development Bank, China Exim Bank, Agricultural Development Bank of China, and Industrial and Commercial Bank of China. It has been estimated that about half of the financing for BRI projects (comprising outstanding loans or equity investment) has been provided by these big four Chinese banks (OECD 2018; Baniya, et al., 2019).

The BRI is also severely criticised for widespread corruption. The Corruption Perception Index (CPI) 2021 scores suggest that the perceived corruption in Belt and Road participants' economies is higher than the global average and is highest among lower-middle- and low-income BRI participating economies. Perceptions of bribery are higher in construction and public works than in any other sector, including the arms industry and oil and gas sectors, according to the Transparency International 2011 Bribe Payers Index.

Environmental Degradation

The BRI plan also poses a great risk of environmental degradation. Experts have categorised the environmental risk posed by BRI as direct and indirect (Lososet, et al., 2019). The environmental risk varies with the size of the project, type of the project (rail, road or energy) and domestic condition of the country. Many BRI projects routes pass through steep terrain, while rail and particularly high-speed rail are constrained to fairly straight paths, and less easily routed around topographical and hydrological barriers. BRI projects lead to a huge loss of forest cover. Construction around the terrain poses risk of soil erosion, landslides, flooding in the region, sedimentation in rivers, and interruptions of water courses. Polluting air and water, habitat destruction and fragmentation, displacement of flora fauna, animal migration, and human-wildlife collusion among other prominent environmental threats posed by BRI projects. It is estimated that BRI projects would possibly increase global carbon dioxide emissions by 0.3 per cent, while 7 per cent or more in case of low-income economies (World Bank, 2019). Further, BRI project would increase global warming by 2°C. The Tsinghua-based Center for Finance and Development estimated that the current carbon footprint of the BRI should be reduced by a 68 per cent to stay within this limit. Otherwise, it could lead alone to warming of nearly 3°C (Héraud, 2019).

New Initiative by Non-participants to BRI

Along with offering connectivity through infrastructure financing, creating its economic and diplomatic influence has been one of the prominent ambitions of Chinese President Xi. To some extent, it has been successful in surpassing the US and other developed European nations as major development partners in select African countries. In a time of heightened US-China rivalry, the US and other G7 nations launched Build Back Better World (B3W) initiative during the 47th G7 summit in 2021. The summit was attended by Australia, India, South Korea and South Africa as guest participants. B3W promises to be a values-driven, market-led, high-standard, and transparent infrastructure partnership to help narrow the US$ 40+ trillion infrastructure gap in the developing world by 2035. It aims to coordinate in mobilising private-sector capital in four areas of focus—climate, health and health security, digital technology, and gender equity and equality. The B3W is intended to be global in scope and to cover low-and middle-income countries. B3W is perceived as a response to China from the US and like-minded countries to counter BRI. More importantly, this initiative is seen as a strategy to build a coalition among low and middle-income countries while offering to finance an alternative grand infrastructure plan to that of China led by the US and other G7 countries (Panda, 2021). Once implemented, B3W aspires to become one of the largest infrastructure-focused initiatives, extending from Latin America and the Caribbean to Africa to the Indo-Pacific. Comparing B3W with BRI would be too early given the nascent stage of the initiative. B3W plan was unveiled less than a year ago compared to 9 years of BRI (White House, 2021).

Downturn in BRI

A recent report released by the Chinese Think Tank Green BRI suggests that investment in BRI has reduced drastically by 54 per cent in 2020 compared to 2019 (Nedopil, 2022). The report also suggests that China has been struggling to finance BRI projects in various parts of the world. This reduction is primarily attributed to the several countries that opted out from their proposed investment as mentioned earlier in the chapter. Countries like Malaysia, and Uganda have scrapped a few BRI projects. Countries have initialled legal investigations against BRI projects. Due to negative sentiments and perceptions emerged among the countries after the Hambantota incidence has further damaged the prospects of several BRI projects. Further BRI scheme has greatly suffered due to the outbreak of the COVID-19. Almost all the countries have been affected by the COVID-19 which in turn affected the economies and their capacity to invest in any projects.

Conclusion

This chapter attempted to address two important aspects of BRI. First, what are the benefits BRI brings for its participants and second what are the risks in getting associated with the BRI projects. The participants have benefitted to some extent from a growth in the percentage of trade. However, contrary to general perception China's trade with BRI partner countries has increased only by 4 per cent in the period 2013-2021. Over the China's foreign direct investment (FDI) countries participating in the BRI reached US$ 161.3 billion.

The study further finds, BRI projects have come with a huge cost to many participants. Countries like Sri Lanka had to lose control of their Hambantota port. Djibouti in the East African region is also on the verge of losing its control of a container terminal built as part of BRI projects. BRI projects have been criticised for their opaque bidding process, widespread corruption and inflated cost. BRI exposes the participant to huge financial risk and drags them to debt trap, especially in small and economically weak nations.

References

ADB. (2017), Meeting Asia's Infrastructure Needs, Asian Development Bank, at https://www.adb.org/publications/asia-infrastructure-needs. Accessed on 25 February 2022.

Baker McKenzie (2017). Belt & Road: Opportunity and Risk, at https://www.bakermckenzie.com/-/media/files/insight/publications/2017/10/beltroad/baker_mckenzie_belt_road_report_2017.pdf?la=en. Accessed on 25 February 2022.

Baniya, S., et al., (2019). "Trade Effects of the New Silk Road: A Gravity Analysis", World Bank Policy Research Working Paper 8694. The Word Bank, Washington DC.

BRF (2019). Full text of joint communique of leaders' roundtable of 2nd Belt and Road Forum. The State Council Information Office, Peoples Republic of China. http://english.scio.gov.cn/beltandroad/2019-04/27/content_76349836.htm. Accessed on 24 April 2022.

BRI News (January 15, 2020). "China's Foreign Trade with Belt & Road Countries Robust in 2019". Business Reporting Desk, at https://www.beltandroad.news/2020/01/15/chinas-foreign-trade-with-belt-road-countriesrobust-in-2019/. Accessed on 15 January 2022.

China.org.cn (May,25 2022). Press conference on integrating domestic and foreign trade and fostering dual circulation development, at http://english.scio.gov.cn/pressroom/2022-05/25/content_78236271.htm. Accessed on 24 June 2022

Chatzky, A. and McBride, J. (January 28, 2020). China's Massive Belt and Road Initiative,

Council on Foreign Relations, at https://www.cfr.org/backgrounder/chinas-massive-belt-and-road-initiative. Accessed on 22 March 2022.

Chellaney, B. (2017). China's Debt-Trap Diplomacy. Project Syndicate, at https://www.project-syndicate.org/commentary/china-one-belt-one-road-loans-debt-by-brahma-chellaney-2017-01?barrier=accesspaylog. Accessed on 26 April 2022.

Ghossein, T., B. Hoekman, and Shingal, A. (2018). "Public Procurement in the Belt and Road Initiative", Background paper, World Bank, Washington, DC.

Habib, A. M. (June 25, 2018). "How China Got Sri Lanka to Cough Up a Port". The New York Times, at https://www.nytimes.com/2018/06/25/world/asia/china-sri-lanka-port.html. Accessed on 23 March 2022.

Héraud, B., (2019). Les nouvelles routes de la soiemettentenpérill'AccorddeParis. Novethic, at https://www.novethic.fr/actualite/environnement/climat/isr-rse/la-nouvelle-route-de-la-soie-pourrait-mettre-en-peril-l-accord-de-paris-147649.html. Accessed on 21 April 2022.

Hurley, J., Scott M., and Gailyn, P. (2018). "Examining the Debt Implications of the Belt and Road Initiative from a Policy Perspective". CGD Policy Paper, at https://www.cgdev.org/sites/default/files/examining-debt-implications-belt-and-road-initiative-policy-perspective.pdf. Accessed on 21 April 2022.

Joshua P. M., (June 19, 2017). "China's One Belt One Road initiative: A view from the United States". Brookings Institute, at https://www.brookings.edu/research/chinas-one-belt-one-road-initiative-a-view-from-the-united-states/. Accessed on 22 February 2022.

Kapoor, K., Thant, A. M. (August 2, 2018). "Myanmar scales back Chinese-backed port project due to debt fears – official". Reuters. At https://www.reut.ers.com/article/us-myanmar-china-port-exclusive/exclusive-myanmar-scales-back-chinese-backed-port-project-due-to-debt-fears-official-idUSKBN1KN106. Accessed on 17 March 2022.

Kyger, L. (January 30, 2020). "China seeks to redraw the global trade map". The Hinrich Foundation, at https://www.hinrichfoundation.com/research/tradevistas/us-china/belt-and-road-initiative/. Accessed on 14 February 2022.

Losos E., Pfaff A., Olander L., Mason S., Morgan S., (2019). "Reducing Environmental Risks from Belt and Road Initiative Investments in Transportation Infrastructure". Policy Research Working Paper 8718, World Bank, Washington, DC.

Made in China 2025, at https://english.www.gov.cn/2016special/madeinchina2025/. Accessed on 13 February 2022.

US Chamber of commerce (2017). "Made in China 2025: Global ambitions built on local protections", at https://www.uschamber.com/assets/archived/images/final_made_in_china_2025_report_full.pdf. Accessed on 11 March 2022.

Nancy, M. G. Et.al. (2019). "The Belt and Road Initiative Opportunities and Risks for Africa's Connectivity", China Quarterly of International Strategic Studies, Vol. 5, No. 1, 117–141.

Nedopil, C. (2021). "Investments in the Belt and Road Initiative", Green Finance & Development Center, FISF Fudan University. Shanghai.

Nedopil, C. (2022). "China Belt and Road Initiative (BRI) Investment Report 2021". Green Finance & Development Center, FISF Fudan University, Shanghai.

MFA (2021) Wang Yi Presides over Asia and Pacific High-level Video Conference on Belt and Road Cooperation. Ministry of Foreign Affairs of the people's Republic of China.

MFA (July 26, 2019). Chinese Embassy in Sweden, Ministry of Foreign Affairs, Peoples Republic of China, The Belt and Road Initiative Progress, Contributions and Prospects, at https://www.mfa.gov.cn/ce/cese/eng/zgxw/t1675676.htm. Accessed on 25 April 2022.

OECD. (2018). "China's Belt and Road Initiative in the global trade, investment and finance landscape", OECD Business and Finance Outlook 2018, OECD Paris, at https://www.oecd.org/finance/Chinas-Belt-and-Road-Initiative-in-the-global-trade-investment-and-finance-landscape.pdf. Accessed on 9 April 2022.

Panda, J. (August 9, 2021). Build Back Better World Initiative: A Partnership Against or Beyond China? MP-IDSA Issue Brief 2021, at https://www.idsa.in/issuebrief/build-back-better-world-initiative-jpanda-090821. Accessed on 7 March 2022.

The White House (June 12, 2021), "Fact Sheet: President Biden and G7 Leaders Launch Build Back Better World (B3W) Partnership". Press release, at https://www.whitehouse.gov/briefing-room/statements-releases/2021/06/12/fact-sheet-president-biden-and-g7-leaders-launch-build-back-better-world-b3w-partnership/. Accessed on 2 March 2022.

The World Bank. (2019). "Belt and Road Economics: Opportunities and Risks of Transport Corridors". The World Bank, at https://www.worldbank.org/en/topic/regional-integration/publication/belt-and-road-economics-opportunities-and-risks-of-transport-corridors. Accessed on 4 March 2022.

Transparancy International (2021), The Corruption Perception Index (CPI) 2021, at https://www.transparency.org/en/cpi/2021. Accessed on 25 February 2022.

Transparency International (2011). Bribe Payers Index 2011, at http://files.transparency.org/content/download/98/395/file/2011_BPI_EN.pdf. Accessed on 25 March 2022.

UNCTAD. (2021). A new centre of gravity: The regional comprehensive economic partnership and its trade effects. UNCTAD, at https://unctad.org/system/files/official-document/ditcinf2021d5_en_0.pdf. Accessed on 4 March 2022.

US Chambers of Commerce (2017). "Made in China 2025: Global ambitions built on local protections", US Chamber of Commerce, at https://www.uschamber.com/assets/archived/images/final_made_in_china_2025_report_full.pdf. Accessed on 2 April 2022.

WBD. (2019). "China's Belt and Road Initiative: Why the Price Is Too High. Podcasts". Wharton Business School, at https://knowledge.wharton.upenn.edu/article/chinas-belt-and-road-initiative-why-the-price-is-too-high/. Accessed on 11 March 2022.

World Bank. (2019). Belt and Road Economics: Opportunities and Risks of Transport Corridors. Advance Edition. Report Number 137911, World Bank, at https://www.worldbank.org/en/topic/regional-integration/publication/belt-and-road-economics-opportunities-and-risks-of-transport-corridors Accessed on 22 February 2022.

4. The United States and China: The Strategic Competition and Response

Stuti Banerjee and *Ankita Dutta*

Abstract

The relations with China are viewed from the spectrum of strategic competition by the United States. In the past three decades, their relations have evolved from conflict to dialogue to cooperation to strategic competition and rivalry. While both the countries have found some common ground on issues related to climate change, the key issues such as trade divergences, high technology, threat perception, etc. have remained unresolved. These issues are further compounded by the rise of China as an economic powerhouse in the region. Its increasingly aggressive actions in its neighbourhood, its expanding military might and divergences on the key global multilateral issues —have further complicated the bilateral relations between the two. The blurring lines between China's economic, military and political strategies such as through the Belt and Road Initiative (BRI) is being increasingly studied by several countries. Viewed from the United States perspective, it represents a significant challenge to the United States' economic, political, climate change, security, and global health interests. The paper looks at the evolving relations between the United States and China and analyses the trajectory of relations by studying the three recent Presidencies of the United States—Barack Obama, Donald Trump and Joe Biden. It looks at the United States administrations' response to China and various policy frameworks adopted.

Introduction

The geo-political rivalry between the United States (US) and China can be viewed through many lenses. It is a competition between democracy and autocracy, between two militaries, between a private capital economy and a state-supported economy, between a pioneer of advanced technologies and one that is trying to replace it, and between an established and rising power. The past decade has been a major inflexion point in the relations between US and China. The rise in Beijing's assertive posturing in the international system, its expanding military presence and increasing economic influence, especially in the Indo-Pacific region, has ensured that the US and other countries are revisiting their strategies towards China.

Within this scenario, the Belt and Road Initiative (BRI), launched by Chinese President Xi Jinping in 2013 represents one of the largest foreign policies undertaken by any country. The Scope of BRI has also expanded from the development of infrastructure through roads, railways and ports to include the aspects of digital connectivity where the emphasis is to improve on telecommunication networks, e-commerce and development of artificial intelligence capabilities. The idea behind the initiative is two-fold—first, is to connect China's modern cities to its underdeveloped region and second, to connect the mainland to Eurasian, Southeast Asian, and South Asian regions. The blurring lines between China's economic, military and political strategies such as through the BRI is being increasingly being studied by several countries. Viewed from the US perspective, it represents a significant challenge to US economic, political, climate change, security, and global health interests. The paper looks at the evolving relations between the US and China and analyses the trajectory of relations by studying the three recent Presidencies of the US-Barack Obama, Donald Trump and Joe Biden. It looks at the US administrations' response to China and various policy frameworks adopted.

Rising China and Responses from the United States

The relations with China are viewed from the spectrum of strategic competition by the US. In the past three decades, their relations have evolved from conflict to dialogue to cooperation to strategic competition and rivalry. While both the countries have found some common ground on issues related to climate, the key issues such as trade divergences, high technology, threat perception, etc. have remained unresolved. These issues are further compounded by the rise of China as an economic powerhouse in the region. Its increasingly aggressive actions in its neighbourhood, its expanding military might and divergences on the key global multilateral issues—have further complicated the bilateral relations between the two. The following section traces the trajectory of the relationship through three US Presidencies—President Obama, President Trump and President Biden.

President Barack Obama's Pivot to Asia

President Barack Obama came into office as "*the first Pacific President*," stressing that his Administration would pay attention to Asian regional issues and that the US would restore its engagements in the region. The assurance to its Asian partners and allies came as China's Asia policy became more assertive. During this period, the US adopted a substantive position on China such as support to Japan recognising that the Senkaku islands are under the administration of Japan and providing support to Seoul as Pyongyang tested nuclear weapons.

At the end of 2011 and at the beginning of 2012, the White House announced the US strategic pivot toward the Asia-Pacific region in order to ensure, as it was expressed by President Obama in his address to Australian Parliament, that "the US will play a larger and long-term role in shaping this region and its future". The strategy rested on the "foundation of strong US ties to countries throughout the region". It was to strengthen military alliance, build stronger trade partnerships, strengthen the region's institutional architecture to reinforce rules-based order and foster durable partnerships to address global challenges (Obama White House, 2015). The ultimate goal, according to National Security Advisor Tom Donilon, was to promote US interests by helping to shape the norms and rules of the Asia-Pacific region, to ensure that "international law and norms be respected, that commerce and freedom of navigation are not impeded, that emerging powers build trust with their neighbours, and that disagreements are resolved peacefully without threats or coercion" (Donilon, 2011).

In the military sphere, the strategy pushed for the increased redeployment of US forces to West Pacific and East Asia. It called for intensifying bilateral and multilateral military cooperation between the US and its allies and partners in the region. With respect to China, it highlighted the need to gain capabilities to counteract against Chinese espionage especially cyber espionage and the creation of an Air-Sea battle concept with a view to potential conflict with the People Liberation Army (PLA) forces especially in the maritime domain (Przemysław Furgacz, N.A.).

Although the Obama administration did not formally articulate a position on BRI, as part of its Asia strategy, in November 2015, it announced the largest free-trade deal in US history, the Trans-Pacific Partnership (TPP, now known as the Comprehensive and Progressive Agreement for Trans-Pacific Partnership, or CPTPP). The agreement covered 40 percent of the global economy by linking 12 countries on the Pacific. While the US officials stated that the TPP was not designed to exclude China, nonetheless, the stringent obligations requiring transparency and trade liberalisation meant that China was unable to join the initiative. The TPP made the US more economically competitive in Asia, and put pressure on China to raise its standards. The trade agreement was to increase the US access to the growing markets of Asia while enhancing the protection of US intellectual property rights and ensuring that US companies are competing in a more fair and impartial regional market (Manyin, 2012). At the same time, the US was also to work with partners to help maintain a reliable and safe flow of cargo across the Indian and Pacific Oceans in a reference to the growing claims of China in the waters of the region.

The Obama administration also made smaller commitments to connecting and investing in the Asia-Pacific and launched its Power Africa Public-Private Partnership to electrify Africa. Power Africa supports healthy competition in African energy markets to ensure that consumers get the best value for money with the goal of 30,000 MW of cleaner energy and 60 million new connections by 2030 (USAID, 2018). Another key initiative the Global Procurement Initiative, launched by the US Trade and Development Agency (USTDA) was aimed at providing developing countries with a tool kit for open and transparent procurement practices, better methods to determine fair value for purchases, and assistance in selecting smarter and more sustainable infrastructure (USTDA, 2013). The stress on ensuring transparency and governance standards, setting up industrial standards all point to a push from the US to encourage China to include them in its initiatives including the BRI projects and to encourage countries to include such standards in their agreements with China.

The US also made a shift in multilateral diplomacy towards the region with intensified efforts to expand and upgrade its participation in multilateral Asia and Asia-Pacific institutions such as the ASEAN Regional Forum and East Asia Summit. The region was also witnessed increased US diplomatic visibility through high-level visits.

Donald Trump Administration—Indo-Pacific as Next Theatre

President Donald Trump continued the engagement with the Asia Pacific region, abet with a few changes. The presidency focused on the working of the Communist Party of China and the threats that it posed to the American economy, politics and military. President Trump asked four of his most senior national security officials, Robert C. O'Brien, Christopher Wray, William Barr, and Michael Pompeo, to explain current US policy on China to the American people. The Trump Administration's policy experiment on China sought to slow China's progress and pressure Beijing's leadership to become more responsive to American priorities and concerns regarding its behaviour. This policy shift was built upon judgments that China's gains in overall national power came at America's expense, and unless China was stopped or slowed, it could eclipse the US and impose its own vision and values on the international system (Hass, 2020).

Unlike his predecessor, the Trump Administration responded to the BRI which had become a global initiative with a maritime component —the Maritime Silk Road Initiative and the Polar Silk Road Initiative that connected China to Europe through sea routes in the Arctic, digital connectivity through the Digital Silk Road and even started a health initiative as part of its health diplomacy.

In an effort to counter the BRI, the US highlighted the lack of ecological study, labour standards, transfer of technology and financial debt to countries as the negative consequences of the China-led project. To counter the BRI, the administration upgraded its own agencies to better compete with China on strategic infrastructure. Further, it worked to mitigate the risks from Chinese technologies such as Huawei to US' interests. Additionally, Washington highlighted the threat emanating from Chinese theft of intellectual property, unfair trade practises and China's use of BRI to increase its coercive leverage and gain strategic assets. Addressing Asia-Pacific Economic Cooperation (APEC) members in 2018, Vice President Mike Pence warned the member countries that they should, "not accept foreign debt that could compromise your sovereignty.... [The US] don't drown our partners in a sea of debt.... We do not offer a constricting belt or a one-way road" (The Trump White House, 2018).

In October 2018, President Trump signed into law the *Better Utilization of Investments Leading to Development (BUILD) Act*, which created the *Development Finance Corporation (DFC)* to replace the US Overseas Private Investment Corporation (OPIC) as the country's official development bank. The initial capital available to the DFC was US$ 60 billion, which represented the doubling of capital which was available to OPIC. The critical aim for DFC is to invest in infrastructure projects in the developing world. The US Agency for International Development's (USAID) Development Credit Authority was also transferred to DFC, and the DFC was given additional powers, such as the ability to do business with non-US companies, take equity stakes in projects, and lend to SOEs. The Trump administration hoped that these new authorities would allow the DFC to provide more flexible financing terms and, with the US government as a partner, lower the political and regulatory risks for participation by the US private sector. The intent was to provide a counterweight to China's state-centric BRI by catalysing private capital and helping the private sector compete in frontier markets. It was also the time that President Trump implemented tariffs and other trade barriers on a number of Chinese products with the goal of forcing it to make changes to what the US claims were unfair trade practices and intellectual property theft. China retaliated by imposing tariffs on American products triggering a trade war with the second largest economy in the world that continues to date.

In a bid to push for infrastructure development, the US also launched the Blue Dot Network (BDN) with Australia and Japan. The BDN is a multi-stakeholder initiative designed to bring together like-minded governments, the private sector, and civil society under shared values to advance global infrastructure development. The BDN aims to promote quality infrastructure investment that is open and inclusive, transparent, economically viable, Paris Agreement aligned, financially, environmentally and socially sustainable, and compliant with international standards, and laws and regulations (US Department of State, NA). Neither China nor the BRI was mentioned in the vision document, nonetheless, the emphasis on debt transparency, and project-level and country-level debt sustainability, build local capacity, with a focus on local skills transfer and local capital market, promote sustainable and inclusive economic growth and development among other criteria listed for certification indicate that it is being promoted as an alternative to the BRI.

On 20 May 2020, the White House released a report in accordance with the *FY2019 National Defense Authorization Act*, titled 'United States Strategic Approach to the People's Republic of China'. The report details the whole-of-government strategy with respect to the People's Republic of China (PRC) and stated that, "The Administration's approach to the PRC reflects a fundamental re-evaluation of how the US understands and responds to the leaders of the world's most populous country and second largest national economy" (The White House, 2020). To counter the growing challenge from China, the Trump Administration adopted a competitive approach having two objectives; the first objective is to strengthen and improve the resilience of American institutions, alliances and partnerships to withstand the challenges that are presented by the PRC. The second is to compel the PRC to cease or reduce its actions that are harmful to the national security of the US, its allies and partners. Senior officials continued to publicly warn countries about the risks of getting involved in BRI, mainly by emphasising the debt burden of BRI projects and China's use of BRI to increase its coercive leverage. National Security Advisor John Bolton argued BRI had the "ultimate goal of advancing Chinese global dominance."

The most notable effort to arrest the rise of China's growing influence in the region was the embrace of the Indo-Pacific concept by the Trump Administration through the 'free and open Indo-Pacific'. The building blocks of this engagement in the Indo-Pacific region were building collective security through a network of regional allies and partners, promoting economic prosperity, and encouraging good governance and shared principles. The Administration rolled out a number of initiatives, including increased engagement in the Indian Ocean and Pacific Islands region, regional transparency and anti-corruption plans, and digital infrastructure and energy cooperation programs, which support these goals. The Administration's Indo-Pacific concept acknowledged the need to respond more forcefully to Beijing's destabilising behaviour and coercion of regional allies, which has undermined both the US interests and the sovereignty of Indo-Pacific partners (Ford, 2020).

One notable development under the Trump Administration was the focus on expanding the US engagement with smaller nations in the Indian Ocean and Pacific Islands regions. In South Asia, the Administration has worked to tighten relationships with countries such as Nepal and Sri Lanka, offering new high-level dialogues and assistance that includes US$ 500 million toward infrastructure development in Nepal and a high-endurance Coast Guard cutter for Sri Lanka (ibid.). These were visible examples of the US efforts to improve its relations with the countries of the region and to counter Chinese bilateral and multilateral initiatives here.

The maritime component of the BRI, its assertive actions in the South China Sea, and China's disregard for the ruling by the Permanent Court of Arbitration have meant that the US has also stepped up its military activity and naval presence in the region in recent years, including freedom of navigation operations (FONOPs). Recognising the increasing connectivity between the Indian Ocean and the Pacific Ocean, the US also renamed its Pacific Command to Indo-Pacific Command in 2018. The Command is the oldest and largest of the eleven commands operated by the US Department of Defense and has been given priority in its efforts to modernise its hardware and software. Given the increasing complexity of the area of operation, the Command has been tasked to build a strategic environment that maintains the balance of power favourable to the US and manages competition with China responsibly.

Admiral Philip Davidson, former commander of US Indo-Pacific Command, stated that "Through excessive territorial claims, debt-trap diplomacy, violations of international agreements, theft of intellectual property, military intimidation, and outright corruption, the Communist Party of China seeks to control the flow of trade, finance, communications, politics, and the way of life" (Lowy Institute, 2020).

The US National Security Agency also undertook a campaign to contain China's influence in the United Nations and other multilateral institutions. The US concern, which is shared by some of its European colleagues, is that China is seeking to gradually alter the language of UN diplomacy to conform to its own diplomatic vision.

All of these initiatives points to the 'whole of government approach' from the US to counter the growing Chinese influence. The National Security Strategy, the National Defence Strategy and the Indo-Pacific Strategy, together have highlighted the need for all agencies of the US Administration to work together with each other and partners to create a balance of power favourable to the US.

Biden Administration—Democracy vs Autocracy

Since President Joe Biden assumed office, US-China relations have remained on edge. The early signs of the discord were visible in the first press conference by President Biden, where he said that "This is a battle between the utility of democracies in the 21st century and autocracies" adding "We have got to prove democracy works" (Remarks by President Biden in Press Conference, 2021)—which can be construed as a reference to China and Russia. In his first address to Congress, he further elaborated that "We're in competition with China and other countries to win the 21st Century" (Remarks by President Biden to Congress, 2021), pledging to maintain a strong US military presence in the Indo-Pacific and promising to boost technological development and trade. This speech, if looked at in a larger perspective, lays down the US outlook toward China and the action that the administration has taken.

Build Back Better World

During the G7 Summit in 2021, President Biden along with the leaders of the G7 launched "Build back Better World" (B3W) initiative for "a values-driven, high-standard, and transparent infrastructure partnership led by major democracies to help narrow the US$ 40+ trillion infrastructure need in the developing world, which has been exacerbated by the COVID-19 pandemic" (B3W Factsheet, 2021). The idea behind the initiative is to coordinate and mobilise private-sector capital to focus on four key areas – climate, health and health security, digital technology and, gender equity and equality. Pegged as a counter to the BRI, the B3W is also global in scope covering Latin America and the Caribbean to Africa and the Indo-Pacific. As the lead partner of the initiative, the US is working towards "mobilising the full potential of its development financial tools including DFC, USAID, EXIM, the Millennium Challenge Corporation, and the US Trade and Development Agency, and complementary bodies such as the Transaction Advisory Fund" (ibid.). This was done with the aim to complement the domestic infrastructure investment under the American Jobs Plan to create jobs at home and to create opportunities to demonstrate the US competitiveness abroad.

The BRI is seen as a Chinese-government driven project which lacks transparency, has poor environmental and labour standards, and has led to debt troubles in many countries. While China or the BRI are not mentioned in the initiative, the reference to both is clear in the framework. The guiding principles of the B3W (ibid.) provide a clear reference to accomplish the initiatives in the best way possible. The emphasis is laid on the initiative to be "value-driven" with the "*Infrastructure development carried out in a transparent and sustainable manner*—financially, environmentally, and socially—will lead to a better outcome for recipient countries and communities". Similarly, it highlights that the initiative will meet the "*High standards* which have become ever more important at a time when governments are grappling with complex decisions on how to tackle climate change, build back local economies, direct scarce financing, and boost employment in an inclusive way", thereby emphasising on good governance and strong standards. *Climate-friendly investments* is also a key feature of the initiative which is further complimented with strong *strategic partnerships* where the projects will be developed "through consultation with communities and assessing local needs as true partners." In terms of financing, the emphasis is laid on mobilisation of private capital through development finance to address the infrastructure gap in the low and middle-income countries. These investments will be by "responsible and market-driven private sector, paired with high standards and *transparency in public funding*, is crucial for long-run development effectiveness and sustainability". To further create transparency in funding, "rigorous standards for project planning, implementation, social and environmental safeguards, and analytical capability" as developed by multilateral development banks and other international financial institutions will be incorporated in the initiative.

The initial steps in operationalising of the initiative has been in Latin America. Latin American countries have been active partners in the BRI and with the Chinese public banks committing to loans of more than US$ 138 billion to regional governments and state-owned enterprises for projects that are mostly in the energy and infrastructure sectors, since 2005 (China-Latin America Finance Databases, N.A.). China is the top trading partner for several of the region's largest economies, including Brazil, Chile, and Peru. To counter the increasing footprints of Beijing, Washington had sent teams on a "listening tour" of Colombia, Ecuador, and Panama. It seems the idea behind these tours was to scout for potential infrastructure investments the US and other G-7 countries can make (Reuters, 2021).

While critically analysing the initiative, the key challenge for the US and the G7 members is that they have to walk a tightrope in terms of ensuring flexibility and cost-effectiveness of the projects while upholding its key policies of fiscal, labour, environmental and human rights standards. While the strength of the initiative lies in the fact that it is focusing on the areas which can constitute as the strength of the seven countries, still the initiative is at a nascent stage and it remains unclear whether the B3W will emerge as a viable alternative to match the scope of BRI.

Focus on the Indo-Pacific

With the focus of the global geopolitics and geo-economics shifting to the Indo-Pacific from the Euro-Atlantic, the US has also calibrated its policies towards the region. While a shift of interest was visible since the Obama Administration's policy of Pivot to Asia and Rebalance to Asia, the trends were further cemented under the Trump Presidency with the changing of nomenclature of its Pacific Command to Indo-Pacific Command, his initiation of trade war with China and his emphasis on enhancing the US presence in the region. These steps have been taken forward by President Biden, who has also pushed for a comprehensive approach to the region as a way of countering the increasingly aggressive behaviour of China. The region is strategically important for the US as the two-way trade between the US and the region totalled US$ 1.75 trillion in 2020, and it supports more than five million Indo-Pacific jobs. Foreign direct investment from the US was approximately US$ 969 billion (US Indo-Pacific Strategy, 2022) in 2020 and has nearly doubled in the last decade.

The strategic concerns are mainly driven by the economic and energy interests of the countries at play. To say so, more than 40 per cent of the global seaborne trade passes through the Strait of Malacca; around 15.5 million barrels of global oil trade passes through the Gulf of Hormuz; and 11 million barrels of oil pass through Malacca and Singapore straits. These strategic interests make SLOC security a vital need as China's assertive posture such as in the case of South China Sea imposes significant obstacles. These are further compounded by China's expanding footprints in the Indian Ocean and its increasing military posture in the Indo-Pacific region which has resulted in security challenges in the region. In this scenario, the strategic challenges faced by the US vis-à-vis China in the Indo-Pacific region are three-fold: the importance of international law and peaceful settlement of disputes; freedom of navigation and over-flight; and unimpeded lawful commerce, including in the South China Sea. The increasing economic, diplomatic, military, and technological might of China in the region was also mentioned in the US Indo-Pacific Strategy released in February 2022.

The US' outlook toward China is also defined in the Strategy which highlights, "the US is investing in the foundations of our strength at home, aligning our approach with those of our allies and partners abroad, and competing with the PRC to defend the interests and vision for the future that we share with others.... Our objective is not to change the PRC but to shape the strategic environment in which it operates, building a balance of influence in the world that is maximally favourable to the US, our allies and partners, and the interests and values we share. We will also seek to manage competition with the PRC responsibly. We will cooperate with our allies and partners while seeking to work with the PRC in areas like climate change and non-proliferation" (US Indo-Pacific Strategy, 2022). Two key initiatives taken by the US in the region include AUKUS and the launch of Indo-Pacific Economic Framework for Prosperity (IPEF).

AUKUS was announced in September 2021, by Prime Minister Morrison, Prime Minister Johnson, and President Joe Biden to determine, by March 2023, the optimal pathway for an Australian conventionally-armed, nuclear-powered submarine capability. AUKUS aims to – first, provide Australia with a conventionally armed, nuclear-powered submarine capability at the earliest possible date, while upholding the highest non-proliferation standards. And second, to develop and provide joint advanced military capabilities to promote security and stability in the Indo-Pacific region; third, to diversify its cooperation in cyber capabilities, artificial intelligence, quantum technology, and undersea capabilities (Fact Sheet AUKUS, 2022). While China was not mentioned in the declaration, the threat-perception emerging from the country was clear. Under the AUKUS agreement, nuclear-powered submarines will give the Royal Australian Navy the capability to go into the South China Sea, where China is increasingly getting aggressive, to protect its so-called assets and conduct patrols—even though this has not been mentioned by the leadership of the three countries. Beijing reacted to the agreement as "extremely irresponsible" and called out the member states for initiating an "arms race" (SCMP, 2021) in the Indo-Pacific. In short, AUKUS seeks to address core US concerns of regional security, deterrence, and balance of power in the Indo-Pacific. It is an attempt to augment US partnerships in the region and its presence through coordination and cooperation with like-minded partners.

Indo-Pacific Economic Framework (IPEF) was launched on 23 May 2022. The rationale behind the framework was enunciated by the Biden administration as "important turning point in restoring US economic leadership in the region and presenting Indo-Pacific countries an alternative to China's approach" (Press Call IPEF, 2022). The IPEF consists of 13 countries,[1] which account for 40 per cent of global GDP and includes some of the world's fastest-growing, most dynamic economies. The framework will focus on four key pillars of economic engagement (Factsheet IPEF, 2022) in the region:

- First, Connected Economy: the idea is to pursue high-standard rules of the road in the digital economy, including standards on cross-border data flows and data localisation, strong labour and environment standards and corporate accountability provisions that promote a race to the top for workers through trade.

- Second, Resilient Economy: to seek first-of-their-kind supply chain commitments that better anticipate and prevent disruptions in supply chains to create a more resilient economy and guard against price spikes. To establish an early warning system, mapping critical mineral supply chains, improving traceability in key sectors, and coordinating on diversification efforts.
- Third, Clean Economy: to seek first-of-their-kind commitments on clean energy, decarbonisation, and infrastructure that promote good-paying jobs. Emphasis on cooperation in the areas of renewable energy, carbon removal, energy efficiency standards, and new measures to combat methane emissions.
- Fourth, Fair Economy: to seek commitments to enact and enforce effective tax, anti-money laundering, and anti-bribery regimes that are in line with our existing multilateral obligations to promote a fair economy.

The IPEF is expected to provide a level-playing field for the member countries as it is not a trade deal or a free trade agreement, nor are the countries expected to discuss reduction of tariffs or increasing market access. The aim of the IPEF is that "the new landscape and the new challenges need a new approach", therefore "IPEF is a 21st century economic arrangement designed to tackle 21st-century economic challenges, ranging from setting the rules of the road for the digital economy, to ensuring secure and resilient supply chains, to helping make the kinds of major investments necessary in clean energy infrastructure and the clean energy transition, to raising standards for transparency, fair taxation, and anti-corruption" (Press Call, IPEF, 2022).

Conclusion

Faced with a China that is more assertive, there is bipartisan support in the US for a tougher approach to China. The US views China as a strategic rival that is growing its influence across regions and domains, the assertive behaviour of China towards its neighbours, and the disruptions due to growing Chinese advances in the technological sector. In a visible shift in policy documentation, China has been termed as a strategic competitor-politically, economically, militarily and technologically. The BRI aims to build connectivity and cooperation while bridging the global infrastructure gap that is constraining the flow of trade. While the BRI has economic aspects to it, the geopolitical goals associated with the project have significant economic and strategic consequences for the US.

When the BRI was announced, it lacked the present geographical breath and multi-domain security significance. The Obama Administration established a two-prong strategy of engagement with China while trying to address the competition from China by executing its own rebalancing strategy. While not addressing the BRI, the Administration made commitments on connectivity and infrastructure. As China started to acquire strategic assets and as the debt crisis along the BRI projects began to emerge, the US under the Trump Presidency worked to build a concentre response. The US employed a 'whole of government approach' with all agencies of the Administration working towards building on one hand, the American competitiveness and on the other, minimising China's ability to leverage its economic influence to extract political concessions that harm American interests.

Rifts continue to remain in the Sino-US relations with the latter increasingly identifying China as a strategic competitor, and China viewing the US as a hegemonic power that is "building barriers". Given the fact that President Biden and President Xi Jinping had met each other during the Obama Administration years, it was hoped that relations would improve after the US elections. However, there has been limited progress. The lack of regular communication is a measure of the rising tensions between the two nations, as they seek to manoeuvre to limit the global influence of the other while realising that they also need to work together on issues of mutual interest such as climate change, pandemic control and economic recovery.

Note

1. Members of IPEF—Australia, Brunei, India, Indonesia, Japan, Republic of Korea, Malaysia, New Zealand, the Philippines, Singapore, Thailand, Vietnam and the US.

References

"China-Latin America Finance Databases", *The Dialogue,* at https://www.thedialogue.org/map_list/. Accessed on 24 May 2022.

Factsheet, Build Back Better World (B3W), White House, 12 June 2021, at https://www.whitehouse.gov/briefing-room/statements-releases/2021/06/12/fact-sheet-president-biden-and-g7-leaders-launch-build-back-better-world-b3w-partnership/. Accessed on 24 May 2022.

Factsheet, Indo-Pacific Economic Framework for Prosperity, White House, 23 May 2022, at https://www.whitehouse.gov/briefing-room/statements-releases/2022/05/23/fact-sheet-in-asia-president-biden-and-a-dozen-indo-pacific-partners-launch-the-indo-pacific-economic-framework-for-prosperity/. Accessed on 24 May 2022.

Factsheet, Implementation of the-Australia, United-Kingdom, United States Partnership, (Aukus), White House, 5 April 2022, at https://www.whitehouse.gov/briefing-room/statements-releases/2022/04/05/fact-sheet-implementation-of-the-australia-united-kingdom-united-states-partnership-aukus/. Accessed on 24 May 2022.

Lindsey Ford (2020), "The Trump Administration and the 'Free and Open Indo-Pacific", Brookings, 2020, at https://www.brookings.edu/wp-content/uploads/2020/05/fp_20200505_free_open_indo_pacific.pdf. Accessed on 24 May 2022.

Lowy Institute (2020), An Address by Admiral Philip S. Davidson on the United States 'Interests in the Indo-Pacific, at https://www.lowyinstitute.org/publications/x., Accessed on 24 May 2022.

Mark E. Manyin and others (2012), "Pivot to the Pacific?", The Obama Administration's "Rebalancing" Toward Asia, Congressional Research Service, at https://sgp.fas.org/crs/natsec/R42448.pdf. Accessed on 25 May 2022.

Press Call on Launch of the Indo-Pacific Economic Framework, White House, 23 May 2022, at https://www.whitehouse.gov/briefing-room/press-briefings/2022/05/23/on-the-record-press-call-on-the-launch-of-the-indo-pacific-economic-framework/. Accessed on 25 May 2022.

PrzemysławFurgacz (N.A.), "The Military and Security Aspects of Obama's Pivot to Asia", at http://citeseerx.ist.psu.edu/viewdoc/download?doi=10.1.1.1022.7521&rep=rep1&type=pdf. Accessed on 25 May 2022.

Remarks by President Biden in Press Conference, White House, 25 March 2021, at https://www.whitehouse.gov/briefing-room/speeches-remarks/2021/03/25/remarks-by-president-biden-in-press-conference/. Accessed on 25 May 2022.

Remarks by President Biden to Joint Session of Congress, White House, 29 April 2021, at https://www.whitehouse.gov/briefing-room/speeches-remarks/2021/04/29/remarks-by-president-biden-in-address-to-a-joint-session-of-congress/. Accessed on 25 May 2022.

Reuters, 27 September 2021, at https://www.reuters.com/world/americas/us-plans-projects-latin-america-countering-chinas-belt-road-2021-09-27/. Accessed on 25 May 2022.

Ryan Hass (2020), "Lessons from the Trump administration's policy experiment on China", Brookings, at https://www.brookings.edu/research/lessons-from-the-trump-administrations-policy-experiment-on-china/. Accessed on 26 May 2022.

SCMP, 16 September 2021, at https://www.scmp.com/news/china/diplomacy/article/3149052/china-hits-out-highly-irresponsible-aukus-defence-pact-between. Accessed on 26 May 2022.

The White House (2020), "United States Strategic Approach to the People's Republic of China", at https://www.whitehouse.gov/wp-content/uploads/2020/05/U.S.-Strategic-Approach-to-The-Peoples-Republic-of-China-Report-5.24v1.pdf. Accessed on 26 May 2022.

The Trump White House (2018), Remarks by Vice President Pence at the 2018 APEC CEO Summit, at https://trumpwhitehouse.archives.gov/briefings-statements/remarks-vice-president-pence-2018-apec-ceo-summit-port-moresby-papua-new-guinea/. Accessed on 26 May 2022.

The Obama White House (2015), "FACT SHEET: Advancing the Rebalance to Asia and the Pacific", at https://obamawhitehouse.archives.gov/the-press-office/2015/11/16/fact-sheet-advancing-rebalance-asia-and-pacific. Accessed on 26 May 2022.

Tom Donilon, "America is Back in the Pacific and will Uphold the Rules", Financial Times, 27 November 2011.

USAID (2018), Power Africa Private Sector Partners, at https://www.usaid.gov/powerafrica/privatesector. Accessed on 27 May 2022.

U.S. Department of State (N.A.), Vision Statement: Blue Dot Network, at https://www.state.gov/blue-dot-network-vision-statement/. Accessed on 27 May 2022.

US Indo-Pacific Strategy, White House, February 2022, at https://www.whitehouse.gov/wp-content/uploads/2022/02/U.S.-Indo-Pacific-Strategy.pdf. Accessed on 27 May 2022.

USTDA (N.A.), The Global Procurement Initiative: Understanding Best Value,at https://ustda.gov/gpi-goals-and-objectives/. Accessed on 27 May 2022.

Part II
BRI in South Asia

5. China-Pakistan Economic Corridor: Pursuing Agenda amid Conflict Situation

Dhrubajyoti Bhattacharjee

Abstract

The China-Pakistan Economic Corridor, a flagship project of BRI, intends to bring China and Pakistan economically and strategically close to each other. It was assumed that this project will bolster Pakistan's economic future with a new paradigm. However, the nature of investment, the controversies associated with the corridor's alignment, the opacity of the investments, the conflict in Balochistan, and the manner in which Pakistani civilian and military administration has become embroiled in the multi-billion-dollar project, has made CPEC more of a challenge for China, Pakistan and the region, than a corridor of opportunity. This chapter will try to assess the nature of the project and the various challenges that it entails.

Amongst the six international economic corridors that have been envisaged in the Belt and Road Initiative (BRI), the China-Pakistan Economic Corridor (CPEC) has been identified as a flagship project. The CPEC directly impinges on the sovereignty and territorial integrity of India, and therefore, a project that lacks legitimacy and is illegal.

The idea of developing the CPEC was visualised by Chinese Premier Li Keqiang during his visit to Pakistan in May 2013 (Bhattacharjee, 2015). It was turned into a reality during President Xi Jinping's visit to Islamabad in 2015. The CPEC was proposed to be an economic and infrastructural project to change the developmental map of Pakistan. The economic corridor connects the Xinjiang Uygur Autonomous Region (XUAR) of China to the Pakistani port of Gwadar through a network of roads measuring around 3,000 km (1,800 miles). It also provides Pakistan with its much-needed economic infrastructure, especially power-generation plants (Shah, 2015). This chapter tries to identify and analyse various phases that CPEC is divided into and the major challenges that CPEC poses not only for Pakistan-China ties but also for the region.

I. Status of the CPEC Projects

CPEC's wide network of roads, railways and pipelines are intended to transport oil and gas from Pakistan's southern Gwadar Port to Kashgar city, via the Khunjerab Pass in the Karakoram range in Pakistan-occupied Kashmir (PoK), to north-western China's XUAR (*China Daily*, 2015). When Nawaz Sharif's Pakistan Muslim League (Nawaz) [PML (N)] came to power in 2013, they were looking for large foreign investments in major power and infrastructural projects, which would boost Pakistani economy in the long term. The proposal of the CPEC was seen by many as more of an achievement for the Sharif leadership. The CPEC is also a major project for China to connect and enhance its sphere of influence in the Indian Ocean by developing the Gwadar port in the province of Balochistan, which would remain the principal pillar of the Corridor.

However, in the last one and a half decades, there has been a significant rise of religious radicalism and extremism in Pakistan, especially after the Peshawar Army School incident in 2014, the Pakistani army came down heavily on such radical groups in the regions of North Waziristan, Khyber Paktunkhwa and Balochistan. From the very beginning, China was apprehensive with regard to the security and law and order situation in the provinces, which would be a major part of CPEC. In 2015, the Pakistani Army had created a Special Army Division constituting more than 10,000 army personnel protecting staff and projects involved in CPEC. However, despite these measures, the insurgent groups have carried out numerous cases of hostage-taking and incidents of violence against Chinese officials and workers. It remains to be an imminent threat and seems to be impacting bilateral ties, especially at the popular level.

Projects under CPEC: Phase One (2014-2020)

The first phase (2014-2020) focuses on energy and infrastructure projects and development of the Gwadar Port city (Chinoy, 2021, p. 4). CPEC has made significant progress in its first phase. The majority of the projects planned in the transportation infrastructure and energy sectors have been implemented and some are still going on. In the first phase of CPEC, 1800 km of new highways and urban mass transit projects were executed along with laying of 820 km of optic fibre cable besides the Orange metro project in Lahore. CPEC also added more than 5,300 megawatts of new power generation capacity to Pakistan's national grid and as per Pakistani narrative, these projects have played a leading role in reducing energy shortages in the country. However, the country still faces massive power outages. Pakistan has grossly overlooked the climate change perspective, where it allowed establishment of Chinese coal-based power plants under CPEC.

Phase Two (2021-25)

The proposed second phase of CPEC initially had its focus on industrialisation, agricultural modernisation, Information Technology and Scientific and Technological cooperation rather than energy and infrastructure development. Development of Special Economic Zones (SEZs) under Phase-II of CPEC had been made as the top priority. To accelerate industrialisation, it was decided to set up SEZ in each province, which is still in the process of planning and seeking investments (Umar, 2022, p. 1). The Pakistan government has not been able to woo investors either from West Asia or Europe.

The first of these, Allama Iqbal Industrial City (AIIC) was built in Faisalabad in early 2020 but still needs investments to make it operational (Hasnain, 2022). However, as per Asad Umar, former Minister of Planning, Development and Reform, the industrial city is fully operational (Umar, 2022, p. 1).

The second SEZ is being set up in Rashakai in Khyber Pakhtunkhwa (KP).The third SEZ is in Dhabeji, Sindh. The Sindh government has awarded the contract for its development. Bostan SEZ in Balochistan has also been launched. Initially, interest was shown by investors, but due to bureaucratic red-tapism, corruption and lack of political will and stability, no such investment has yet been made. The provision of infrastructure, including gas and electricity, to these SEZs is still in the process of construction.

As part of the second phase, for power generation, most of the coal power plants are either under construction or near completion. Punjab and Sindh have three proposed coal power plants each whereas Gwadar has one. In Khyber Pakhtunkhwa the Suki-Kinari dam is under construction for hydropower generation; in Punjab the Karot Hydro Power plant is also under construction. In Pakistan-occupied Kashmir (PoK), a joint venture called Azad Pattan Power Limited (APPL) has been initiated between China Gezhouba Group having 80 per cent shares and Pakistan's Laraib Group will be holding 20 per cent shares. All the hydropower projects under APPL will transfer the ownership of these projects to Pakistan after operating the facilities for a period of thirty years. In PoK, the Kohala Hydro Power plant, the Phandar Project and the Gilgit KIU Hydro Power are still under feasibility study along with some solar and wind projects. The ±660kV Matiari-Lahore (HVDC) transmission project has started commercial operation since September 2021.

The other projects in Phase Two are infrastructural projects and creation of SEZs. Amongst the infrastructural projects KKH Phase II, which is from Havelian Thakot of a stretch of 120 km and the Karachi Lahore motorway of 392 km, are completed. The rest of the infrastructural projects are still under feasibility study. The four CPEC rail-based mass transit projects have yet to see any sort of construction work (Pakistan-China Institute, 2022). The East Bay Expressway construction is still undergoing and the construction of the New Gwadar International Airport has slowed down. Due to the ongoing law and order challenges, not many airlines have shown interest in carrying out operations from the airport after construction.

As claimed by CPEC officials, 46 projects have been completed or are under-construction, with a total investment of US$ 25.4 billion (Umar, 2022, p. 1), which cannot be validated by any government document available in the open source. This shows the lack of transparency in the construction of these projects.

Most of the projects proposed in Balochistan are all under construction. Work is yet to start on the rest of the projects (Pakistan-China Institute, 2022). In the ninth Joint Coordination Committee (JCC) meeting various other projects have been proposed but none of the projects have seen any feasibility study report (CPEC New Provincial Projects, 2022). Feasibility studies of the ninth proposed SEZ under CPEC have been shared in April 2022 with their Chinese counterpart (Proposed Special Economic Zones, 2022).

There is the mention of two more phases of CPEC till 2030. Projects under these two phases will be to enhance and strengthen human capacity building through joint institutional setups imparting knowledge in economics and international trade, business management, technology, agriculture, engineering, which includes artificial intelligence (AI) and corporate law, etc. These phases will also involve boosting the capacity of SEZs and generating local investments. However, there is a lack of transparency with regard to the timeframe when all such projects under CPEC will be handed over to Pakistani State and private institutions as well as the terms and conditions involving joint projects and the terms and conditions of repayment of Chinese loans in the form of soft investments.

It should be noted here that the China Electric Power Equipment and Technology Co. Ltd. (CET)/State Grid Corporation of China (SGCC) has sought Rs 12.35 billion (PKR) as Transmission Service Payment (TSP) for September 2021 to February 2022. The project will be able to start commercial operations only after clearing the above-mentioned dues (India Blooms, 2022). As the country presently goes through political and economic instability, after the dismissal of Imran Khan's government, the future of the second phase to be completed on time is highly unlikely. However, it has been proposed that by 2030, all the proposed projects will be completed (CPIC, 2022).

II. Strategic Aspects and Challenges

The level of corruption that is ingrained into every stratum in Pakistan has become a major impediment for projects to be completed. As there is lack of transparency and detachment of various governmental institutions, there is no quality check or accountability.

The CPEC is perceived in Pakistan as not only helping the country economically but it is also seen as a long-term commitment by China to deepen ties. It was expected to boost their close strategic and military partnership and provide reassurance to Pakistan (Chinoy, 2021, p. 8). However, in the last two years, many of the projects either have been stalled or are in the process of planning. With the rise of violence against Pakistani military and the Chinese workforce employed in Pakistan by local insurgent groups functioning in the region, there is a growing sense of insecurity. It is also a question that if Pakistan is unable to pay back the humungous debt that it has already taken from China, in what form will China recover such unpaid debts. Such economic insecurity that has a deep-seated strategic dimension may negatively impact the 'all weathered friendship' between Pakistan and China.

China has invested significantly in PoK, which is Indian territory. A large section of the CPEC also passes through the areas of Gilgit-Baltistan in PoK. India has protested against such investments as it infringes on the sovereignty of India. As per the Ministry of External Affairs (MEA), "Government's concerns arise in part from the fact that the inclusion of the so-called illegal 'China-Pakistan Economic Corridor' (CPEC) as a flagship project of 'OBOR/BRI', directly impinges on the issue of sovereignty and territorial integrity of India. This so-called illegal 'China-Pakistan Economic Corridor' (CPEC) passes through parts of the Union Territories of Jammu and Kashmir and Ladakh which are under illegal occupation of Pakistan" (MEA, 2020).

During the last few years, large-scale protests by local residents of Gilgit and Baltistan have been witnessed. The protests were against the projects carried out under CPEC, rising unemployment, high inflation and rise in prices of essential commodities and the "colonial attitude" of both the Pakistan and Chinese leaderships towards the region (Times Now News, 2021).

It has been noted that Pakistani Army was engaged in the forceful evacuation of people from their traditional homesteads and farmlands in several areas of Gilgit, Baltistan and Balochistan to acquire land for the CPEC. For example, land acquisition for the Sahiwal coal power plant project was done in a controversial manner. People were forced to sell their agricultural land. In the case of those who were unwilling to do so, the police brought charges of terrorism against them to force them to part with their lands (Chinoy, 2021, p. 13). An expert from the Amsterdam-based European Foundation for South Asian Studies (EFSAS), said,

> Despite the fact that this corridor would cross the region and produce a number of negative environmental and ecological impacts, Gilgit Baltistan is already facing serious environmental problems in relation to climate change because of air and water pollution, inadequate waste disposal, natural resources depletion, deforestation, loss of biodiversity and glacier melting ... Gilgit Baltistan has notable reserves of copper, coal, iron, silver, and gold among other metals and minerals. The factories which will emerge during the construction of this corridor will use all the minerals of Gilgit Baltistan as raw material for which the population will not be paid royalty. (*Business Standard*, 2017)

III. Lack of Transparency of Contracts

In a report by AIDDATA, a US-based international development research lab, observed that Chinese loans under CPEC constitute 95.2 per cent and 73 per cent of total commitments in energy and transport sectors. These loans are at or near commercial rates as opposed to grants and have short and long-term periods. Islamabad is the seventh largest recipient of Chinese overseas development financing with 71 projects worth US$ 27.3 billion currently underway. The interest rate is 3.76 per cent for an average loan with 13.2 years' maturity (when full repayment with interest is due) and 4.3 years of grace period, it said. It further stated that Pakistan received about half of all Chinese development finance in the form of "export buyer's credit", i.e., money lent by Chinese institutions to Pakistan in order to facilitate the purchase of equipment and goods to be bought by Chinese implementation partners (Malik, et al., 2021).

Figure 5.1: Total Development Financing in Pakistan

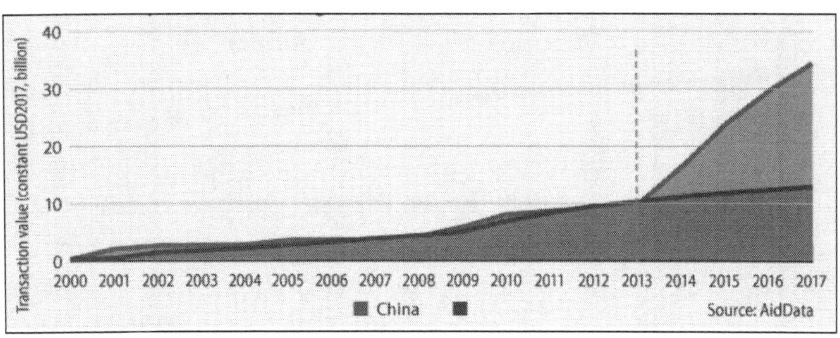

Source: AidData.

It can be noted here that Imran Khan's party, Pakistan Tehreek-e-Insaf (PTI), when in opposition, had demanded complete transparency in CPEC investments. But when they were in government, they did nothing to make public the costs or conditions of the CPEC deals with China's government, companies and banks, keeping the matter strictly under wraps just as its predecessor had done, and one can foretell that this will be repeated by forthcoming governments as well (*Dawn*, 2021).

Jonathan Hillman while stating the nature of CPEC stated "Expectations have been nothing if not exaggerated. Promises have been broken, as only a fraction of CPEC's projects have materialized" (Hillman, 2021, p. 149). Andrew Small, a Senior Transatlantic Fellow with the Asia program at the German Marshall Fund of the United States, has pointed out that China is not interested to invest any more in new projects and is more interested to complete the existing projects, downgrading the entire project. He wrote, "This is a change in scale from the aspirations that once characterised the scheme, which one Chinese official characterised as moving from "mega projects" to "peanut projects" (Small, 2020).

IV. The Balochistan Issue

Chinese workers have been targeted frequently in Balochistan, which is one of the reasons behind the fear amongst Chinese workers based in the province. Violence has been rising especially since 2018, when there was a general realisation of the negative impact of the projects on the local populace, which are being carried out under the garb of CPEC. In a media interview, Brahamdagh Bugti, exiled leader of the Baloch Republican Party had stated that the Chinese projects in Balochistan aim at colonising the province, which must be resisted. He stated that all the projects that have been carried out in the past, were not for the benefit of the people of Balochistan but for the benefit of the rulers in Islamabad (*DW News*, 2020).

Senator Akram Baloch, when asked about the viability of the Saindak Copper Gold Project, stated that the Pakistan government exploits the resources of the region and never takes the locals into confidence. He questioned the claims by the Pakistan federal government about large Chinese investments being made in the province, Balochistan remains extremely poor with no proper health facilities, education and housing or even clean drinking water (*DW News*, 2020). Abdul Malik, former Chief Minister of Balochistan has stated that the province is not getting its due share of royalties from these projects, which could have been used for the upliftment of the province (*DW News*, 2020). He further asked, "How can you expect the local people not to be resentful if their share of jobs in provincial institutions such as GDA or the Gwadar Port Authority is minimal" (*Dawn*, 2020).

China's acquisition of Gwadar port has further strengthened the insurgency as local Baloch firms and labour have been excluded in favour of Chinese companies and workers. This has been the problem of Chinese mode of investment. CPEC has served to further exacerbate the divide between Islamabad and the region, due to the exclusionary and Punjab-centric planning (*Greek City Times*, 2022).

Local fishermen had willingly handed over their fishing areas for the construction of the Gwadar port, expecting better returns. However, the federal government instead handed over fishing permission to Chinese fishermen, which triggered widespread unrest. Chinese large fishing trawlers were also involved in illegal fishing which led to a month-long protest in November 2021 under the leadership of Jamaat-i-Islami (JI). The protesters had presented nineteen demands, including taking actions to free the sea of the 'trawler mafia', enabling fishermen to openly go into the waters.

As per Hillman, Gwadar "is still largely disconnected from the rest of the country and has struggled to provide basic services, including reliable potable water and electricity. If large cargo ships suddenly began arriving, the port and its weak infrastructure reaching inland would not be able to handle them" (Hillman, 2021, p. 147).

Pakistan's determination to protect Chinese investment has prompted the military to strengthen its grip and use heavy-handed tactics against any opposition to the projects, deepening resentment among the Baloch people. This has led to extra-judicial kidnappings and killings. This has further led to strengthening of the insurgency. Anger against the Chinese and the Pakistani state, who are seen as usurpers and colonial masters, is real and powerful (Chinoy, 2021, pp. 17-18).

V. Debt Trap and Pakistan's fledgling economy

It has been witnessed on multiple occasions, that during a severe financial crisis, China has made attempts of bailing out Pakistan. China, in 2022 has agreed to the request of rolling over US$ 4.2 billion, which had to be paid back by 31 March 2022 (*Economic Times*, 2022). However, debt servicing is now the strongest factor hurting the economy of Pakistan. It is also responsible for the decline in the country's foreign reserves, as Pakistan has to acquire more loans to pay instalments of previous loans. With the recent loans been taken from the International Monetary Fund (IMF), which was followed by structural adjustments that has furthered weakened the Pakistani currency, and the ongoing political instability, it seems highly unlikely that Pakistan will be able to overcome the ongoing economic crisis any time soon.

With regard to the various projects and investments by China in Pakistan, there have been accusations of lack of transparency, as well as providing undue advantage to Chinese firms in getting projects, and unfair treatment of local companies (*Dawn*, 2020). It is to be noted that when Pakistan tried to approach non-Chinese investors, such as the Asian Development Bank, for funding on soft loans for a railway track project called ML1 fearing the Chinese debt trap, this attempt was significantly discouraged by China (Jorgic, 2018; *Dawn*, 2019). Pakistani senators have time and again raised the fear that the CPEC may become another East India Company (*Dawn*, 2016).

Though it does not seem that debt trap is going to be an immediate threat to the ongoing projects under CPEC, with changing global equations, Pakistan also cannot claim to be out of the threat or challenges being posed by burgeoning foreign debt. If the situation so arises, where Pakistan is unable and defaults in paying back its foreign debt, it might have to lease major projects to China, as Sri Lanka was forced to do with regard to Hambantota port. This will pose a severe strategic threat to South Asian stability as a whole, as economic instability will have a negative impact on the growth of the region.

Conclusion

CPEC has proved to be a challenge rather than an opportunity for both Pakistan and China as well as the region. The strategic aspect remains much evident, as both sides have pursued their respective agendas even in conflict situations, undermining the interests of the local populace. Corruption in every level of administration and bureaucracy in Pakistan, the civil-military rifts, red tapism among others have forced China to rethink about future investments in Pakistan. Under the garb of CPEC, the Pakistan army has made attempts to alter the population demography in Gilgit-Baltistan, as well has resorted to extra-judicial kidnappings and killings in Khyber Pakhtunkhwa and Balochistan in the veil of providing security to CPEC projects. Pakistan has wilfully allowed China to establish coal-based power projects based on outdated technologies that will make a deep negative impact on the environment.

References

Ahmadani, Ahmad, (2022). "Energy crisis worsening, amid hot weather", Pakistan Today, Profit, 7 April 2022, at https://profit.pakistantoday.com.pk/2022/04/07/energy-crisis-worsening-amid-hot-weather/. Accessed on 2 April 2022.

Ali, T., Huang, J. and Xie, W., (2022). "Bilateral Economic Impacts of China–Pakistan Economic Corridor", Agriculture, 2022, 12(2), 143. https://doi.org/10.3390/agriculture12020143. Accessed on 2 April 2022.

Alice Wells' remarks "Another doomed attempt to defame Sino-Pak relations: Chinese embassy", *Dawn*, 21 May 2020, at https://www.dawn.com/news/1558763. Accessed on 2 April 2022.

Antonopoulos, Paul, (2022). "Chinese-owned port instigates insurgency in Pakistan's Balochistan", *Greek City Times*, 22 March 2022, at https://greekcitytimes.com/2022/03/22/chinese-pakistans-balochistan/. Accessed on 3 April 2022.

"Backgrounder: China-Pakistan Economic Corridor", *China Daily*, 22 April 2015, at https://www.chinadaily.com.cn/world/2015xivisitpse/2015-04/22/content_20503693.htm. Accessed on 1 April 2022.

"Balochistan CM caught on video distributing cash among Gwadar protestors", *IANS News*, 17 December 2021, at https://ianslive.in/news/balochistan_cm_caught_on_video_distributing_cash_among_gwadar_protesters-835786/LatestNews/0. Accessed on 1 April 2022.

Bhattacharjee, Dhrubajyoti, (2015). "China Pakistan Economic Corridor", Issue Brief, 12 May 2015, Indian Council of World Affairs, at https://www.icwa.in/show_content.php?lang=1&level=3&ls_id=5103&lid=835. Accessed on 3 April 2022.

Brautigam, Deborah, (2020). "A critical look at Chinese 'debt-trap diplomacy': The rise of a meme", Area Development and Policy, Volume 5, Issue 1, 2020, pp. 1-14.

Chansoria, Monika, (2015). "China Makes its Presence Felt in Pak Occupied Kashmir", The Sunday Guardian, 27 April 2015, at http://www.sunday-guardian.com/analysis/china-makes-its-presence-felt-in-pak-occupied-kashmir. Accessed on 3 April 2022.

"China agrees to rollover USD 4.2 billion Pakistan debt: Shah Mehmood Qureshi", *Economic Times*, 30 March 2022, at https://economictimes.indiatimes.com/news/international/world-news/china-agrees-to-rollover-usd-4-2-billion-pakistan-debt-shah-mehmood-qureshi/articleshow/90549273.cms. Accessed on 2 April 2022.

"China Pakistan Economic Corridor", Pakistan-China Institute, 2022, at http://cpecinfo.com/. Accessed on 2 April 2022.

"Chinese firm seeks Rs 12.35bn dues from Pakistan for power project", India Blooms, 9 March 2022, at https://www.indiablooms.com/world-details/SA/33723/chinese-firm-seeks-rs-12-35bn-dues-from-pakistan-for-power-project.html. Accessed on 2 April 2022.

Chinoy, Sujan R. (2021). "China Pakistan Economic Corridor: The Project and its Prospects", MP-IDSA Occasional Paper, No. 58, January 2021.

CPEC New Provincial Projects, Pakistan-China Institute, 2022, at http://cpecinfo.com/cpec-new-provincial-projects/. Accessed on 2 April 2022.

"CPEC violating rights of Gilgit-Baltistan residents: European think tanks", Business Standard, 17 October 2017, at https://www.business-standard.com/article/international/cpec-violating-rights-of-gilgit-baltistan-residents-european-think-tanks-117101700377_1.html. Accessed on 2 April 2022.

"Ex-CM wants greater role of Baloch people in CPEC projects", *Dawn*, 10 February 2020, at https://www.dawn.com/news/1533576. Accessed on 1 April 2022.

Hasnain, Khalid, (2022). "Punjab set to launch another four economic zones", *Dawn*, 6 March 2022, at https://www.dawn.com/news/1678538., Accessed on 3 April 2022.

Hillman, Jonathan E. (2021). *The Emperor's New Road: China and the project of the Century*, Washington DC, CSIS.

"India should be Upfront in Voicing Opposition to China-Pakistan Economic Corridor", *Business Standard*, 21 April 2015, at http://www.business-standard.com/article/news-ians/india-should-be-upfront-in-voicing-opposition-to-china-pakistan-economic-corridor-115042100473_1.html. Accessed on 1 April 2022.

Jorgic, Drazen,(2018). "Fearing debt trap, Pakistan rethinks Chinese 'Silk Road' projects", Reuters, 30 September 2018, at https://www.reuters.com/article/us-pakistan-silkroad-railway-insight-idUSKCN1MA028. Accessed on 3 April 2022.

Kiani, Khaleeq, (2019). "Govt puts major CPEC power project on hold", *Dawn*, 14 January 2019, at https://www.dawn.com/news/1457449. Accessed on 3 April 2022.

Malik, Amar A. Parks, Bradley, Russell, Brooke, Lin, Joyce Jiahui, Walsh, Katherine, Solomon, Kyra, Zhang, Sheng, Elston, Thai-Binh and Goodman, Seth, "Banking on the Belt and Road: Insights from a new dataset of 13,427 Chinese development projects", AIDDATA, A Research Lab at William and Mary, Virginia, September 2021.

"Pakistan: CPEC instigates insurgency in Balochistan", ANI News, 17 March 2022, at https://www.aninews.in/news/world/asia/pakistan-cpec-instigates-insurgency-in-balochistan20220317192600/. Accessed on 3 April 2022.

Pei, Minxin, (2014). "Why China Keeps Throwing Trillions in Investments Down the Drain", Fortune, 1 December 2014, at http://fortune.com/2014/12/01/china-investment-losses-infrastructure/. Accessed on 3 April 2022.

Proposed Special Economic Zones, Pakistan-China Institute, 2022, at http://cpecinfo.com/proposed -special-economic-zones/. Accessed on 3 April 2022.

"Protests rock Pakistan over inflation, unemployment as locals lose faith in CPEC in Gilgit-Baltistan region", Times Now News, 22 December 2021, at https://www.timesnownews.com/international/article/protests-rock-pakistan-over-inflation-unemployment-as-locals-lose-faith-in-cpec-in-gilgit-baltistan-region/842605. Accessed on 3 April 2022.

"Question No. 606 BRI and CPEC", Lok Sabha, Unstarred Question No. 606, 02 February 2020, Ministry of External Affairs, Government of India, at https://www.mea.gov.in/lok-sabha.htm?dtl/32353/QUESTION+NO606+BRI+AND+CPEC. Accessed on 1 April 2022.

Raza, Syed Irfan, (2022). "CPEC could become another East India Company", *Dawn*, 18 October 2016, at https://www.dawn.com/news/1290677. Accessed on 3 April 2022.

Shah, Saeed, (2015). "China's Xi Jinping Launches Investment Deal in Pakistan", *The Wall Street Journal*, 20 April 2015, at http://www.wsj.com/articles/chinas-xi-jinping-set-to-launch-investment-deal-in-pakistan-1429533767. Accessed on 3 April 2022.

Shaikh, Rizwan and Chen, Chien-Kai, "China's Debt Trap in Pakistan? A case study of the CPEC Project", South Asia Research, Vol. 41(3), August 2021, pp. 1-16.

Siddiqua, Ayesha, (2021). "In Gwadar protest success, you are missing out this war within Pakistani establishment", The Print, 29 December 2021, at https://theprint.in/opinion/in-gwadar-protest-you-are-missing-out-war-within-pakistani-establishment/789574/. Accessed on 2 April 2022.

Small, Andrew, (2020). "Returning to the Shadows: China, Pakistan, and the Fate of CPEC", German Marshall Fund of the United States at Harvard University, 23 September 2020, at https://www.gmfus.org/news/returning-shadows-china-pakistan-and-fate-cpec. Accessed on 2 April 2022.

Timeline of CPEC Progress, CPIC, 2022, at https://www.cpicglobal.com/pakistan-overview/cpec/. Accessed on 3 April 2022.

"Transparency needed", Dawn, 1 October 2021, at https://www.dawn.com/news/1649464. Accessed on 1 April 2022.

Umar, Asad, (2022). "CPEC 2.0: Expanding the bilateral economic relationship", Government of Pakistan, 2022, p. 1, at http://cpec.gov.pk/brain/public/uploads/documents/CPEC_2.0_Eng.pdf. Accessed on 3 April 2022.

"Why Chinese investment is stoking anger in Pakistan's Balochistan province", DW News, 15 July 2020, at https://www.dw.com/en/why-chinese-investment-is-stoking-anger-in-pakistans-balochistan-province/a-54188705. Accessed on 2 April 2022.

6. China and Bangladesh under the Rubric of BRI

Teshu Singh

Abstract

The Belt and Road Initiative (BRI) is a signature project of President Xi Jinping. It has positioned China at the centre of the international system, with its physical, financial, cultural, technological, and political influence flowing to the rest of the world. It is trying to redrawing the world's map, with new railroads and bridges, fibre-optic cables and 5G networks, and ports. Bangladesh joined the BRI in 2016. Bangladesh has very cautiously moved with the BRI. Unlike other countries in South Asia like Sri Lanka, Bangladesh has not fallen into the debt trap with China. The paper aims to analyse the growing China-Bangladesh ties under the rubric of the BRI. As a part of the strengthening of the relations, China has initiated various projects in Bangladesh. The chapter explores the status of the project and its dynamics.

Introduction

Initiated in 2013, the One Belt One Road (OBOR) that later became the Belt and Road Initiative (BRI) is a manifestation of the Chinese Dream. Since then, it represents a vision for national rejuvenation and the creation of a new global order led by China. The two initiatives namely the 'Silk Road Economic Belt' and the 'Maritime Silk Road' together form the BRI. During his trip to Kazakhstan, Chinese President Xi Jinping made a speech on 7 September 2013, at Nazarbayev University, Kazakhstan. In his speech, he explained China's policy of good neighbourly and friendly cooperation toward countries in Central Asia

(MFA, 2013). Additionally, at the Indonesian Parliament on 2 October 2013, President Xi Jinping proposed the revival of the "Maritime Silk Road" (MSR), which is a symbol of cultural and historical linkages between China and Southeast Asia. Together these two initiatives are called the BRI (Wu and Zhang, 2013).

The BRI is the signature project of President Xi Jinping since 2013. Xi Jinping's ambition for Chinese centrality on the global stage is intricately captured in his idea of BRI. In its original conception, the BRI was a vehicle for Chinese-led hard infrastructure development along the six corridors. Over a period of time, it has diversified and now its offshoots include digital, health, and polar Silk Roads and all countries are welcome to participate (*Economy*, January/February 2022).

On 28 March 2015, the National Development and Reform Commission (NDRC) jointly with the Ministry of Foreign Affairs and Commerce Ministry released a detailed action plan for BRI. The document emphasises that BRI is the centrepiece of Chinese foreign and domestic economic strategy (NDRC PRC, 2015). The document highlights the BRI as the lynchpin of Chinese foreign and domestic economic strategy. Subsequently, the BRI was incorporated into the Constitution of the CPC in 2017 and it also figured in the 14th Five-Year Plan.

It may be noted that since 2012 there have been changes in the Chinese Foreign Policy. In 2013, Xi Jinping delivered a speech titled "Let the Sense of Community of Common Destiny Take deep Root in Neighbouring Countries." This is in sharp contradiction to Deng Xiaoping's *taoguangyanghui* (keeping a low profile). Xi Jinping is propagating *fenfayouwei* (striving for achievements) (Miller, 2017).

It is evident, BRI will remain the pillar of the Chinese foreign policy. The BRI is based on five cooperation priorities or "Five Connectivity" is the term given to the basic cooperative framework of the BRI, namely, policy coordination, facilities connectivity, unimpeded trade, financial integration and people-to-people bonds (Kun, 2019). Amongst the six international economic corridors that have been announced under BRI, the Bangladesh China India Myanmar Economic Corridor (BCIMEC) seeks to integrate Bangladesh into the larger BRI. It may be noted that BCIMEC which has been previously mentioned as part of BRI when it was launched in 2013, did not figure in the list of 35 corridors mentioned in the new list of projects under the BRI (Varma, 2020). On the contrary, Chinese foreign Spokesperson, Geng Shuang reiterated "It is very much on board" and stated that the 13th meeting of the BCIM forum was held on the sidelines of China, South Asia Business Forum" (Varma, 2019). Conspicuously, although the two countries cooperation in the area of connectivity began in 1999 following the initiation of the Kunming Initiative that was later renamed the China-Bangladesh-India-Myanmar Economic Corridor (BCIMEC) the inauguration of the BRI in 2013 gave greater importance to the China-Bangladesh bilateral relations.

Bangladesh joins Belt and Road Initiative

China and Bangladesh established diplomatic relations in 1976. In 1980, China started investing in Bangladesh. There are various facets of China-Bangladesh relations but majorly defence cooperation forms the base of bilateral cooperation. According to a 2020 report by the Stockholm International Peace Research Institute (SIPRI), Bangladesh is China's second-largest buyer of military hardware globally. It is almost one-fifth of China's export from 2016 to 2020. The arms sales from China to Bangladesh form 70 per cent of Bangladesh's total purchases (SIPRI, 2021). It also highlights that Pakistan, Bangladesh and Algeria were the largest recipients of the Chinese arm sale from 2016 to 2020 (*Financial Express*, 2021).

In 2016, President Xi Jinping visited Bangladesh. During his visit, Bangladesh officially joined BRI. The bilateral relations were elevated from a "comprehensive partnership of cooperation" to a "strategic partnership of cooperation". During the visit, President Xi Jinping promised US$ 40 billion investment in Bangladesh. A total of US$ 24.45 billion was allocated for bilateral assistance for infrastructure projects and US$ 13.6 billion for joint ventures. In addition, US$ 20 billion in loan agreement was also committed (*bd24news*, 2016).

The two countries signed 27 projects to implement with Chinese assistance under an umbrella deal. President Xi Jinping also promised to give soft loans of US$ 21.5 billion for the projects. It was agreed that China would provide Bangladesh with over US$ 9.45 billion in credit for the 12 projects (Ahmad and Byron, 2017).

Table 6.1: List of BRI Projects

Sl. No.	Name of the Project Foreign Assistance	million (US$)
1.	Padma Bridge Rail Link Project *	2667.93
2.	Dhaka-Sylhet four-lane highway project	2110
3.	Development of the national ICT infra-network project for the Bangladesh Government	156.56
4.	Construction of tunnel under Karnaphuli River	705.80
5.	Installation of Single Point Mooring (SPM) with double pipeline	500.466
6.	Rajshahi WASA Surface Water Treatment Plant	350
7.	System loss reduction by replacing 5 million electromechanical energy metres with electronic energy metres	165.98
8.	Expansion and strengthening of the Power System Network under DPDC area	1650.51
9.	Power Grid Network Strengthening Project under PGCB	1321.83
10.	Construction of Dhaka-Ashulia elevated expressway	1393.98
11.	Establishing six full-fledged TV stations of Bangladesh Television	127.88
12.	Modernisation of telecommunication network for digital connectivity	231.00
13.	Construction of a dual-gauge track parallel to the existing Joydebpur-Mymensingh-Jamalpur section	581.26
14.	Construction of double line between Joydebpur and Ishurdisections	752.79
15.	Establishing digital connectivity	1000
16.	Marine Drive Expressway and coastal protection works from Sitakunda-Chittagong-Cox's Bazar	2856.56
17.	Expansion and modernisation of Mongla port facilities	249.17
18.	Extension of underground mining operations of Barapukuria Coal Mine	256.41
19.	Gazaria 350 MW coal-fired power plant	433
20.	Conversion of MG railway track to DG railway track in the Akhaura-Sylhet section	1756.05
21.	Prepayment metering project for Bangladesh Power Development Board's (BPDP) distribution zone	521.56
22	New inland container port near Dhirasram railway station	200
23.	Replacement of overloaded distribution transformer to provide reliable electricity to the RE region	230.59
24	Water supply, sanitation, drainage, and solid waste management for small municipalities	150

25	Modernisation and expansion of public sector jute mills of Bangladesh	280
26	Chinese economic and industrial zone in Chittagong	280
27	Modernisation of rural and urban lives through ICT	500

Source: Rubiat Saimum, "The Prospect of Belt and Road Initiative in the Context of Bangladesh", *China Report* (2020): 1–20 Sage Publications Los Angeles/London/New Delhi/Singapore/Washington DC/Melbourne DOI: 10.1177/0009445520930396

Note: *The Padma Bridge was inaugurated on 25 June 2022. The Foreign Ministry of Bangladesh has stated that the bridge is not a part of the BRI and Bangladesh has not taken any foreign funding for the construction of the structure (*The Daily Star*, 2022).

Status of the Projects under BRI

At present, nine projects are running under the BRI in Bangladesh. The success of projects under BRI in Bangladesh is very much dependent on the sustainable financing and economic feasibility of the projects (Rahman, 2021).

Bangladesh's first toll road project was signed on 6 December 2018. The government of Bangladesh had signed a contract with a China-Bangladesh consortium to upgrade the 48-km Dhaka Bypass Road to a dual carriageway. The up-gradation was intended to improve connectivity between the north and northwestern parts of Bangladesh and the Chittagong Port. Reportedly, from 2009 to 2019, China invested around US$ 9.75 billion in projects related to Transportation in Bangladesh (Hasan, 2021).

China is working on the power sector in Bangladesh. They are working on a Power Grid Network Strengthening project at an investment of US$ 1.32 billion and also an expansion and strengthening of power system network that might help in the intelligent operation of the power grid in Bangladesh with an investment of US$ 2.04 billion (Samsani, 2021).

Chinese companies were granted the majority of contracts to develop a new deep-sea port at Payra in the middle of the country, which will include an LNG terminal, an oil refinery, a coal terminal to service a power plant, and a container terminal. It may be noted that the Payra port project has not faced much criticism as compared to other ports in Sri Lanka (Hambantota) and Pakistan (Gwadar). The reason for it could be because the Payra project has not used a "field of dreams" approach (build it and they will come). Payra port has very interesting geography. It lies deep within the Ganges delta and must be approached by a 75-km-long canal being dredged through mudflats. Bangladeshi authorities have indicated that the port is an unlikely place for a naval base (Brewster, 2019). The Payra 1,320 MW ultra-supercritical coal-fired power plant is Bangladesh's largest thermal power plant. The plant is expected to generate about 8.58 billion kWh of electricity annually. The operation of the plant implies that Bangladesh has entered a new era after attaining 100 per cent electricity coverage across the country (Cui and Wu, 2019).

The Chinese government will also provide Bangladesh with grant assistance of 300 million RMB (about US$ 50 million) for the construction of the eighth Bangladesh-China Friendship Bridge. According to Bangladesh's Economic Relations Department (ERD), the eighth friendship bridge will be constructed on the Kocha River in southern Bangladesh. The length of the bridge is 1400 metres and Bangladesh Roads and Highway Department will carry out the project. The bridge will play an important role in accelerating the movement of people and goods of the Barisal and Khulna divisions. At present, a ferry operates on the river which takes more than one hour crossing it (*China Daily*, 2021). China will fund the ninth Bangladesh-China Friendship Bridge and other infrastructure development projects. The location and other related infrastructure projects will be settled through negotiations between the two governments (*Xinhua*, 2017).

The progress related to the Padma Bridge (Padma Multipurpose Bridge Project) is of great significance. The Padma Bridge project has come under scrutiny (*The Daily Star*, 2022). In a recent development, the Ministry of Foreign Affairs of Bangladesh has argued that the Padma Multipurpose Bridge has been entirely funded by the Government of Bangladesh and no foreign funds from any bilateral or multilateral funding agency have financially contributed to its construction. Bangladeshi and foreign construction firms were engaged for the implementation of the project. Prior to this development, the Padma Bridge was perceived as a part of the BRI (*The Daily Star*, 2022).

The construction of the Padma Bridge is of vital importance for Bangladesh. The bridge will connect the 19 south-west districts with the rest of the country. It will greatly enhance connectivity across Bangladesh and South Asia. According to reports, a single Padma Bridge would boost Bangladesh's GDP by more than 1 per cent. It will benefit at least 30 million people in the southwestern part of Bangladesh (Hasan, 2019).

The Padma Multipurpose Bridge is the largest and most challenging infrastructure project in the history of Bangladesh. The bridge will link the northeast and southwest sections of Bangladesh. It is also an important channel for connecting up with the "Trans-Asian Railway." The bridge is called the "Dream Padma Bridge" of Bangladesh and will end the practice of crossing the Padma River by ferries and boats (Cui and Wu, 2022).

Challenges to the Project

Red tape from both sides has delayed the projects related to BRI. In Bangladesh, the projects have to get approvals from several committees which in turn makes it a cumbersome process. The procedure in China is more tedious. According to an official of the Ministry of Finance, Bangladesh "the situation is even more dragged-out in China." For example, if the Chinese side does not agree to, or fails to understand even a particular word in the project documents, they send the file back to Bangladesh for the process to start afresh (Byron and Chakma, 2019).

The financial limitation from the Chinese side has also hampered the pace of BRI projects. Only a few officials of the bank deal with foreign loans, so the funds are released very slowly. The intense lobbying by Chinese firms to win the contracts for the development projects cause further delays, the Finance Ministry official said (Byron and Chakma, 2019). Since 2016, US$ 1.8 billion was committed on average each year, which is in line with what the multilateral lenders do. "Also as per Chinese Exim bank officials, Beijing does not commit more than US$ 3 billion a year to any country as it deems any amount higher than this might be beyond the repayment capacity of the country" (Byron and Chakma, 2019). Another loan agreement involving US$ 280.49 million was struck as part of a US$ 1.12 billion project to strengthen the power grid network under the Power Grid Company of Bangladesh (PGCB) (Byron and Chakma, 2019).

At times, tax evasion has also withheld the projects. Bangladesh authorities have found that a Chinese company, China Road and Bridge Corporation (CRBC), which is a subsidiary of China Communications Construction Company (CCCC) engaged in the construction of roads and bridges in Bangladesh, was involved in tax evasion while importing construction material for government projects. Earlier in December 2020, the National Board of Revenue (NBR) launched an investigation into ZTE

Bangladesh, a subsidiary of the Chinese ZTE Corporation with many business operations in different sectors of the country, on the suspicion of tax evasion. Bangladesh revenue board sent separate letters to different entities to all the concerned partners as a part of investigations (ANI, 2019).

Sometimes, China has been cautious about Bangladesh getting closer to the US. On a conjecture about Bangladesh joining QUAD, the Chinese Ambassador to Dhaka, Li Jimingin warned the country against joining the Quadrilateral Security Dialogue that some in Beijing view as a prospective anti-China group. He said; "Relations with China would be damaged if Bangladesh joins the QUAD." Foreign Minister A.K. Abdul Momen responded within a day, reminding China that Bangladesh was free to make its own foreign policy choices and to pursue alignments and relationships in its interest. He also observed that Beijing would wade into the internal choices of another country (*Prothom Alo* (English), 2021).

China, Bangladesh and the Geopolitics around BRI

The BRI has been seen as an opportunity for Bangladesh to achieve its national development goals of becoming a developed country by 2041. China has implemented several infrastructure projects. In 2022, most of the projects are nearing completion in Bangladesh. According to *China Daily*, Bangladesh has set out plans to rise up from the status of a least developed country to that of a developing nation by 2026-and cooperation with China is seen as a key enabler of this target" (Das, 2022).

Bangladesh is important to China due to its geopolitical location, and as a result, investment has steadily increased. China is making inroads into South Asia with its access to the Indian Ocean. This move is aimed at enhancing its presence in the Indian Ocean so as to reduce its dependence on the Malacca Strait, counted among the world's busiest shipping lanes. Bangladesh is strategically important both for the US and China as part of the Indo-Pacific Strategy and BRI, respectively (Rahman, 2021).

Although, Bangladesh joined BRI in 2016, it did not allow Chinese investment in deep-sea ports which could prove suitable for a future Chinese Navy presence. Dhaka cancelled the Sonadia deep-sea project, and instead agreed to one in Payra, which is "accessible only through a 75-km-long canal, a very unlikely place for a naval base". Bangladesh has moved on with the BRI project in a very cautious manner. Unlike the other South Asian countries like Pakistan and Sri Lanka, Bangladesh has carefully managed its relationship with China and has not fallen into the 'debt trap'. Consciously, it did not allow Chinese investment in deep seaports such as Sonadia and agreed only for the Payra port project. Consequently, Bangladesh pitched in the idea of building a port at Sonadia with multiple international stakeholders. The palpable reason for this was environmental concerns, and possibly due to further geopolitical caution and wariness of Chinese credit. However, the deal could not be worked out. Bangladesh opted for a Japan-backed port at Matabari (Cox Bazaar District) and China got the deep seaport project at Payra. There was a huge protest in Dhaka on China handling the Payra port as it could bring China close to the Indian Ocean. However, there is a caveat; China has built the Kyaukpyu port in Myanmar. Across the BRI, policymakers and commentators talk about "balance" with grave concern. In the jostling between great powers, the agency of countries stuck in between is often overlooked, but the nuances of great power competition are rarely lost on those in-betweens most keenly affected (Mardell, 2020).

As Tom Miller has stated that there has been a change in Chinese foreign policy with the launch of the BRI. Prior to the launch of the initiative, one of the basic tenets of the foreign policy was 'non-interference' and 'non-alignment' in domestic politics of the country. However, for the last five years, China is trying to build a "community of shared destiny" in Asia which basically runs contradictory to the principle of non-interference. Some experts argue that China has begun to influence and interfere in Bangladesh's domestic policy. Along with the economic investments, China is also instrumental in political coordination in Bangladesh (*Prothom Alo*, 2016).

At the site of the Payra power plant, there were clashes between local workers and Chinese expatriates. A Chinese electrician was killed and seven other employees of the 1320 MW Payra Power Plant were injured in a clash between Bangladeshi and Chinese employees in Patuakhali's KalaparaUpazila (Patuakhali, 2019).

China has also withdrawn funding for a few BRI infrastructure projects in Bangladesh after the recipient country re-evaluated the programs and revised their costs. The future of the two rail projects is indefinite as of now. The reports after the re-evaluation of infrastructure projects proposed cutting cost of rail projects. The expected US$ 1.045 billion in costs for the Joydebpur-Ishwardi dual-gauge double-line rail were to be reduced by 12.91 per cent and the US$ 1.272 billion budget for the Akhura-Sylhet dual gauge rail was to be reduced by 20.8 per cent. Cumulatively, total savings would come to nearly US$ 572 million for Bangladesh. China has responded by not funding the Joydebpur-Ishwardi double-line project and for the Akhura-Sylhet dual project, they discontinued the work. Bangladesh also asked for a review of the costs of another project, the US$ 902.33 million Joydebpur-Jamalpur dual-gauge rails, which was also supposed to be funded by China under a government-to-government arrangement. The railway officials suggest that in G2G projects with China, funding, conditions for appointing contractors and project cost calculation processes are similar. Consequently, Joydebpur-Jamalpur dual-gauge rail-track project might also lose Chinese funding if the expected costs are reduced (Islam, 2021).

China, Bangladesh and Debt Trap

Bangladesh has explained its position on the issue of taking loans and the issue of 'debt trap'. Minister of State for Foreign Affairs Mohammed Shahriar Alam stated that Bangladesh "never will" (Sui, 2019) ask China for more loans as it looks for ways to finance its future development. Ahead of the Second Belt and Road Forum (2019), Alam said any amount of debt can be "dangerous" for countries not achieving high economic growth, adding that "Bangladesh has gained the economic power" to service its own loans linked to Beijing's BRI (Sui, 2019).

A comparative analysis of the external debt ratio with other BRI member countries that are falling into the so-called "debt trap" suggests that Bangladesh is in a good position to manage its external debt compared to its counterparts. For example, Sri Lanka's debt ratio to nominal GDP is 104 per cent and Pakistan has 41 per cent, respectively. On the other hand, Bangladesh's foreign debt stock is around US$ 78.04 billion in the fiscal year 2020-21. It is around 22 per cent of the GDP. Overall, debt issue is not a concern for Bangladesh (Rahman, 2019).

A report by the Center for Global Development (CGD) has shown that 68 BRI countries are at risk of debt distress according to measures of debt sustainability. Comparatively, according to the report, Bangladesh appears to be at a low risk as compared to the other countries. According to the World Bank and the International Monetary Fund, a country will cross the danger mark if its external debts exceed 40 per cent of GDP. According to the Ministry of Finance of Bangladesh, the total outstanding foreign loan of the country was nearly US$ 44.06 billion, depicting per capita loan to be around US$ 278 in 2019-2020 fiscal year. Bangladesh is unlikely to fall into the Chinese debt trap. Of Bangladesh's total external debt in the 2019-20 fiscal year, 38 per cent was from the World Bank, 24.5 per cent from the Asian Development Bank (ADB), 17 per cent from the Japan International Cooperation Agency (JICA), 6.81 per cent from China, 6.18 per cent from Russia and 1.3 per cent from India (Shahzzad, 2021).

Chinese Assistance during the Pandemic

Besides the investments under the rubric of BRI, during the COVID-19 pandemic, in 2020, China provided Bangladesh with 3 million surgical and N-95 masks, 1,10,000 sets of personal protective equipment (PPE) kits, sanitizers, testing kits, thermometer guns, and ventilators (*Xinhua*, 2020). China sent a 10-member medical team to Bangladesh in June 2020, for two weeks to provide consultation and train Bangladeshi medical professionals on pandemic control, patient treatment, and laboratory tests (*The Financial Express*, 2020). Along with mask diplomacy, health philanthropy has also been employed by various Chinese companies toward China's partner countries during this pandemic. The Jack Ma Foundation and Alibaba Foundation donated 40,000 testing reagents and 3,00,000 masks to Bangladesh (*Xinhua*, 2020). Cultural Counselor of the Embassy of China in Bangladesh handed over Anti-COVID-19 medical materials to Bangladesh Shilpakala Academy, Bangladesh National Museum and other 4 Bangladesh local cultural and art organisations on 23 April 2020 (MFA, 2020). Bangladesh has got another 5 million doses of COVID-19 vaccines (*Xinhua*, 2021). This is in addition to the 2 million jabs that Bangladesh had already received from China until July 2021. Bangladesh joined China-led South Asian Foreign Ministers' meeting on COVID-19 cooperation (PTI, 2021).

The geostrategic location of Bangladesh is of immense importance. Chinese interest in the ports of the Bay of Bengal has implications for regional stakeholders. To sum up, the BRI projects were seen as an opportunity to fill the infrastructure gap in Bangladesh. BRI projects have been delayed due to several factors. However, Bangladesh has very cautiously moved with the projects as it has learned lessons from other South Asian countries.

References

Ahmad, R and Rejaul Karim Byron. (2017). "China-Funded Projects: Dhaka seeks to speed up deals", The Daily Star, 15 November, at https://www.thedailystar.net/frontpage/china-funded-projects-dhaka-seeks-speed-deals-1491319. Accessed on 15 January 2022.

ANI. (2021). "Chinese companies linked to CPEC projects evade tax commitments in Bangladesh", *Economic Times,* 18 December, at https://economictimes.indiatimes.com/news/international/world-news/chinese-companies-linked-to-cpec-projects-evades-tax-commitments-in-bangladesh/articleshow/88354100.cms?from=mdr. Accessed on 18 January 2022.

Ashraf, S.(2016). "Xi Jinping's visit to enhance ties", *Prothom Alo*, 29 August, at https://en.prothomalo.com/bangladesh/Xi-Jinping-s-visit-to-enhance-ties-Syed-Ashraf. Accessed on 1 February 2022.

Brewster, D. (2019). Bangladesh's road to the BRI. *The Interpreter* , 30 May, at https://www.lowyinstitute.org/the-interpreter/bangladesh-road-bri, Accessed on 5 February 2022.

bd24news.com. (2016). China sign 27 deals as President Xi visits Dhaka, 15 October, at https://bdnews24.com/bangladesh/2016/10/14/bangladesh-china-sign-27-deals-as-president-xi-visits-dhaka. Accessed on 7 February 2022.

Belt and Road Initiative, at https://www.beltroad-initiative.com/belt-and-road/. Accessed on 12 February 2022.

Byron, R. Karim and Jagaran Chakma. (2019), China Funded Projects: Red tape holds back progress. The Daily Star, 19 October, at https://www.thedailystar.net/frontpage/news/china-funded-projects-red-tape-holds-back-progress-1815790. Accessed on 5 March 2022.

China Daily. (2021). China provides Bangladesh fund for 8th friendship bridge , 8 April, at https://www.chinadaily.com.cn/world/2016-04/08/content_24362098.htm. Accessed on 10 March 2022.

Das, A. (2022). "Dhaka builds ambitions on BRI", *China Daily*, 4 April, at https://global.chinadaily.com.cn/a/202104/06/WS606b9f8ca31024ad0bab39d7.html. Accessed on 18 March 2022.

Cultural Counselor Sun Yan hands over Anti-COVID-19 Medical Materials to Bangladesh local cultural and art organizations, (2020), 29 April, at https://www.mfa.gov.cn/ce/cebd//eng/zmjw/t1774904.htm. Accessed on 19 March 2022.

Economy, E. (2022). "Xi Jinping's New World Order: Can China Remake the International System?", *Foreign Affairs*, January/February, at https://www.foreignaffairs.com/articles/china/2021-12-09/xi-jinpings-new-world-order. Accessed on 18 March 2022.

Financial Express Online Desk. (2021). "Pakistan, Bangladesh, Algeria major recipients of Chinese arms", 17 March, at https://thefinancialexpress.com.bd/national/pakistan-bangladesh-algeria-major-recipients-of-chinese-arms-1615990443. Accessed on 18 March 2022.

NDRC PRC, (2015), "Vision and actions on jointly building Belt and Road," 28 March, at http://www.china.org.cn/china/Off_the_Wire/2015-03/28/content_35182638.htm. Accessed on 22 February 2022.

Ghatack, P. (2019), "Bangladesh's Ruling Party Signs MoU with China's Communist Party", *Benar News*, 21 March, at https://www.benarnews.org/english/news/bengali/china-mou-03212019171549.html. Accessed on 18 February 2022.

Hurley J., Scott Morris, and GailynPortelance. (2018). "Examining the Debt Implications of the Belt and Road Initiative from a Policy Perspective", March, at https://www.cgdev.org/sites/default/files/examining-debt-implications-belt-and-road-initiative-policy-perspective.pdf. Accessed on 21 January 2022.

Hasan, P. (2021). "BRI provides benefits for Bangladesh", *China Daily*, 11 October, at https://global.chinadaily.com.cn/a/202110/11/WS6163e762a310cdd39bc6e219.html. Accessed on 25 February 2022.

Hasan, P. (2022). "BRI provides benefits for Bangladesh", *Pakistan Today*, 19 March, at https://www.pakistantoday.com.pk/2022/03/19/bri-provides-benefits-for-bangladesh/. Accessed on 27 February 2022.

Huaxia. (2021). "Bangladesh gets another 5 mln doses of Chinese COVID-19 vaccine," *Xinhuanet*, 18 September, at http://www.xinhuanet.com/english/asiapacific/2021-09/18/c_1310196542.htm. Accessed on 27 February 2022.

Islam, S. (2021). "Belt and Road projects in limbo as Bangladesh cuts budgets", *Nikkie Asia*, 28 June, at https://asia.nikkei.com/Spotlight/Belt-and-Road/Belt-and-Road-projects-in-limbo-as-Bangladesh-cuts-budgets. Accessed on 2 March 2022.

Jiao W. and Zhang Yunbi, (2013). "Xi in call for building of new 'maritime silk road'", *China Daily*, 4 October, at https://www.chinadaily.com.cn/

china/2013xiapec/2013-10/04/content_17008913.htm. Accessed on 12 January 2022.

Kun, Z. (2019). "Five-Connectivity measures BRI impact", *China Watch*, 24 January, at http://www.chinawatch.cn/a/201901/24/WS5c493294a310df3a7f3711b9.html. Accessed on 28 January 2022.

Mardell, J. (2020). "The BRI in Bangladesh: Walking the tightrope between Beijing and Delhi. Place of Publication?", 11 August, at https://merics.org/en/short-analysis/bri-bangladesh-walking-tightrope-between-beijing-and-delhi. Accessed on 25 January 2022.

Miller, T. (2017). *China's Asian Dream*, London: Zed Books.

"Padma Bridge not part of Belt and Road Initiative", (2022). The Daily Star, June 18, at https://www.thedailystar.net/news/bangladesh/development/news/mega-projects-wont-negatively-impact-economy-pm-3048206. Accessed on 24 June 2022.

Prothom Alo English. (2021). "China Has Crossed the Line When Talking About Quad: Foreign Minister", 11 May, at https://en.prothomalo.com/bangladesh/government/china-has-crossed-the-line-when-talking-about-quad-foreign-minister. Accessed on 28 January 2022.

Patuakhali. (2019). "Chinese worker killed in clash at power plant", The Daily Star, 20 June, at https://www.thedailystar.net/backpage/news/chinese-worker-killed-clash-power-plant-1759597. Accessed on 25 January 2022.

PTI, (2021). "Bangladesh to join China-led initiative on COVID-19 cooperation among South Asian nations", *Economic Times*, 26 April, at https://economictimes.indiatimes.com/news/international/world-news/bangladesh-to-join-china-led-initiative-on-covid-19-cooperation-among-south-asian-nations/articleshow/82261812.cms?from=mdr. Accessed on19 February 2022.

PTI, (2021). "China warns of 'substantial damage' to ties if Bangladesh joins US-led Quad alliance; Dhaka calls it 'aggressive'", *Economic Times*, 11 May, at https://economictimes.indiatimes.com/news/defence/china-threatens-bangladesh-says-ties-will-be-hit-if-it-joins-quad/articleshow/82544639.cms?from=mdr. Accessed on 29 January 2022.

Padma Multipurpose Bridge Project, at http://www.padmabridge.gov.bd/. Accessed on 25 January 2022.

MFA, (2013). "President Xi Jinping Delivers Important Speech and Proposes to Build a Silk Road Economic Belt with Central Asian Countries", 7 September, at https://www.mfa.gov.cn/ce/cegy//eng/zgyw/t1076334.htm#:~:text=President%20Xi%20Jinping%20Delivers%20Important,Belt%20with%20Central%20Asian%20Countries&text=On%20Sept.,Future%22%20at%20Kazakhstan's%20Nazarbayev%20University. Accessed on 15 January 2022.

Rahman, S. Abdur. (2021). "The BRI in Bangladesh: 'Win-Win' or a 'Debt Trap'?", *The Diplomat*, 9 November, at https://thediplomat.com/2021/11/the-bri-in-bangladesh-win-win-or-a-debt-trap/#:~:text=Currently%2C%20nine%20projects%20are%20running,Dasher%20Kandi%20Sewerage%20treatment%20plant. Accessed on 28 January 2022.

Samsani, S. (2021) "China-Bangladesh strategic linkages", 11 May, at https://www.orfonline.org/expert-speak/china-bangladesh-strategic-linkages/. Accessed on 28 January 2022.

Shazzad, H. (2021). "Is Bangladesh at risk of falling into the Chinese debt trap?",The Daily Star, 8 November, at https://www.thedailystar.net/views/opinion/news/bangladesh-risk-falling-the-chinese-debt-trap-2224391. Accessed on 30 January 2022.

Siu, P. (2019). "Bangladesh eyes alternatives to China's belt and road loans as it seeks to fund future development", *South China Morning Post*, 23 April, at https://www.scmp.com/week-asia/economics/article/3007190/bangladesh-eyes-alternatives-chinas-belt-and-road-loans-it?module=perpetual_scroll_0&pgtype=article&campaign=3007190, Accessed on 5 February 2022.

"Use of Ritonavir, Resochin, Ribavirin, Arbidol can be effective: Chinese experts", *The Financial Express*, 14 June, 2020, at https://www.thefinancialexpress.com.bd/health/use-of-ritonavir-resochin-ribavirin-arbidol-can-be-effective-chinese-experts-1592131775. Accessed on 5 February 2022.

Varma, K J M. (2020). "BCIM missing out of list of China's BRI projects". PTI, 5 April, at https://www.theweek.in/wire-updates/international/2019/04/28/fgn16-china-bcim.html. Accessed on 17 March 2022.

Varma, K J M. (2019). "Bangladesh-China-India-Myanmar-Economic corridor project not abandoned, says China", *The Print*, 10 June, at https://theprint.in/world/bangladesh-china-india-myanmar-economic-corridor-project-not-abandoned-says-china/248341/. Accessed on 29 January 2022.

Wezeman, Pieter D., Alexandra Kuimova, and Siemon T. Wezeman. (Stockholm International Peace Research Institute, SIPRI, March 2021) "Trends in International Arms Transfers, 2020," SIPRI Fact Sheet, at https://sipri.org/sites/default/files/2021-03/fs_2103_at_2020.pdf. Accessed on 19 February 2022.

Xinhua, Bangladesh receives Supplies from Jack Ma, Ali Baba. (2020). *Xinhua*, 29 May, at http://www.xinhuanet.com/english/2020-04/07/c_138955230.htm. Accessed on 19 February 2022.

"Xi Jinping Meets with Chairperson of Bangladesh Nationalist Party Khaleda Zia." (2016). Ministry of Foreign Affairs of the People's Republic of China, 14 October, at https://www.fmprc.gov.cn/mfa_eng/topics_665678/

XJPDJPZMJLGJXGSFWBCXZYDGAJXDJZGJLDRDBCHW/t1406620.shtml. Accessed on 14 March 2022.

Xinhua. (2017). "China to fund Bangladesh for construction of infrastructure development projects", 12 May, at http://www.xinhuanet.com/english/2017-05/11/c_136274644.htm, Accessed on 19 March 2022.

Yige, C and Wu Chaolan. (2022). "Pathway to brighter future: Belt and Road Initiative in South Asia", *People's Daily*, 2 April, at http://en.people.cn/n3/2022/0402/c90000-10079566-4.html. Accessed on 29 March 2022.

7. BRI in Sri Lanka and Maldives: Economic, Political and Security Dynamics

Samatha Mallempati

Abstract

The significance of Sri Lanka and the Maldives in the Indian Ocean strategic and security space has attracted many foreign powers in the past. Both the countries have found themselves in the middle of power competition during the Cold War period. The rise of China in the 21st century, as an important global player and its thrust on reviving its centuries-old ocean trade routes (maritime silk route) which can sustain its fast-growing economy by cultivating relations with littoral states, has shifted the global attention to China's activities in the Indo-Pacific/Indian Ocean region. In this context, China's active engagement with two Indian Ocean Island states Sri Lanka and the Maldives, strategically important neighbours of India has raised considerable interest. Both island states chose to become the part of Belt and Road Initiative (BRI) started by China, providing impetus to China's expanding maritime role and furthering China's economic and security interests in the region. In this context, the chapter will try to look at China-Sri Lanka and China-Maldives relations in the 21st century, investments by China, domestic responses to China's role and political and security implications.

Introduction

China's active presence in Sri Lanka and the Maldives needs to be looked at in the larger context of post-Cold War global power dynamics. The end of Cold War enhanced the idea of multipolar world where China tried to increase its influence in the Asian region and cultivate its age-old trade and cultural relations within the framework of Maritime Silk Route/BRI with littoral States in the Indian Ocean Region including with Sri Lanka and the Maldives. The inroads China has made in these two island states have implications for India due to geographical proximity and possible security implications. India has been seen as a "net security provider" in the Indian Ocean (Brewster, 2013). It seems both the island states are increasingly willing to play an important role in securing peace and rule-based Indian Ocean by balancing relations with regional and major powers, while taking advantage of geopolitical and strategic location to further their own economic and security interests. The support extended to BRI can be seen in this context. The sections below will try to look at Sri Lanka-China and Maldives-China relations, reasons for supporting the BRI, economic aspects of BRI projects, domestic responses and concerns, as well as political, strategic and security factors.

China-Sri Lanka Relations

China's engagement and inroads into Sri Lanka is not new. China-Sri Lanka relations were described as a model for small country and big country relations by the former President of China Hu Jintao (USC US-China Institute, 2007). China-Sri Lanka cultural and trade relations go back to thousands of years and it is said that the Chinese scholar-monk, Fa Xian spent two years in Anuradhapura in the 5th century in translating Buddhist scriptures, which were later taken to China. Chinese admiral Zheng He used Sri Lanka as a base for sailing as far as West, up to the Horn of Africa (Kaplan, 2011, p. 194). Five hundred years later the triangular tablet he erected in 1410 was unearthed in Galle and the message inscribed talks about a peaceful world built on trade (Kaplan, 2011, p. 195).

Even before the establishment of formal diplomatic relations, China-Ceylon Rice-Rubber Pact was signed in 1952. The Pact helped the then Pro-West United Nations Party (UNP) government (1948-56), to steer through adverse economic conditions and food crisis (Yatanoor, 1997, p. 98). The foundation for diplomatic relations was laid with the visit of China's Premier Zhou Enlai in 1957 to Sri Lanka, as a special guest to participate in the Independence Day celebrations. While welcoming Zhou, S.W.R.D. Bandaranaike, the Prime Minister of Sri Lanka, stressed that "Ceylon (Present day Sri Lanka) look upon the contribution which China is making in shaping the new world" (Cooke, 2017, p. 15). This statement was a testimony to how Sri Lanka looked at China's role in world politics. Sri Lanka also organised a Colombo Conference during India-China War in 1962 that brought together Ghana, Egypt, Cambodia, Burma and Indonesia to discuss a way out of war. In 1963, Agreement on Commercial Maritime Relations between China and Sri Lanka was seen by experts as inimical to India's interest in the region. However, Sri Lanka defended the agreement on grounds that it will benefit in the transport of rice, textiles and other imports from China and Sri Lanka's own shipping lanes would get an advantage over the Chinese ports (Cooke, 2017, p. 18). The 1982 China-Sri Lanka Joint Trade Committee, the Agreement on Economic and Trade Cooperation of 1984 and the Sri Lanka-China Joint Commission of 1991 streamlined the economic relations. Total trade between Sri Lanka and China was doubled from US$ 125.6 million to US$ 256.2 million from 1990 to 2000 (Deyshappriya, 2019, p. 370). Sri Lanka also took the side of China when it came to issues like Taiwan's independence (USC US-China Institute, 2007). Sri Lanka co-sponsored the draft resolution to restore Chinese legitimacy in the United Nations in 1971 and supported China to get an observer status in the South Asian Association for Regional Cooperation (SAARC). As opposed to the West, China chose to support Sri Lanka at the multilateral forums such as the United Nations, regarding Sri Lanka's human rights situation. This has also brought the two countries closer.

Relations in the 21st Century

In this background, Sri Lanka-China relations have seen robust growth in the 21st century. Official bilateral visits helped in expanding the scope of economic relations. During the visit of President Mahinda Rajapaksa to China in February-March 2007, the year 2007 was designated as "China-Sri Lanka Friendship Year", to mark the establishment of 50 years of diplomatic relations (USC US-China Institute, 2007). During the visit, a Memorandum of Understanding (MoU), on investment promotion was signed other than the Economic and Technical Cooperation Agreement and Friendship City Agreement between the Chinese city of Guangzhou and the district of Hambantota. Because of the high-level interactions, China's investments in building infrastructure in Sri Lanka has commenced even before the war ended in 2009. China built Bandaranaike International Centre in Colombo, Puttalam Coal Power project, and discussions were held between the two countries for the development of the Hambantota Development Zone which included harbour development, a bunkering system and tank farm. During 2005-2016, disbursements by China for various projects to Sri Lanka increased from US$ 11 million to US$ 440 million.

Relations further deepened after both the countries signed, China-Sri Lanka's "Strategic Cooperative Partnership Agreement" in 2014, during the visit of China's President Xi Jinping to Sri Lanka (MFA, PRC, 2021). The Plan of Action that was signed during the visit to strengthen the strategic cooperation, emphasised on "common traditional values, development aspirations and strategic interests, as a source of strength for continuation of traditional friendship between the two countries" (MFA, Government of Sri Lanka, 2014).

The Plan of Action also reiterated Sri Lanka's support to One-China Policy and China's support to Sri Lanka in maintaining national unity and territorial integrity (MFA, Government of Sri Lanka, 2014). Some of the objectives both countries tried to achieve to realise the strategic partnership over the years are, maintaining high-level mutual visits, strengthening cooperation in port construction, industrial parks near the ports, strengthening maritime security and coordination in multilateral frameworks such as the United Nations (UN) (Embassy of the PRC in Sri Lanka, 2014). The Plan of Action also mentions about long-term financial assistance from China to Sri Lanka in developing projects such as Ruwanpura Expressway, Northern Expressway, Gin-Nilwala River diversion, Kelani River Basin, Thalpitigala Reservoir, rehabilitation of national airports, expansion and modernisation of Petroleum Refinery and related infrastructure including pipelines, water supply and wastewater management (MFA, Government of Sri Lanka, 2014). Economic cooperation is also an integral part of strategic cooperation and by setting up a Joint Working Group on Trade in 2013, Sri Lanka tried to benefit from the trade in tea, rubber, fish and fish products, coconut and jewellery, etc. with China, in which Sri Lanka has a comparative advantage (Fernando, 2017, p. 84). To further the economic cooperation both the countries are looking forward to sign an FTA. So far 6 rounds of negotiations took place to formalise the FTA. Sri Lanka also became a founding member of the Asian Infrastructure Investment Bank (AIIB) in 2014.

Other than the development projects proposed, the notable outcome of China's President Xi's visit to Sri Lanka in 2014, was the support extended by Sri Lanka to China to build the 21st Century Maritime Silk Road. To this end, both sides agreed to work on completing Hambantota Port Project, Colombo Port Project, and Hambantota Port Development Project (Phase II) and also announced the establishment of a Joint Committee on Coastal and Marine Cooperation. Therefore, President Xi Jinping's visit to Sri Lanka in 2014 was considered, a new chapter in bilateral relations. After the visit both the countries tried to advocate a sustainable Asian security concept (MFA, Government of Sri Lanka, 2014).

This idea has found support in Sri Lanka's foreign policy calculus. In Sri Lanka's strategic and political circles, there is an understanding that global economic power is shifting towards Asia and by the year 2030, the Asian region will overtake North America and Europe in Gross Domestic Product (GDP) and investments in technology (Embassy of Sri Lanka in Korea, 2017). This view was echoed by the Prime Minister of Sri Lanka, Ranil Wickramasinghe in his statement at the BRI Forum in 2017, held in Beijing. He said that the 'BRI will accelerate the growth process in Asia and Sri Lanka's participation in the BRI will help in strategic repositioning in the region' (Embassy of Sri Lanka in Korea, 2017). To emerge as a commercial hub, investments by China, including three major ports—Colombo, Hambantota and Trincomalee, and the two international airports—Colombo and Mattala, are connected by road and rail to the proposed Special Economic Zones (SEZs). These initiatives were expected to transform Sri Lanka into shipping, aviation and a logistics hub. While supporting the initiative, Sri Lanka also took a position, probably to assuage the legitimate concerns of India, that the success of hub will also depend on the maintenance of long-term stability in the Indian Ocean by promoting peaceful and non-military cooperation, ensuring unimpeded commerce based on the multilateral trading system (Embassy of Sri Lanka in Korea, 2017) This position was reverberated in the joint statement released by Sri Lankan political parties on the 100th anniversary of the Communist Party of China (CPC) (Embassy of MFA, PRC in Colombo, 2021).

Investments by China in Sri Lanka

The high-level interactions based on the strategic cooperation framework, have contributed to financing by China for a number of development and infrastructure projects, which also extended to cooperation between financial institutions and companies of both the nations. The Exim Bank of China, China Commercial and Industrial Bank (CCID) and China Development Bank (CDB) have provided loans for various projects in Sri Lanka. So far, the three agencies together completed thirty-one projects. It is to be noted that majority of projects are loan-based with 2 to 6 per cent interest rates. The China Harbour Engineering Company (CHEC), China Merchant Port Holding Company (CMPHC), the Sri Lanka Ports Authority (SLPA) and concerned Ministries are acting as implementing agencies. These agencies have invested heavily in the major port development, road and rail network and energy projects, which are considered important to realise the BRI of China. The table below provides information about some of the ongoing and completed projects supported by China.

Table 7.1

Project	**Loan/investment Amount in US$ million**
Colombo Katunayake Expressway (A1, A2, A3 & A4) was completed in 2013	248.2
Hambantota International Airport Project was completed in 2013	190
Northern Road Rehabilitation Project (C1A, C1B, C11A, C11B, C7, C2, C3) was completed in 2013	424

Southern Transport Development Project was completed in 2017	138
Colombo Lotus Tower Project was completed in 2018	88.6
Hambantota Hub Development Project was completed in 2020	252.5
Hambantota Port Development Project was completed in 2019	1335.7
Construction of Extension of Southern Expressway Section 4, 2 and 1 was completed in 2020	1545
Construction of Outer Circular Highway Project Phase III (Kadawatha to Kerawalapitiya) was completed in 2020	494
CICT Colombo Terminal (Investment) completed in 2014	500
Colombo Port City (Investment) is an ongoing project expected to be completed in 2042	1300
Puttalam Coal Power I & II completed in 2011	1346
Colombo East Container Terminal (investment) to be completed in 2024 in three phases	710

Source: Department of External Resources, Sri Lanka

These projects are aimed at increasing the connectivity at the domestic level as well as with global supply chains for Sri Lanka and were designed to benefit not just the economy of Sri Lanka but also to help China to maintain its domestic oil and energy needs through uninterrupted supply.

In post-2009, single largest FDI came from China to build the Colombo International Container Terminal (CICT), the first green filed terminal investment. The deep-water terminal helped the Colombo port to become a major player as a transhipment hub (Fernando, 2017, p. 85).

The project which drew considerable international attention was the Hambantota Port. The much-talked about port, was in the cards since 2002, but could not be implemented due to fund crunch and domestic civil war. In 2003, SNC Lavalin, a Canadian engineering firm, completed a feasibility study for the port, but was rejected by a task force. But in 2006,

Ramboll, a Danish consulting firm, completed a second feasibility study. It took a relatively optimistic view of the port's potential and concluded that it can take the load off the ports at Colombo, Galle, and Trincomalee and by 2040, the port would be able to handle, nearly 20 million Twenty-foot Equivalent Units (TEU) (CSIS, 2018).

Mahinda Rajapaksa who came to power in 2005 ceased the opportunity, to develop the southern parts of the country, including Hambantota, his own constituency by building a cricket stadium, port and an international airport all through Chinese funding. Hambantota has been chosen because it is a midway point on the sea routes between China on the one hand and the Middle East and Africa on the other. These regions are source of energy for China and the port and oil bunkering storage facilities at Hambantota are seen as assets to both the countries (2007, p. 22). The development of Hambantota a somewhat backward district in the South of Sri Lanka was seen as a departure from how Sri Lanka was seen globally, mostly as a "byword for ethnic conflict" and by developing the port, Sri Lanka wanted to send a message that the country was ready to emerge as a strategic node for global maritime commerce (Kaplan, 2011, p. 193). However, the port could not develop to cater to the ships passing through the East-West maritime route and ended up as loss-making port, nearly 46.7 billion Sri Lankan rupees. Due to low business, the government could not pay the loans taken for the project. In 2017 the National Unity Government (NUG) led by Maithripal Sirisena and Ranil Wickramasinghe, decided to lease the port for 99 years to China. A concession agreement was signed with the CMPHC, with a 70 per cent stake and the remaining 30 per cent by the SLPA (Stacey, 2017). The US$ 1.2 billion agreement has given the powers to CMPH to develop the port areas and adjacent areas as industrial zones and the SLPA will be responsible for security services. By developing Hambantota as an industrial hub, the government of Sri Lanka tried to ease the debt burden and believed that the full potential of the port will be realised in the future.

The proposal to develop an industrial zone by acquiring the land near Hambantota port met with protests by trade unions in 2017. The proposal was also challenged in the court. The Hambantota Parliamentarian Namal Rajapaksa opposed the decision of the National Unity Government and accused the government of playing geopolitics with national assets (Stacey, 2017). China countered the allegations that the government headed by Sirisena, had awarded the Hambantota Port to China for 99 years, and has a provision for extension beyond 99 years (*DD News*, 2022). To quell domestic and international concern and criticism regarding the security of Sea Lanes of Communication due to presence of China in this strategically located port, the government of Sri Lanka decided to shift the Galle Southern Naval Command next to Hambantota Port. There are more than 700 naval officers engaged in maritime security efforts who are based, next to the harbour premises leased by China.

The Colombo Port City Project is another project, which has been seen by many as "economic game changer" (Phadnis, 2022). The Colombo Port is ranked 22nd in the world and the port city is being developed by China by reclaiming 269 hectares of land from the sea. The Port City was expected to create nearly 200,000 lakh jobs for Sri Lankans. In 2015 the NUG of Sri Lanka halved the project citing financial irregularities and ecological issues. But the project construction was renewed in 2016. Colombo Port City Economic Commission Act was also passed in 2021 to streamline, ease of doing business in the port city which is expected to bring US$ 15 billion over a 25-year period. The Act was passed with two-thirds majority in the Parliament by the ruling SLPP. However, possibility that the Act may create an entity that may not adhere to Sri Lanka's Constitution and state institutions through the Colombo Port City Special Economic Zone became a concern (Centre for Policy Alternatives, 2021). Apart from the controversy regarding the composition of the commission, the power it yields pertaining to matters such as leasing of the area, in approving environmental standards and in granting licences to do business were taken up by political parties and civil society of Sri Lanka. Civil society groups and opposition filed nearly eighteen petitions against the Act, and sought a national referendum and the passage of it in the Parliament by two-thirds majority (*Economic Times*, 2021).

Concerns

Overall, according to a comprehensive report on BRI in Sri Lanka by the Chatham House, Chinese infrastructure projects have contributed to improving road connectivity and renewable energy. For instance, according to the report, the Puttalam power plant that was built with China Exim Bank loans emerged as a longer-term solution to the country's electricity supply problems (Wignaraja, 2020, p. 10). The comprehensive report also highlighted that projects under BRI can generate job opportunities for the local population. At the same time, it also mentioned about various risks involved in implementation, in terms of environmental concerns, transparency and challenges on the security front such as the possibility of dual-use facility, allowing military submarines, etc. (Wignaraja, 2020, p. 18). In 2014, two Chinese submarines and a warship docked at Colombo port and it is seen as an example of future use of ports developed by China for military use.

Concerns regarding increasing debt Sri Lanka owed to China have been flagged from time to time. The value of Sri Lanka's external public debt to China doubled from US$ 2.2 billion to US$ 5 billion between 2012 and 2018 has led to concerns (Wignaraja, 2020, p. 12). The US Vice President Mark Pence while emphasizing on China's debt trap diplomacy citing Sri Lanka's Hambantota Port said,

> Sri Lanka, which took on massive debt to let Chinese state companies build a port of questionable commercial value. But the country could no longer afford its payments, so Beijing pressured Sri Lanka to deliver the new port directly into Chinese hands. It may soon become a forward military base for China's growing blue-water navy. (White House Archives, 2018)

Though Sri Lanka's major lenders are market sources and international financial institutions such as the World Bank and the ADB, followed by bilateral sources such as Japan, China and India, loans taken from China to build mega infrastructure projects are believed to be difficult to repay due to higher interest rates, lack of transparency in agreements signed and sustainability of projects in a small economy like Sri Lanka. China often downplayed the criticism that 'joint projects are expensive and not profitable to Sri Lanka (Embassy of the PRC in the US, 2022).

The economic crisis in Sri Lanka has also brought back the debate on feasibility of projects supported by China in Sri Lanka. Due to economic crisis, for the first time in history, Sri Lanka announced a default on its external debt. The increase in total external outstanding debt of Sri Lanka from US$ 35.1 billion by end of April 2021 to US$ 51 billion by April 2022 is a real worry for the Sri Lankan economy (Department of External Sources, 2021). The FDI received by Sri Lanka also fell to approximately US$ 550 million in 2020, significantly less than the US$ 1.2 billion in 2019 and US$ 2.3 billion in 2018 (US Department of State, 2022).

Chinese Foreign Minister's Wang Yi's visit to Sri Lanka at the beginning of 2022, sought to reassure continuity in relations despite the few setbacks at the bilateral level that were witnessed in the under the SLPP government. In December 2021, China withdrew three wind projects, planned near Jaffna (Abeyagoonasekera, 2021, p. 64). These developments indicate that China wants to go beyond commercial relations with Sri Lanka and it is looking forward to making inroads into the Sri Lankan Tamil community through economic and cultural diplomacy, which India needs to watch out carefully for security reasons. Sri Lanka's refusal to pay for contaminated organic fertiliser sent to Sri Lanka by a Chinese company led to the blacklisting of the People's Bank of Sri Lanka by China in October 2021. After months of speculations regarding the pay, the issue was resolved just before China's Foreign Minister Wang Yi's visit to Colombo. Sri Lanka agreed to pay nearly US$ 6.9 million to the Chinese company that supplied contaminated fertilizer (*Tamil Guardian*, 2022). The decision by the Sri Lankan government to settle the issue was criticised by professional groups 'on grounds of transparency in handling public money by government institutions' (*Nikkei Asia*, 2022). Despite the recent visible differences, trade relations between Sri Lanka and China have improved considerably. Trade with China exceeded US$ 5 billion in 2021 as well as Sri Lanka's trade with India. China stood as the largest import partner for Sri Lanka, recording more than US$ 4.7

billion of imports in 2021. Tourist arrivals saw a dip from China due to the pandemic (Central Bank of Sri Lanka, Annual Report-2021, p. 151). Despite these concerns, it seems that China is determined to engage with Sri Lanka on its own terms. China's proposal in January 2022, to have a forum on the development of island countries in the Indian Ocean to bring synergy in development strategies of China and island states may further bring Island states such as Sri Lanka into China's orbit (MFA, PRC, 2022).

Maldives-China Relations

The Maldives, an archipelago in the Indian Ocean, has seen many political upheavals in the last ten years, which received significant international attention. Not just the political developments that garnered the attention of the world, Maldives' engagement with China and its support to BRI generated much interest in the internal politics of the Maldives and its role in larger geopolitics of the Indian Ocean region. Given the history of strong economic and political relations Maldives has with India, its approach towards China became a focal point of discussion in security calculus of the region. The widely scattered islands of Maldives in the Indian Ocean (750 km from North to the South), offer strategic vantage points to monitor vital shipping lanes in the Indian Ocean (Lintner, 2019, p. 170).

Substantial high-level exchanges took place after Maldives and China established diplomatic relations in 1972. The Maldives opened its mission in China in 2008 and China opened its diplomatic mission in Male in 2011. The Economic and Technical Cooperation Agreement was signed in 1984, which was extended from time to time. Since 1988, China is involved in building a Male Housing Project, which has been described as being the most critical 'building block of China-Maldives Friendship' (Fernando, 2017, p. 240). Maldivian President Maumoon Abdul Gayoom visited China in September 2006 and met with Chinese President Hu Jintao. After the formation of the first democratically elected government in the Maldives in 2008, both the countries have also focused on tourism development. Tourism is one of the main sources of revenue for the Government of Maldives contributing to 28 per cent of GDP and nearly 60 per cent of revenue. China remained as the top source of tourist arrivals to the Maldives from 2010 to 2018, and the position is taken over by India since 2019 (Ministry of Tourism, Government of Maldives, 2021) Mutual Visa Exemption Fees also helped to boost tourism from China to the Maldives.

The debate over the role of India and China in the Maldives came into public discussion due to the GMR controversy. The US$ 500 million project to develop the Male international airport by GMR was scrapped unilaterally in 2012 by the government led by President Waheed due to protest against the company and later the contract was given to state-owned Chinese company.

China's investments in Maldives saw a momentum during Abdulla Yameen government that came to power in 2014. During the visit of Chinese President Xi Jinping in September 2014 to the Maldives, both the countries agreed to cooperate, in "the joint construction of the 21st Century Maritime Silk Road and build a future-oriented comprehensive friendly and cooperative partnership" (Embassy of the PRC in Barbados, 2014). Both the countries also decided to promote bilateral trade and investment through the mechanism of the Economic and Trade Joint Committee. The Chinese have undertaken projects such as the construction of roads and housing units, expansion of Male International Airport (US$ 830 million), development of a power station, construction of a bridge to connect Malé with Hulhule, investments in tourism and agriculture sectors. The President of Maldives Yameen has decided to call the US$ 400 million grant aid Male-Hulhule Bridge as "Maldives-China Friendship Bridge", which was inaugurated in 2018. China's investments in Maldives's tourism service industry have also been promoted since then. Other important project supported by China is Laamu Atoll Link-Road Project. In July 2105, Yameen administration passed a controversial Land Acquisition Bill through a constitutional amendment that allowed foreigners to own land which can be reclaimed from the sea and who can invest more than US$ 1 billion (*Maldives Independent*, 2015). Given the fact that China has the technology to reclaim the land and finances required, the bill was seen as beneficial to China's interest in the region to further its BRI objectives. In 2019, the Maldives Democratic Party (MDP) government repealed the controversial law. In 2019, the Uninhabited

Land Act of Maldives was passed by the MDP government, that allows foreigners with US$ 1 million to lease land on uninhabited islands for purposes other than tourism for a maximum of 21 years (US Department of State, 2021). Foreigners can also lease land up to a maximum of 50 years for investments over US$ 10 million. In December 2021, China's firm Sino Soar Hybrid Technology Co. Ltd. (Beijing), won a bid to develop hybrid solar-diesel power system in the inhabited islands of an atoll south of capital Male. Notably, Maldives became the second South Asian country to sign an FTA with China in 2017, after Pakistan. China stood as the largest import partner for the Maldives from 2018 to 2021, followed by India.

Concerns

The MDP criticised the way the FTA was rushed to the Parliament by Yameen administration and passed without much consultation within the country. The Government just allowed an hour for the entire Parliamentary process to approve the 1000-plus page document (Chaudhury, 2017). It is not yet clear, if the MDP government will go ahead with full implementation of the FTA.

The MDP leader, former President and current Speaker of the Parliament of Maldives has been vocal against China's increasing role and investments in the Maldives. Nasheed stated that, Chinese-funded infrastructure projects were carried out at inflated costs and are designed to allow China to demand an ownership stake in the future if Maldives fail to repay the loans. China refuted the allegations (*Maldives Independent*, 2019).

According to Maldives Monitory Authority, the total external debt has increased over the years and by the end of 2021, it totalled US$ 2,448.6 million (Maldives Monitory Authority, 2022, p. 69). Despite the differences in Maldives-China relations and the debt figures among political parties of Maldives, China remained as an important trading and investment partner for the Maldives even under the present MDP government led by President Solih. China was asked to restructure the debt by the Maldives, but the request is pending.

The economy of Maldives suffered due to travel restrictions and lockdowns during the pandemic. The tourism sector accounts for 50 per cent of GDP and due to loss in tourism revenue, it is estimated that Maldives need nearly US$ 1.2 billion in financial help to keep the economy on track in coming years (UNCTAD, 2020). Due to these reasons, Maldives will continue to engage with China. The visit of China's Foreign Minister Wang Yi to the Maldives on 9 January 2022 coincided with 50 years of establishment of China-Maldives diplomatic relations. The visit statement mentioned that "China-Maldives relations have become a model of friendly exchange, mutual benefit and win-win results between countries" (MFA, PRC, 2022). Maldives Foreign Minister Abdulla Shahid said that "the results of the Belt and Road cooperation between the Maldives and China have been fruitful, benefiting people's livelihood and profoundly changing the face of Maldivian society" (MFA, PRC, 2022).

Despite the MDP leader Nasheed's overt criticism of China's role in Maldives, other political leaders within the MDP and opposition parties in Maldives yet to come forward in criticism of China.

Political and Strategic Factors

Sri Lanka's and Maldives' geo-strategic location connecting the Indo-Pacific Region, has been a critical factor in China's engagement with the two island states. China's role in India's south is also seen as an example of soft diplomacy, driven by its need for increasing uninterrupted flow of energy to sustain its economic growth (Kaplan, 2011, p. 283).

China was world's top crude oil importer in 2019. China's new "refinery capacity and strategic inventory stockpiling, combined with flat domestic oil production, were the major factors contributing to the increase in China's crude oil imports" (The US Energy Information Administration, 2020). Nearly, 55 per cent of China's crude oil imports come from countries within the Organisation of the Petroleum Exporting Countries (OPEC). China's involvement in Sri Lanka and the Maldives is also the result of its "Malacca dilemma" and to avoid the dilemma, China is actively pursuing to become a regional power not only in the western Pacific but also in the Indian Ocean (Kaplan, 2011, p. 289). China's role in the Indian Ocean may invite contestations by countries having stakes in the region. China's assertive postures in the seas and the BRI are seen as a challenge to established rule-based system. India has been advocating, free, open, inclusive Indo-Pacific region which includes the entire Indian Ocean and the western Pacific. India's concept of SAGAR (Security and Growth for All in the Region) also advocates the idea of Indo-Pacific that is founded upon a cooperative and collaborative rules-based order (Siddiqui, 2019).

Sri Lanka which advocated the idea of "Indian Ocean as a Zone of Peace" in 1971, sees itself at the crossroads of Indo-Pacific as well as BRI. In this context, Sri Lanka's support to BRI is seen as a balancing act in the region. Sri Lanka, while supporting the BRI initiative, has also been emphasising on the importance of freedom of navigation and rule-based order, to avoid strategic competition in the region (Colombage, 2020). Sri Lanka is also cautious about the securitisation of region involving various powers (Colombage, 2020). Therefore, often Sri Lanka emphasised on neutral foreign policy. It is no doubt that Sri Lanka is willing to play a bigger role in the Indian Ocean arena, while covertly conscious of India's legitimate security interests and concerns in the region. Sri Lanka repeatedly emphasised that it will not be a strategic security concern to India, as it is very much under the maritime and air security umbrellas of India (*Tamil Guardian*, 2020).

The economic crisis Sri Lanka is facing in 2022, has forced the island nation to look at India for assistance. The unprecedented crisis in Sri Lanka has compelled the country to default on its debt for the first time in its independent history (*Financial Express*, 2022). Sri Lanka's foreign reserves also fell to just US$ 50 million in April 2022. Sri Lanka is trying to negotiate a loan from International Monitory Fund (IMF), to restructure its debt. This may require Sri Lanka to change its economic policies. China being an important partner for Sri Lanka has expressed its concern about Sri Lanka going to IMF, as it might impact the bilateral relations (Economy Next, 2022). Unlike India, China's response was not so forthcoming to the economic crisis. India stood as a reliable partner for Sri Lanka to tackle the crisis. India provided nearly US$ 4 billion to Sri Lanka to import essential items from India. China provided only US$ 76 million as humanitarian assistance to Sri Lanka.

Similar to Sri Lanka, by supporting the BRI, Maldives is also trying to carve its own space in the geo-politics of the region. The Maldives tilt towards China after 2014 was accompanied by political turbulence in the country, tilt towards authoritarian rule and undermining of democratic institutions. In August 2017, three Chinese naval ships docked in waters of Maldives to engage in training programmes with the Maldives National Defence Force. The MDP government which came to power in 2018, tried to rebalance relations with India and also with the West. The India-First Policy of Maldives government has tried to assuage India's legitimate security concerns and India's foray in building large infrastructure projects such as the US$ 500 million Greater Male Connectivity Project, is seen as a positive move. The strategic engagement has also increased in recent years. India provided technical support, lending and granting naval or maritime vessels and installing coastal surveillance systems in Maldivian territories (Rasheed, 2021). India-Maldives signed a US$ 50 million defence line of credit in February 2021 to facilitate capacity building in the maritime domain. The Maldives also seems to be willing to deal with major powers in the Indo-Pacific region. It signed a Defence Cooperation Agreement with the US in 2020.

Conclusion

China's engagement with Sri Lanka and Maldives indicates that it has made substantial inroads in the Indian Ocean region by involving the two island states through BRI projects. What is to be watched is how the domestic politics of Island states will play out in the future and whether India's legitimate security concerns are addressed in a transparent manner. Unlike China's funding for various infrastructure projects, undoubtedly India's external assistance to two island states in recent years proved that India is a reliable and stable partner. India's Neighbourhood First Policy has also contributed to strengthening relations in the areas of economy and security. The Colombo Security Conclave is an example in this regard, where countries have agreed to strengthen regional security by collaborating on maritime safety and security, countering terrorism and radicalisation, combating trafficking and transnational organised crime (Ministry of External Affairs, GoI, 2022). China lauded India's efforts in helping Sri Lanka to tackle the economic crisis is a reflection of acceptance by China of India's unwavering role in the region. But geographic rivalry often defined India-China relations. This rivalry, coupled with not-so-transparent BRI project implementation and the advantage China has in the field of security in South Asia through sales of arms and support to political regimes which can be inimical to India's interests are issues which need careful observation.

References

Abeyagoonasekera, A. (2021). *Conundrum Of An Island: Sri Lanka's Geopolitical Challenges.* Singapore: World Scientific.

Brewster, D. (2013). "India: Regional net security provider", Ministry of External Affairs, 5 March 2022, at https://mea.gov.in/articles-in-indian-media.htm?dtl/22468/India+Regional+net+security+provider

Business Standard (2021). Adani seals deal to develop Western Container Terminal at Colombo Port, 20 March 2022, at https://www.business-standard.com/article/companies/adani-grp-seals-deal-to-develop-western-container-terminal-at-colombo-port-121093001398_1.htm

Central Bank of Sri Lanka, Annual Report-2021 (2022). "External Sector Developments and Policies", Colombo: Central Bank of Sri Lanka, 15 May 2022, at https://www.cbsl.gov.lk/en/publications/economic-and-financial-reports/annual-reports/annual-report-2021

Centre for Policy Alternatives (2021). "Colombo Port City Economic Commission Billand key Areas of Concern", at https://www.cpalanka.org/wp-content/uploads/2021/05/CPA-commentary-on-the-Port-City-Bill-03.05.2021-1.pdf

Centre for Strategic and International Studies (2018). "Game of Loans: How China Bought Hambantota". Centre for Strategic and International Studies, 2022, at https://www.csis.org/analysis/game-loans-how-china-bought-hambantota

Chaudhury, D. R. (2017). "Maldives-China FTA could plunge Maldives into political crisis", *The Economic Times*, 1 May 2022, at https://economictimes.indiatimes.com/news/defence/maldives-china-fta-could-plunge-maldives-into-political-crisis/articleshow/61873

Colombage, J. (2020). "Keynote address by Foreign Secretary Admiral Professor Jayanath Colombage at the Pathfinder Indian Ocean Security Conference",

Foreign Affairs Ministry, Sri Lanka, 1 March 2022, https://mfa.gov.lk/keynote-address-by-foreign-secretary-admiral-prof

Conference on Chia-Sri Lanka Relations. (2007). "Conference on Chia-Sri Lanka Relations", Colombo: Bandaranaike Centre for International Studies (BCIS) and China Institute of International Studies, China.

Cooke, G. I. (2017). "Sino-Lanka Relations: A Diplomatic Perspective", in G. I. Senanayake, *Sixty Years if China-Sri Lanka Relations 1957-2017*, p. 15. Colombo: BCIS.

Daily FT. (2021). "Trade Unions to Protect the ECT' make representations to clergy against deal with India", February 22, 2022, at https://www.ft.lk/front-page/Trade-Unions-to-Protect-the-ECT-make-representations-to-clergy-against-deal-with-India/44-712297

DD News (2022). "China counters Sri Lankan media report terming Hambantota port 99-year lease extendable", 2 March 2022, at https://ddnews.gov.in/international/china-counters-sri-lankan-media-report-terming-hambantota-port-99-year-lease

Department of External Sources, G. O. (2021). "Foreign Debt Summary", 2 March 2022, at http://www.erd.gov.lk/index.php?option=com_content&view=article&id=102&Itemid=308&lang=en

Deyshappriya, R. (2019). "Sri Lanka-China Economic Relations in Comparative Perspective: Ample Room to Grow", *China Report*, 364-392.

Economic Times (2021). "Sri Lanka's Supreme Court Terms Chinese Port City Bill Inconsistent with Constitution: Parliament Told", 2 April 2022, at https://economictimes.indiatimes.com/news/defence/sri-lankas-supreme-court-terms-chinese-port-city-bill-inconsistent-with-

Economy Next (2022). "China 'sad' that Sri Lanka went to IMF and defaulted: envoy", 28 April 2022, at https://economynext.com/china-sad-that-sri-lanka-went-to-imf-and-defaulted-envoy-93468/

Embassy of Ministry of Foreign Affairs of the Republic of China, Colombo (2021). "100th Anniversary of the Communist Party Of China (CPC) Joint Statement of Sri Lanka Political Parties", 10 January 2022, at http://lk.china-embassy.org/eng/zsgx/202108/P020210911639474548365.pdf

Embassy of the People's Republic of China in Barbados (2014). "Xi Jinping Holds Talks with President Abdulla Yameen of MaldivesJoin Hands to Establish the Future-Oriented Comprehensive Friendly and Cooperative Partnership Between China and Maldives", 23 January 2022, at https://www.mfa.gov.cn/ce/cebb/eng/zgyw/t1191946.htm

Embassy of the People's Republic of China in the United States (2022). "Foreign Ministry Spokesperson Wang Wenbin's Regular Press Conference", 19

March 2022, at http://www.china-embassy.org/eng/lcbt/wjbfyrbt/202201/t20220110_10480654.htm

Embassy of the Peoples Republic of China in Sri Lanka (2014). "Xi Jinping Holds Talks with President Mahinda Rajapaksa of Sri Lanka the Two Heads of State Decide to Join Hands to Promote China-Sri Lanka Strategic Cooperative Partnership for Solid and In-Depth Development", 8 January 2022, at http://lk.china-embassy.org/eng/zgxw/201409/t20140919_1424509.htm

Embasy of Sri Lanka Korea (2017). "Speech by Ranil Wickramasinghe, Prime Mnister of Sri Lanka at the second session of the Leader's Round Table of the Belt and Road Forum for International Development", 12 February 2022, at http://www.slembassykorea.com/kor/bbs/board.php?bo_table=s1_3_kor&wr_id=20&page=6

Fernando, S. (2017). "Economic Relations between Sri Lanka and China", in G. I. Mihiri (ed.), *Sixty Years if China-Sri Lanka Relations 1957-2017.* Colombo: BCIS.

Financial Express (2022). "Sri Lanka defaults on debt for first time as economic crisis deepens", 25 May 2022, at https://www.financialexpress.com/economy/sri-lanka-defaults-on-debt-for-first-time-as-economic-crisis-deepens/2532380/

Ganeshan Wignaraja, D. P. (2020). "Chinese Investment and the BRI in Sri Lanka", 30 January 2022, from Chatham House: https://www.chathamhouse.org/2020/03/chinese-investment-and-bri-sri-lanka-0/about-authors

Kaplan, R. D. (2011). *Monsoon: The Indian Ocean and the Future of American Power.* New York: Random House.

Lintner, B. (2019). *The Costliest Pearl: China's Struggle for India's Ocean.* UK: Hurst & Co.

Liu, P. (2018). "The Security Structure in South Asia and Its Impacts on Belt and RoadInitiative", in W. R. Zhu (ed.), *Annual Reporton the Developmentof the Indian Ocean.* Beijing: Springer.

Maldives Independent (2015). "Majlis approves foreign freeholds in second amendment to constitution," 6 March 2022, at https://maldivesindependent.com/politics/majlis-authorizes-foreign-ownership-of-land-in-second-constitutional-amendment-101193

*Maldives Independen*t. (2019). "Nasheed reignites 'debt trap' row with Chinese ambassador", 23 April 2022, at https://maldivesindependent.com/politics/nasheed-reignites-debt-trap-row-with-chinese-ambassador-149679

Maldives Monitory Authority (2022). *Annual Report-2021,* 28 March 2022, at https://www.mma.gov.mv/documents/Annual%20Report/2021/AR2021.pdf?v=2

Ministry of External Affairs, Government of India (2021). "Question No. 2655 Scrapping of Trilateral Agreement by Sri Lanka", 16 February 2022, at https://www.mea.gov.in/rajya-sabha.htm?dtl/33676/QUESTION_NO2655_SCRAPPING_OF_TRILATERAL_AGREEMENT_BY_SRI_LANKA

Ministry of External Affairs, Government of India (2022). "Joint Press Statement of the 5th NSA Level Meeting of the Colombo Security Conclave held on 09 – 10 March 2022, in Maldives", 16 March 2022, at https://mea.gov.in/press-releases.htm?dtl/34943/Joint+Press+Statement+of+the+

Ministry of Foreign Affairs of Republic of China. (2021). "International Situation and China's Diplomacy in 2021", 13 January 2022, at https://www.fmprc.gov.cn/mfa_eng/wjb_663304/wjbz_663308/2461_663310/202112/t20211230_10477324.html

Ministry of Foreign Affairs of the People's Republic of China (2022). "Wang Yi Holds Talks with Maldivian Foreign Minister Abdulla Shahid", 30 January 2022, at https://www.fmprc.gov.cn/mfa_eng/wjdt_665385/wshd_665389/202201/t20220109_10480370.html

Ministry of Foreign Affairs of the Republic of China (2022). "Wang Yi: Carry Forward the Spirit of the Rubber-Rice Pact to Expand China-Sri Lanka Strategic Cooperative Partnership", 24 March 2022, at https://www.mfa.gov.cn/mfa_eng/zxxx_662805/202201/t20220110_104

Ministry of Foreign Affairs, Government of Sri Lanka (2014). "Plan Of Action Of The Democratic Socialist Republic Of Sri Lanka Andthe People's Republic Of China To Deepen Thestrategic Cooperative Partnership", 18 February 2022, at https://www.mfa.gov.lk/images/stories/Newspapers/plan%20of%20final.pdf,

Ministry of Tourism, Government of Maldives (2021). *Tourism Year Book 2018-2021*, 16 March 2022, at https://www.tourism.gov.mv/en/statistics/annual/year-

Nikkei Asia (2022). "Sri Lanka settles $6.9m fertilizer bill with Chinese supplier", 14 January 2022, at https://asia.nikkei.com/Politics/International-relations/Sri-Lanka-settles-6.9m-fertilizer-bill-with-Chinese-supplier2

Phadnis, A. (2022). "Colombo Port City: Sri Lanka's Economic Game Changer", *Business Standard*, 20 March 2022, at https://www.business-standard.com/podcast/international/colombo-port-city-sri-lanka-s-economic-game-changer-122031400094_1.html

Rasheed, A. A. (2021). "The Role of the Maldives in the Indo-Pacific Security Space in South Asia", E-International Relations, 5 April 2022, at https://www.e-ir.info/2021/02/09/the-role-of-the-maldives-in-the-indo-pacific-security-space-in-south-asia/

Robert, K. D. (2011). *Monsoon: The Indian Ocean and the Future of American Power.* New York: Random House.

Siddiqui, H. (2019). "India's concept of Indo-Pacific is inclusive and across oceans", Ministry of EXternal Affairs, Government of India, 18 January 2022, at https://mea.gov.in/articles-in-indian-media.htm?dtl/32015/Indias_concept_of_IndoPacific_is_inclusive_and_across_oceans.

Sigdel, A. (2020). *India in the Era of China's Belt andRoad Initiative: How Modi Responds to X.* London: Lexington Books.

Stacey, K. (2017). "China signs 99-year lease on Sri Lanka's Hambantota port", 30 January 2022, at https://www.ft.com/content/e150ef0c-de37-11e7-a8a4-0a1e63a52f9c.

Subramanian, N. (2022). "Maldives issues decree to ban anti-India protests", *Indian Express*, 3 May 2022, at https://indianexpress.com/article/world/maldives-issues-decree-to-ban-anti-india-protests-7881122/.

Tamil Guardian. (2022). "China forces Sri Lanka to pay up", 17 January 2022, at https://www.tamilguardian.com/content/china-forces-sri-lanka-pay,

Tamil Guardian (2020). "We don't want to be caught up in this power game', Sri Lanka's Foreign Secretary expresses concerns over Quad military alliance", 9 March 2022, at https://www.tamilguardian.com/content/we-don-t-want-be-caught-power-game-sri-lanka-s-foreign

The US Energy Information Administration (2020). "China's crude oil imports surpassed 10 million barrels per day in 2019", 5 April 2022, at https://www.eia.gov/todayinenergy/detail.php?id=43216

UNCTAD (2020). "Impact of COVID-19 on tourism in small island developing states", 9 February 2022, at https://unctad.org/news/impact-covid-19-tourism-small-island-developing-states.

US Department of State (2021). "2020 Investment Climate Statements: Maldives", 8 April 2022, at https://www.state.gov/reports/2020-investment-climate-statements/maldives/

US Department of State (2022). "2021 Investment Climate Statements: Sri Lanka", 23 January 2022, at https://www.state.gov/reports/2021-investment-climate-statements/sri-lanka/

USC US-China Institute (2007). "Joint Press Communiqué of The People's Republic of China and the Democratic Socialist Republic of Sri Lanka", 2 April 2022, at https://china.usc.edu/joint-press-communique-peoples-republic-china-and-democractic-socialist-republic-sri

White House Archives (2018). "Remarks by Vice President Pence on the Administration's Policy Toward China", 9 March 2022, at https://trumpwhitehouse.archives.gov/briefings-statements/remarks-vice-president-pence-administrations-policy-toward-china/

Yatanoor, C. (1997). *Sri Lanka's Foreign Policy under the Presidentship of J. R. Jayewardene.* Delhi: Kalinga Publications.

8. China's BRI in Nepal: Complexities and Concerns

Naresh Kumar B. K.

Abstract

This chapter examines evolving dimensions of Chinese engagement with Nepal in the context of the Belt and Road Initiative (BRI). After briefly reviewing the Nepal-China relations, the chapter empirically analyses the BRI projects in Nepal. While emphasising on economic benefits of its investments in various projects under BRI, China has masked the strategic component of its ventures. Though the BRI began with much optimism and fanfare in Nepal, the projects remain almost a non-starter on the ground or have witnessed very slow progress. The chapter argues that, gradually, buoyancy is replaced by concerns over the Chinese debt trap and Nepal's preference for grants over loans. These factors would only hinder the progress of the projects in the foreseeable future.

Introduction

Taking advantage of the high economic growth rate that China achieved since 1980s, it is trying to expand its presence in countries across the globe. In South Asia, China's attempt to consolidate her economic, strategic, political and military foothold needs no elaboration. Nepal is also one such country where China is making serious attempts to establish a firm foothold by taking advantage of the institutional faultlines in the country. It is trying to make forays into Nepal's political, economic and socio-cultural spheres by exploiting the fragile economic situation and development deficit. Roads, railways, airports, inland container depots (ICDs) and optical fibre cable networks are being developed, besides emerging as a big player in the hydropower sector. Media is another area where China has entrenched itself deeply. It has engaged some of the prominent media houses of Nepal, both print and electronic. Attempts to use several social, cultural and religious organisations as interest groups to influence the Nepalese government in its favour are also ongoing.

Since 2010, China-Nepal bilateral trade has increased. Despite the continuing trade imbalances between the two countries, China has substantially increased its exports to Nepal, including goods traditionally sourced from India. Nepal's request for assistance to build facilities to have strategic petroleum reserves in at least at three places is also under consideration by China. Bilateral trade is skewed in favour of China with imports amounting to US$ 1.88 billion and only US$ 8 million in exports during the FY2020-21 (Department of Customs, N.A.). In 2010, Chinese tourists visiting Nepal were recorded as 46,360, which more than doubled to 1,23,805 in 2014. Following the COVID-19, the numbers have come down drastically. The total number of Chinese tourists visiting Nepal in 2020 stood at 19,257 as compared to 1,69,543 in 2019 (Ministry of Culture, Tourism and Civil Aviation, 2021). Efforts for recognition of Mandarin as one of the language papers in government-run schools continues even as 100 odd Chinese volunteers were engaged in teaching the language in different schools. China is assiduously pursuing its entrenchment in Lumbini, the birthplace of Lord Buddha, apparently in a bid to bolster its endeavour to assume the leadership of World Buddhism.

During 2015-16, two key developments drove China to further bolster its engagement with Nepal. They are (a) April 25, 2015 earthquake and relief and rescue operations; and (b) Madhesi blockade. The period also witnessed an overall enhancement of the Chinese footprint in a wide range of areas including political, economic, infrastructure building, media cooperation, etc. Chinese participation in the earthquake rescue and relief operations has generated a lot of goodwill. Beijing pledged US$ 750 million for post-earthquake reconstruction and rehabilitation. Then Prime Minister KP Oli concluded an 8-day (20-27 March 2016) official visit to China during which several agreements and MoUs were signed. Significant amongst them are (a) transit transport; (b) construction of oil storage facilities and assistance for exploration of oil and natural gas in Nepal; and (c) preparation of a project report to extend China's railway line to Nepal which envisages Rasuwagadhi-Kathmandu and Kathmandu-Pokhara-Lumbini rail links. The transit agreement, which has been covered extensively in the Nepalese media, allows Nepal to access Chinese ports to conduct its foreign trade.

At present, transportation infrastructure linking Nepal with China is minimal due to the difficult terrain. To improve connectivity, China is planning to extend the Qinghai-Tibet Railway (QTR) network to Kathmandu, from there up to Lumbini. While the Lhasa-Xigatse line of that section has been operational since August 2014, the construction of Xigatse-Kerung line (35 km from Rasuwa district in Nepal) is proposed.

Nepal and Belt and Road Initiative

Nepal signed (May 2017) an agreement with China indicating its intention to join BRI even before the formal agreement was announced on May 12 in Kathmandu. Nepal followed up by forming three committees: (a) Project identification committee; (b) Project implementation committee; and (c) Project coordination committee, to decide on what projects should be taken under BRI and coordinate timely implementation. Initially, the SEZ at Damak in Jhapa District, Cross-border Economic Cooperation Zone and Budhi Gandaki Hydropower project were slated as BRI projects. Of late, however, there is slow progress over BRI projects in Nepal.

Given the negative experiences of some countries vis-à-vis BRI projects, especially concerns over debt trap, Nepal wants the projects to be carried out on grant/aid basis rather than on loans. On the eve of scheduled visit (March 25-27, 2022) of Chinese Foreign Minister Wang Yi, the Nepali Congress Spokesperson Prakash Sharan Mahat delineated the approach of the Sher Bahadur Deuba-led government to the BRI projects. He stated, "We should focus on developing road networks under the BRI but we cannot do so through costly loans. So our priority is to secure grants or soft loans. Also, the projects should be implemented through international bidding so that firms from other than China's can also compete for the projects" (Giri, 2022).

China-Nepal Trans-Himalayan Multi-Dimensional Connectivity Network and China-Nepal cross-border railway were included in the Joint Communiqué of the Second Belt and Road Forum for International Cooperation (BRF) held in Beijing in April 2019 (The Second Belt and Road for International Cooperation, 2019). During the Second BRI Forum, Nepalese President Bidya Devi Bhandari remarked that:

> For a landlocked country like Nepal, connectivity is of paramount importance in its socio-economic development. With enhanced connectivity, vast opportunities for trade, investment, tourism and people-to-people relations will open up. The development of 'Trans-Himalayan Multi-Dimensional Connectivity Network', including Nepal-China Cross-Border Railway, will boost connectivity not only between Nepal and China but other countries in the region. (Ministry of Foreign Affairs, 2019)

During the visit of Chinese President Xi Jinping to Nepal in October 2019, the two countries "agreed to intensify the implementation of the Memorandum of Understanding (MoU) on Cooperation under the Belt and Road Initiative to enhance connectivity, encompassing such vital components as ports, roads, railways, aviation and communications within the overarching framework of trans-Himalayan Multi-Dimensional Connectivity Network" (Ministry of Foreign Affairs, 2019). Both the countries also agreed to conduct the feasibility study of the cross-border railway project (ibid.). Despite the two sides previously agreed to intensify the implementation of the MoU on Cooperation under the BRI since June 2018 (Ministry of Foreign Affairs, 2018), the BRI projects have not gained much traction in Nepal. Following is an assessment of the BRI projects as well as a few other major Chinese projects in Nepal.

Railway Network

China plans to extend the Qinghai-Tibet Railway (QTR) line from Xigatse to Keyrong and connect Kathmandu (further to Pokhara and Lumbini) as part of China-Nepal cross-border railway. China had agreed (March 2016) to provide financial and technical support for the feasibility study and preparation of a Detailed Project Report (DPR) of the proposed Rasuwagadhi-Kathmandu and Kathamndu-Pokhara-Lumbini Railway Project (Ministry of Foreign Affairs of Nepal, 2016). The proposed railway line between Keyrong and Kathmandu would be 72 km long in Nepal with 98.8 per cent covered in tunnels and bridges at an estimated cost of US$ 2.93 billion (Chitrakar, N.A.). As per the pre-feasibility study for the Kathmandu-Pokhara Railway, the total length of the railway line would be 187 km, having 44 tunnels and 42 bridges and it is estimated to cost US$ 2.83 billion (Investment Board of Nepal, 2020). The Kathmandu-Lumbini railway line with a total length of 152 km will have six tunnels and 16 bridges. The railway line from Keyrong is proposed to pass through two different routes viz., Keyrong-Kathmandu-Pokhara and Keyrong-Baireni-Kurintar-Lumbini. Significantly, a study conducted by the Chongyang Institute for Financial Studies, Renmin University, titled "Feasibility of China-Nepal Railway and Collaborative Construction of Belt and Road by Two Nations" pointed out that a minimum of 40 years would be required to recover the investment in the CNR project (*The Hong Kong Post*, 2022). Further, the possible returns from the project are not very attractive as Nepali exports basket is filled with only primary goods whereas China exports secondary/manufacturing goods and it could use this railway to dump its products in Nepal as well as other markets of South Asian Countries (ibid.). Experts also argue that the extension of QTR Railway into Nepal may serve 'dual purpose' for China.

Budhigandaki Hydropower Project: Chinese SOE, China Gezhouba Group Corporation, was awarded the contract to develop the 1200 MW Budhigandaki Hydropower project, largest in terms of capacity, with an estimated cost of US$ 2.5 billion which would be financed by China. The contract was awarded by the Nepal Government without international bidding. The project however faced opposition from Naya Shakti Nepal, a party led by former Prime Minister Baburam Bhattarai. More significantly, the Agriculture and Water Resources Committee and Finance Committee of the Parliament recommended that the project should be scrapped since the due procedure was not followed in awarding the contract. The Committees also observed that awarding a contract to a Chinese company which failed to deliver the Chamelia Hydropower Project on time was questionable. The project was subsequently shelved and the Government of Nepal decided to develop the project with domestic resources.

Special Economic Zone (SEZ)

China has committed (15 May 2017) to invest US$ 1 billion for setting up a Special Economic Zone (SEZ) to be known as "Friendship Industrial Park", in Damak (Jhapa District), close to the porous Indo-Nepal border and the constituency of former PM KP Oli. The SEZ, which would be taken up as a BRI project, would have manufacturing units producing different items, both consumer and consumer durables. A total of 192 small, medium-sized and large factories are expected to be set up inside the Nepal-China Friendship Industrial Park in the first phase (*Xinhua*, 2021). The industrial park, amongst others, is likely to have enterprises of producing white goods, transportation equipment, and textile and garments and food processing (ibid.). Govinda Thapa, President of the Damak Clean Industrial Park claimed that "the Chinese companies are expected to establish at least 25 large factories targeting Nepali and South Asian markets" (china.org.cn, 2020). Chinese assistance to set up the industries would be as per the agreement signed in 2018 between the Nepali Ministry of Trade and Commerce and the State Administration for Industry and Commerce of China.

Pokhara Regional International Airport (PRIA): A Chinese company, CAMC Engineering Company of China was awarded the contract for construction of PRIA in May 2014 and the work commenced in July 2017 (Prasain, 2021). The cost of constructing the airport is estimated to be US$ 215.96 million, which the EXIM Bank of China had agreed to provide (ibid.). The EXIM Bank also agreed to extend 25 per cent of the estimated cost as an interest-free loan, while the remaining 75 per cent would be made available as a soft loan with a 2 per cent interest (Sharma, 2020). Although the project was not enlisted as a BRI project, it significantly enhances the connectivity between the two countries. The work was being carried out under Engineering Procurement and Construction (EPC) model. It was expected to be completed by July 2021. However, owing to the COVID-19 pandemic, the Civil Aviation Authority of Nepal extended the deadline to July 2022 (Prasain, 2021). The airport was handed over to Nepal by a Chinese State Councilor and Foreign Minister Wang Yi in March 2022, (Baral, 2022) despite only 93 per cent of the work was completed (Myrepublica, 2022).

Digital Connectivity: While digital connectivity in Nepal was not brought under the ambit of BRI, it is well-known that digital connectivity is one of the core components of the Chinese initiative under Digital Silk Road launched in 2015. Major digital connectivity projects in Nepal undertaken by China include laying of optical fibre cable and 4G LTE expansion project.

Optical Fibre Cable: An agreement to provide internet protocol (IP) to Nepal with a terrestrial cable route was signed (December 2016) between Nepal Telecom (NT) and China Telecom Global (CTG) which is a subsidiary of China Telecom, a State-Owned Enterprise (Giri, 2017). This was envisaged to facilitate cross-border terrestrial connectivity between China and Nepal through the optical fibre cable. It started commercial operation in January 2018 (*The Himalayan Times*, 2018). With the commercial operationalisation of Nepal-China Optical Fibre Link Project, the CTG plans to provide internet service to India and beyond with Nepal as a transit hub. So far, Nepal has been connected internationally through Indian telecom service providers via Birgunj, Bhairahawa and Biratnagar.

4G LTE Expansion Project: Two Chinese companies, China Communications Service International and ZTE were awarded the contract for 4G LTE expansion project by Nepal Telecom in February 2019 (*The Kathmandu Post*, 2019). The estimated cost of the project was around US$ 152 million (ibid.).

Concerns and Pushback against BRI

Barring cross-border railway projects, there is not much progress on other projects (Giri, 2019). Nepal has proposed to include the following projects under the BRI: upgrading the Rasuwagadhi-Kathmandu road; Kimathanka-Hile road construction; road construction from Dipayal to the Chinese southern border; the Tokha-Bidur road; the Galchhi-Rasuwagadhi-Kerung 400 kV transmission line; the Kerung-Kathmandu rail; the 762 MW Tamor hydroelectricity project; the 426 MW Phukot Karnali hydroelectric project; and the construction of Madan Bhandari Technical Institute (Giri, 2019). These projects are yet to reach the negotiation phase.

There was a high degree of optimism in Nepal when Kathmandu became a signatory of the BRI. However, of late, the BRI projects have failed to gain momentum. It could be attributed to several factors. According to former Foreign Minister Pradeep Gyawali: it took time to select projects and later the number of selected projects was trimmed down from thirty-five to nine; pandemic hit when the government was working on project implementation plan and its framework (Giri, 2022). The slow progress of projects raised concerns about Chinese commitment under the BRI. With Nepal Government making its preference clear for grants rather than loans, it is speculated that implementation of the projects may be delayed.

Of late, there are also concerns over the issue of 'debt trap'. China has been accused of burdening countries with unsustainable debts (Wang, 2022). It may be noted that according to the *International Debt Statistics 2022* of the World Bank, the total debt of low and middle-income countries (LMICs) owed to China at the end of 2020 stood at the US$ 170 billion (The World Bank, 2021). Similarly, Aid Data in its study titled *Banking on the Belt and Road: Insights from a New Global Dataset of 13,427 Chinese Development Projects* claimed that LMICs hidden debts (which these countries not reported to the Debt Reporting System of the World Bank) amounted to the US$ 385 billion (Aid Data, 2021). The opaque nature of deals and lack of detailed information further created apprehensions amongst the host countries over Chinese lending and Nepal is no exception.

A Canada-based think-tank, the International Forum for Rights and Security (IFFRAS) reported that around 5,000 protestors called attention to the illegal activities at the site of Damak SEZ, a proposed BRI project (International Forum for Rights and Security, 2022). It further claimed that the reports of BRI loan recipient countries falling into debt traps have made Nepalese people further worry about the BRI projects in their country (ibid.). Further, in March 2022, the Rashtriya Bidhyarthi Parishad, the student wing of the Rashtriya Ekata Abhiyan, staged a demonstration against China and its flagship BRI in Bara district (Khabarhub, 2022). The demonstrators demanded making public the details of the Chinese BRI project agreements. They also denounced excessive Chinese interference in Nepal's internal affairs, encroachment of Nepali territory at various places along the northern border, China-imposed unofficial blockade at border points—affecting Nepali traders, and apathy shown towards Nepali students who have yet to complete their medical degrees from Chinese Universities (due to restrictions in China) among others (ibid.).

BRI vs US Indo-Pacific Strategy

It may be noted that Chinese Foreign Minister Wang Yi visited Nepal from 8-10 September 2019, (Ministry of Foreign Affairs of Nepal, 2019) the first high-level visit from China after the visit of Defence Minister Gen. Chang Wanquan in March 2017. Following his visit, the Chinese Foreign Ministry released a statement which quoted the then NCP Executive Chairman Prachanda saying Kathmandu disapproved of the Indo-Pacific Strategy. The statement said, "Nepal firmly adheres to the non-alignment policy, disapproves of the so-called Indo-Pacific Strategy, opposes any attempt to stop the development of China, and always believes that China's development is an opportunity for Nepal and is willing to learn from China's successful experience" (Giri, 2019). This made the US to seek clarifications from the Government of Nepal as to whether they endorsed a similar view. However, in the run-up to ratification, several media reports claimed that Beijing was trying to sabotage MCC Nepal-Compact. It was reported that China was "playing a role" in souring Nepal's relations with third countries, particularly with the US, and is currently actively propagating, lobbying and spending against the MCC (Khabarhub, 2021). Reports also claimed a Chinese official, Chen Chao, the Deputy Minister of International Affairs under the Central Committee of the Communist Party of China, in a video conversation with UML leader Shankar Pokhrel, had urged the latter to "reconsider" the party's position on MCC before endorsing it (ibid.). The Compact was finally ratified in February 2022 (Pradhan, 2022). Chinese media have also contributed to the politicisation of the MCC Nepal Compact. Such a tussle between two major powers has worried Nepal as it does not want to be entangled in the geostrategic competition between the US and China.

Conclusion

There is no doubt that the BRI is part of China's strategy to reshape the global geopolitics to serve their interests. Nepal is one of the prime examples of geopolitical power play between major powers as evidenced by clash over BRI and the USIPS. India and Nepal share a unique relationship of friendship and cooperation characterised by open borders and deep-rooted people-to-people contact. Chinese aggressive forays into Nepal and other countries of the region through multifaceted engagement, including the BRI, without addressing the legitimate strategic concerns of India would only lead to regional rivalry. With concerns over debt trap and Nepalese preference for grants over loans, the BRI projects may witness slow progress in the near future.

References

Aid Data. (2021). "Banking on the Belt and Road: Insights from a New Global Dataset of 13,427 Chinese Development Projects", 24 March 2022, at https://docs.aiddata.org/ad4/pdfs/Banking_on_the_Belt_and_Road__Insights_from_a_new_global_dataset_of_13427_Chinese_development_projects

Baral, K. M. (2022). "Has China handed over Pokhara intl' airport in haste?", *The Annapurna Express*, 13 May 2022, at https://theannapurnaexpress.com/news/has-china-handed-over-pokhara-intl-airport-in-haste-5116

china.org.cn. (2020). "Construction work in China-Nepal friendship industrial park to kick off early next year", 9 May 2022, at http://t.m.china.org.cn/convert/c_tvMI7IGC.html

Chitrakar, A. (N.A.). "Railway Projects in Nepal", UNESCAP, 12 August 2021, at https://www.unescap.org/sites/default/files/Item5_Nepal_0.pdf

Department of Customs (N.A.). "Foreign Trade Statistics 2020-21", 17 May 2022, at https://customs.gov.np/page/fts-fy-207778

Giri, A. (2022). "Chinese foreign minister visiting on March 25-27", *The Kathmandu Post*, 22 March 2022, at https://kathmandupost.com/national/2022/03/22/chinese-foreign-minister-visiting-on-march-25-27

Giri, A. (2022). "Five years on, BRI projects are nowhere on the horizon", *The Kathmandu Post*, 20 May 2022, at https://kathmandupost.com/national/2022/05/20/five-years-on-bri-projects-are-nowhere-on-the-horizon

Giri, A. (2019). "Nepal trims projects under BRI from 35 to 9 at Chinese call", *The Kathmandu Post,* 31 March 2022, at https://kathmandupost.com/national/2019/01/18/nepal-trims-projects-under-bri-from-35-to-9-at-chinese-call

Giri, A. (2019). "Nepal's Disapproves of Washington's Indo-Pacific Strategy, Beijing Says", *The Kathmandu Post,* 19 September 2021, at https://kathmandupost.com/national/2019/09/11/nepal-disapproves-of-indo-pacific-strategy-china-s-foreign-ministry-says

Giri, A. (2019). "With just 10 months left in BRI pact, not a single project has made any real progress", *The Kathmandu Post,* 31 March 2022, at https://kathmandupost.com/national/2019/07/17/with-just-10-months-left-in-bri-pact-not-a-single-project-has-made-any-real-progress

Giri, S. (2017). "Nepal needs to wait longer to use Chinese bandwidth", *The Kathmandu Post,* 11 April 2022, at https://kathmandupost.com/money/2017/06/19/nepal-needs-to-wait-longer-to-use-chinese-bandwidth

International Forum for Rights and Security (2022). "Anti-China protests in Nepal over land encroachment and BRI investment", IFFRAS, 31 March 2022, at https://iffras.org/anti-china-protests-in-nepal-over-land-encroachment-and-bri-investment/

Investment Board of Nepal (2020). "Kathmandu-Pokhara Railway Project", Investment Board of Nepal, July 2021, at https://ibn.gov.np/wp-content/uploads/2020/04/Kathmandu-Pokhara-Lumbini-Railways.pdf

Khabarhub (2021). "China 'playing foul' on MCC; Nepali communist leaders under China's pressure", 11 April 2022, at https://english.khabarhub.com/2021/21/227696/

Khabarhub (2022). "Student wing of Rastiya Ekata Abhiyan holds protest against China and BRI in Bara", 17 March 2022, at https://english.khabarhub.com/2022/12/241297/

Ministry of Culture, Tourism and Civil Aviation (2021). "Nepal Toruism Statistics 2020", 21 May 2022, at https://www.tourism.gov.np/files/NOTICE%20MANAGER_FILES/NTB_Statistics_2020%20_final.pdf

Ministry of Foreign Affairs (2018). "Joint Statement between Nepal and the People's Republic of China", 26 May 2022, at https://mofa.gov.np/joint-statement-between-nepal-and-the-peoples-republic-of-china/

Ministry of Foreign Affairs. (2019). "Joint Statement between Nepal and the People's Republic of China", 3 May 2022, at https://mofa.gov.np/joint-statement-between-nepal-and-the-peoples-republic-of-china-2/

Ministry of Foreign Affairs of Nepal (2016). "Joint Statement between the People's Republic of China and Nepal", 29 July 2021, at https://mofa.gov.np/joint-press-statement/

Ministry of Foreign Affairs of Nepal (2019). "Press Release regarding the visit of Chinese Foreign Minister", 10 September 2021, at https://mofa.gov.np/press-release-regarding-the-visit-of-chinese-foreign-minister/

Ministry of Foreign Affairs (2019). "Statement delivered by the Rt. Hon. President at the High-Level Meeting of the Second Belt and Road Forum for International Cooperation", 29 January 2022, at https://mofa.gov.np/statement-delivered-by-the-rt-hon-president-at-the-high-level-meeting-of-the-second-belt-and-road-forum-for-international-cooperation/

Myrepublica (2022). "93 percent work of Pokhara airport completed", 11 April 2022, at https://myrepublica.nagariknetwork.com/news/93-percent-work-of-pokhara-airport-completed/

Pradhan, T. R. (2022). "Parliament ratifies MCC compact after years of delay", *The Kathmandu Post*, 24 April 2022, at https://kathmandupost.com/national/2022/02/27/nepal-parliament-ratifies-mcc-compact

Prasain, S. (2021,). "Covid-19 pushes back completion of Pokhara international airport", *The Kathmandu Post*, 11 July 2021, at https://kathmandupost.com/money/2021/07/09/covid-pushes-back-completion-of-pokhara-international-airport

Sharma, L. P. (2020). "Construction of new international airport in Pokhara on track despite lockdown", *The Kathmandu Post*, 11 July 2021, at https://kathmandupost.com/money/2020/06/14/construction-of-new-airport-in-pokhara-on-track-despite-lockdown

Sigdel, A. (2020). *India in the Era of China's Belt and Road Initiative: How Modi Responds to Xi.* London: Lexington Books.

The Himalayan Times (2018). "Nepal-China optical fibre link operationalised", 11 April 2022, at https://thehimalayantimes.com/nepal/sino-nepal-cross-border-optical-fibre-link-starts-operations-today

The Hong Kong Post (2022). "Nepal-China Railway Project to become a White Elephant", 6 April 2022, at https://thehongkongpost.com/2022/04/02/nepal-china-railway-project-to-become-a-white-elephant/

The Kathmandu Post (2019). "Two Chinese firms roped in for 4G LTE expansion project", 11 April 2022, at https://kathmandupost.com/money/2019/02/04/two-chinese-firms-roped-in-for-4g-lte-expansion-project

The Second Belt and Road for International Cooperation (2019). "Joint Communique of the Leaders' Roundtable of the 2nd Belt and Road Forum for International Cooperation", 29 January 2022, at http://www.beltandroadforum.org/english/n100/2019/0427/c36-1311.html

The World Bank (2021). "International Debt Statistics 2022", 17 April 2022, at https://openknowledge.worldbank.org/bitstream/handle/10986/36289/9781464818004.pdf?sequence=4&isAllowed=y

Wang, K. (2022). "China: Is it burdening poor countries with unsustainable debt?", BBC, 19 March 2022, at https://www.bbc.com/news/59585507

Xinhua (2021). "Nepal PM lays foundation stone for largest industrial park", 9 May 2022, at http://www.xinhuanet.com/english/asiapacific/2021-03/01/c_139773894.htm

9. China, Afghanistan and BRI

Anwesha Ghosh

Abstract

When the Taliban seized power in Afghanistan on 15 August 2021, most countries closed down their diplomatic mission in Kabul and started evacuating their citizens out of Afghanistan. But China was one of the few notable exceptions. It was among the first nations to develop a diplomatic channel with the Taliban regime and declared that it was ready for a "friendly and cooperative" relationship with the regime—the groundwork for that prompt decision, however, was laid down much earlier. Over the years, China had maintained direct communication with the Taliban, and both sides have met on several occasions, bilaterally and internationally, underscoring China's warming ties with the Islamist group. This paper begins by briefly looking at the history of China's engagement with the Taliban and then focuses on Beijing's major interests in Afghanistan. It then engages with the BRI and argues that the combination of geography and security has made Afghanistan a second-class actor concerning BRI as a result, integration of war-torn country into BRI has not featured in Beijing's list of priorities so far. At the end, the chapter offers some projections about Sino-Taliban relations and observes that China is unlikely to commit itself to any substantial investment or playing any greater role in Afghanistan and rather stick to a wait-and-watch policy.

Introduction

In the immediate aftermath of the Taliban recapture of Kabul on 15 August 2021, the US and its allies decided to suspend their diplomatic missions and began their evacuation operations from Kabul. China, however, decided to keep its embassy open and declared that it was ready for a "friendly and cooperative" (France 24, 2021) relations with the Taliban—the groundwork for that prompt decision, however, was laid down much earlier. Over the years, China had maintained direct communication with the Taliban, and both sides have met on several occasions, bilaterally and internationally, underscoring China's warming ties with the Islamist group and the Taliban's growing clout on the global stage. Following the Taliban takeover, China was the first foreign country to pledge emergency humanitarian aid (worth US$ 31 million) to Afghanistan (BBC, 2021). The Taliban regime, who were facing a humanitarian catastrophe and economic meltdown, welcomed Beijing's prompt delivery of food and medical supplies. Based on the Sino-Taliban historic relations, China's core security and economic interests and leverage over Pakistan and the Taliban regime's quest for a partner with economic prowess that can fill the economic void left by the US, it is likely that China and the Taliban regime will develop stronger ties in the days to come. Even if that is the case, this chapter argues that integrating Afghanistan under Belt and Road Initiative (BRI) might not feature in Beijing's list of priorities at present. It begins by briefly discussing Sino-Taliban linkages and engagement over the years and then turns to look at China's overarching interests in the country. It then discusses BRI in the context of Afghanistan and situates it within the larger context of China's overarching interests in the country. The final segment makes some projections about the future of Sino-Taliban engagements and concludes by stating that China's immediate interest is Afghanistan's natural resources, based on the experiences of undertaking relatively smaller projects to extract mineral resources from Afghanistan, Beijing is likely to take a further call on infrastructural projects related to BRI.

China's Engagement with the Taliban: Historical Backdrop

Since the establishment of diplomatic relations between China and the then-Kingdom of Afghanistan in 1950, engagement between the countries remained limited largely to the economic domain Beijing preferred to maintain a distance from political and security issues in Afghanistan (Ghosh, 2019). The PRC condemned the Soviet military intervention and reportedly the People's Liberation Army (PLA) provided support (in terms of training, arms, military advisors and finances) to the Mujahideen resistance alongside the Central Intelligence Agency (CIA) (Bartholomew, 2010). Several thousands of these mujahideen fighters were trained in camps inside Xinjiang; China also provided them with considerably high-grade equipment including machine guns and surface-to-air missiles worth up to US$ 400 million (Starr, 2004). When the Taliban came to power in 1996, Beijing chose to follow a policy of low-level engagement with the group via diplomatic channels as a way to ensure safety and stability at its border. In 1999, the PLA agreed to provide low-level military support to the Taliban via Pakistan, in exchange for severing assistance to the Uyghurs (Nourrit, 2021). Subsequently, economic and technical cooperation began with Chinese telecommunication firms repairing power grids (Iqbal, 2016).

Post-9/11, when Afghanistan re-attracted the world's attention towards itself, China preferred to be a mere spectator to the dramatic events that unfolded there. Only after an interim government was established, the bilateral relations began to assume some pace. Post-Bonn Afghanistan witnessed a rapid realignment in China's Afghan policy from Beijing's 'covert engagement' with the Taliban right up till the 9/11 attacks to an abrupt severing of links with the Taliban and a quick restoration of its diplomatic links with a Western-backed government (Malik, 2002). Instead of aid, China had sought to invest its energies in commercial ventures and Beijing's efforts in this direction began in earnest in 2007 once the country was opened up for foreign investment. The state-backed China Metallurgical Group's US$ 3.5 billion successful bid for MesAnyak mines—the world's largest unexploited copper fields was a significant development (Partlow, 2009). A few years into the intervention, there was a significant resurgence of the Taliban, the Chinese saw merit in re-establishing their clandestine links with the Taliban via Pakistan (Panda, 2021). These linkages were principally aimed to serve Chinese economic interests in the region with an eye at maintaining stability in Xinjiang. For instance, reports suggested that the Taliban may have received Chinese-made weapons via Iran (Synovitz, 2007), while analysts raised suspicions that the Haqqani-led group had intentionally kept attacks away from Chinese infrastructure projects like the MesAynak copper mine outside Kabul (Amini, 2017).

Despite its investments, China was largely viewed as a periphery actor in Afghanistan till 2014. It was after the announcement by the Obama administration that the US would withdrawal its troops from Afghanistan in 2014, Beijing was faced with a real possibility of a resurgence of instability and terrorism at its borders which triggered a change in China's Afghanistan Policy. China began meeting with the Taliban regularly (Sun, 2020), under a pragmatic strategy to foster favourable ties with all factions in Afghanistan in anticipation of a US withdrawal. In 2018, China, Pakistan and Afghanistan signed an MoU on counterterrorism and agreed to coordinate to call on the Taliban to return to the negotiating table (ET, 2018). China was seen meeting the Taliban in 2018 (Bokhari, 2018) and 2019 (Reuters, 2019) as the Trump administration negotiated a peace deal with the Taliban. The visit of the nine-member Taliban delegation to China to seek Beijing's advice on Trump's proposed deal for a peace framework only demonstrated China's considerable influence over the Islamist group.

Since the rapid US withdrawal from Afghanistan under President Joe Biden, Beijing has been forthcoming in its support to the Taliban regime in the country. About a month before the fall of Kabul, when the Taliban was steadily gaining territories in Afghanistan, China's State Councilor and Foreign Minister Wang Yi had hosted a nine-member Taliban delegation in Tianjin to discuss the reconciliation and reconstruction process in Afghanistan and described the group as "a pivotal military and political force" in the country (*The Hindu*, 2021). Chinese Foreign Ministry spokesperson, Hua Chunying, highlighted at a press conference on 16 August 2021 that Beijing had maintained contact with the Taliban and played a "constructive role in promoting the political settlement of the Afghan issue" (Embassy of China, 2021). She further added that China "hoped" for a smooth transition in Afghanistan and that the Taliban would implement its promise of forming an "inclusive Islamic government".

Post-August 2021, China's main assistance to the Taliban came in the form of humanitarian aid and donation of COVID-19 vaccines. On the diplomatic front, China has made efforts to rally international support and aid for rebuilding Afghanistan, particularly by calling the international community to lift sanctions and unfreeze Afghan foreign assets. Correspondingly, Beijing and Pakistan have come together to urge the Western powers to engage the Taliban and to provide assistance to the country. The Taliban regime is aware that Beijing's backing is crucial for obtaining international legitimacy and thus have tried to accommodate Chinese concerns. China strongly slammed President Biden's executive order to free US$ 7 billion (out of more than 9 billion frozen Afghan assets) and split the money between humanitarian aid for Afghanistan and a fund for 9/11 victims. China's Foreign Ministry's spokesperson Wang Wenbin reacted to US' decision by stating- "Without the consent of the Afghan people, the US willfully disposes of assets that belong to the Afghan people, even keeping them as its own. This is no different from the conduct of bandits" (*The Print*, 2022). Although Beijing has refrained from outright recognising the Taliban government so far, Chinese media have jumped on the opportunity to highlight economic opportunities the new Islamic leadership presents for China, particularly for lithium mining, which now seems at the forefront of their developing relations. Yet, officially China has consistently stated that its security interests are at the centre of its interaction with the group, and the Taliban seem to have responded. The history of the pragmatic relationship between China and the Taliban serves as a useful basis for understanding Beijing overarching interests in Afghanistan.

Beijing's Overarching Interests in Afghanistan and BRI

The evolution of China's relations with Afghanistan over the past decades can be linked to Beijing's economic interests and security concerns, which were coherent and synchronised with its overarching strategy to the wider region. Afghanistan is geostrategically located in a hotspot linking the Middle East, Central and South Asia, and Europe. China views the country as a major geopolitical puzzle piece between Pakistan and Iran, both of which have already deepened their ties with Beijing under the Belt and Road (BRI) and China-Pakistan Economic Corridors (CPEC) initiatives (FPJ, 2021). In terms of security, Beijing sees "three evils"—terrorism, separatism, and religious fundamentalism—as threats to its national security and has openly urged the Taliban to make a clean break with other terrorist groups, particularly the East Turkestan Islamic

Movement (ETIM) and Islamic State (*The Diplomat*, 2021). China would want the Taliban to fight off these forces to prevent cross-border terrorism and spread of radicalism into Xinjiang.

As far as economic incentives are concerned, China is attracted by Afghanistan's untapped US$ 1 trillion worth of mineral resources and has expressed interest in Afghanistan's mining sector since the 2000s. These untapped resources in Afghanistan are particularly attractive because they can cater to the growing demand of Chinese domestic demands for energy and primary commodities. However, China's economic interests directly correlate with security concerns. Safe investments require a stable and secure environment and because of the lack of the same, China's past initiatives were fraught with difficulties. For example, the MesAynak copper mine, which was leased to the China Metallurgical Group for 30 years, is one well-known example. The project had to be stalled due to security troubles and concerns surrounding preservation of ancient Buddhist ruins in the area. Although if recent reports are to be believed China is negotiating with Taliban authorities to start mining at the site (Shah, 2022), but it remains to be seen how much progress is made in the coming months. Moreover, since 2013, China has made substantial investments in Central Asia and Pakistan via the China-Central Asia-West Asia and China-Pakistan Economic Corridor (*The Diplomat*, 2022). All these investments around Afghanistan have heightened Beijing's susceptibility to conflict and instability in the region and have encouraged China to take cautious steps toward incorporating the war-torn country under BRI.

BRI and Afghanistan

The first Memorandum of Understanding (MoU) on the BRI between Afghanistan and China was signed in 2016 (OBOR, 2021), and then several initiatives were agreed between the two countries. The central element of BRI is, of course, infrastructure development to encourage connectivity. For Afghanistan, BRI seemed to be an attractive proposition as it provided an opportunity to enable it to transform its aid-dependent economy to one that is self-sufficient, stable and reliable.

Afghanistan's regional economic connectivity ambitions have been closely tied to its strategic location, productive agriculture zones and mineral resources. There was a general belief in the Afghan Republic that optimising growth in these three areas will lead to a sustainable and self-sufficient economy. The Afghan government under Ashraf Ghani had made involvement with the BRI a priority, representing it as a regional cooperation framework (RECCA, 2016) in which Afghanistan and China stood to benefit in the areas of financial services, natural resources extraction and energy development. During a state visit to China in May 2016, the former Chief Executive of Afghanistan, Abdullah Abdullah, and his Chinese counterpart signed an MoU to boost areas of cooperation under the BRI. Through this MoU, it appeared that China regarded Afghanistan as a partner that is "well placed" to help it connect to the wider region via the BRI (RECCA, 2016).

The erstwhile Afghan government identified three areas namely, movement of goods, energy and data; in which Afghanistan had a unique advantage under BRI (RECCA, 2016). A Research Study (Safi and Alizada, 2018) quoted the former Adviser on Infrastructure and Technology to President Ghani, Mohammad Humayon Qayoumi, who cited the Five Nations Railway as one of the critical pieces in Afghanistan's connectivity plans. Under the movement of energy, he cited the TAPI natural gas pipeline, the CASA-1000, the TAP 500-kV and the Kabul-Kunar River Basin as points of connectivity. And under the movement of data, Qayoumi pointed to the Digital Silk Road and specifically the fibre optic link with China through Afghanistan's Wakhan Corridor, achieved through an agreement signed in August 2017, as one of the most important points of connectivity between the two countries.

To realise its vision of becoming a major regional economic trade and infrastructure platform by building connectivity between China and the rest of Eurasia by way of the ocean-based Maritime Silk Road and the land-based Silk Road Economic Belt, China proposed building northern, central and southern belts and Afghanistan fitted well into its southern proposed belt, which starts from China and proceeds to South-East Asia, South Asia and the Indian Ocean (Safi and Alizada, 2018). The Five Nations Railway Project (linking China to Afghanistan via the

Sherkhan Port), Corridor 3 of the Afghanistan National Railway Plan (Kunduz-Torkham railway) and the Digital Silk Road were all initiatives that the former Afghan government and China had undertaken to realise Afghanistan's position within the southern belt of the BRI. Additionally, there was the Sino-Afghan Special Railway Transportation Project, which links China to Afghanistan via the Hairatan port, which received the first freight train from Nantong, China in August 2016 (RECCA, 2016). Covering a total distance of 2,100 km, the Five Nations Railway is a vast and ambitious project that will not only give Afghanistan connectivity to Europe through Iran but will also link the country to China through Central Asia and thereby connecting China with Iran. With the US departure, Afghanistan's newly ensconced Taliban regime expectedly will be looking to China for major investments in the coming few months and the Taliban made it a point to express its interest in China's BRI. Zabiullah Mujahid, the Taliban spokesperson, said that the Taliban "desires" to join the China-Pakistan Economic Corridor, or CPEC, the flagship US$ 50 billion Pakistan component of China's BRI (*Hindustan Times*, 2021). But the question remains how much Beijing will be willing to invest.

So far, given the volatile situation in the country, few projects were actually conducted within the framework of the BRI. Apart from security concerns, Afghanistan's harsh climatic and mountainous topography also made the construction of routes difficult. Not surprisingly, no BRI land corridor crosses Afghanistan. The closest—China-Central Asia-West Economic Corridor (CCAWEC) and the China-Pakistan Economic Corridor (CPEC)—go around the country and over the years China has been reluctant to explain in which manner Afghanistan will be linked to the BRI, as well as concrete investments in Afghanistan under the project (Jayaram, 2016). The political and diplomatic interaction between the Afghan Republic and China was materialised through important agreements, such as the "Treaty of Friendship, Cooperation and Good Neighbourly Relations", the "Agreement on Trade and Economic Cooperation" or the creation of the "China-Afghanistan Joint Economic and Trade Committee", among others (Jose, et al., 2019) but these did not bring any substantial change in Afghanistan's role in BRI. Although Afghanistan could have certainly benefitted from BRI and the latter may help its economic development and regional integration, but China never saw Afghanistan as a key element of BRI. Due to Afghanistan's minimal infrastructure and capacity to have a key role in the BRI, China remained the dominant decision-maker about how Afghanistan can be drawn into the initiative. As the project took shape, it became clearer that China prioritised certain countries, like Pakistan, and ignored some others, such as Afghanistan (Safi and Alizada, 2018), and it is not yet clear how Afghanistan will be connected to the BRI. The combination of geography and security has made a second-class actor concerning BRI as a result, integration of Afghanistan into BRI has not featured in Beijing's list of priorities so far.

Projections for Sino-Taliban Relations

Post-US withdrawal, Afghanistan faces endemic socio-economic crisis, staggering poverty and unemployment, inequality and aid dependency that is threatening the current regime and they are desperately looking at China to fill the economic void left by the US. China was against an extended US presence but has condemned the mishandled withdrawal for creating a security vacuum culminating in regional instability. While the Taliban recently stated that they will ensure the security of Chinese investors, the security threat remains high as there are other militant rivalries and activities on the ground that threaten China's interests. In early October 2021, the Islamic State Khorasan linked their suicide bomb attack on a mosque in Kunduz, Afghanistan, as retaliation for the Taliban's close cooperation with Beijing, which the ISK regarded as mistreating the Uyghurs.

A recently published UN Report (UNSC, 2022) states, "there are no recent signs that the Taliban has taken steps to limit the activities of foreign terrorist fighters in the country". However, there is a detail in the report that indicates otherwise and suggests that the Taliban is placing operational restrictions on a group that is of particular interest to China—like the Turkestan Islamic Party (TIP). According to member states cited in the report, "this Uyghur Islamist group has now been relocated from its traditional stronghold on the border with China-Badakhshan province—to other parts of Afghanistan, namely Baghlan, Takhar, and other provinces. This was reportedly done in an effort by the Taliban to "protect and restrain the group" (UNSC, 2022). Although it is unclear how this move serves to "protect" the group, it is reasonable to assume that the efforts to restrain it were made with Beijing in mind, particularly as the TIP was moved away from the border. It remains to be seen whether the Taliban are able to contain the TIP and deliver on its promises to China not to facilitate any Uyghur militancy in Afghan territory in the days to come.

China will continue to play the economic card, especially when it comes to natural resources. After the Taliban takeover of Kabul in August 2021, many of the Chinese technical persons (who were involved in various commercial projects across Afghanistan) fled the country, however, in recent weeks, several Chinese mining companies along with technical personnel have visited Kabul. Reports suggested that China is slowly moving to claim Afghanistan's vast mineral wealth centred on a mountain south of Kabul (FPJ, 2021). Apart from the movements pertaining MesAynak, Beijing is also in talks to begin work on oil-and-gas reserves in the north of the country, Amu Darya. Both projects were on hold for years because of the war, which ended when the Taliban seized power in August. To test the waters, China may start with mineral extraction projects and based on its experiences of that, Beijing might decide on the next projects. Beijing has largely avoided to implement the large-scale infrastructure projects agreed upon with Afghan authorities of the previous regime. The Afghan territory is also important for China as a route to transport gas and oil from Turkmenistan and the Caspian Sea to East Asia as it is the shortest and cheapest route. But implementation of such big projects would need a stable environment, how far that would be possible remains questionable.

The Taliban on its part may consider deploying special security forces to safeguard Chinese ventures and personnel working on these projects. Chinese companies may also hire security from Chinese private security companies, who had the experience and exposure of working in Afghanistan. These arrangements are likely to yield mutual benefits as the Taliban urgently need investors to politically and economically consolidate while Chinese high-interest loans are devoid of democratisation conditionality (Nourrit, 2021). Building peace through economic development may be more effective in failed states than dented Western Style militarised nation-building (Nourrit, 2021) and China might see it as an opportunity to generate loyalties and strategic assets in Afghanistan.

Meanwhile, another development to watch out for will be the Afghanistan-China-Pakistan axis. The 'all-weather friendship' between Islamabad and Beijing will allow the former to emerge as a trump card for China in its outreach to the Taliban. China could achieve more infrastructure-driven success than the US in Afghanistan on the grounds of its extensive leverage with Pakistan (Panda, 2021). In this context, for countries like India, a major threat of the Taliban takeover is probably going to be Chinese intelligence extending its impressive ties with its Pakistani partners (HRW, 2021). As India tries to navigate the troubled waters in Afghanistan, which over the past two decades had become a key development partner, and crafts its response to the Taliban, the China factor will continue to cast a shadow over New Delhi's position on the Taliban.

Conclusion

To conclude, it can be argued that, factors such as historic linkages between China and the Taliban, their mutual interest and China's leverage over the Taliban's principal backer Pakistan—are likely to provide a foundation for a more dynamic engagement between the two sides. China is still waiting for the international community to confer diplomatic recognition to the Taliban, and will continue to lobby for the same. In the meantime, China would continue its engagement with the Taliban and test the new regime's ability to ensure conditions that would be conducive for undertaking Chinese commercial ventures in Afghanistan. Extraction of natural resources is likely to be China's immediate priority, based on the experiences of those projects, Beijing will take further calls on infrastructural projects related to BRI. It is important to remember; Afghanistan is important to China—but the key reason for that is not the BRI. China did not assign to Afghanistan a relevant role in BRI, ever since the project was announced by President Xi Jinping. No meaningful aberrations from the original plan were discernible in China's strategy for Afghanistan after 2016 either. Afghanistan is playing a marginal and subsidiary role in the BRI and this is not likely to change even with the Taliban regime in power.

References

Amini, M. (2017). "China's Plan to Mine for Copper Beneath an Ancient City Gets thrown off by Corruption charges", CNBC.

BBC. (2021). "China offers $31M in emergency aid to Afghanistan", BBC.

Bartholomew. (2010). *2009 Report to Congress of the US-China Economic and Security Review Commission.* Washington: Diane Publishing.

Bokhari, K. S. (2018). "China courted Afghan Taliban in Secret Meetings", *Financial Times.*

Embassy of China. (2021). "Foreign Ministry Spokesperson Hua Chunying's Regular Press Conference", Embassy of the People's Republic of China in the Republic of Finland.

FPJ. (2021). "With Taliban in power China eyes highly lucrative rare-earth mines in Afghanistan", at https://www.freepressjournal.in/business/with-taliban-in-power-china-eyes-highly-lucrative-rare-earth-mines-in-afghanis

France 24. (2021). "China ready for 'friendly relations' with Taliban, welcomes Afghan development projects", 16 August.

Ghosh, A. (2019). "China's growing influence in Afghanistan and its implications for the Peace Process", ICWA, at https://www.icwa.in/show_content.php?lang=1&level=3&ls_id=3856&lid=2935

HRW. (2021). "Pakistan's Support for the Taliban", Human Rights Watch, at https://www.hrw.org/reports/2001/afghan2/Afghan0701-02.htm

Iqbal, H. (2016). "New Trends in Chinese Foreign Policy and the Evolving Sino-Afghan Ties", Institute of Regional Studies, *Regional Studies*, Vol. XXXIV, No. 2, Spring 2016, pp. 37-64.

Jayaram, N. (2016). *Economic Impact of OBOR on Afghanistan.* Mantraya.

Jose, et al. (2019). "The Belt and Road Initiative: An Architype of New Development Model", in B. S. Francisco Jose (ed.), *"The Belt and Road Initiative: An Architype of New Development Model"*, p. 512. Palgrave Macmillan.

Malik, M. (2002). "Dragon on Terrorism: Assessing China's Tactical Gains and Strategic Losses Post 11 September", October, Calrisle, PA: Strategic Studies Institute, pp. 1-63.

Mariam Safi and Bismellah Alizada. (2018). *Integration Afghanistan into the BRI Initiative.* Kabul: Friedrich Ebert Stiftung.

Nourrit, J. (2021). "China's relations with Taliban-led Afghanistan", China Institute, SOAS, 18 October, at https://blogs.soas.ac.uk/china-institute/2021/10/18/chinas-relations-with-taliban-led-afghanistan/

OBOR. (2021). "Afghanistan: The heart of the New Silk Road strategy?", OBOR Europe, 6 November, at https://www.oboreurope.com/en/afghanistan-new-silk-road/

Panda, J. (2021). "Beijing's Strategic Moments with Taliban: Policy, Strategy and Worldview", IDSA Issue Brief, at https://www.idsa.in/issuebrief/beijings-strategic-moments-taliban-jpanda-03092

Partlow, J. (2009). "Afghan Minister Accused of Taking Bribe", *The Washington Post*, 17 November.

RECCA. (2016). *10 Years RECCA, From Negotiation to Investment, Construction, and Trade: A Decade of Progress.* Kabul: Ministry of Foreign Affairs, Islamic Republic of Afghanistan.

Reuters. (2019). "Afghanistan's Taliban Meets Chinese Government in Beijing22 September 2019", Reuters, 22 September.

Shah, S. (2022). "China Perseus Mineral wealth in Afghanistan" , *The Wall Street Journal*, 13 March, at https://www.wsj.com/articles/china-pursues-afghanistans-mineral-wealth-after-u-s-exit-11647172801

Starr, S. F. (2004). *Xinjiang: China's Muslim Borderland.* New York: M.E Sharp.

Sun, Y. (2020). "China's Strategic Assessment of Afghanistan", War on the Rocks, 8 April, at https://warontherocks.com/2020/04/chinas-strategic-assessment-of-afghanistan/

Synovitz, R. (2007). "Afghanistan: U.S. Worried Iran Sending Chinese Weapons To Taliban", RadioFreeEurope, 14 September, at https://www.rferl.org/a/1078675.html

The Diplomat. (2021). "China in Afghanistan: How Beijing Engages the Taliban", 25 December, at https://thediplomat.com/2021/12/china-in-afghanistan-how-beijing-engages-the-taliban/

The Diplomat. (2022). "How the Rise of Islamic State Khorasan in Afghanistan Feeds Uyghur Militancy", 17 February, at https://thediplomat.com/2022/02/how-the-rise-of-islamic-state-khorasan-in-afghanistan-feeds-uyghur-militancy

The Economic Times. (2018). "China, Pakistan and Afghanistan sign MoU to cooperate on counter terrorism", 17 December, at https://economictimes.indiatimes.com/news/defence/china-pakistan-and-afghanistan-sign-mou-to-cooperate-on-counter-terrorism/articl

The Hindu. (2021). "China Foreign Minister Wang Yi hosts Taliban, calls them 'pivotal force'", 28 July, at https://www.thehindu.com/news/international/taliban-leader-meets-chinese-fm-assures-not-to-allow-terrorist-forces-to-operate-from-afghanistan

The Hindustan Times. (2021). "Taliban say they 'desire' to join China-Pakistan Economic Corridor projects", 7 September, at https://www.hindustantimes.com/world-news/taliban-say-they-desire-to-join-china-pakistan-economic-corridor-projects-101630976453

The Print. (2022). "China slams US for 'willfully' disposing off Afghan assets, says conduct no different from 'bandits'", 15 February, at https://theprint.in/world/china-slams-us-for-willfully-disposing-off-afghan-assets-says-conduct-no-different-from-bandits/833252/

UNSC. (2022). "Security Council ISIL (Da'esh) and Al-Qaida Sanctions Committee Removes 3 Entries from Its Sanctions List", at https://www.un.org/press/en/2022/sc14767.doc.htm

Zia, H. (2018). "Afghanistan's Role in the Belt and Road Initiative", Daily Outlook Afghanistan, 11 October, at http://www.outlookafghanistan.net/topics.php?post_id=21989)

Part III
BRI in China's Neighbouring Regions: Eurasia, East Asia, and Southeast Asia

10. China's BRI and its Neo-mercantilist Approach in Central Asia

Punit Gaur

Abstract

The importance of the Silk Road as a network of numerous inter-linked trade routes connecting Eastern Europe and Africa to South Asia and East Asia, with present-day Eurasia or Central Asia, is well established. For the last three decades (post-USSR disintegration period), various initiatives have been taken for the revival of the historic Silk Road to augment overland commercial connectedness in the region. However, the US military operations and then the withdrawal, the Taliban dispensation in Afghanistan and the uncertainty in Central Asia have so far rendered the idea of its revival unviable. It is important to note that the present-day major international powers have distinct concepts of the revival of the Silk Road that seems to be moving forward at varying paces, operating parallel to each other. On the other hand, China is expanding its association with the Central Asia region and beyond through its BRI (Belt and Road Initiative) policy adopting a neo-mercantilist approach. In this context, this chapter aims to elaborate on China's approach and challenges for the Central Asia region.

Introduction

In ancient times, the Silk Road involved the trade of fine Chinese silk, spices, perfume, grapes, coriander, Baltic amber, and Mediterranean coral (Hopkirk, 1984). Christopher Beckwith delineates the rise and fall of the great Central Eurasian empires, including those of the Scythians, Attila the Hun, the Turks and Tibetans, Genghis Khan and the Mongols associated with this route (Beckwith, 2009). Ancient Silk Road is also known for spreading great world religions like Buddhism, which emerged from India; in this context, the Silk Road was the "first engagement in globalisation" (Norell, et al., 2011).

The Central Asian saga forms a powerful narrative in the aura of the Silk Road. Since the disintegration of the Soviet Union and the emergence of newly independent republics, Central Asia—containing the magical cities of Bukhara and Samarkand and terrain as diverse as the Kazakh steppes, the Karakum desert, and the Pamir Mountains—has been in a constant state of transition (Thubron, 2007). Various "powers" are vying for a place of significance in the world. In this power struggle, the Central Asian region is once again emerged as a place of immense geopolitical importance (Anand, 2012).

China presented BRI as a new and advanced phase of cooperation with Central Asian countries. China issued an important document namely "Vision and Actions on Jointly Building the Silk Road Economic Belt and the 21st Century Maritime Silk Road," in March 2015. As emphasised in the document, the BRI initiative "is intended at endorsing the orderly and free flow of economic factors, highly efficient distribution of resources and profound integration of markets; reassuring the countries along the Belt and Road to attain economic policy coordination and carry out larger and more in-depth regional cooperation of higher values; and mutually creating an open, inclusive and balanced regional economic cooperation architecture that benefits all" (Farkhod, et al., 2019).

China has aggressively endorsed BRI projects in Central Asia since 2013. However, there are no generally recognised classifications or main determinants of what makes a project part of BRI. Therefore, it is hard to distinct BRI analytically from other ongoing projects within the bilateral cooperation between China and the Central Asian countries, as many bilateral agreements are now being brought under the Silk Road and BRI umbrella (Dave, 2018).

China's Belt and Road Initiative

The Chinese idea of a BRI emerged long ago when Chinese Premier Li Peng visited Central Asia in the mid-1990s. As China's economic boom gained momentum in the 1990s and continued through the first decade of the 21st century, the country understandably searched for ways to diversify its fast-increasing energy needs. China is developing multidimensional transport corridors, interconnected logistics and communications networks through its BRI. Through interregional policy coordination across Eurasia, China strives for objectives to extend and develop its relationship with Europe, Africa and the Persian Gulf (Gaur, 2019).

Scholars from across the globe have their connotations of the Chinese discourse on BRI. Some scholars highlight its economic and domestic political objectives. Some scholars called BRI as further evidence of a more assertive posture of China. However, it led China to have increasingly tense relations with its East Asian neighbours and its increasingly competitive relations with the US. Still, China imitates a premeditated agenda that can be slanted towards marginalising the US in Asia, consolidating China's regional domination, and flagging America's international position (Leverett and Bingbing, 2016).

In a persistent pursuit of this strategy, Chinese leader Xi Jinping presented the concept of the New Silk Road in Astana in 2013—an aggregation of land and maritime routes, including the Silk Road Economic Belt (SREB) and the Maritime Silk Road (MSR). The SREB is a Chinese plan to amalgamate the economies of Asia and Europe with the Chinese economy along the Eurasian route. The expansion of transport infrastructure and communication networks connecting railways, roads, and fibre optics highways would link South Asia, Southeast Asia, Central Asia, and Europe along an integrated land corridor. The Chinese SREB/ BRI is an ambitious project to enhance international cooperation and joint development (Gaur, 2019).

The Maritime Silk Road is another major aspect of BRI that is gaining significant importance in light of China's attempt to create an overland Silk Road. The Maritime Silk Road emphasises improved connectivity, but, more importantly, it is designed to enhance China's geostrategic position in the world. It is an effort to initiate a "grand strategy" with global implications, which could be advantageous in fortifying cooperation and elevating it to a new level of maritime partnerships. Nevertheless, China has yet to cultivate the much-needed political and strategic trust (Chaturvedi, 2014).

The primary reasons for this renewed Chinese interest have been attributed to domestic factors: the need to maintain stability on its borders, especially in the western part of China, secure export markets and energy supplies, expand inland transport routes and fill the gap between the eastern and western parts of China's development (Szczudlik-Tatar, 2013). Another proposition in this sphere has been made regarding security and economic imperatives in Xinjiang, home to Muslim Turkic nationalities who have historically challenged Beijing's jurisdiction, thus prompting and shaping China's relations with Kazakhstan, Kyrgyzstan, Tajikistan, Turkmenistan, and Uzbekistan (Karrar, 2006). The historical rhetoric that China has built around the charisma of the Silk Road has been challenged by experts like Tansen Sen. He claims that the objective is to link China's historical and contemporary roles in promoting peace and prosperity in the Asian region. However, the history of ancient expeditions is complicated, with goals and practices unacceptable in the modern context. "Not mentioned ... are the backdrops of conflict and the push to spread a Sino-centric world order" (Sen, 2014).

The rise of China poses a geopolitical challenge to the US and other countries, especially in the context of China's current trade and coercive economic practices, which is associated with its signature foreign policy of the BRI (Hang, 2017). Today it has become an important policy initiative of the Chinese state that involves the highest level of government functionaries (Kaczmarski, 2015).

China's BRI in Central Asia

China is investing in Central Asia through its BRI. It is funding various infrastructure projects in Central Asian countries. The hydrocarbon-rich Central Asian region provides an important source and a relatively safe alternative. Thus, China has built pipelines to import natural gas from Turkmenistan and oil from Kazakhstan. In addition, China has established road and rail connections with the CAR and extended them beyond the CAR to other countries of the Commonwealth of Independent States (CIS) and further to Europe. Central Asian countries also need money, especially to extract value from their enormous mineral resources. Except for Kazakhstan, none of the other Central Asian countries has been able to generate enough domestic finances for growth since independence.

Market-oriented economies and active partnerships in international trade networks are priorities for this landlocked region to attract more diversified projects globally (Taliga, 2021).

Central Asian countries are natural resource-rich, while China is the world's biggest consumer of oil and gas, providing ample grounds to cooperate and collaborate. Due to China's overcapacity of labour-intensive, low-value-added and polluting manufacturing facilities, it wants to expand its markets beyond its borders. China also wants unhindered access to the region's resources, especially when three countries in the Central Asian region have direct borders with China. Chinese companies, particularly in traditional industries, have inadequate domestic growth, so they observe new opportunities overseas (Taliga, 2021). Therefore, it is said that "The BRI is first and foremost a response to China's domestic economic woes, serving to postpone the decisive moment when Chinese production will need to be transitioned from a low-cost model ('Made in China') to a value-added production model ('Created by China')" (Laruelle, 2021).

China is determined to play a substantial role in Central Asia's fast-growing renewable energy markets. China's investment in Central Asian countries is wide-ranging; it is renovating old powerplants, especially coal, and simultaneously transferring its know-how, experience, and technology to the hydropower sector.

The Central Asian region is also considered for higher incomes and low competition. Governments of these countries are also willing to provide tax heavens and other subsidies for overseas investors in various fields. According to China Global investment tracker, Chinese companies invested nearly US$ 50 billion in four Central Asian countries from 2005 to 2020. Chinese companies invested roughly US$ 35.58 billion in Kazakhstan, respectively US$ 4.73 billion in Kyrgyzstan, US$ 2.15 billion in Tajikistan, and US$ 5.79 billion in Uzbekistan. Data also show that the total volume of Chinese investments and contracts within the BRI from 2013 to 2020 was US$ 755.17 billion (as of 20 November 2020), of which US$ 297 billion was in the energy sector, US$ 185.34 billion in transport, US$ 73.22 billion in real estate, US$ 57.44 billion in metals, US$ 22.58 billion in utilities and US$ 15.67 billion in chemicals (Talinga, 2021).

China's Neo-mercantilist Approach

Neo-mercantilism is a national trade policy based on classical mercantilism. Mercantilism is concerned with enriching and empowering the nation, and the state, to the maximum possible degree by obtaining and keeping as much economic activity within the nation's borders (Krasner, 1978). Of particular importance are ensuring financial independence in manufacturing and advanced industries or those with military or national security applications (such as food or energy supplies). Achieving economic autarkies is an element of neo-mercantilism (Hettne, 1993).

The neo-mercantilism encourages exports of technologically advanced or manufactured products while importing raw materials. It is designed to artificially elevate the nation's production by producing for their own and their trading partner's consumption. It maintains artificially high employment and economic activity, which reduces the welfare burden on the government (Hettne, 1990). Theoretically, it aims to increase economic growth with minimal government involvement and low tax obligations. With this reference, China's BRI is a project that aims to connect the East and West through the far-reaching development of infrastructure. It is the existence of Chinese extension and is meant to encourage an entire array of Chinese interests. This interest is highly intricate and can be seen as China's neo-mercantilist approach. The early focus of the initiative is on the countries within Central Asia (Tony Yu, 2017).

In this context, BRI is a creation of the Chinese neo-mercantilist approach. Neo-mercantilism varied from the mercantilism of the 17th to the early 20th century, when merchants were frequently complicit in the imperialism of the great powers in quest of augmented political supremacy and personal prosperity. However, neo-mercantiaism is more controlled because of national and international legal frameworks, disinclination to involve in armed conflicts, and a prevalent admiration of human rights (Ziegler and Menon, 2014). Chinese neo-mercantilism supports global trade and its institutions while also pursuing a government-led globalisation approach to accrue capital and wealth for the nation. China's strategy preferences state-owned enterprises (SOEs) and focuses on establishing free trade areas similar to the China-ASEAN Free Trade Area, initiated in 2010 (Ziegler and Menon, 2014).

China's emergence as a global economic power is primarily due to two essential factors, a sizeable foreign exchange reserve in China and a large amount of foreign direct investment (FDI) going into China compared to the US (Davies, 2013). An accepted, politically stimulating explanation for these facts can be seen in the context of China's rapid rise in the foreign exchange reserve largely due to its mercantilist policy. Its exports rely on a purposely undervalued currency, inexpensive labour, and foreign investors, particularly those from the US.

BRI aims to achieve five objectives: policy coordination, infrastructure building (including railways and highways), unconstrained trade, economic integration and people-to-people contacts (Garlick, 2020). Whereas the historical Silk Road resulted from bottom-up trade actions motivated primarily by nations outside China, the BRI was intended by China's ruling elites. It symbolises the foremost endeavour by China to plan and implement a cross-continental mercantilist strategy with global and geopolitical consequences.

China's production sectors have been facing overcapacity for more than a decade. The Chinese leadership believes in resolving the problem of overproduction by searching for new markets, especially in neighbouring countries through BRI. The initiative provides more chances to develop China's less-developed border regions, especially the northern region. China also aspired to prospect new investment alternatives that protect and expand the value of the capital stockpiled in recent decades (Gaur, 2019).

However, there are fundamental challenges also associated with China's BRI strategy. China's neo-mercantilism had essential shortcomings in the context of some issues in the countries of Central Asia, particularly regarding culture, environment and ethnicity. China's authoritarian approach may also obstruct practical cooperation with democratic governments.

China's Neo-mercantilism: Challenges for Central Asia

There is a need to understand China's approach of neo-mercantilism towards Central Asia through its BRI. First, China's official foreign policy framework rotates around non-interference in the internal domestic affairs of partner nations. Still, China has successfully made countries economically dependent and interfered in its political and domestic affairs through its debt trap policy (Deborah, 2020). China's engagement through BRI to Central Asian countries has also posed a double challenge to Central Asian countries. BRI consists of resource deals with Central Asia, which only benefits China's economy. Although, the shared benefit comes to Central Asia in much-needed necessities like roads, bridges, schools, hospitals and railways, agribusiness, power creation and energy distribution, ICT networks, employment opportunities and training programmes; at the same time, huge sums are invested in Central Asia's infrastructure, with projects being granted to Chinese contractors, who mainly employ Chinese workers. Nevertheless, all these shared benefits greatly benefit the Chinese rather than Central Asia, and now it has become a challenge for Central Asian countries (David, 2018).

The second and possibly most convincing point to understand the 'expansionist' mindset of China through BRI is neo-mercantilism. China's commercial commitment to the rest of the world is mainly depicted by mercantile theory (Arvind, 2011). China's export improving policies inspire a poise of payment in China's favour, manoeuvring their currency to keep it devalued in support of inexpensive capital exports and forced high savings. This procedure leaves China's state capable of huge surplus reserves. This foreign corporatism aligns with state and business endeavours and can be viewed as neo-mercantilism (Qiao, 2013).

Third, as the considerable Chinese migrant population continues to grow in the Central Asia region, but its presence is not explicit. Still, vicious clashes occasionally arise between Chinese migrants and locals, leading to social disruption in the respective countries. Protests have broken out in several China-controlled factories and construction sites against China's reported reluctance to use the local workforce, offering modest wages and adequate work conditions, and against the ecological effect of Chinese enterprises (Lelik, 2016). Although political authority effectively deters public contention in Central Asian countries, uncertainty surrounding China's growing influence continues to channel resentment against Chinese interests. The land is a highly contentious issue, the perception of it being leased to the Chinese voluntarily stirrings nationalist views, condemning their national elites for 'selling out' to the Chinese. Periodic dissents against the reported lease of lands to the Chinese for agricultural or commercial use have often broken out in Kazakhstan and Kyrgyzstan (Hofman, 2016).

Fourth, Central Asia is a strategic and growing energy source, market access, and offers business opportunities for China. A flexible trading approach has been adopted for the users of capital. China's state-aligned multinationals are also trying to enhance economic prosperity and benefit Central Asia by utilising its rich resources and changing them into substantial infrastructural developments. Foreign direct investments and soft loans are measures meant to cultivate the development of Central Asia, but at the same time, it is also a challenge in the future especially when many countries are already facing social and economic challenges due to the debt trap policy of China (Sanjar, et al., 2019).

Last but not least, earlier, China's role in Central Asia was reflected in its association on the receiver side, primarily when the US and Russia engaged in infrastructure-for-aid deals. Over the last decade, China has increased its presence in Central Asia. The mere fact that China's footprint in Central Asia is within a new set of non-Western bounds supports an impressive display of economic arrangements in the context of infrastructure expansion. However, due to the Russian-Ukraine crisis and sanctions on Russia, many projects of China's BRI, especially the rail and road corridors, are distracted and compelling China to reconsider regional trade, development and security strategies (Nathan, 2022). Central Asian countries, especially those who are still recovering from the ripple effects of the pandemic, would also like to reduce their dependency on China.

Conclusion

China deploys neo-mercantilist policies to serve its national development. Nationalism is the core of the mercantilist approach of China to establish the ancient imperial grandeur through the BRI. The Chinese leaders used nationalism to strengthen the authoritarian state, which helped them manage domestic and to pursue foreign affairs and neo-mercantilist policy further. The global expansion of China's neo-mercantilism can be seen in its BRI for further strategic enlargement to create a new global economic and political order.

China's objectives in Central Asia include looking for upstream resources for its national oil companies. Chinese energy investments are also the fragment of a more considerable economic penetration of the Central Asian economies, especially to gradually replace Chinese consumer goods from Russia. However, the Chinese security objectives are focused on containing the "three evils" of terrorism, separatism, and extremism and preserving regional stability. As a result of its neo-mercantilist policies through BRI, China increased its influence through trade and other soft power mechanisms. However, to some extent, the pandemic and the Russian-Ukraine crises have affected China's influence in Central Asian countries. It will be interesting to see if China changes the policy or continues with it, especially in the Central Asian region.

References

Anand, V. (2012/08/13). "Afghanistan and America's New Silk Road Strategy", at https://www.vifindia.org/article/2012/august/13/afghanistan-and-america-s-new-silk-road-strategy. Accessed on 27 April 2022.

Aparna Raman (2017). "Partnerships with Asia: China's Role in South-South Development Cooperation", *Jindal Journal of Public Policy*, Vol. 3, Issue 1, pp. 160-172.

Beckwith, C.I. (2009). *Empires of the Silk Road: A History of Central Eurasia from the Bronze Age to the Present*, Princeton University Press.

Business Standard, Arvind Subramanian (2011). "Learning from Chinese Mercantilism", 25 January 2011.

Charles E. Ziegler and Rajan Menon (2014). "Neomercantilism and Great-Power Energy Competition in Central Asia and the Caspian" *Strategic Studies Quarterly*, Vol. 8, No.2, pp. 17-44.

Chaturvedi, R.R. (2014). "New Maritime Silk Road: Converging Interests and Regional Responses," ISAS Working Paper, no. 197, pp. 1-20.

Dave B., (2018). "China's Silk Road Economic Belt Initiative in Central Asia: Economic and Security Implications", in Marlene L. (ed.), *China's Belt and Road Initiative and Its Impact in Central Asia*, pp. 97-108. Washington, D.C.: The George Washington University, Central Asia Program.

David Dollar (2018). "Is China's Development Finance a Challenge to the International Order?" *Asian Economic Policy Review*, Vol. 13, no. 2, pp. 283-298.

Davies, K. (2013). "China Investment Policy: An Update", OECD Working Papers on International Investment, 2013/01, OECD Publishing.

Deborah Brautigam (2020). "A critical look at Chinese 'debt-trap diplomacy': the rise of a meme", *Area Development and Policy*, 5:1, 1-14.

Farkhod A. et al., (2019). "BRI in Central Asia: Overview of Chinese Projects", *Central Asia Regional Data Review*, 20: 1-5.

Fu-Lai Tony Yu (2017). "Neo-Mercantilist Policy and China's Rise as a Global Power", Contemporary Chinese Political Economy and Strategic Relations, Vol. 3, No. 3, Dec. 201 7, pp. 1043-1073.

Garlick J. (2020). "The Regional Impacts of China's Belt and Road Initiative". *Journal of Current Chinese Affairs*, Vol.49, no.1, pp. 3-13.

Gaur P., (2019). "New Silk Road Diplomacy: India's Challenges and Responses", Central Asia and the Caucasus, no. 20 (1), pp. 56-61.

Hang, Nguyen T.T. (2017). "The Rise of China: Challenges, Implications, and Options for the United States" *Indian Journal of Asian Studies* vol. 30 no. 1/2 pp 47-64.

Harry T., (2021). "Belt and Road Initiative in Central Asia: Desk Study", ITUC.

Hettne, B. (1992). *The Double Movement: Global Market versus Regionalism.* Tokyo: United Nations University.

Hettne, B. (1993). "The Concept of Neomercantilism", in: Magnusson, L. (ed.) *Mercantilist Economics. Recent Economic Thought Series*, vol 33. Springer, Dordrecht.

Hofman I., (2016). "Politics or profits along the 'Silk Road': what drives Chinese farms in Tajikistan and helps them thrive?". *Eurasian Geography and Economics.* 57, 3, 457-481.

Hopkirk, P. (1984). *Foreign Devils on the Silk Road: The Search for the Lost Cities and Treasures of Chinese Central Asia*, Oxford University Press, Oxford.

Kaczmarski, M. (2015). "The New Silk Road: A Versatile Instrument in China's Policy".

Karrar, H.H. (2010). "The New Silk Road diplomacy: China's Central Asian foreign policy since the Cold War".

Laruelle, M. (2018). "China's Belt and Road Initiative and Its Impact in Central Asia", Washington, D.C.: The George Washington University, Central Asia Program.

Lelik A., (2016). "Kyrgyzstan: Bishkek Hopes Chinese Investment Can Produce Industrial Breakthrough". Eurasianet.

Leverett F. and Bingbing W. (2017). "The New Silk Road and China's Evolving Grand Strategy", *The China Journal*, no. 77, pp. 110-132.

Nathan H. (2022, March 21). "Russian invasion dealing China a Silk Road economic setback". Eurasianet.

Norell, M., et al. (2011). *Travelling the Silk Road: Ancient Pathway to the Modern World*, Sterling Signature Publication, New York.

Qiao Yu (2013). "Relocating China's Foreign Reserves", Brookings, Washington DC.

Rezakhani, K. (2010). "The Road That Never Was: The Silk Road and Trans-Eurasian Exchange," *Comparative Studies of South Asia, Africa and the Middle East*, Vol. 30, No. 3, pp. 420-433.

Sanjar T., et al. (2019). "Study on China's Investment in Central Asia", *International Journal of Innovation Education and Research*, Vol 7 No 4, pp. 299-314.

Sen, T. (2014). "Silk Road Diplomacy—Twists, Turns and Distorted History," Yale

Global.

Stephen D. Krasner, (1978). *Defending the National Interest: Raw Materials Investments and U.S. Foreign Policy*, Princeton University Press, Princeton.

Szczudlik-Tatar, J. (2013). "China's New Silk Road Diplomacy," PRISM Policy Paper, No. 34 (82).

Thubron, C. (2007). *Shadow of the Silk Road*, HarperCollins Publishers, Noida, India, 2007.

11. Russia-China Cooperation and the BRI

Himani Pant

Abstract

Russia's relations with China entered a new phase of cooperation in 2014 when the former's economic isolation from the West began owing to the crisis in Ukraine. Eight years later Russia's relationship with the West has reached a new phase of hostility given its recognition of Donetsk and Lugansk as independent republics and its 'special military operation' in Ukraine since 24 February 2022. Amid this geopolitical churning, there is also a renewed focus on the Russia-China partnership and the impact of the crisis on China's ambitious Belt and Road Initiative (BRI). This chapter examines the dynamics of Russia-China relations and compares the BRI with Russia's own regional integration project-Eurasian Economic Union (EAEU). It highlights the scope and limits of their coordination and explores the impact of the renewed conflict in Ukraine on the BRI.

Introduction

The idea of forming the BRI was first voiced expressly by China's President Xi Jinping during his speech in Astana in September 2013. Ironically, this period also witnessed rising antagonism between Russia and the West following Ukraine's abrupt departure from the Association Agreement with the European Union (EU) in November of the same year. Ukrainian President Viktor Yanukovych's decision to abandon the EU deal was premised on the rationale of not antagonising Russia. With widespread protests over the abrupt departure from the said deal and mounting pressure to quit, Yanukovych fled Kiev on 22 February 2014 and took refuge in Russia. Soon afterwards, Russia held a (debated) referendum in the Crimean Peninsula and occupied it. While the international status of Crimea still remains disputed and is regarded as an 'annexation', Russia regards Crimea as an integral part of its territory (Pant, 2022). As the events in Ukraine's Maidan unfolded over the course of the next few months, a major departure was visible in Russia's foreign policy- a course that had been in the making for some time but which gained unprecedented momentum amid the 2014 Ukraine crisis. In this respect, 'competing rationalities' (Averre, 2009) over Ukraine served as a final jolt to Russian foreign policy which had prioritised integration into the wider West since the 1990s despite occasional differences.

The economic sanctions imposed by the United States (US), the EU and other countries not only fuelled Russian nationalism but also "compelled Moscow to pivot to China, turning two natural competitors into close strategic partners" (Chellaney, 2022). Russia's pivot to Asia or China, thus, marked "a new 360-degree vision, in which Moscow serves as a vantage point for a novel geopolitical construct: Eurasia writ large" (Trenin, 2017, p. 106). A changed outlook toward China can also be deciphered in the speeches by the Russian officials in the aftermath of the crisis. For instance, Prime Minister Dmitry Medvedev noted in his opening remarks at a meeting on the development of cooperation with the countries of the Asia-Pacific region that there was "no doubt that China will remain our key partner today and, in the future" (Medvedev 2014).

It must be noted, however, that Russia's economic outreach to China had predated the crisis. Russia and China began their gradual rapprochement in the 1980s and two decades later signed the 2001 Treaty of Good Neighbourliness and Friendly Cooperation which paved way for the settlement of Russian-Chinese border disputes (MFA PRC, 2001). Nevertheless, the economic isolation from the Western markets intensified this process and Moscow decided to reach out to China "to foster an economic partnership in a more direct fashion than before" (Gabuev, 2016). Moscow took several measures in order to overcome the barriers that it had put in place to restrict cooperation with Beijing earlier. As a result of this new accommodating approach towards Beijing, some major informal barriers were removed. This included reversal of Russia's long-standing policy of withholding sales of its most advanced weapon systems as well as easing of the restrictions that had previously limited Chinese participation in large infrastructure and natural resource projects. The country also reviewed its relationship with China in Central Asia which had up till then been defined as largely competitive with very limited opportunities for collaboration (Gabuev, 2015, p. 4).

President Putin's visit to Shanghai in May 2014 took place during the peak of the Ukraine crisis when it had already begun to experience the consequences of Ukraine-related economic sanctions imposed on it. The West had targeted core sectors of the Russian economy such as finance, energy, defence, transport, raw materials among others, and had also imposed several individual sanctions. In turn, Russia had also imposed counter-sanctions which exacerbated the situation further. During Putin's aforementioned visit, a 30-year gas deal between Russian state-owned company Gazprom and China's National Petroleum Corporation (CNPC) estimated to be about US$ 400 billion was reached. The deal had strong geopolitical undertones, as it highlighted the "deepening strategic entente of Russia and China" (Lukin, 2021, p. 7) even though it was clear that in economic terms, the profits would be much less compared to what Russia had been used to earning in its dealings with Europe. However, the isolation from the West provided Russia an option to diversify its energy supplies and it was able to receive capital from China at a crucial time.

Meanwhile, a gas deal was also a win-win situation for China. In addition, easing of the barriers by Russia allowed Chinese companies to buy assets in the former's natural-resource sector and to bid on infrastructure contracts such as roads and railways. Chinese investments in Russia's industrial sector, something which had hitherto been seen as a politically sensitive move were also approved. Russia's pivot to Asia following the Ukraine crisis, thus, facilitated China's access to key strategic sectors of the Russian economy along with a large market for consumption of Chinese technology for the first time. Apart from access to Russia's oil and gas fields, it received advanced military systems from Russia such as an ambitious arms deal of about US$ 3 billion of Russia's "long range S-400 surface to air missile (SAM) system" and Su-35, among others. These arms transfers ushered in a new phase in military-technical cooperation between the two countries. Since 2014, the Moscow-Beijing partnership has evolved exponentially despite frequent misgivings about the longevity of their understanding.

Economic ties form the backbone of the Russia-China partnership. China continues to be Russia's largest trading partner for more than a decade. Despite the momentum affected by the coronavirus pandemic in 2020, the relations continued to grow and showed considerable improvement in 2021 with over US$ 146 billion in total trade (Reuters, 2022). Furthermore, while the two had aimed to boost total trade to US$ 200 billion by 2024, they have now revised the target to US$ 250 billion given the steady progress (TASS, 2022). It is worth noting that the trade amounted to a mere US$ 16 billion in 2003. The current numbers, thus reflect a consistent economic growth over the years.

However, the partnership continues to be asymmetrical. The Figure 11.1 shows bilateral trade between Russia and China and demonstrates how it works in China's favour.

Figure 11.1: Bilateral trade between Russia and China

Year	Exports to China (in billion $)	Imports from China (in billion $)
2013	35.63	53.21
2014	37.49	50.77
2015	28.6	34.94
2016	28.01	38.02
2017	38.91	48.05
2018	56.01	52.22
2019	56.79	54.16
2020	49.06	54.9
2021	68.02	73

Source: Federal State Statistics Service of Russian Federation (Rosstat).

Russia's exports to China include mainly oil, coal, natural gas, fertilisers, metals, etc. With the deepening of the Ukraine crisis since February 2022, it has also emerged as a major wheat supplier to China after the latter lifted all wheat-import restrictions on the country (SCMP, 2022). On the other hand, its imports from China mainly comprise of electronics and machinery, industrial goods and other consumer goods like textiles and apparel; vehicles; ships; aircraft, etc. (CRS, 2022). The composition of trade continues to widen in the aftermath of the Ukraine crisis.

Russia has also become an important part of China's BRI in these years despite its occasional misgivings about the project. Connectivity projects such as the Power of Siberia pipeline to transfer natural gas to China is an important dimension of this dynamic. Russia already supplies gas to China via its Power of Siberia pipeline, which began pumping supplies in 2019, and by shipping liquefied natural gas (LNG). It exported 16.5 billion cubic metres (bcm) of gas to China in 2021 (Reuters, 2022). During the recent Beijing summit on the sidelines of the Winter Olympics in China in February 2022, both countries agreed on a further supply of gas from Russia to China, the payment of which was decided to be settled in Euros instead of US dollars.

Figure 11.2: Russia-China Plan New Gas Pipeline

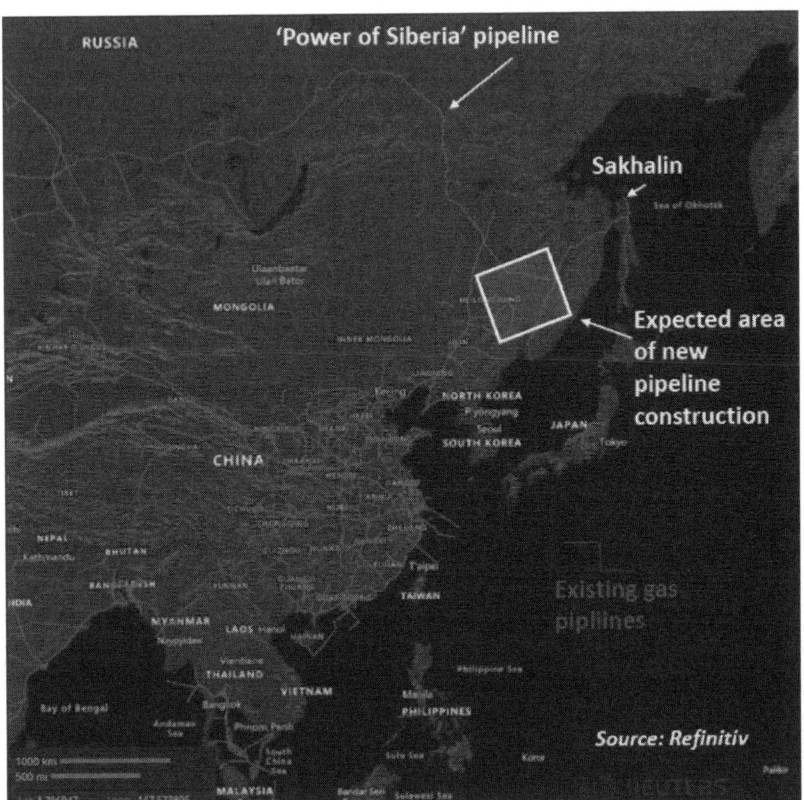

Source: Reuters, 2022.

Eurasian Economic Union and the Belt and Road Initiative

Apart from the bilateral dimension, Russian and Chinese geopolitical interests intersect in Eurasia, particularly in East and Central Asia as well as the Arctic region. While this creates inevitable probabilities for competition and conflict, the two countries have managed to "keep their differences in key Eurasian zones under control while displaying a significant degree of mutual coordination and collaboration" (Lukin, 2021, p. 3). One such instance of coordination was displayed in 2015 as the two sides agreed to harmonise their respective integration projects, the BRI and EAEU.

EAEU

Russia, Belarus, Kazakhstan and Kyrgyzstan signed a treaty on forming a Customs Union and Common Economic Space in 1999. The treaty was based on the model proposed by the Kazakh President, Nursultan Nazarbayev in 1994 who envisioned "the formation of a unified customs zone to facilitate "free movement of goods, services, capital and workforce" (Kazantsev, 2008, p. 1076). This culminated in the creation of a Eurasian Economic Community (EEC or EurAsEC) a year later. In May 2014, the Treaty of the Eurasian Economic Union was signed and it came into effect on 1 January 2015. In its current form, the EAEU is an economic union of five member states: Armenia, Belarus, Kazakhstan, Kyrgyzstan, and Russia. It is designed to provide freedom of movement of goods, services, capital, and labour among these participating countries. Despite its limitations, particularly economic ones, the EAEU is viewed as a means for Russia to maintain its influence in the post-Soviet space. At the same time, as an organisation led by Russia, it has been projected as a balance against China and its "pursuit of becoming a superpower in Eurasia, particularly in South-East and Central Asia" (Mekhdiev, et al., 2019, p. 1). The EAEU aims to a form of "protective integration" (Clark, 2020) to secure Russian hegemony in the post-Soviet space through a restrictive customs union (Kirkham, 2016).

During Chinese President, Xi Jinping's visit to Moscow in May 2015 to attend the Victory Day parade, Russia agreed to harmonise the EAEU with the BRI and signed a joint declaration on "Cooperation in Coordinating Development of the Eurasian Economic Union and the

Silk Road Economic Belt" (MFA PRC, 2015; The Kremlin, 2015). It marked the beginning of a new outline for the development of Russia-China relations. Under the framework of the BRI-EAEU agreement, both sides decided to align their complementary economic advantages to cooperate in different sectors, in order to tap full potential (Hui, 2019) and agreed to cooperate on a bilateral level as well as within the SCO.

Figure 11.3: EAEU and BRI

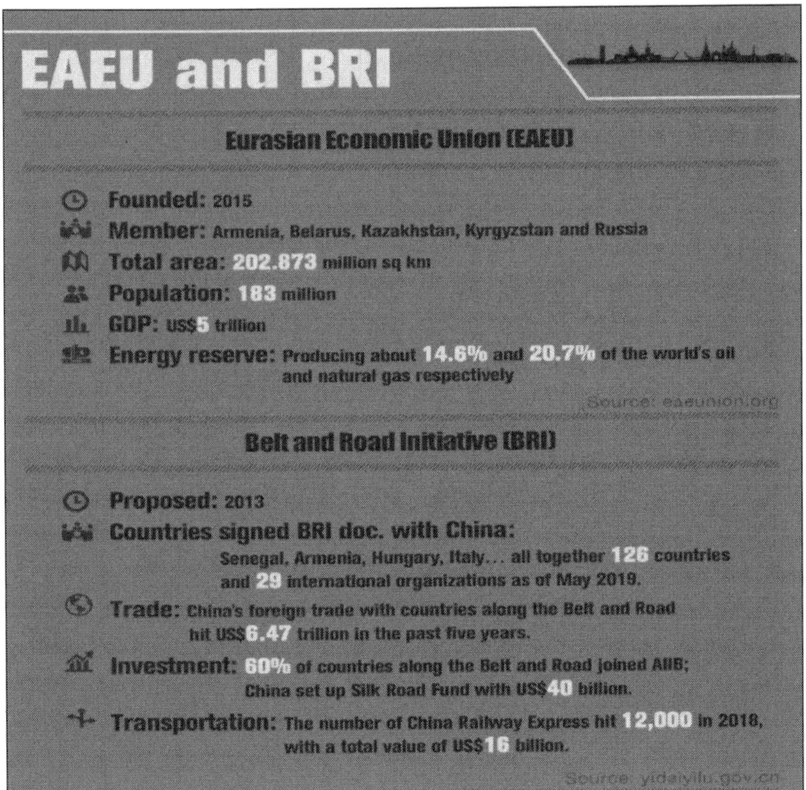

Source: EAEU, CGTN.

The Joint Statement noted that both sides would work towards achieving cooperation in trade and investment facilitation; joint investment projects; enhancing infrastructure connectivity; free trade agreement between the EAEU and China in a long-term promotion of SMEs; payments in national currencies; cooperation within the Asian Infrastructure Investment Bank (AIIB), Silk Road Fund, SCO

Interbank Consortium; global trade and investment governance, etc. (ibid.). It is important to note in this context that Russia's President and not the Eurasian Economic Commission's chairman signed the document on behalf of the EAEU (Shakhanova and Garlick, 2020). As a step further, Moscow also suggested: "extending economic cooperation to the Association of Southeast Asian Nations" (Trenin, 2017, pp. 113-114). This commitment to align the two projects was reaffirmed during President Putin's visit to Beijing the following year (MFA PRC, 2016). In October 2016, China and the EAEU started one-year negotiations on trade and economic cooperation including five rounds of talks, three meetings of joint working groups and two ministerial consultations. On 17 May 2018, China and the EAEU signed an agreement on trade and economic cooperation, covering customs cooperation, trade facilitation, and intellectual property rights along with new topics like e-commerce. This was the first major systematic arrangement ever reached between the two sides. This time, the document was signed by Vice-Minister of Commerce Fu Ziying, Chairman of the Board of the Eurasian Economic Commission (EEC) Tigran Sargsyan and representatives of the EAEU members at the Astana Economic Forum that had convened the same day. The agreement covers 13 aspects such as customs cooperation, trade facilitation, intellectual property rights, sectoral cooperation and government procurement, including new topics like e-commerce and competition. China and the EAEU agreed to further simplify procedures of customs clearance and cut costs of trade in goods by strengthening cooperation and exchange of information between each other (*Xinhua*, 2018).

So far, some headway has been made on two projects in Russia under the BRI framework. One example is a 770-km high-speed Moscow-Kazan railway in which the Russian Ministry of Transport and Chinese Railways collaborated. This is projected as the first segment of a bigger transnational high-speed railway connecting Russia and China. An additional trilateral agreement includes the building of the Northern Rail Corridor from Russia that connects the ports of the Russian Far East and the east and northeast of China to Europe via Trans-Siberian Railway branches that run through Russia, and routes that traverse Mongolia and Kazakhstan (UNESCAP, 2018). While the feasibility and success of these endeavours depend on the geopolitical environment, these nevertheless reflect the understanding between both the countries.

However, Russia has also been wary of joining China-led endeavours, such as the BRI even as the country has been making constant efforts to harmonise its objectives and interests with those of China (Trenin, 2017, p. 113). Consequently, Moscow has pushed for multilateral institutions like the Shanghai Cooperation Organisation (SCO), Russia-India-China (RIC) trilateral initiative, etc. in order to balance China's influence. The country's push for SCO expansion to include India yielded results when in June 2017, India and Pakistan formally joined the SCO. While the addition of new members (in this case even complex due to border issues between India and Pakistan) casts adverse effects on reaching consensus, it serves Moscow's objective of 'diluting China's superiority' (Trenin, 2017, pp. 113-114). The geopolitical and consequently geo-economic situation around Russia makes it vital for it to build a strong system of relations with emerging powers such as China and India (Mekhdiev, et al., 2019, p. 4).

Despite the optics about integration of the two projects, it is important to note that the strategic ties between the two countries are mostly confined outside the domain of the BRI framework. Though both sides have spent years claiming a close relationship and commitment to the project, "Russia has long been an absent partner" (Shah, 2020). There is also little tangible evidence to show that Russia is even an official partner country of the BRI. As Igor Denisov (2020) puts it, "Russia is not part of the BRI. It is only a supporter of Chinese global outreach as long as it is in Russia's interests". For instance, as Russia's economy began to recover following a tough economic period in the aftermath of the 2014 Ukraine crisis, there were also indications of the country's disenchantment with the BRI. Russia's Foreign Minister, Sergei Lavrov's absence from the 2019 BRI Forum was viewed as "a subtle change in Russia's approach towards the BRI" (Shah, 2020) given its concerns over China's heavy investments in infrastructure and investment in Russia's backyard- its sphere of influence. In addition, given China's opaqueness about the definite contours of BRI and exact extent of third-party participation in the initiative, it is hard to determine Russia's role in the BRI.

Moreover, major transportation projects proposed by the EAEU to China remain shelved. In addition, China is yet to categorise any of the EAEU projects under the BRI ambit.

Impact of Russia-Ukraine Conflict on BRI

Though short of a formal alliance, the Russia-China partnership continues to grow and has been described by its respective leadership as a "friendship without limits" (Xi and Putin, 2022). However, while the developments in Ukraine have pushed Russia closer to China, they have also highlighted the challenges to their partnership. Russia's recognition of the Donbas region and military intervention in Ukraine since 24 February 2022 has generated an even stricter response from the Western countries towards Russia. This carries inevitable adverse consequences for China's BRI given that territories of Russia and the Russian-led EAEU form an integral part of the project.

This region comprises of the majority of territories which form a part of BRI's overland route—the Silk Road Economic Belt, which has to pass this region to reach its ultimate destination in Western Europe (Shakhanova and Garlick, 2020). Amid the ongoing geopolitical turn, China would have to inevitably look at other land corridors to reach the European market. BRI's other corridors such as the Central Asia-West Asia (CAWA) corridor has already attracted significant attention as an alternate route linking China with Europe as it bypasses Russia, Belarus as well as Ukraine. Given the volatile situation in Ukraine, the ongoing conflict in Ukraine has also halted BRI engagement in the country. The global economic impact of the Ukraine conflict and consequent economic sanctions has already manifested in several parts of the world. This carries adverse economic consequences for China as it seeks to enhance its economic footprint, especially given its strong economic ties with Russia.

Given the Russia's deteriorating relations with the West, association with the country has already created challenges for China which has continued to maintain a neutral stance in the conflict. At a time when the reservations of the West regarding China's assertiveness in general and concerns regarding the role of new and emerging technologies are rising, the instability in Russia and Ukraine have inevitable repercussions for China.

Conclusion

Russia and China are not allies but their relations have prospered at an unprecedented phase since 2014. A partnership of convenience, the relationship could best be described as 'transactional' that carries mutual benefits. However, the relationship continues to be asymmetrical in the economic sphere with China occupying a dominant position. Russia, on the other hand, has endeavoured to make up for its lack of capital by maintaining its position as the security provider in the neighbouring region as well as by supplying crucial defence equipment.

The conflict in Ukraine has highlighted the resilience of their partnership given China's refusal to criticise Russia. However, it has also exposed the limitations of their partnership, which could pose obstacles to future engagement. While the two share the common interest of creating a counterbalance to the US, their respective antagonism with the Western economies are likely to have adverse implications on China's integration projects. Unlike Russia, China has the economic might which it has been using towards enhancing its global footprint and BRI forms an important component of this objective. As Russia's differences with the world increases, it may be difficult for China to sustain its balancing act in future.

References

Averre, D. (2009). "Competing Rationalities: Russia, the EU and the 'Shared Neighbourhood'", *Europe-Asia Studies*, Vol. 61(10), pp. 1689-1713.

Brunnstrom, D. and Martina, M. (2022). "China unsettled by Ukraine, but don't underestimate Xi's Taiwan resolve – CIA head," Reuters, 8 March, at https://www.reuters.com/world/china/china-unsettled-by-ukraine-dont-underestimate-xis-taiwan-resolve-cia-head-2022-03-08/. Accessed on 10 March 2022.

CGTN (2019). "China-proposed BRI aligns well with EAEU", at https://news.cgtn.com/news/3d3d774e7a45544d35457a6333566d54/index.html. Accessed on 16 April 2022.

Chellaney, B. (2022). "Can punishing Russia become an end in itself?", The Hill, 4 April, at https://thehill.com/opinion/international/3257740-can-punishing-russia-become-an-end-in-itself/. Accessed on 20 April 2022.

Clarke, M. (2011). *Xinjiang and China's Rise in Central Asia—A History,* Routledge, pp. 158-168.

Clarke, M. (2020). "The Neglected Eurasian Dimension of the 'Indo-Pacific': China, Russia and Central Asia in the Era of BRI". *Security Challenges,* Vol. 16(3), pp. 32-38, at https://www.jstor.org/stable/26924337. Accessed on 20 March 2022.

Congressional Research Service (2022). "China's Economic and Trade Ties with Russia", 22 May, at https://crsreports.congress.gov/product/pdf/IF/IF12120. Accessed on 30 May 2022.

Eichensehr, K. E. (2021). "Biden Administration Imposes Sanctions and Seeks to Cement Alliances to Counter China and Russia", *American Journal Of International Law*, Vol. 115:3, pp. 536-545, at https://doi.o rg/10.1017/ajil.2021.28. Accessed on 26 March 2022.

Fang, Y. (2020). "From the Eurasian Economic Union to the Greater Eurasian Partnership: The View of Chinese Scholars on Eurasian Integration", Russian Council, 28 February, at https://russiancouncil.ru/en/blogs/yufang/from-the-eurasian-economic-union-to-the-greater-eurasian-partnership-t/. Accessed on 10 February 2022.

Gabuev, A. (2016). "Friends with benefits. Russian-Chinese Relations After the Ukrainian Crisis", Carnegie Moscow Center, at https://carnegiemoscow.org/2016/06/29/friends-with-benefits-russian-chinese-relations-after-ukraine-crisis-pub-63953. Accessed on 10 January 2022.

Ghiasy, R. (2018). "China's Belt and Road Initiative: Security implications and ways forward for the European Union", Stockholm International Peace Research Institute, at http://www.jstor.org/stable/resrep24430. Accessed on 5 April 2022.

Hillman, J. E. (2020). "China and Russia: Economic Unequals", Center for Strategic and International Studies (CSIS), at http://www.jstor.org/stable/resrep25230. Accessed on 24 March 2022.

Hui, L. (2019). "BRI has bolstered China-Russia relations". Quoted in China Daily, 22 April, at https://www.chinadaily.com.cn/a/201904/22/WS5cbd237aa3104842260b7792.html. Accessed on 30 April 2022.

Kirkham, K. (2016). "The Formation of the Eurasian Economic Union: How Successful is the Russian Regional Hegemony?", *Journal of Eurasian Studies*, Vol. 7, no. 2, pp. 111-28.

Kuhrt, N., and Buranelli, F. C. (2018). "Russia and the CIS in 2017: Russia in Asia: Succumbing to China's Embrace?", *Asian Survey*, Vol. 58 (1), pp. 55-64, at https://www.jstor.org/stable/26390402. Accessed on 19 January 2022.

Lo, B. (2022). "Turning Point? Putin, Xi, And the Russian Invasion of Ukraine", Lowy Institute, 25 May, at https://www.lowyinstitute.org/publications/turning-point-putin-xi-and-russian-invasion-ukraine. Accessed on 30 May 2022.

Lukin, A. (1999). "Russia's image of China and Russian-Chinese relations". *East Asia*, 17(1), pp. 5-39.

Lukin, A. (2021). "Road and Belt, Iron Silk Road and Russian-Chinese geopolitical cooperation and competition", OrdnungspolitischeDiskurse, Vol. 3. OrdnungsPolitisches Portal (OPO).

Medvedev, D. (2014). "Meeting on the development of cooperation with the countries of the Asia-Pacific region", 12 May, at http://government.ru/news/12293/. Accessed on 20 April 2022.

Mekhdiev E, Pashkovskaya I, Takmakova E, Smirnova O, Sadykova K, Poltorykhina S. (2019). "Conjugation of the Belt and Road Initiative and Eurasian Economic Union: Problems and Development Prospects", *Economies*, Vol. 7 (4): .118, at https://doi.org/10.3390/economies7040118. Accessed on 4 February 2022.

MFA PRC (2001). "Treaty of Good-Neighborliness and Friendly Cooperation between the People's Republic of China and the Russian Federation", 24 July, at https://www.fmprc.gov.cn/mfa_eng/wjdt_665385/2649_665393/200107/t20010724_679026.html. Accessed on 18 January 2022.

MFA PRC (2015). "Xi Jinping Holds Talks with President Vladimir Putin of Russia", 8 May, at https://www.mfa.gov.cn/ce/cgbelfast//eng/zgxw_1/t1263258.htm. Accessed on 11 April 2022.

Pant, H. (2022). "Ukraine Crisis and its Implications. Indian Council of World Affairs", 3 March, at https://www.icwa.in/show_content.php?lang=1&level=3&ls_id=7147&lid=4835. Accessed on 4 March 2022.

Peyrouse, S. (2017). "The Evolution of Russia's Views on the Belt and Road Initiative", *Asia Policy*, 24, 96-102, at https://www.jstor.org/stable/26403207. Accessed on 4 March 2022.

Ramani, S. (2021). "Russia and China in Africa: Prospective Partners or Asymmetric Rivals?", South African Institute of International Affairs, at http://www.jstor.org/stable/resrep38659. Accessed on 29 March 2022.

Reuters (2022). "Russia, China agree 30-year gas deal via new pipeline, to settle in euros", 4 February, at https://www.reuters.com/world/asia-pacific/exclusive-russia-china-agree-30-year-gas-deal-using-new-pipeline-source-2022-02-04/, Accessed on 4 February 2022.

Reuters (2022). "Factbox: China-Russia trade has surged as countries grow closer", 1 March, at https://www.reuters.com/markets/europe/china-russia-trade-has-surged-countries-grow-closer-2022-03-01/. Accessed on 2 March 2022.

Shakhanova, G., and Garlick, J. (2020). "The Belt and Road Initiative and the Eurasian Economic Union: Exploring the 'Greater Eurasian Partnership,'" *Journal of Current Chinese Affairs*, 49(1), 33-57, at https://doi.org/10.1177/1868102620911666. Accessed on 2 March 2022.

Shah, A. (2020), "Russia Loosens its Belt", *Foreign Policy*, at https://foreignpolicy.com/2020/07/16/russia-china-belt-and-road-initiative/. Accessed on 11 February 2022.

South China Morning Post (2022). "As Ukraine crisis deepens, China lifts all wheat-import restrictions on Russia", 24 February, at https://www.scmp.com/economy/china-economy/article/3168278/ukraine-crisis-deepens-china-lifts-all-wheat-import. Accessed on 1 March 2022.

TASS (2022). "Xi Jinping aims to increase trade with Russia to $250 bln — Kremlin", 4 February, at https://tass.com/economy/1398199?utm_source=google.com&utm_medium=organic&utm_campaign=google.com&utm_referrer=google.com. Accessed on 4 February 2022.

The Kremlin (2015). "Joint Statement of the Russian Federation and the People's Republic of China on Cooperation in Conjugation of Construction of the Eurasian Economic Union and the Silk Road Economic Belt", 8 May, at http://kremlin.ru/supplement/4971. Accessed on 4 February 2022.

Torbakov, I. (2016). "Managing Imperial Peripheries: Russia and China in Central Asia", in Thomas Fingar (ed.), *The New Great Game: China and South and Central Asia in the Era of Reform*, p. 259, Stanford University Press.

Torjesen, Stina (2008). "Russia as a Military Great Power: The Uses of the CSTO and the SCO in Central Asia", in Elana Wilson Rowe and StinaTorjesen (eds), *The Multilateral Dimension in Russian Foreign Policy*, pp. 195-206, Routledge, London.

Trenin, D. (2017). "Russia and 'Grand Eurasia': Will It Work? Horizons", *Journal of International Relations and Sustainable Development*, Vol. 9, pp. 106-119, at https://www.jstor.org/stable/48573711. Accessed on 12 Mach 2022.

Tsygankov, Andrei P. (2005). "Vladimir Putin's Vision of Russia as a Normal Great Power", *Post-Soviet Affairs*, Vol. 21, 2, pp. 132-58.

Xi Jinping (2013). Speech by H.E. Xi Jinping. President of the People's Republic of China. Nazarbayev University, 7 September, at https://www.fmprc.gov.cn/ce/cebel/eng/zxxx/t1078088.htm. Accessed on 18 January 2022.

Xi Jinping and Putin, V. (2022). "Joint statement of the Russian Federation and the People's Republic of China on the International Relations Entering a New Era and the Global Sustainable Development". Beijing, 4 February, at http://en.kremlin.ru/supplement/5770. Accessed on 4 February 2022.

Xinhua (2018). "China, EAEU sign agreement on trade, economic cooperation", 18 May, at http://english.www.gov.cn/news/international_exchanges/2018/05/18/content_281476151403330.htm. Accessed on 20 March 2022.

12. Japan's Approach to BRI: Between Cooperation and Competition

Jojin V. John

Abstract

Japan's response to China's Belt and Road Initiative (BRI) has evolved from an initial balancing approach to complex engagement featuring conditional cooperation and outright competition driven by a complex mix of strategic, economic and normative considerations. BRI prompted the revitalisation of Japanese infrastructure diplomacy leading to the announcement of the Partnership for Quality Infrastructure (PQI), a normative and substantive policy framework. Central to the Japanese balancing strategy has been the promotion of the 'quality infrastructure' principle as a global standard. The conditional cooperation strategy under which Japan agreed to cooperate with China on infrastructure development in a third country, on the one hand, aimed to help Japanese companies to take advantage of the economic opportunities and, on the other hand, intends to reform BRI from within to adhere to international norms and standards. The competitive dimension of the Japanese response involves stepping up Tokyo's infrastructure development commitments and building an international coalition under the Free and Open Indo-Pacific framework. Mapping the evolution of Japan's BRI response, the paper illustrates that Tokyo had been treading a middle path between endorsement and containment while enhancing its position as a leading infrastructure development actor by upholding a normative and rules-based order.

Since its announcement in 2013, China's 'One Belt One Road', which later came to be known as the 'Belt and Road Initiative (BRI)', has gained significant attention in international politics. With the aim of connecting Asia to Europe and Africa via land and sea and with a promise to invest around US$ 8 trillion (John, Scott, and Portelance, 2019), BRI has often been described as the largest infrastructure programme undertaken in human history (Williams, Robinson, and Bouzarovski, 2020). While Beijing promotes BRI primarily as an economic programme, it's geopolitical and strategic implications are huge because of its sheer size and scope. BRI also manifests a departure in Chinese foreign policy from the decades-old keeping a low profile strategy to an assertive foreign policy outlook. Many observers have argued that BRI is the cornerstone of China's quest for hegemony (Beeson and Crawford, 2020).

BRI, since its inception, has also emerged as a significant issue of foreign and security for most countries. Japan, too was no exception. Even though Japan does not figure under the geographic scope of any BRI project, its implications have been multi-dimensional. First, BRI has emerged as a competitor and challenger to Japan's established position and influence in Asia as a leading player, especially in the infrastructure development sector (Katada and Liao, 2020). Second, Tokyo perceives BRI as a significant challenge to regional stability and security. It undermines the principles and standards of the liberal international order that Japan dearly wants to preserve (IPP, 2018).

The chapter is an attempt to provide an account of the Japanese response to BRI. The evaluation of the Japanese response to BRI has been explored in three sections. The first section of the paper evaluates the Japanese response during the early years since the launching of BRI (2013-2017), during which Tokyo largely focused on revitalising its infrastructure diplomacy with the announcement of the Partnership for Quality Infrastructure (PQI), while reserved its position on BRI. Section two evaluates the second phase (2017-2022) of the Japanese policy toward BRI, which features a hedging strategy that includes an attempt for conditional engagement with BRI while pursuing a multi-dimensional balancing approach. Implications of the COVID pandemic on Japan's approach to BRI are also discussed in the conclusion section of the chapter.

'Cold Shouldering' and Revitalising Infrastructure Diplomacy (2013-2017)

Japan has been long engaged in infrastructure diplomacy in Asia through its Official Development Assistance (ODA) programme and Asian Development Bank (ADB) (Pascha, 2019). Southeast Asia has been the focus of the Japanese aid programme. However, it has expanded its focus to other regions, including South Asia, Central Asia and Africa. Such efforts were part and parcel of Japanese economic diplomacy. The latest drive for bolstering Japanese infrastructure export has been witnessed even before the announcement of the BRI. In 2010 Democratic Party of Japan (DPJ) administration (2009-12), under the 'New Growth Strategy' advanced policies to support Japanese companies' infrastructure development operations abroad (Yoshimatsu, 2017). The policies to advance infrastructure export received much attention with the return of Prime Minister Shinzo Abe to office in 2012. The export of infrastructure was seen as a vital component of Abenomics, PM Abe's economic strategy to revitalise Japanese economic growth (Kantei, 2014). The Abe administration established the "Management Council for Infrastructure Strategy" in this regard. It unveiled the 'Infrastructure Export Strategy' in 2013, intending to triple infrastructure sales from 10 trillion yen in 2010 to 30 trillion yen by 2020 (Yoshimatsu, 2017). It laid out specific targets and guidelines for different regions. Under this strategy, the Abe administration identified the Association of Southeast Asian Nations (ASEAN) as 'a market where Japan will never lose and be behind' (Yoshimatsu, 2017).

The announcement of the BRI in 2013 changed the landscape of Japanese infrastructure diplomacy. The Abe administration initially showed little response to the BRI, mainly because the substance of Beijing's proposals was so vague that Tokyo could not correctly evaluate the initiative. For instance, during the Summit between Japanese Prime Minister Shinzo Abe and Chinese President Xi Jinping in Jakarta in April 2015, President Xi insisted that the international community had widely welcomed China's proposals for BRI and the AIIB. In response, Abe asked him to explain the maintenance of good governance and debt sustainability for borrowers regarding the AIIB. PM Abe pointed out Japan is closely watching how the BRI would evolve in future (MOFA,

2015). Unlike BRI, in which Japan took a wait-and-see approach, on AIIB, Tokyo was antagonistic and decided not to join the initiative (Katada, 2016).

Even though the Japanese government had reservations about the initiative the aggressive branding of the BRI forced Tokyo to revamp its infrastructure diplomacy. In 2014, the Abe government set up another institution to promote Japanese infrastructural exports—Japan Overseas Infrastructure Investment Corporation for Transport and Urban Development (JOIN) (MLITT, 2014). It became the first Japanese private-public fund, specialising in overseas infrastructure investment and collaborating with companies, banks, and the government. Together with establishing JOIN, the Japanese government revised rules to allow the Japan Bank for International Cooperation (JBIC) to become more risk-taking (JBIC, 2015). In May 2015, PM Abe announced the Partnership for Quality Infrastructure (PQI) initiative. Announcing PQI, Abe pledged 'to spread high-quality and innovative infrastructure throughout Asia, taking a long-term view'. Under the new initiative, Tokyo promised to provide US$ 110 billion for quality infrastructure investment in Asia from 2016 to 2020 (MOFA, 2015). The four pillars of the Japanese infrastructure development plan under PQI include expanding infrastructure development assistance with all available tools under Japanese disposal, collaboration with the Asian Development Bank, financing of high-risk projects through various means, including the enhanced functions of the Japan Bank for International Cooperation (JBIC) and the promotion of quality infrastructure as an international standard (MOFA, 2015). The fourth pillar, which aimed to promote PQI as an international standard, has been the most important element of the revised Japanese infrastructure diplomacy. It set out to establish quality as a new normative principle in infrastructure financing and development that has been targeting Chinese practices under BRI, especially issues of openness, transparency, economic efficiency, and debt sustainability (Koga, 2019).

Pushing the narrative of quality infrastructure, PM Abe made a veiled attack on BRI. Announcing PQI, PM Abe highlighted that the need of the hour is not quantity but quality in infrastructure development (Abe, 2015). The emphasis on quality was a counter-narrative underscoring the superiority of Japanese infrastructure compared to a quantity-driven investment spearheaded by Beijing under the BRI (Pascha, 2020). Following the announcement of the PQI, Tokyo took action to raise awareness of quality principles for infrastructure investment. During a speech at the ASEAN Business and Investment Summit in November 2015, Prime Minister Abe urged participants to expand quality infrastructure "with superior economic efficiency, in harmony with the environment, with maximum energy efficiency, which is also made to last long" (Abe, 2015).

Japan took advantage of G7 Ise-Shima Summit that it hosted in May 2016 as a platform for fleshing out a normative standard for international infrastructure development based on quality infrastructure (MOFA, 2016). During the Summit, 'Principles for Promoting Quality Infrastructure Investment' (G7 Principles) was adopted. The G7 Principles identified effective governance, social and environmental impacts, public-private partnership, addressing social and environmental impacts, and benefit for the local community as five principles of quality infrastructure development (MOFA, 2016). During the Summit, the Abe administration also announced the 'Expanded Partnership for Quality Infrastructure initiative, enhancing its commitment by promising to provide US$ 200 billion from 2017 to 2021 (METI, 2016).

Towards reinvigorating its infrastructure diplomacy, Tokyo reformed its foreign aid policy. The Abe administration amended the ODA charter in 2015, emphasising the strategic importance of ODA and the partnership it has developed (Jain, 2019). A primary factor that prompted a change in Japanese aid policy was Tokyo's losing out to the Chinese in the HSR project between Jakarta and Bandung in September 2015. The incident forced Japan to adjust its lending policies and focus on promoting "high-quality" infrastructure development. In stepping up its competition with China in infrastructure development, Japan exempted the condition of central government guarantees in providing yen loans directly to sub-sovereign entities of developing countries (Zhao, 2018).

The Abe administration unveiled the 'Free and Open Indo-Pacific Strategy' (FOIPS) at the 6th Tokyo International Conference on African Development (TICAD VI) held in Kenya in August 2016, articulating Japan's vision for regional order. Connectivity through quality infrastructure has been an essential component of the FOIPS. It encapsulates Japan's regional strategy that evolved in response to the growing Chinese assertiveness in the region aimed to maintain the status quo through Japan's proactive role, strengthening its alliance with the US and partnership with like-minded countries (MOFA, 2016).

Hedging through Conditional Engagement (2017-2022)

There has been a visible shift in Japan's approach to BRI since mid-2017, with Tokyo signalling interest in conditional engagement. Tokyo's changed approach to BRI was part and parcel of an overall improvement in Japan-China relations that substantially deteriorated during the first half of 2010 following heightened security tension on account of their conflict over territory in the East China Sea (John, 2018). Another factor contributing to Japan's charm offensive to BRI has been the political change in Washington and the emergence of a 'transactional approach' in the US foreign policy under President Donald Trump (Basu, 2020).

A key development that showed the Abe administration's interest in engaging with BRI was the Japanese participation in the first Belt and Road Forum in Beijing in May 2017. The Japanese delegation to the BRI Forum was led by Toshihiro Nikai, then Secretary-General of Liberal Democratic Party (LDP) and leading China hand in Japan. Further, PM Abe, soon after the BRI Forum, stated that "Japan is ready to extend cooperation with the Belt and Road Initiative (BRI)" (Abe, 2017). On a positive note, Abe said, "One Belt, One Road Initiative holds the potential to connect East and West as well as the diverse regions found in-between". However, PM Abe laid three criteria for Japanese cooperation. First, "it is critical for infrastructure to be open to use by all, and to be developed through transparent and fair procurement." Second, the projects must be "economically viable". And lastly, projects "should be financed by debt that can be repaid" without damaging "the soundness of debtor nation's finances". He also said that he "would expect 'One Belt One Road' initiative will fully incorporate such a common frame of thinking, and come into harmony with the free and fair Trans-Pacific economic zone" (Abe, 2017). During his Summit meeting with Xi on the sidelines of the Hamburg G20 Summit in July 2017, Abe described the "One Belt One Road Initiative" as a "vision with potential" and repeated his willingness to cooperate (Asahi, 2017).

As a way forward, during his meeting with Chinese Premier Li Keqiang on the sidelines of the China-Japan-Korea Trilateral in Tokyo in December 2017, PM Abe proposed the idea of joint business projects in 'third country' involving private enterprises. PM Abe said that under a "Free and Open Indo-Pacific Strategy, Japan can cooperate significantly with China which has put forward the One Belt, One Road initiative" (Abe, 2017). The Abe administration signalled its intention to offer financial support to Japanese private sector companies for projects under BRI (*Nikkei*, 2017). Furthermore, in June 2018, a revised version of Japan's basic policy on infrastructure exports referred to the promotion of cooperation with China for the first time (Kantei, 2018). It was based on the agreement reached between PM Abe and Chinese Premier Li Keqiang in May 2018, where they pledged to set up a joint public-private committee to coordinate economic cooperation in third countries. In this regard, the Committee for the Promotion of Japan-China Business Cooperation in Third Countries was held in September 2018, and the Japan-China Forum on Third Country Business Cooperation was held in October 2018. The interest of the Japanese business in exploiting the business opportunities in BRI projects has been an important factor that influenced Tokyo's approach. In July 2017, the Japanese business lobby, the Japanese Chamber of Commerce and Industry in China, had set up a liaison office in Beijing to share information among member companies (*Nikkei*, 2017).

During the visit of PM Shinzo Abe to Beijing in October 2018, Japan and China agreed to cooperate on infrastructure projects under the framework of a 'third country partnership'. At a forum attended by PM Abe and Premier Li Keqiang, private companies from both countries inked documents to undertake more than 50 projects (MOFA, 2018). Joint projects include the construction of a smart city in Thailand involving Japanese contractor JFE Engineering Corp. and Chinese construction company JSCC. Forum also witnessed an agreement between China Development Bank and Japan Bank for International Cooperation to finance infrastructure projects in third countries (Mainichi Shimbun, 2018). While describing the effort as a "win-win" situation, PM Abe stressed the importance of "international standards" to ensure that infrastructure projects are open, transparent, economically viable and should also account for the financial health of the recipient countries (Mainichi Shimbun, 2018). Furthermore, Abe directly appealed to the importance of the four standards to Chinese Premier Li Keqiang at a summit meeting in May 2018 and to Chinese President Xi Jinping in October 2018 (Mainichi Shimbun, 2018).

While proposing conditional cooperation with BRI, Tokyo strengthened its infrastructure diplomacy featuring enhanced financial commitments, promoting PQI as a global standard, and building an international coalition with like-minded countries and regional organisations through bilateral and multilateral partnerships. Following its successful campaigning that resulted in the announcement of G7 Principles on Quality Infrastructure Development, Tokyo pursued the agenda at other multilateral forums, including the Asia-Pacific Economic Cooperation (APEC) and G20 (Yoshimatsu, 2021). Japan played an instrumental role in revising the APEC's 2014 Guidebook on Quality of Infrastructure Development and Investment. Though APEC has already incorporated quality principles in its standard for infrastructure financing by its member states, it was weak in its behavioural codes for both borrowers and lenders in carrying out infrastructure projects. The revised guideline was released in 2018, incorporating the principles of openness, transparency, economic efficiency and financial sustainability to match the G7 Principle adopted in 2016 (METI, 2018). Japan also pushed the quality infrastructure standard at the G20 by taking advantage of its role as the host, leading to the adoption of the G20 Principles for Quality Infrastructure Investment (the G20 Principles) in June 2019. Considering G20's prominence in global economic governance as the world's leading and most comprehensive forum, the adoption of the G20 Principle has been the culmination of Japan's four years of persistent efforts to make the 'quality' a standard for infrastructure investment. Subsequently, Japan has been working closely with multilateral agencies and Banks' to enhance the awareness of G20 Principles and make them into their practice (Yoshimatsu, 2021). For instance, the Japanese government partnered with the World Bank Group to establish the Quality Infrastructure Investment (QII) Partnership in 2019 to provide grant support for incorporating the G20 Principles into the banks infrastructure projects and raise awareness of the quality dimensions of infrastructure (World Bank, 2016).

This phase also witnessed significant momentum on the part of Japan to build an international coalition on the issue of infrastructure development aimed at promoting the quality infrastructure standards and pooling resources to balance BRI through alternate infrastructure financing. In this regard, Japan has been working closely with the US and Australia and launched the Trilateral Partnership for Infrastructure Investment in the Indo-Pacific in November 2018 (MOFA, 2018). Its objective was to provide regional countries with an alternative, transparent source of infrastructure funding and encourage the participation of private enterprises. In November 2019, under the trilateral framework, Blue Dot Network (BDN) was initiated as a body to certify the international quality standards of infrastructure projects based on the G20 (Yanagida, 2021). Though primarily a certification body, BDN also provides access to US$ 60 billion in capital in loans or equity through the US International Development Finance Corporation (US-IDFC).

Infrastructure cooperation also has emerged as an important pillar of Australia, India, Japan and the US, Quadrilateral Dialogue or the QUAD. At the Japan-US-Australia-India consultation in November 2018, senior officials in charge of foreign affairs committed to supporting overall economic development that "fosters the development of quality infrastructure based on international standards, such as openness, transparency, economic efficiency, and debt sustainability" (MOFA, 2018). At the first QUAD physical summit in September 2021, the QUAD infrastructure partnership was announced (White House, 2021). On the multilateral front, Japan has also backed the American-led Build Back Better World (B3W) initiative at the Cornwall G7 Summit in June 2021. B3W is widely perceived as an alternative to BRI for the infrastructure development of low- and middle-income countries encouraging the participation of non-governmental actors (Panda, 2021).

On the bilateral front, Japan has been working closely with its QUAD partners, EU and ASEAN. While the US-Japan cooperation on Free and Open Indo-Pacific (FOIP) initially focused on security, it has evolved to become more comprehensive with the inclusion of issues like regional connectivity and infrastructure development. The emphasis has been on three fronts; promotion of the quality infrastructure standards, synchronisation of aid and infrastructure agencies of the two countries and digital infrastructure partnership in the third country (Yanagida, 2020). Digital cooperation has received much attention, especially amidst the COVID pandemic. Significant progress in this direction has been the signing of an agreement on Japan-US Cooperation on Energy Infrastructure in Third Countries in 2017 (METI, 2017) and the launching of the US-Japan Global Digital Connectivity Partnership (GDCP) in May 2021 (State Department, 2021).

The highlight of Japan-EU infrastructure partnership has been the signing of the "Partnership on Sustainable Connectivity and Quality Infrastructure" in September 2019 (MOFA, 2019). The agreement was based on a strong convergence of interest articulated at April 2019, Japan-EU Summit. At the Summit, Tokyo and Brussels, affirmed their commitment to establishing a Connectivity Partnership based on sustainability as a shared value, quality infrastructure and their belief in the benefits of a level playing field (Godehardt and Karoline, 2020). They agreed to work on all dimensions of connectivity, bilaterally and multilaterally, including digital, transport, energy and people-to-people exchanges based on the principles of quality infrastructure (MOFA, 2019). To contribute to the funding of the EU-Japan partnership's implementation, the European Investment Bank (EIB) signed two memoranda of understanding: one with the Japan Bank for International Cooperation (JBIC) and another with Nippon Export and Investment Insurance (NEXI).

While Japan-India relations have been on the upswing over the last decade, the agenda of infrastructure development acquired salience, especially after the announcement of the BRI. Considering their shared apprehension about BRI (*Hindustan Times*, 2019), it's only natural for the two countries to work together in promoting an alternative narrative of international infrastructure development in the Indo-Pacific. Since 2017, Tokyo and New Delhi have placed "quality infrastructure" at the centre of their bilateral relationship. During PM Abe's visit to India in 2017, the two countries issued a joint statement that strongly endorsed the principles of quality infrastructure and signed a long list of agreements pertaining to Japanese investments in Indian infrastructure development based on the quality principle (MOFA, 2017). The list of cooperation included infrastructure development in the Northeastern states of India, rail projects, including the Mumbai-Ahmedabad high-speed rail and metro projects in six major cities, and energy, sanitation, and "smart city" cooperation. Another important aspect of India-Japan infrastructure cooperation has been its regional dimension with an agreement to work together to integrate the Indian Ocean region and to improve connectivity links between Asia with the east coast of Africa through the joint initiative of the Asia-Africa Growth Corridor (AAGC) (ERIA, 2017). As it was announced right after the Belt and Road Forum, the AAGC has been widely perceived as a countermeasure to China's BRI. Apart from the AAGC the two countries have also been exploring infrastructure cooperation in various parts of the Indo-Pacific under the framework of the India-Japan third country partnership.

Since the adoption of the Fukuda Doctrine in 1977, Japan has emerged as the lead player in infrastructure development in Southeast Asia (Tomoo and Sayaka, 2019). The announcement of BRI forced Japan to reinvigorate its infrastructure diplomacy as it faced significant competition from Beijing. For instance, Beijing's successful bid to contract Indonesia's High-Speed Rail in 2015 over Japan resulted in a revamping of the Japanese approach through the announcement of PQI not only committed more resources but also pushed the standard of quality infrastructure (Berger, 2019). Despite BRI's growing attention, Japan's infrastructure investment in ASEAN is substantially larger. Since 2000, Japan has invested roughly US$ 230 billion in infrastructure, in comparison to China's US$ 155 billion (Alegado, 2018). In August 2017, Japan enhanced its commitment to infrastructure development in ASEAN by supporting the Master Plan on ASEAN Connectivity 2025 (ASEAN, 2021). At the 22nd ASEAN-Japan Summit on November 4 2019 in Bangkok, ASEAN and Japan adopted the Joint Statement on Connectivity to further strengthen ASEAN-Japan cooperation in regional connectivity. Furthermore, at the Japan-ASEAN Summit Meeting held in November 2020, Tokyo announced the Japan-ASEAN Connectivity Initiative, in which Japan proposed that it would help strengthen land, sea, and air corridor connectivity through infrastructure development together with human resource development of 1,000 individuals over the next three years (Yanagida, 2020A). Japan has also pursued cooperation with ASEAN on digital infrastructure. In this regard, Japan and Southeast

Asian states agreed to collaborate together through the "ASEAN-Japan Fourth Industrial Revolution Initiative" which aims to facilitate private sector-led innovation, human development, and e-commerce (ASEAN, 2018).

Conclusion

Japan's response to China's BRI has been complex and has been evolving along with the evolution of BRI. It can be understood in two different phases. During the first phase (2013-2017), Japan's initial 'cold shoulder' rhetoric addressed China's infrastructure advances without naming them directly and stressed the importance of economic feasibility, creditworthiness, and quality as prerequisites for infrastructure development, thereby emphasising Japan's competitive edge. BRI also prompted the revitalisation of Japanese infrastructure diplomacy leading to the announcement of the Partnership for Quality Infrastructure (PQI) in 2015, a normative and substantive infrastructure development initiative. The phase also witnessed Japan's announcement of FOIPS, which articulates the Japanese vision of regional order in the Indo-Pacific, intending to balance Chinese assertiveness in the region.

During the second phase, the Japanese response featured a hedging strategy that involved conditional cooperation with BRI while pursuing multi-dimensional infrastructural diplomacy. Under the framework of 'China-Japan partnership in the third country', Japan proposed to engage with BRI subject to the adoption of international standards. A major factor that underpinned Tokyo's proposal of conditional engagement has been an effort to stabilise Japan-China relations in the context of the political change in the US with the election of President Donald Trump and the uncertainty caused by the intensification of the US-China strategic competition. Apart from stabilising the bilateral relations, Tokyo's conditional engagement strategy was also motivated to take advantage of economic opportunities for Japanese enterprises and to induce quality infrastructure standards in BRI practices. Japan saw an opportunity to socialise China into the standards of quality infrastructure in a situation where BRI was facing severe international criticism and pushback from partner countries after three years of its launch. The adoption of quality standards in BRI projects, as indicated at the second BRI Forum in 2019 and Beijing's adherence to the G20 Principle of Quality Infrastructure, has been the result of persistent efforts on the part of Japan to internationalise norms and principles of quality infrastructure. Simultaneously, Tokyo also intensified its efforts to balance BRI by building an international coalition on infrastructure development with like-minded countries at the multilateral and bilateral levels. Japan has been active in promoting infrastructure partnerships under QUAD, G7, and US-Japan-Australia trilateral and through bilateral partnerships with the US, EU, Australia, India and ASEAN. So far, the Japanese approach to BRI has featured a complex hedging strategy through unilateral, bilateral and multilateral balancing and conditional engagement. The overall objective seems not to contain BRI but to influence Chinese infrastructure development practice and, more broadly, its international behaviour adhering to international norms and standards, thus preserving rule-based international order.

References

Abe, Shinzo. (2015). "The Future of Asia: Be Innovative", MOFA Japan, 22 May, at https://www.mofa.go.jp/ic/dapc/page1e_000042.html. Accessed on 25 April 2022.

Abe, Shinzo. (2017). "Asia's Dream: Linking the Pacific and Eurasia", 5 June, at https://japan.kantei.go.jp/97_abe/statement/201706/1222768_11579.html. Accessed on 25 April 2022.

Abe, Shinzo. (2017). "Welcome Reception for the Third Japan-China Business Leader and Former High-Level Government Official Dialogue", at https://japan.kantei.go.jp/98_abe/actions/201712/4article4.html. Accessed on 25 April 2022.

Abe, Shinzo. (2015). "Address by Prime Minister Shinzo Abe on the occasion of the ASEAN Business & Investment Summit", 21 November, at https://japan.kantei.go.jp/97_abe/statement/201511/asean.html. Accessed on 25 April 2022.

Alegado, S. (2018). "Japan Still Beating China in Southeast Asia Infrastructure Race", Bloomberg, 9 February, at https://www.bloomberg.com/news/articles/2018-02-08/ japan-still-beating-china-in-southeast-asia-infrastructure-race. Accessed on 25 April 2022.

Asahi Shimbun. (2017). "Abe, Xi in accord on trade project but differ over North Korea", 9 July, at http://www.asahi.com/ajw/articles/AJ201707090013.html. Accessed on 25 April 2022.

ASEAN. (2018). "Chairman's Statement of the 21st ASEAN-Japan Summit Singapore", 14 November, at https://www.mofa.go.jp/files/000419668.pdf. Accessed on 25 April 2022.

ASEAN. (2021). "Overview of ASEAN-Japan Dialogue Relations", at https://asean.org/wp-content/uploads/2021/12/Overview-ASEAN-Japan-Relations-full-version-as-of-1-Dec-21.pdf. Accessed on 25 April 2022.

Basu, T. (2020). "China-Japan-US triangle: Abe's balancing act", at https://www.lowyinstitute.org/the-interpreter/china-japan-us-triangle-abe-s-balancing-act. Accessed on 25 April 2022.

Beeson, M., and Crawford, C. (2020). "Putting the BRI in Perspective: History, Hegemony and Geoeconomics", *Chinese Political Science Review.* doi:10.1007/s41111-022-00210-y. Accessed on 25 April 2022.

Berger, B. H. (2019). "ASEAN Connectivity and China–Japan Infrastructure Export Competition Challenges facing ASEAN Integration", Asia Society, at https://asiasociety.org/sites/default/files/2019-04/Chapter%2014%20ASEAN%20Connectivity%20and%20. Accessed on 25 April 2022.

ERIA. (2017). "Asia Africa Growth Corridor: Partnership for Sustainable and Innovative Development: A Vision Document", at https://www.eria.org/Asia-Africa-Growth-Corridor-Document.pdf. Accessed on 25 April 2022.

Godehardt, N., andKaroline, P.-V. (2020). "Connectivity and Geopolitics: Beware the 'New Wine in Old Bottles', Approach", at https://www.swp-berlin.org/10.18449/2020C35. Accessed on 25 April 2022.

Hindustan Times. (2019). "India and Japan can provide an alternative to BRI", at https://www.hindustantimes.com/editorials/india-and-japan-can-provide-an-alternative-to-bri/story-l55redw0C0HFywg082nHRJ.html. Accessed on 25 April 2022.

IPP. (2018). "Aim of China Belt and Road Initiative and Proposal of National Strategy to be Taken", Japan Institute for Peace Policies, 20 March, at https://ippjapan.org/archives/2646. Accessed on 25 April 2022.

Jain, P. (2019). "Japan's Foreign Aid and 'Quality' Infrastructure Projects: The Case of the Bullet Train in India", at https://www.jica.go.jp/jica-ri/publication/workingpaper/l75nbg0000153t43-att/JICA_RI_WP_No.184.pdf. Accessed on 25 April 2022.

JBIC. (2015). "Japan Bank For International Cooperation Guidelines For Confirmation Of Environmental And Social Considerations", at https://www.jbic.go.jp/wp-content/uploads/page/2013/08/36442/Environemtal_Guidelines2015.pdf. Accessed on 25 April 2022.

John, H., Scott, M., and Portelance, G. (2019). "Examining the Debt Implications of the Belt And Road Initiative from a Policy Perspective", *Journal of Infrastructure, Policy and Development*, 3(1): 139-175.

John, J. (2018). "Japan-China Relations: A New Dynamics", ICWA, at https://www.icwa.in/show_content.php?lang=1&level=3&ls_id=4917&lid=1741. Accessed on 25 April 2022.

Kantei. (2014). "Japan Revitalization Strategy: Japan's Challenge for the Future", at https://policy.asiapacificenergy.org/node/1322. Accessed on 25 April 2022.

Kantei. (2018). Press Conference by the Chief Cabinet Secretary, 8 June, at https://japan.kantei.go.jp/tyoukanpress/201806/8_p.html. Accessed on 25 April 2022.

Katada, S. (2016). "The TPP, AIIB, and Japan's Foreign Economic Strategy", East-

West Centre, at https://www.eastwestcenter.org/system/tdf/private/api125.pdf?file=1&type=node&id=35659. Accessed on 25 April 2022.

Katada, S. N., and Liao, J. (2020). "China and Japan in Pursuit of Infrastructure Investment Leadership in Asia", *Global Governance: A Review of Multilateralism and International Organizations,* 26(3), 449-472.

Koga, K. (2019). "Japan and Southeast Asia in the Indo-Pacific", in K. Springer (ed.), *Japan and Southeast Asia in the Indo-Pacific.* Perth US-Asia Center, Perth.

Mainichi Shimbun. (2018). "Japan, China to cooperate in third-country infrastructure projects", 26 October, at https://mainichi.jp/english/articles/20181026/p2g/00m/0fp/093000c. Accessed on 25 April 2022.

METI. (2016). "The 'Expanded Partnership for Quality Infrastructure' initiative directed toward the G7 Ise-Shima Summit Meeting announced", METI Japan, at https://www.meti.go.jp/english/press/2016/0523_01.html. Accessed on 25 April 2022.

METI. (2017). "Japan and the United States Affirm Advancement of Cooperation in the Fields of Energy and Infrastructure", at https://www.meti.go.jp/english/press/2017/1107_001.html. Accessed on 25 April 2022.

METI. (2018). "APEC Guidebook on Quality of Infrastructure Development and Investment Revised", at https://www.meti.go.jp/english/press/2018/1117_001.html. Accessed on 25 April 2022.

MLITT. (2014). JOIN is inaugurated today, Ministry of Land, Infrastracture, Trasport and Tourism, at https://www.mlit.go.jp/en/report/press/sogo05_hh_000018.html. Accessed on 25 April 2022.

MOFA. (2015). "Japan-China Summit Meeting", MOFA Japan, 23 April, at https://www.mofa.go.jp/a_o/c_m1/cn/page1e_000041.html. Accessed on 25 April 2022.

MOFA. (2015). "Partnership for Quality Infrastructure: Investment for Asia's Future", MOFA Japan, at https://www.mofa.go.jp/policy/oda/page18_000076.html. Accessed on 25 April 2022.

MOFA. (2016). "G7 Ise-Shima Principles for Promoting Quality Infrastructure", MOFA Japan, at https://www.mofa.go.jp/files/000160272.pdf. Accessed on 25 April 2022.

MOFA. (2016). "Free and Open Indo-Pacific Strategy", MOFA Japan, at https://www.mofa.go.jp/files/000406631.pdf. Accessed on 25 April 2022.

MOFA. (2017). "Japan-India Joint Statement", at https://www.mofa.go.jp/files/000289999.pdf. Accessed on 25 April 2022.

MOFA. (2018). "Japan-Australia-India-U.S. Consultations", at https://www.mofa.go.jp/press/release/press1e_000099.html. Accessed on 25 April 2022.

MOFA. (2018). "Prime Minister Abe Visits China", MOFA Japan, at https://www.mofa.go.jp/a_o/c_m1/cn/page3e_000958.html. Accessed on 25 April 2022.

MOFA. (2018). "Joint Statement of the Governments of Australia, Japan, and the United States of America on the Trilateral Partnership for Infrastructure Investment in the Indo-Pacific", at https://www.mofa.go.jp/mofaj/

files/000420368.pdf. Accessed on 25 April 2022.

MOFA. (2019). "Partnership on Sustainable Connectivity and Quality Infrastructure between the EU and Japan", at https://www.mofa.go.jp/files/000521432.pdf. Accessed on 25 April 2022.

Nikkei Asia Review. (2017). "Japan to help finance China's Belt and Road projects", 6 December, at https://asia.nikkei.com/Politics-Economy/International-Relations/Japan-to-help-finance-China-s-Belt-and-Road-projects. Accessed on 25 April 2022.

Nikkei Asian Review. (2017). "Nippon Express climbs aboard China's Belt and Road Initiative", 30 September, at https://asia.nikkei.com/Business/Companies/Nippon-Express-climbs-aboard-China-s-Belt-and-Road-Initiativ. Accessed on 25 April 2022.

Panda, J. (2021). "Build Back Better World Initiative: A Partnership Against or Beyond China?", at https://www.idsa.in/issuebrief/build-back-better-world-initiative-jpanda-090821. Accessed on 25 April 2022.

Pascha, W. (2019). "The new dynamics of multilateral cooperation mechanisms in East Asia", in Y. Li, and M. Taube (eds), *How China's Silk Road Initiative is Changing the Global Economic Landscape.* Routledge.

Pascha, W. (2020). "The quest for infrastructure development from a 'market creation' perspective: China's 'Belt and Road', Japan's 'Quality Infrastructure' and the EU's 'Connecting Europe and Asia'", *International Economics and Economic Policy*, 17, 687-704.

State Department. (2021). "Joint Statement on the Launch of the U.S.-Japan Global Digital Connectivity Partnership", at https://www.state.gov/joint-statement-on-the-launch-of-the-u-s-japan-global-digital-connectivity-partnership. Accessed on 25 April 2022.

Tomoo, K., and Sayaka, U. (2019). "Japanese Infrastructure Investment in Southeast Asia", S. Rajaratnam School of International Studies, at http://hdl.handle.net/11540/10170. Accessed on 25 April 2022.

White House. (2021). Fact Sheet: Quad Leaders' Summit, at https://www.whitehouse.gov/briefing-room/statements-releases/2021/09/24/fact-sheet-quad-leaders-summit/#:~:text=On%20September%2024%2C%20President%20Biden,Leaders'%20Summit%20of%20the%2. Accessed on 25 April 2022.

Williams, J., Robinson, C., and Bouzarovski, S. (2020). "China's Belt and Road Initiative and the emerging geographies of global urbanisation", *Geographical Journal*, 128-140.

World Bank. (2016). "QII: Advancing Green, Resilient, Inclusive Development", at https://www.worldbank.org/en/programs/quality-infrastructure-investment-partnership/overview. Accessed on 25 April 2022.

Yanagida, K. (2020). "Strengthening US-Japan-Southeast Asia Cooperation on Connectivity in the Indo-Pacific", at https://www.eastwestcenter.org/system/tdf/private/apb538.pdf?file=1&type=node&id=38921.Accessed on 25 April 2022.

Yanagida, K. (2020a). "Japan's Connectivity Initiatives in the Free and Open Indo-Pacific: An Economic Assessment", Konrad-Adenauer-Stiftung, Singapore, at https://www.kas.de/documents/288143/10822438/Panorama_2019_02_4c_v5d_KensukeYanagida. Accessed on 25 April 2022.

Yanagida, K. (2021). "Japan's Connectivity Initiatives in the Indo-Pacific", at https://www.nbr.org/publication/japans-connectivity-initiatives-in-the-indo-pacific/. Accessed on 25 April 2022.

Yoshimatsu, H. (2017). "Japan's export of infrastructure systems: pursuing twin goals through developmental means", *The Pacific Review*, at doi:10.1080/09512748.2016.1276953.

Yoshimatsu, H. (2021). "Japan's strategic response to China's geo-economic presence: quality infrastructure as a diplomatic tool", *The Pacific Review*, at doi:10.1080/09512748.2021.1947356.

Zhao, H. (2018). "Chinese and Japanese infrastructure investment in Southeast Asia: from rivalry to cooperation?", at https://www.ide.go.jp/English/Publish/Reports/Dp/689.html?media=pc. Accessed on 25 April 2022.

13. BRI: Responses from South Korea

Jojin V. John

This chapter is an account of South Korea's (Korea hereafter) approach to China's Belt and Road Initiative (BRI). Though not directly a part of any designated BRI project, Korea has shown a keen interest since its announcement. Having established a strong economic relations with China over the last decades, the initiative was seen as a new economic opportunity. In particular, Seoul viewed BRI as complementing its own efforts to integrate the Korean Peninsula to Eurasia through multi-modal transport and industrial linkages. Successive Korean governments have also seen BRI as an opportunity to induce reform and opening up of North Korea. However, influenced by the growing negative narrative of BRI and the intensification of the US-China strategic competition pushed Korea to undertake a cautious approach to BRI.

Korea-China Relations: Brief Background

After having fought the Korean War (1950-53) on the opposite side, China and Korea had no diplomatic relations during the Cold War period. Following their diplomatic normalisation in 1992, bilateral ties have seen rapid development. The status of the relations was periodically upgraded to reflect the expansion of the relations, "friendly cooperative relationship" in 1992, "collaborative partnership for the 21st century" in 1998, "comprehensive cooperative partnership" in 2003, "strategic cooperative partnership" in 2008, and "enriched strategic cooperative partnership" in 2014 (Ye, 2017).

Economic relations remained the centre pillar of Korea-China relations. By 2004 China had become South Korea's leading trading partner. In 2015, Seoul and Beijing inked a free trade agreement. Bilateral trade reached a record figure of US$ 240 billion in 2017. South Korea's trade with China exceeds its combined trade with US and Japan, the second and third largest trade partners. China has become the top destination for South Korean investment, with a total stock of about US$ 52 billion (John, 2018).

Despite the rapid expansion of bilateral relations, the two countries had intermittent troubles. Following the sinking of the South Korea corvette Chenonon and Yeongpyondong shelling by North Korea in 2010, different perspectives between China and Korea were staged concerning the future of the Korean Peninsula, such as policy orientations of the two towards their common neighbour, North Korea, and perception and acceptance of the role of the US in the East Asian security structure (Ye, 2017). As a result, bilateral mutual trust rapidly deteriorated. However, the relations were patched up with the political change in both countries. President Park Guen-hye and President Xi Jinping both came to power in 2013, and spearheaded unprecedented enthusiasm to embrace the most robust level of relations since normalisation. In July 2014, President Xi visited Seoul, breaking the tradition of visiting Pyongyang first as the new Chinese leader. Many interpreted Park's attendance at the Chinese celebration of the 70th anniversary of the end of World War II in 2015 as the peak of China-Korea relations.

After the DPRK's fifth nuclear test and ballistic missile launch 2016, differences in the two countries' policy priorities began to grow more apparent. Korea's decision to install the US THAAD missile defence system in July 2016 further deteriorated the relations between Seoul and Beijing. In response to the THAAD installation, Beijing imposed "informal" sanctions on certain sectors of the bilateral economic interaction and snubbed diplomatic engagement. The Hyundai Research Institute estimated the Chinese sanctions cost a loss of 8.5 trillion won (US$ 7.5 billion) in South Korea's gross domestic product for 2017 (John, 2018).

Soon after assuming office in May 2017, President Moon Jae-in reached out to normalise the relations. By adopting a 'Three No" position on the THAAD issue, the Moon administration managed to make a breakthrough in the relations. In the context of an intensification of China-US strategic competition, the Moon administration adopted an approach of 'balanced diplomacy', to maintain Korea's alliance relations with Washington and economic partnership with Beijing.

Korea's Approach to Belt and Road Initiative

Park Guen-hye, the daughter of former President of Korea Park Chung-hee, advocated unification as a jackpot and made the unification of the Korean Peninsula the main focus of her administration's foreign policy (Ji-Eun, 2014). Recognising that support from Beijing, as well as that of Washington, is necessary for the unification of the Korean peninsula, President Park had made an unusual effort to strengthen Seoul's relationship with China (Hwang, 2014). The overall positive attitude of the Park Geun-hye administration towards Beijing, as well as the policy of moving deeper into Eurasia, which the South Korean administrations consistently pursued, provided the context for Korea's interest in BRI. Korean support for BRI under President Park was expected Chinese backing for her approach to North Korea (Yuanzhe, 2016). The 'One Belt One Road (OBOR) initiated in 2013, which was later renamed 'Belt and Road Initiative' (BRI), with its "Vision and Actions" plans to make the three northeastern provinces of China (Liaoning, Jilin, and Heilongjiang) to become sea-land 'windows' linking Russia, Mongolia, and other areas in the Far East complemented Park administration's Eurasia Initiative (EAI) (MOEF, 2015).

Under the vision of EAI unveiled in 2013, the Park administration called for the interconnection of transportation, logistics, and energy networks across Europe and Asia. It promoted the "Silk Road Express" vision and was keen on exploiting the potential of the Arctic Ocean to develop intermodal transport and logistics network in the region (Taehwan, 2015). Seoul aimed to connect South Korea, North Korea, Russia, China, Central Asia, and Europe railways through the Silk Road Express and create an energy network of power grids and gas and oil pipelines in Eurasia. By implementing EAI and further involvement in Eurasia integration processes, Seoul is expected to save transportation costs and diversify trade markets for energy and mineral resources and agricultural products. The project also has been envisaged to contribute to peace building on the Korean Peninsula. In particular, EAI envisaged "building corridors of trust and peace on the Korean Peninsula" through the Rajin-Khasan logistics project implemented by Russia and North Korea and the more active role of the Pyongyang (MOFA, 2015). Seoul counted on the synergy effect of the combination of its own and Chinese initiatives (Jaeho, 2015). However, the EAI has been put on the back burner due to the troubled inter-Korean relations. In this regard, the Park administration has been seeking Chinese help to pursue North Korea's participation. Beijing has already been engaged in implementing business projects related to transportation infrastructure in North Korea (Jin and Ducruet, 2007).

Korea's growing relations with Beijing has also been reflected in its decision to join the Beijing-initiated Asian Infrastructure Development Bank, despite Washington's protest. Furthermore, at the 13th Korea-China Finance Ministers 'Meeting, Seoul and Beijing selected EAI and BRI as the focus of bilateral cooperation in 2015. In October 2015, during a meeting between President Park and Chinese Premier Li Keqiang, the leaders noted the similarities between the South Korean Eurasian Initiative and China's BRI. They signed an MoU on regional development initiatives and overseas market research (MOFA, 2015). They also agreed to fund a joint study to explore the potential of third-country cooperation.

However, the discussion and implementation of joint plans were suspended following the decision of the Park administration in July 2016 to deploy the US THAAD anti-missile systems in the aftermath of North Korea's 5th nuclear test and long-range missile tests. This decision caused an adverse reaction from China, which imposed 'informal 'economic sanctions against Korean exports to China and restricting Chinese tourist flow to Korea (John, 2018). The THAAD incident deteriorated the relations to its lowest point since Seoul and Beijing established diplomatic relations.

From the very beginning, Moon Jae-in, who assumed office in May 2017, has taken measures to reset the relations with China. Unlike his predecessor, who focused on unification, the Moon administration emphasised establishing a peace regime in the Korean Peninsula and strengthening inter-Korea ties. Along with the Korean Peninsula peace initiative, the Moon administration advocated 'balanced diplomacy' in its relations with Beijing and Washington in the context of intensifying strategic rivalry between the two. Soon after assuming office Moon sent a delegation to the First Belt and Forum in May 2017, which was seen as an opportunity to improve relations with Beijing (Snyder and Byun, 2017). Korea also sent a delegation to the second BRF Forum in 2019 led by Deputy Prime Minister and Finance Minister Hong Nam-ki.

President Moon's approach to BRI was driven by an effort to find synergy between BRI and his New Northern Policy (NNP) and New South Policy (NSP), the two-pronged initiative announced to replace the Park administration's EAI (Lee, 2019). Under the framework of the NNP, the Moon administration aimed to develop economic cooperation with the countries of Eurasia, which, in terms of their industrial and economic characteristics, are divided into three groups: Russia, China (primarily the three northeastern provinces) and Central Asia. The NNP was closely related to the concept of the "New Economic Map on the Korean Peninsula" aimed at "economic unification" of the Korean Peninsula—through the development of the economic ties between the two Korean and the creation of a common market. In practice, this concept is planned to be implemented through the creation of three regional economic belts connecting the South and North Korea and promoting Northeast Asian regional economic integration. NSP, on the other hand, was emphasised to improve Seoul's relations with ASEAN and India.

The NNP had many areas of convergence with BRI, particularly projects involving the three Northeastern provinces of China. From a Korean perspective, the cooperation aimed to develop and promote projects in connection with the China-Mongolia-Russia Economic Corridor initiative, increasing the use of the Trans-China Railway (TCR) and Trans-Mongolian Railway (TMGR) and ultimately reconnecting ROK and North Korean railways (PCNEC, 2018). During his first visit to China in December 2017, President Moon highlighted convergence between BRI and Seoul's connectivity initiatives in the region by saying that,

> The core of the Belt and Road Initiative is the construction of six economic corridors. However, there is an empty space here. The Belt and Road Economic Corridor is not connected to the eastern end of Eurasia and the Korean Peninsula, where the continent and ocean meet. If the connection between the Trans-Korean Railway and the Trans-Siberian Railway, which Korea is actively promoting, meets the economic corridors of China, Mongolia and Russia, the railway, air, and sea transport networks of the Eurasian continent will form in all directions... I am confident a link between the One Belt, One Road initiative and New North, New South policies will lead to peace and joint prosperity in the region. (Moon, 2017)

During the visit, Seoul and Beijing reaffirmed their 2015 agreement to promote the third-country partnership. Furthermore, an MoU was signed between Korea's Trade Insurance Corporation and China's Construction Bank to support the joint advancement of companies in the infrastructure market. During President Moon's visit, China has also given the sanction for constructing three industrial parks to be jointly operated by South Korean and Chinese firms. The industrial parks are located in Yancheong in Jiangsu Province, Yantai in Shandong Province and Huizhou in Guangdong Province. The agreement to establish the three industrial park projects was signed during the Park administration. However, they were on hold for more than a year as the deployment of the THAAD strained bilateral ties. Beijing has been promoting the three projects as part of Seoul-Beijing cooperation under the BRI. In addition to the three industrial parks, the two countries have established a Korea-China International Cooperation Demonstration Zone in Changchun in the Jilin province of China, which the Chinese side has been promoting as part of the BRI initiative (PRN, 2020). However, the Korean side has dismissed Beijing's claim that they are part of the two countries' BRI cooperation.

Since 2018 with positive trends in inter-Korean rapprochement, the hopes for the implementation of the trans-Korean Railway project revived as well. In 2018, Seoul and Beijing agreed to revise and improve the previously concluded Memorandum of Understanding on the South Korean Eurasian Initiative and the Chinese BRI (MOEF, 2018).

During a meeting with Chinese Premier Li Keqiang in December 2019, ROK President Moon Jae-in proposed China's cooperation to realise Seoul's vision of East Asian rail community with the participation of both Koreas, Japan, China, Russia, Mongolia and the US. The Chinese premier, in turn, expressed the readiness of the PRC to participate in this project (CheongWaDae, 2019). However, the unresolved North Korean nuclear problem is an obstacle to its implementation. The efforts to foster collaboration between the BRI and NNP/NSP have been continued despite the disruptions caused by the COVID-19 pandemic. During the Korea-China Joint Economic Committee took place in December 2021, Seoul and Beijing adopted the Korea-China Joint Plan for Economic Cooperation (2021-2025), a plan for economic cooperation between the two countries for the next five years, During the meeting they also agreed to foster collaborative efforts between Korea's New Southern and Northern Policies and China's BRI (MOFA, 2021).

Apart from President Moon's peace initiative, potential economic benefit has also been the key motivating factor for Korea's interest in the BRI. Participation in BRI was expected to bring profit to South Korean companies and contribute to the growth of the economy, while delay or non-participation can result in a loss of positions and the displacement of South Korean businesses from the countries involved in this initiative (Hundt and Kim, 2019). However, in the context of the intensified strategic competition between the US and China, among the Korean elites, it is widely believed that Korea should distinguish between mutually beneficial cooperation and political interests in everything related to policy towards China. It was suggested to carry out selective economic cooperation with China while adhering to the strategic focus on the US (Han, 2015). In a context where BRI was increasingly interpreted as China's strategy toward achieving hegemony, Seoul has become more cautious in its approach to BRI. The balancing act in Moon's foreign policy has also been reflected in Korea's approach to BRI.

Conclusion

Compared to other allies of the US, Korea's response to the Chinese BRI has been quite different. Korea's approach to the BRI has been shaped by a combination of economic, geopolitical and inter-Korea factors. Unlike other US allies, Korea views BRI as a potential economic opportunity and complements its efforts to enhance peace and security in the Korean Peninsula. Korea's efforts to strengthen its relations with Beijing under President Park and President Moon and their respective Eurasian economic connectivity initiatives shaped Seoul's optimistic outlook towards the BRI. Though the North Korean policies of the Park and Moon administrations were different, both viewed collaboration with BRI as means to achieve their respective objectives. President Moon even referred to the historical significance of BRI for the Korean Peninsula, which he dubbed "the last stop on the Silk Road" (Moon, 2017).

However, political and security factors have been a major stumbling block to Korea's participation in the BRI projects. During the Park administration, despite the headway made towards strengthening relations with Beijing, the diverging security interest between Seoul and Beijing has emerged to become a major factor that limited Korea's cooperation in BRI. It is also important to note that BRI was still in its early stage during the Park administration, and the negative implications of BRI were not a significant issue at that time. Unlike the Moon administration, President Park was less constrained by the US-China strategic rivalry in its approach to the BRI, which became a major issue after the inauguration of President Doland Trump in 2017. The pressure to choose a side forced the Moon administration to adopt a 'balanced diplomatic' approach to its relations with the US and China, which further limited Korea's manoeuvring space for Korea's participation in BRI. The second half of the Moon Presidency has witnessed a more cautious approach to BRI. Despite proposing to explore the synergy between NNP/NSP and BRI, the Moon administration has become reticent about Korea's position on BRI in an attempt to maintain independent and balanced posturing between BRI and the US-led Indo-Pacific initiative. To overcome the geopolitical limitation in pursuing an economic interest, Seoul has been pushing the idea of a third-country partnership with China without framing such activities under the BRI framework.

The political change in Korea with the inauguration of Yoon Seok-yeol as the new President in May 2022 is expected to cause a change in Korean approach to BRI. Yoon administration has advocated a new approach to Korean foreign policy, marking a clear departure from the Moon administration. In an attempt to overhaul the balance diplomacy practised by President Moon, the new administration has called for strengthening Korea's alliance relations with the US and reset in Korea's China policy. With a hard-line approach to North Korea and a proactive role in Indo-Pacific, Korea's foreign policy approach is more aligned with the US, hence is expected to have an impact on Korea's approach to relations with China and BRI in particular. However, the new Korean administration will continue to promote mutually beneficial economic projects with China as long as it does not contradict its relations with the US.

References

CheongWaDae. (2019). "Results of Meeting with People's Republic of China Premier Li Keqiang", 23 December, at https://english1.president.go.kr/BriefingSpeeches/Briefings/486. Accessed on 23 May 2022.

Han, W. (2015). "The China Paradox", 1 June, at https://koreajoongangdaily.joins.com/news/article/article.aspx?aid=3004874&ref=mobile. Accessed on 23 May 2022.

Hundt, D., and Kim, S. (2019). "Elite Opinion and the 'Belt and Road' Debate in South Korea", *Pacific Affairs*, 27-48.

Hwang, J. (2014). "The ROK's China Policy under Park Geun-hye: A New Model of ROK-PRC Relations", CFR, 14 August, at https://www.brookings.edu/research/the-roks-china-policy-under-park-geun-hye-a-new-model-of-rok-prc-relations/. Accessed on 23 May 2022.

Jaeho, H. (2015). "China's "One Belt, One Road" Project Can Sync up with Korean Trade Efforts," *Global Times*, at https://www.globaltimes.cn/content/938849.shtml. Accessed on 23 May 2022.

Ji-Eun, S. (2014). "Unification may be jackpot: Park", *Korea Joongang Daily*, at https://koreajoongangdaily.joins.com/news/article/article.aspx?aid=2983129. Accessed on 23 May 2022.

Jin, C. J., and Ducruet, C. (2007). "Rajin-Seonbong, new gateway of Northeast Asia", *The Annals of Regional Science*, 927-950.

John, J. (2018). "Towards a "New Normal": Explaining Developments in South Korea-China Relations", ICWA, 27 February, at https://www.icwa.in/show_content.php?lang=1&level=3&ls_id=4935&lid=1734. Accessed on 23 May 2022.

Lee, J. (2019). "Korea's New Southern Policy: Motivations of 'Peace Cooperation' and Implications for the Korean Peninsula", Asan Institute, 21 June, at http://en.asaninst.org/contents/koreas-new-southern-policy-motivations-of-peace-cooperation-and-implications-for-the-korean-peninsula/. Accessed on 23 May 2022.

MOEF. (2015). "Korea and China Select Eurasia Initiative and "One Belt and One Road" as Focus for Bilateral Cooperation This Year", at http://english.moef.go.kr/pc/selectTbPressCenterDtl.do%3Bjs. Accessed on 23 May 2022.

MOEF. (2018). "Korea and China Agree on Strengthening Economic Cooperation", at https://english.moef.go.kr/ec/selectTbEconomicDtl.do?boardCd=E0007&seq=4435. Accessed on 23 May 2022.

MOFA. (2015). "Diplomatic White Paper", at https://www.mofa.go.kr/www/brd/m_4106/down.do?brd_id=8701&seq=357609&data_tp=A&file_seq=2. Accessed on 23 May 2022.

MOFA. (2015). "President Park Geun-hye attends MOU signing ceremony between Korea and China, 31 October, at https://www.mofa.go.kr/www/brd/m_4076/view.do?seq=356908&srchFr=&srchTo=&srchWord=&srchTp=&multi_itm_seq=0&itm_seq_1=0&itm_seq_2=0&company_cd=&company_nm=. Accessed on 23 May 2022.

MOFA. (2021). "Outcome of 25th Meeting of Korea-China Joint Economic Committee", 2 December, at https://www.mofa.go.kr/eng/brd/m_5676/view.do?seq=321941. Accessed on 23 May 2022.

Moon, Jae-in (2017). "President Moon, Keynote Speech at the Korea-China Third-Country Industry Cooperation Forum", 16 December, at https://www.news1.kr/articles/?3181975. Accessed on 23 May 2022.

PCNEC. (2018). "Establishment of New Northern Economic Cooperation Promotion Strategy and Basic Plan", 28 December, at https://bukbang.go.kr/bukbang/info_data/references/?boardId=bbs_0000000000000013&mode=view&cntId=13&category=%EC%A0%95%EC%B1%85&pageIdx=7. Accessed on 23 May 2022.

PRN. (2020). "Global Promotional Conference Of China-rok (changchun) International Cooperation Demonstration Zone Held In Beijing",PR Newswire, 5 September, at https://en.prnasia.com/releases/apac/global-promotional-conference-of-china-rok-changchun-international-cooperation-demonstration-zone-held-in-beijing-290558.shtml. Accessed on 23 May 2022.

Snyder, S., and Byun, S.-W. (2017). "North Korea, THAAD Overshadow Beijing and Seoul's 25th Anniversary", *Comparative Connections*, pp. 81-90.

Taehwan, K. (2015). "Beyond Geopolitics: South Korea's Eurasia Initiative as a New Nordpolitik", Asan Institute, 16 February, at https://theasanforum.org/beyond-geopolitics-south-koreas-eurasia-initiative-as-a-new-nordpolitik/. Accessed on 23 May 2022.

Ye, M. (2017). *China-South Korea Relations in the New Era: Challenges and Opportunities.* Lanham, MD: Lexington Books.

Yuanzhe, R. (2016). "China's Perspective on the China-ROK Strategic Partnership", Jstor, at http://www.jstor.com/stable/resrep10996.7

14. China-Mongolia Relations and the Economic Corridor

Sudeep Kumar

Abstract

The chapter explains the historical engagements between Mongolia and China. In the pre-Cold War era, the Mongolia was dominated by the erstwhile Soviet Union. In the post-Cold War era, however, China dominates Mongolia while the contested political space is divided between pro-Russian and pro-Chinese legislators in the Mongolian parliament. Both China and Russia seem to have a tacit understanding of providing a security umbrella and economic cover to Mongolia. However, the rise of China has intensified the debate about the "China Threat" in the Mongolian policy circle and issues such as its geopolitical implications and sovereignty and security concerns are dominating the debate. In this context, the chapter tries to critically assess the transport and connectivity aspects of the Belt and Road Initiative (BRI), China-Mongolia-Russia Economic Corridor (CMREC), in particular the section of Tianjin-Ulaanbaatar-Ulan-Ude Central Route, its current status and geopolitical dimensions, ecological concerns and other issues related with it.

China-Mongolia Relations: Introduction

The establishment of China's Manchu-ruled Qing dynasty in 1644 divided the Mongolian region into Inner Mongolia and Outer Mongolia. Since 1636, Inner Mongolia, as a political-geographical unit, has been part of the Chinese empire and its subsequent governments. However, Outer Mongolia came under Manchu-Qing domination between 1691 and 1921 (Soni, 2009).

The fall of China's Qing Empire in 1911 resulted in the establishment of the Sun Yat-Sen led the Republic of China, which created a favourable environment for the declaration of the independence movement in Outer Mongolia. Furthermore, the declaration of independence movement created a backlash and repercussions for the Sun Yat-Sen led government in the Inner Mongolian region of the Republic of China (1911-49). After a decade-long independence movement, an independent Outer Mongolian state was established in 1921. Against this backdrop, the Republican China was critical of Outer Mongolia's declaration of the independence movement and knew its implications for its administered Inner Mongolian region. For this reason, the Sun Yat-Sen administration argued that Outer Mongolia was an integral part of the territory of the Qing Empire; therefore, it should remain under the control of the successive Chinese governments. Historically, the rise of Qing China had not been possible without occupying the geostrategic locations of the Inner Mongolian region. Qing rulers built an alliance with Inner Mongolian tribes to protect themselves from the dangers of any potential external threats on its northern borders. Furthermore, Qing China built 'the Great Wall' to protect themselves from the attacks of the tribes in the Outer Mongolian region.

In the present context, the discussion on the rise of China and its geopolitical implications is of great significance for Mongolia's foreign policy in the 21st century. At the same time, expanding geopolitical interests and its preference for a "stable" neighbourhood has become a preferred policy choice for China. Similarly, Mongolia seeks to overcome its landlocked geography by connecting Central Asian, North-East Asian, Far Eastern, Chinese and Russian markets (Soni, 2006).

Mongolia is a landlocked state located between two big neighbours China and Russia. Mongolia seeks to maintain a balance between development and security. To achieve this goal, Mongolia's 1992 constitutional reforms paved the way for the process of democratisation, which built institutions and pursued constitutional democratic polity to become a modern sovereign nation-state within the international community (Bedeski, 2008).

Against this backdrop, there have been three prominent factors in determining China-Mongolia Relations over the years, which are as follows: (a) Chinese claims to Outer Mongolia and the Mongolian memory of Manchu oppression (1691-1921); (b) China's subjugation of Inner Mongolian populations and Mongolian fear of complete Sinicisation (1636 Onwards); (c) China's discriminatory policies in Inner Mongolia (Green, 1986).

Until the disintegration of the Soviet Union in 1989, China-Mongolia relations were subordinate to Soviet Union-Mongolia relations. In the post-Cold War era, China became a significant political and trading partner that led to the substantial rise in Chinese investments in infrastructure development, which helped consolidate Chinese economic and strategic interests in Mongolia (Soni, 2009). As of now, it seems that Mongolia has been able to maintain an optimal balance between its immediate neighbours, Russia and China. At the same time, it is trying to gradually increase the roles of the foreign powers such as Japan, South Korea, India, and the European Union (EU) as the 'Third Neighbours' to reduce Mongolian overreliance on China and Russia (Soni, 2018).

The "China Threat" Debate

The BRI was launched to expand Chinese strategic interests, which makes Mongolia cautious. Within the context of the BRI and CMREC, China is involved in various infrastructure and connectivity projects in Mongolia. However, the major concern is that China can influence local leaders and administrators to meddle in the political process of Mongolia. The democratic election and change in political leadership shift the political inclinations between China and Russia. Because of this reason, even Chinese policymakers acknowledge conceivable risk factors in successfully implementing CMREC projects (Pei, 2015). China's one-party system and its strategic investments have the leverage to exploit the fault lines in Mongolia's democratic election process in the long term. However, some Chinese experts believe that the change in democratic government and approach of the Western world can impact and delay the implementation of BRI and CMREC projects in Mongolia (Xue, 2016).

The developing countries, including Mongolia, are at a risk for BRI investments because of the under-developed or closed market, infrastructure and connectivity projects, and juvenile legal system; hence, these possible risks including different political systems and their performance, will produce discrepancies in the perception of BRI investments. Another risk factor is the conflict of interests due to the differences in economic strategies between China and many BRI countries; for example, in this case, the BRI participating countries giving preferential treatment to local labour-intensive industries using domestic legislation (Alicia, 2013).

The China-Mongolia-Russia Economic Corridor provides insights into the intricacies of China's BRI and its "debt-trap" diplomacy, which has been of particular concern for Mongolian policymakers. Against this backdrop, Mongolia has been following a "Double Balancing Policy"[1] to maintain balanced relations with landlocked neighbours China and Russia while looking for 'Third Neighbours'. For example, Mongolia encouraged China's entry into the oil sector to balance the Russian dominance. At the same time, Mongolia seeks to reduce its coal exports to avoid overdependence on the Chinese market. Mongolia has encouraged foreign investors, such as India, Japan, South Korea, the EU, and others, with the sole intention of balancing the overdependence of Chinese and Russian investments (Alicia, 2013). Interestingly, both China and Russia are watching the incoming foreign direct investments with scepticism; however, they are unwilling to take the risks of confrontation or criticism in Mongolia's political, economic, and social circle.

Mongolia is not a full member of the Chinese-dominated Shanghai Cooperation Organisation (SCO) and Russian-dominated Eurasian Economic Union (EEU), which indicates its willingness to conduct independent external economic and foreign policies. It is to be noted that Mongolia joined SCO as an observer state in 2004. Mongolia looks to Russia as a security provider while it now considers China as an economic opportunity. Russia's actions like debt cancellation, free visa regime, and vaccine diplomacy have strengthened people-to-people contacts between Mongolia and Russia. But, a common concern for Russia and Mongolia is that Russia finds itself in a tight spot to match China's increasing economic footprint in Mongolia (Radchenko and Jargalsaikhan, 2021). Recently, Mongolia welcomed China's construction of roadways, the improved fuel supplies and haulage services along the Central Route of the CMREC. However, the main challenges, such as Mongolia's landlocked location as a geostrategic buffer state, low financing, and rail gauge incompatibility between Russian and Chinese standards, have been the main reasons behind the delayed implementation of the CMREC projects. Given the traditional Sino-Russian strategic competition in Mongolia, perhaps short and mid-term investments from India, Japan, South Korea, the EU, and others could help develop Mongolia as a pivotal transit and logistic hub for the Eurasian region (Bazarsad, Sukhbaatar and Jargalsaikhan, 2021).

BRI in Mongolia: An Overview

The BRI encompasses six international corridors to link the Eurasian landmass through transport and connectivity projects. At the same time, the usage of maritime routes for trade and transit purposes to connect China to Oceania, African and European markets via the South China Sea and the Indian Ocean is called the '21st Century Maritime Silk Road'. President Xi launched the 'Silk Road Economic Belt' in September 2013 in Astana, and the 21st Century Maritime Silk Road in October 2013 in the Parliament of Indonesia. As a meta-project, BRI keeps expanding by linking all existing projects, free economic zones and ongoing projects at the bilateral, regional and multilateral levels. In the first Belt and Road Forum for the International Cooperation (14-15 May 2017), the BRI launched—the Digital Silk Road - to build digital connectivity through 5G networks. One year later, China launched—the Polar Silk Road—to develop the Arctic shipping lanes through its first Arctic Policy White Paper in 2018. Under the BRI framework, China's priorities include five areas of cooperation to boost policy coordination, infrastructure connectivity, free flows of trade and investment, financial integration, and people-to-people contacts (Parepa, 2020). China prioritises 'policy coordination' to implement the other four areas of cooperation to implement the BRI projects successfully. The policy document, 'Vision and Actions on Jointly Building Belt and Road', calls for the promotion of cooperation, construction of macro-policy exchanges and communication mechanisms, expansion of common interest, enhancement of political trust, and achievement of a new cooperative consensus (Chen and Wu, 2019).

The BRI's primary motivations could be domestic such as closing the developmental gap between coastal and non-coastal regions, utilising excessive manufacturing capacity, using its foreign currency reserve, and securing high-quality development in the manufacturing sector to bolster internal political stability through steady economic growth ultimately. All these factors are important in generating political legitimacy for the Chinese Communist Party (Hillman and Sacks, 2021).

Within the six land corridors of BRI, the China-Mongolia-Russia Economic Corridor (CMREC) is the shortest land corridor between Mongolia and its neighbours and it opens up alternative transit routes to facilitate trade and investment in the Eurasian region. Moreover, CMREC involves China, Mongolia, and Russia, which have comprehensive strategic partnerships (Kumar, 2022).

On 11 September 2014, Xi proposed a trilateral regional initiative to link China's BRI, Mongolia's Development Road Initiative (referred to as Steppe Road), and Russia's Trans-Eurasian Railway Network. As a buffer state between China and Russia, Mongolia's geostrategic location is crucial for linking the BRI, Steppe Road, and Trans-Eurasian Railway Network to provide economically viable export routes for three countries—for Chinese manufactured items; for Russian oil and gas; and for Mongolian natural resources such as coal, iron, silver, copper, crude oil, and gold. On 23 June 2016, China, Mongolia and Russia signed a tripartite agreement in Tashkent to build CMREC projects, aiming to improve transport connectivity through road, rail and port construction; and cooperation in trade and investment, energy, agribusiness, communication technology, environment and ecological protection (Jinbo, 2019).

CMREC and its Geopolitical Dimension

The complex historical relations have influenced the contemporary China-Mongolia bilateral relations, whereas China's occasional remarks that "*Mongolia was part of China*" worsened societal ties over the years. It is to be noted that Mongolia became a part of the Manchu empire under China's Qing dynasty (1644-1911). Another irritant in bilateral relations is the issue of His Holiness 14th Dalai Lama, the paramount Tibetan spiritual leader. As a Buddhist country, Mongolia cannot deny its Buddhist populace the right to worship the Dalai Lama. His visit to Mongolia in 2014 generated strong reactions when China closed its border and began to impose fees on the imported commodities from Mongolia. China also suspended bilateral official talks and put its US$ 4.2 billion loans on hold.

In 2015, furthermore, the leasing of agricultural land to China in Dornod Aimag, a Mongolian province, further intensified the domestic criticisms against Chinese investments in Mongolia (Pieper, 2020).

Coming to Russia-Mongolia Relations, Mongolia was never a part of the erstwhile Soviet Union. In the 1940s-50s, the joint construction of the Trans-Mongolian Railroad Network (2200 km long) was carried out by the Soviet Union and Mongolia. Since then, Russia has inherited 50 per cent ownership of the Trans-Mongolian Railroad Network. At present, any railroad track-up-gradation project requires Russia's prior involvement or approval. Russia's military and technical ties make Mongolia a geostrategic buffer state to safeguard the security interests of its Far Eastern region. After adopting the 1992 Constitution, Mongolia institutionalised its military neutrality considering the security interests of Russia and China. However, Russia's traditional military and technical ties with Mongolia are stronger than Mongolia's present relations with China (Jargalsaikhan and Batmunkh, 2021).

Under the 'Third Neighbour Policy', Mongolia has a strategy to engage India, Japan, and South Korea, it's the 'Steppe Road Initiative' is aimed at reducing the vulnerabilities because of the landlocked geographical location. Being a non-member of the Russia-dominated Eurasian Economic Union, Mongolia sees itself as a transit nation between China's BRI and Russia-dominated Eurasian Economic Union (Campi, 2019). In the 2016 China-Mongolia-Russia Economic Corridor Plan, China and Russia included the 'Third Country Clause' to accommodate the Mongolian concerns regarding increasing financial and political dependence (Bille, 2019).

The Russian factor in China-Mongolia relations further added another layer of complexity in terms of speedy implementation of the China-Mongolia-Russia Economic Corridor. However, China and Russia have a shared interest in keeping Mongolia away from the large-scale investments from the 'Third Neighbours'. Hence, both neighbours try their best to avoid a conflict of interests in Mongolia and are more accommodative of mutual concerns of strategic nature. In 2016, China halted the 'Egiin GoI' hydropower project because of Russian concerns and its geographical proximity to the largest freshwater, Lake Baikal. Mongolia's attempts to diversify its electric power supply would also affect the adjacent Russian southern bordering region because most hydropower stations are built on the Angara River in the Irkutsk region (Kohn, 2016).

Another case of geostrategic competition between China and Russia can be seen in the Tianjin-Ulaanbaatar-Ulan-Ude Central Route (Central Route, hereafter), which has a single-track railway freight corridor and an international roadway between China, Mongolia, and Russia. This single-track railway freight corridor was built by the Soviet Union and has been in use for many decades. In 2018, China completed the construction of the international roadway for transit trucking service along the central route. The Central Route connects Ulan-Ude (Eastern Siberian City) and Ulaanbaatar (Mongolian Capital) to the Tianjin port via Erenhot (a Chinese border town in Inner Mongolia). Mongolia has been over-dependent on this Central Route to import and export to China (Monitor, 2020).

Figure 14.1: CMREC Projects

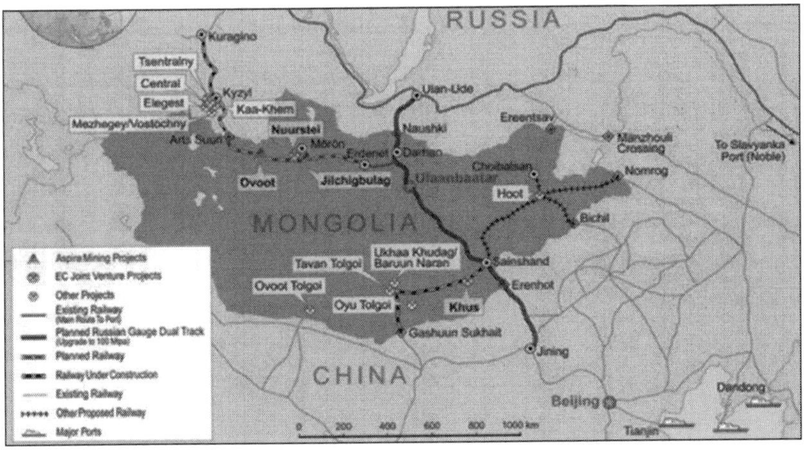

Source: https://beltandroad.ventures/beltandroadblog/china-mongolia-russia-economic-corridor

China constructed roadways along the Central Route, the upgradation of the single-track railway freight corridor into a double-track electrified railway freight corridor did not happen due to geopolitical competition between China and Russia. China has adequate capital and finance to upgrade this single-track railway freight corridor. But, the ground reality indicates that all Chinese railroad projects are only on paper in Mongolia, awaiting implementation. For better access to China's vast market, technology, labour, and infrastructure, there have been constant demands by some groups of Mongolian people to allow the narrower Chinese track gauge (1435 mm) in Mongolia. Russia does not allow the change in railroad standards as it is a matter of geopolitical influence, considering that any infrastructure development project has always had the dual-use potential for civil-military purposes (Radchenko and Jargalsaikhan, 2021).

For many years, Russia has been critical of Chinese investments in Mongolia. Recently, a tripartite consensus has been reached to upgrade the Tianjin-Ulaanbaatar-Ulan-Ude Central Route into a double-track electrified railway line by 2030. However, the precondition is to use the Russian locomotives in the up-gradation process, which will be bought on the additional loans from the Russian Banks. A few years back, the Mongolian Parliament approved building two Chinese railroad projects with narrower track gauge standards (1435 mm) from the Tavan Tolgoi coal mine and Khuut coalmine to the Erenhot border port. In 2020, however, the Supreme Court of Mongolia overturned the decision regarding narrowing the gauge for the railroads; therefore, Mongolia remains strictly committed to a 1520 mm broader track gauge favouring the existing Russian-Mongolian rail system. In other words, the traditional Russian-Mongolian military and technical ties will balance the Chinese geostrategic influence in the CMREC freight corridor projects (Pieper, 2020). The major takeaway is that the tug-of-war between the Mongolian ruling government on one side, and its opposition parties with a Supreme Court mandate on the other, does not allow the building of dual-use Chinese railroad projects, with narrower track gauges (1435 mm), in Mongolia.

Mongolia's Ecological Stakes

Mongolia has diverse landscapes such as dense forests, rivers and freshwater lakes in the north, the Gobi Desert in the south, the Daurian Steppe Grassland in the east, and the Altai Mountains in the west. Its largest river basin is the Selenge Basin which provides significant water shares to the freshwater Lake Baikal in Russia. More than 70 per cent of the water resources flow from its northern region to the southern part of Mongolia. There have been many concerns regarding China-funded hydropower projects to meet energy demand for its mining activities, which causes severe biodiversity impacts on the endangered migratory bird species and the ecosystem in the Selenge Basin-Lake Baikal complex (Zoinet, 2020).

Figure 14.2: The Human Presence in Mongolia's Landscape

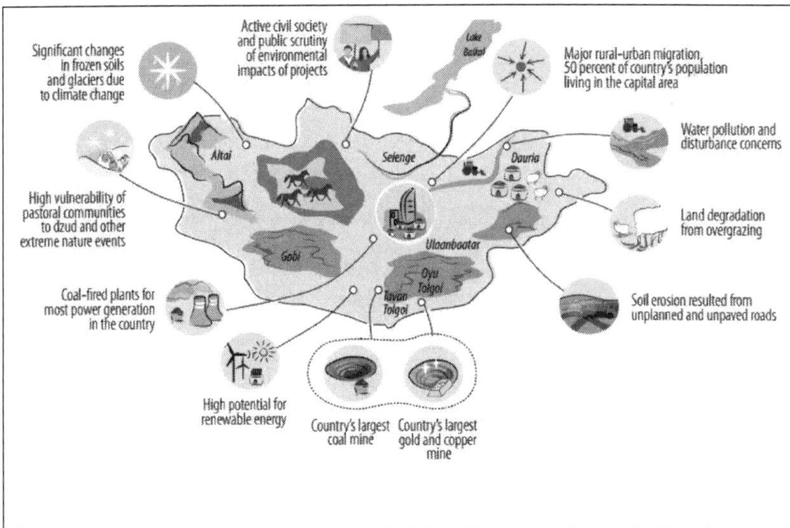

[1] *Dzud* is a Mongolian term for a severe winter in which large number of livestock die, primarily of starvation because they are unable to graze and in other cases directly from the cold.

[2] A traditional *ger* (Mongolian) is a portable, round tent covered with skins or felt and used as a dwelling by several distinct nomadic groups in the steppes of Central Asia.

Source: https://zoinet.org/wp-content/uploads/2020/07/BR-Mongolia-FINAL-WEB2-.pdf.

In Mongolia, many environmentalists complain about environmental hazards, including air and water pollution, soil erosion, habitat destruction and fragmentation, and timber depletion. Due to the risks of oil and gas spilling around proposed pipeline projects, the people's livelihood can be threatened in these ecologically fragile areas. Moreover, Mongolia is also concerned about the overgrazing of the Steppe Grassland, due to the substantial rise in goat stocks, to meet the increasing demands for authentic cashmere. The growing cashmere exports via the truck transit routes became the root cause of the desertification of the Steppe Grassland in Mongolia. At the same time, the mining activities and rapid urbanisation led to the disruption of the ecological system to a large extent. The extensive mining-based resource industries put pressure on rural land and water resources, thus, forcing rural habitats to migrate without access to clean water, basic sanitation, and electricity in cities. In winter, these migrants depend solely on coal-burning for heating and cooking purposes, leading to the worst air pollution in Ulaanbaatar (Ye, 2017).

Even Chinese experts acknowledge that the environmental laws and ecological concerns limited CMREC investment and thus made recommendations to increase the ecological awareness drive and fulfil the social responsibility concerning environmental protection in Mongolia (Ulagpan, 2021).

In Mongolia, Chinese investment solely depends on coal-based thermal power plants for electricity generation in the energy sector; for example, more than 93 per cent of power is generated through coal-based electricity plants. Mongolia has failed to kick-start sustainable means for electricity generation like hydropower, wind and solar. The primary reason behind the non-implementation of hydropower projects is the rivers' relatively smaller size and capacity, which remain frozen most of the year. Another possible reason behind the overdependence on coal-based thermal power generation is that the proposed CMREC project could not create a regional integrated power supply and transmission network in the Gobi Desert to tap the full potential of wind and solar energy.

The environmental impacts of the mining sector are another cause of concern; for example, in 2015, China-funded Mongolia's hydropower plant project on the Orkhon River met with massive protests. The massive protests were regarding the dangers of the hydroelectric power project and its negative impacts on the connected pipeline project to the water system of Lake Baikal, a habitat to more than 3,000 unique species in the neighbouring ecosystem in Russia. The development of road and railway routes cause habitat loss for numerous species, deforestation, wildlife and timber trafficking. The building of the transportation corridors is disrupting the herder's activities facing active deforestation area within Heilongjiang province in China; and Republic of Buryatia, Irkutsk Oblast, Zabaykalsky Krai and Lake Baikal in Russia; in the northern region of Mongolia. Mongolia's centuries-old unique nomadic lifestyle faces a severe existential crisis amid rapid deforestation and environmental degradation in its vast steppe grasslands. In addition, the rapid urbanisation and mining boom to extract rich natural resources put pressure on its fragile ecosystem (Shuying, 2017).

Issues and Concerns

Mongolia however, is cautious about the economic and political risks associated with the proposed Chinese projects. Mongolia is concerned regarding access to the European market within BRI connectivity projects. Contrary to the logic of connectivity, it seems China does not believe in the principle of reciprocity in trade and investment. By taking advantage of economic globalisation, China exports their manufactured commodities abroad but denies equal and reciprocal access to foreign investors in the Chinese market. Moreover, China is putting pressure on Mongolia to respect Chinese sensitivities on its core interests, including the Tibet issue and banning the visit of His Holiness Dalai Lama (Ankhtuya, 2021).

Within the first ten months in 2021, Mongolia's foreign trade with 151 countries was around a total trade volume of US$ 13.2 billion. During the same period, Mongolia exported 86 per cent of its total exports to China, while the total imports were 39.7 per cent from China (Monitor, 2020). In 2017, when Mongolia signed the US$ 5.5 billion bailouts by the International Monetary Fund (IMF), the Chinese debt was approximately 10 per cent of its external debt. In 2020, however, Mongolia's nominal external debt was around 220 per cent of its total GDP (Bazarsad, Sukhbaatar and Jargalsaikhan, 2021). In addition, Mongolia's quest to diversify its trade and investment portfolio can be driven toward reducing its overdependence on the Chinese economy in the long run. Against this backdrop, Mongolia did not permit three Chinese banks (Industrial and Commercial Bank of China, Export-Import Bank of China, and Bank of China) to operate and finance the infrastructure projects in Mongolia (Junmian, 2021).

Mongolia's trade route with the world passes through the Erenhot port (a Chinese land port in Inner Mongolia) that has been transformed into an important rail freight hub. At Erenhot port, China has built massive infrastructure and railroad facilities to increase the passing capacity and total cargo volume annually. With 8000 freight trains,

Erenhot port recently became a significant transportation channel that carries cargo up to Malaszewicze in Poland. The Erenhot port now serves 53 China-Europe freight trains for delivering goods to ten European countries (Huaxia, 2021). Already, 1497 freight trains passed through the port with 10.2 million tonnes of cargo until July 2021 (Monitor, 2020). But the problem lies on the Mongolian side of the international border due to the incompatibility between the Russian-Mongolian rail track gauge (1520 mm) and the Chinese rail track gauge standard (1435 mm). It takes a longer time in overall border transit because of the required change in bogies of the freight trains (Zoinet, 2020).

Beyond the Tianjin-Ulaanbaatar-Ulan-Ude Central Route Railroad Corridor, there are proposal about Tavan Tolgoi Railroad Project that seeks to link Mongolia's Tavan Tolgoi Coal Mine to the Erenhot port. So far, there is hardly any progress in the implementation of these projects. The non-upgradation of the Central Route Railway Freight Corridor limited Mongolia's regional trade and impacted its economic development to its full potential (Kumar, 2022). Although Mongolia highlights its status as a transit nation between China's BRI and Russia-dominated Eurasian Economic Union, the ground realities suggest that its 'Third Neighbour Policy' aimed to access Japanese, South Korean, Indian, and EU markets are largely dependent on Chinese transit routes, while maintaining a careful balancing act between Russia and China.

Note

1. Mongolia's Double Balancing policy aims to balance its overdependence on both its immediate neighbours China and Russsia against each other, while attempts to find additional "Third Neighbours" to diversify its trade portfolio.

References

Alicia J.C. (2013). "New Sino-Mongolian Oil Deal Undercuts Russia's Old Role", *Eurasia Daily Monitor.* 13(10): 13-16.

Alicia, J.C. (2013). "Sino-Mongolian Coal Relationship Continues Downward Spiral", *Eurasia Daily Monitor.* 13(17): 6-8.

Ankhtuya. (2021). "Mongolia's Foreign Trade Volume Increased by 26.3 per cent", at https://news.mn/en/796603/. Accessed on 2 March 2022.

Bazarsad, I., Sukhbaatar, C., and Jargalsaikhan, M. (2021). "Sino-Mongolian Economic Interconnectivity: Big Talks, Little Progress", at https://en.iss.gov.mn/?p=290. Accessed on 2 March 2022.

Bazarsad, I., Sukhbaatar, C., and Jargalsaikhan, M. (2021). "Sino-Mongolian Economic Interconnectivity: Big Talks, Little Progress",at https://en.iss.gov.mn/?p=290. Accessed on 2 March 2022.

Bedeski, R. E. (2008). "Mongolian Futures: Scenarios for a Landlocked State". Stockholm: Institute for Security and Development Policy.

Billé, F. (2016). *Sinophobia: Anxiety, Violence, and the Making of Mongolian Identity*. Honolulu, Hawaii: University of Hawai'i Press.

Campi, A. J. (2019). *Mongolia's foreign policy: Navigating a changing world. Boulder*. Colorado: Lynne Rienner.

Chen, Y., and Wu, Y. (2019). "Report on the Policy Coordination Index for the Belt and Road Initiative (2018)", *China and the World*, 02(03), 1950018-1-27. doi:10.1142/s2591729319500184

Green, E. E. (1986). "China and Mongolia: Recurring Trends and Prospects for Change", *Asian Survey*, 1337-1363.

"Greening the China-Mongolia-Russia Economic Corridor: A Visual Synthesis". (2020), at https://zoinet.org/wp-content/uploads/2020/07/BR-Mongolia-FINAL-WEB2-.pdf. Accessed on 2 March 2022.

Hillman, J., and Sacks, D. (2021, March). "Findings | China's Belt and Road: Implications for the United States", at https://www.cfr.org/report/chinas-belt-and-road-implications-for-the-united-states/findings. Accessed on 2 March 2022.

Huaxia. (2021). "China-Mongolia Border Port Sees Cargo Volume Rise",5 March 2022, at http://www.xinhuanet.com/english/2021-08/06/c_1310111801.htm

Jargalsaikhan, M., and Batmunkh, M. (2021). "What are Russian interests in Mongolia?", at https://library.fes.de/pdf-files/bueros/mongolei/18519.pdf. Accessed on 2 March 2022.

Jinbo, W. (2019). "The China-Mongolia-Russia Economic Corridor", in F. Cai and P. Nolan (eds.), *Routledge Handbook of the Belt and Road*, pp. 197-201. Abingdon, London: Oxon.

Junmian, Z. (2021). "Erenhot handles 8,000 China-Europe Freight Trains", at http://www.china.org.cn/business/2021-10/25/content_77830043.htm. Accessed on 2 March 2022.

Kohn, M. (2016). "Russia Stalls China's $1 Billion Hydropower Loan for Mongolia", at https://www.bloomberg.com/news/articles/2016-07-10/russia-stalls-china-s-1-billion-hydropower-loan-for-mongolia. Accessed on 2 March 2022.

Kumar, S. (2022). "China-Mongolia-Russia Economic Corridor: An Assessment", Indian Council of World Affairs, at https://www.icwa.in/show_content.php?lang=1&level=3&ls_id=6870&lid=4679. Accessed on 2 March 2022.

Monitor, G. (2020). "Belt and road: China-Mongolia-Russia Corridor", at https://www.geopoliticalmonitor.com/fact-sheet-china-mongolia-russia-corridor/. Accessed on 2 March 2022.

Monitor, G. (2020). "Belt and road: China-Mongolia-Russia Corridor", at https://www.geopoliticalmonitor.com/fact-sheet-china-mongolia-russia-corridor/. Accessed on 2 March 2022.

Monitor, G. (2020). "Belt and road: China-Mongolia-Russia Corridor", at https://www.geopoliticalmonitor.com/fact-sheet-china-mongolia-russia-corridor/. Accessed on 2 March 2022.

Parepa, L. (2020). "The Belt and Road Initiative as Continuity in Chinese Foreign Policy", *Journal of Contemporary East Asia Studies*, 9(2), pp. 175-201.

Pei, C.Y. (2015). "Foreign Aid Political Risk Analysis". International AID. No. 5, pp. 40-45.

Pieper, M. (2020). "The New Silk Road Heads North: Implications of the China-Mongolia-Russia Economic Corridor for Mongolian Agency within Eurasian Power Shifts", *Eurasian Geography and Economics*,62(5-6), pp. 745-768.

Radchenko, S., and Jargalsaikhan, M. (2021). "Mongolia: Russia's best friend in Asia?", at https://theasanforum.org/mongolia-russias-best-friend-in-asia/. Accessed on 2 March 2022.

Russia-Mongolia-China Road Corridor to be ready in 2018. (2017), at https://www.silkroadbriefing.com/news/2017/09/08/russia-mongolia-china-road-corridor-ready-2018/. Accessed on 2 March 2022.

Soni, S. K. (2009). "China's Periphery Policy: Implications for Sino-Mongolian Relations", *India Quarterly*, pp. 251-69.

Soni, S. K. (2006). *Mongolia-China Relations: Modern and Contemporary Times.* Pentagon Press, New Delhi.

Soni, S. K. (2018). "The Geopolitical Dilemma of Small States in External Relations: Mongolia's Tryst with Immediate and Third Neighbours", *The Mongolian Journal of International Affairs*, 27-44.

Shuying, Z. (2017). "Legal Risk Prevention and Control under One Belt and One Road", *Construction Enterprise Management*, No. 3 (2017), pp. 41-46.

Ulagpan, Y. (2021). "Belt and Road Initiative: Opportunities and Challenges for Mongolia", at https://apjjf.org/2021/3/Ulagpan.html. Accessed on 2 March 2022.

Xue, R.C. (2016). "Analysis of One Belt And One Road: Orientation, Risk and Probing for a Path of Smooth Progress", *Journal of Seeking Knowledge Guide*, No. 10, pp. 26-31.

Ye, H.J. (2017). "'The Belt and Road' Strategic Risk Challenge and Countermeasure", *Journal of Mudanjiang College of Education*, 3(5), pp. 72-76.

15. Economic Statecraft through BRI in Southeast Asia

Temjenmeren Ao

Abstract

It is close to a decade since the announcement of the Silk Road Economic Belt and the 21st Century Maritime Silk Road by President Xi Jinping in 2013. The paper is a study on China's Belt and Road Initiative (BRI) in Southeast Asia, which given its geography as well as the economic opportunities makes it crucial. The paper outlines the projects under the BRI in Southeast Asia while also examining some concerns that challenge the utility of the initiative.

Broad Outline of the BRI Framework: An Agenda or Strategy or Programme?

On 28 March 2015, a document titled 'Vision and Actions on Jointly Building the Silk Road Economic Belt and 21st Century Maritime Silk Road', was jointly issued by the National Development and Reform Commission (NDRC), the Ministry of Foreign Affairs and the Ministry of Commerce, PRC. According to this document the BRI is open to all countries for building peace and cooperation, based on the principle of openness and inclusiveness. Through the BRI there would be the promotion of "... practical cooperation in all fields and build a community of shared interest, destiny, and responsibility featuring mutual political trust, economic integration and cultural inclusiveness...." The BRI drew its inspiration from the concept of the Silk Road which was an ancient network of trade routes that connected China to the Mediterranean via Eurasia; established during the Han Dynasty around two millennia ago. The BRI is not just a development plan which focuses on building transportation infrastructure but it is also important for securing China's energy needs along with protecting its national and security interests (Karpathiotaki, Tian, Zhou and Huang, 2021).

China's BRI also previously known as the One Road, One Belt (OBOR) is aimed at the integration of Silk Economic Belt with the 21st Century Maritime Silk Route. The economic belt route of China would develop as well as integrate with six proposed economic corridors, such as the China-Pakistan Economic Corridor (CPEC), Bangladesh-China-India-Myanmar Economic Corridor (BCIM), China-Central Asia-West Asia Economic Corridor, the China-Mongolia-Russia Economic Corridor, the New Eurasia land Bridge Economic Corridor, and the Indo-China Peninsula Economic Corridor.

Apart from opening greater access to large and new markets, the aim for undertaking this massive infrastructure initiative would enable China to secure its energy needs from its sources to its manufacturing bases on the mainland (*The Economist*, 2016). Until 1993, China was self-sufficient in terms of its energy demand. However, the rapid economic modernisation and growth that witnessed a spike in demand in the 1990s along with a stagnant domestic supply saw China transforming itself from a net exporter to a net importer of energy resources. The highly contested energy sources in West Asia are already dominated by Western oil conglomerates which made it difficult for China to secure oil and gas fields. Therefore, China looked toward countries in Central Asia, Southeast Asia, and Africa where the presence of Western companies were limited on account of many factors such as imposition of sanctions (Panwar, 2009).

The Chinese position is that while it has been moving from being an oil surplus to oil deficit economy it has been trying to develop an external oil strategy that has much in common with the Japanese model. In 1998, the China National Petroleum Corporation was restructured into a group of joint companies and became active participant in the world energy scene. Chinese entities such as Petro China, SINOPEC Corp., and CNOOC Ltd. have all made initiatives towards the exploration and development of various global energy hotspots, and Chinese companies are operating in some thirty countries across the globe (Kambara and Howe, 2007). Through the BRI, China intends to establish an efficient energy corridor from its sources in Central Asia and Southeast Asia to its manufacturing bases in China.

Southeast Asia in the BRI Framework

Southeast Asia straddles some of the busiest maritime and aerial commercial routes in the world that are key to China's economic rise and survival. Southeast Asia is also one of the fastest-growing regions in the world and has been resilient despite the global economic slowdown (Chan, 2017). Chinese President Xi Jinping proposed the Maritime Silk Road (MSR)—now part of the BRI—during his visit to Indonesia in October 2013. It is an attempt to promote economic integration and connectivity between China and Southeast Asia by reviving the ancient MSRs with a modern network of high-speed rail, motorways, pipelines, and ports stretching across the region (Hong, 2017).

Further, through the BRI China sees an opportunity to develop its landlocked western provinces, as it would open access to the markets of Southeast Asia. For Southeast Asia, the BRI also presents a opportunity since investment in infrastructure would be crucial for the region's economic development and growth. According to the Asian Development Bank (ADB), of the total estimated US$ 3 trillion investment which is needed from 2016-2030 in order to maintain the current development momentum in Southeast Asia; 36 per cent would be required in the transport sectors. Traditional investments from the West in Southeast Asia are either not keeping up with the region's needs or are turning away from infrastructure. This gap leaves room for more BRI investments in Southeast Asia, given that China's economic ties with the region have remained strong (Yu, 2021). Singapore, Vietnam, Thailand, Malaysia, Cambodia, and Myanmar are all ranked amongst the top ten most connected to China via trade. In the past decade, China's supply chain connectivity have increased across the BRI regions with the Southeast Asian economies being the most connected. Further, it is found that in Southeast Asia, Chinese companies are also outsourcing lower value-added processes to Cambodia and Laos (Yan, 2018).

The Sea Route under the BRI covers the entire region of Southeast Asia. One route starts from the eastern coast of China into Europe through the South China Sea and the Indian Ocean. The other route begins from China's coast and traverses through the South China Sea to East Indonesia. This would enable China to attain not only transit but also make inroads into the markets in Africa and Europe through

Southeast Asia. This would help expand China's access into Eurasia and Europe, while also further accelerating its trade and commerce in South and Southeast Asia.

The Second Belt and Road Forum held at Beijing in April 2019, indicated that more countries are opening up to the idea of the BRI at a time when there was growing erosion of the global international trade system with increasing protectionism in the midst of the US-China trade war. The nations of Southeast Asia remain a key element of the BRI and despite their concerns see it as a necessity towards supporting its infrastructure development and preserving the multilateral trading order, since both remain key factors for promoting economic growth. This was evident given the fact that all of the ASEAN nations expect Indonesia—on account of the Presidential elections—had their top leaders attending the second forum of the BRI. Despite frictions stemming from the South China Sea and lingering concerns over the debt tally of BRI projects, Southeast Asian governments remain keen on the project (Tiezzi, 2019). Some of the ongoing projects in the region which were being supported by Chinese-led investments were integrated and made part of the infrastructure and connectivity plans under the BRI framework.

Figure 15.1: Total BRI-related Capital Flows to Southeast Asia

(Figures in US$ billion) (Yan, 2018)

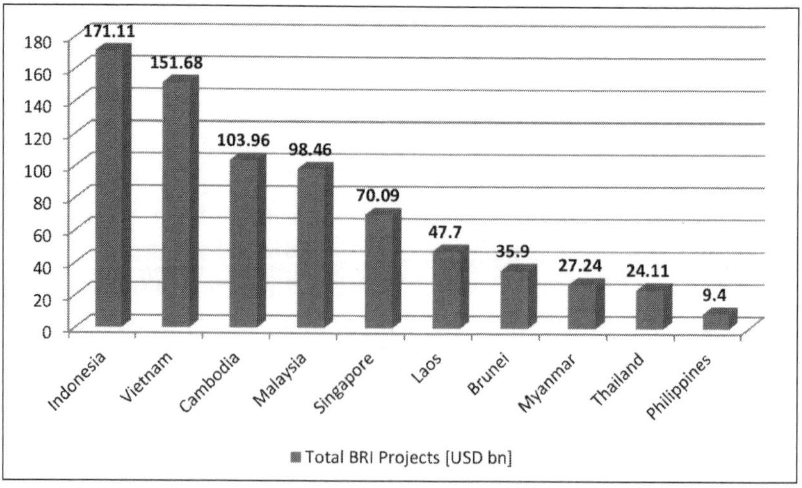

The bar diagram in Figure 15.1 indicates the total BRI-related capital flows to Southeast Asian countries, this includes direct investment, portfolio investment, and official investment. The data indicates that Indonesia has been the largest recipient in terms BRI related capital flows with US$ 171.1 billion, followed by Vietnam with US$ 151.1 billion. The largest sum of investment under the BRI in Southeast Asia is in the transport and logistics sector followed by investment in the energy-related sectors. Under transport and logistics, there is huge BRI investment in the railway sector. Some of these are the Kuala Lumpur-Kota Bahru Rail estimated to cost US$ 14.3 billion, the Preah Vihear-Kaoh Kong Railway in Cambodia estimated at US$ 9.6 billion, and the Vietnam-Boten Railway Project with investment of US$ 5.8 billion. There is also the US$ 7.3 billion Kyaukpyu Deep Sea Port construction in Myanmar. In the energy sector, there is China General Nuclear which has made a US$ 5.9 billion investment in Malaysia, and the Chinese energy entity Zhejiang Hengyi which has invested US$ 3.4 billion in Brunei's oil sector (Yan, 2018).

BRI investments in Southeast Asia grew from US$ 16.8 billion in 2014 to US$ 29.3 billion in 2019, accounting for 27.6 per cent of all BRI investments worldwide. Under this 46.2 per cent of the BRI investments in Southeast Asia was in the construction sector (Yu, 2021). The following sub-sections will cover the engagements of some of the Southeast Asian countries in the BRI.

Cambodia

Cambodia is one of China's closest partner countries in Southeast Asia and is a staunch supporter of the BRI. The close diplomatic and political relationship between Cambodia and China has facilitated a broad spectrum of China-financed and China-built projects including both transport infrastructures such as roads and bridges as well as energy infrastructures such as dams and power plants. Cambodian PM Hun Sen led a large delegation to attend the first BRI Forum in Beijing on 14-15 May 2017 and followed it up with a State visit from 16 to 17 May. During the visit, China pledged US$ 240 million in grants to Cambodia with 13 agreements being signed that included infrastructure development, trade, maritime cooperation, and tourism under the BRI framework (Vannarith, 2017).

Both countries signed a MoUs towards implementing the BRI of which the Sihanoukville Special Economic Zone (SSEZ) in the Cambodian coastal city being the most high profile. The SSEZ is a comprehensive 'special economic zone' that includes a port and hosts a wide range of businesses, including factories as well as casinos (Ferchen, 2021). Another major project is the 190 km long Phnom Penh-Sihanoukville Expressway which is currently underway and is expected to be completed by March 2023 (Kha, 2019).

As indicated in Figure 15.2, the Phnom Penh-Sihanoukville Expressway Project is Cambodia's first and most important strategic corridor that will help reduce travel time between Phnom Penh and Sihanoukville seaport by two hours. This will help reduce transport costs and improve the logistics in the region. Being built at a cost of US$ 2.019 billion, the road is being constructed by PPSHV Expressway Co. Ltd., a subsidiary of China Road and Bridge Corporate and technical assessment is by Malaysia-based Minconsult SDN. BHD (Vanyuth, 2021).

Figure 15.2: Construction of New Highway from Phnom Penh-Sihanoukville Expressway Project

(Tenth Regional EST Forum in Asia, 2017)

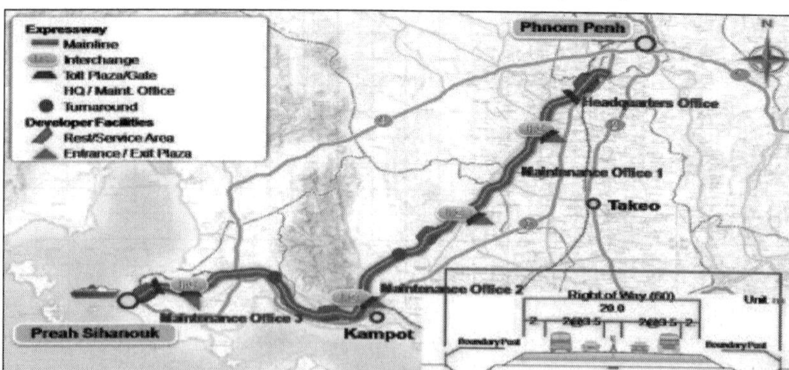

By 2017, Chinese companies were reportedly responsible for 70 per cent of industrial investment in Cambodia, held at least 369,000 hectares of land concessions, and had development rights for around 20 per cent of Cambodia's coastline. The Koh Kong Port in Koh Kong Province is an example of a significant Chinese infrastructure investment. It is part of a pilot zone on a 45,000-hectare concession that was provided to a

Chinese company for 99 years with a 100 per cent equity stake. Phase 1 of the Koh Kong Port project is currently underway, while two man-made lakes, a power plant, four-lane highway, resort, and golf course are already completed (Mobley, 2019).

Indonesia

Since President Yudhoyono (2004-2014) and the current President Jokowi there has been much emphasis on infrastructure development since it was realised that in order to achieve its growth target of 6-7 per cent, the Indonesian government needed to focus on the development of power sector, maritime connectivity, and transportation. However, one of the obstacles to Indonesia's infrastructure development has been financing and funding these projects. The budgetary constraint is the main concern of the government to finance infrastructure projects with its ability to raise funds through debt issuance also being restricted by law. Under the existing law, government budget deficit cannot exceed 3 per cent of GDP. The large amount of investment needed to sustain the country's economic development and the financial constraints has resulted in the Indonesian government being open to any initiatives that could promote its infrastructural growth. Against this backdrop, the BRI's objective to promote infrastructure and connectivity development was in line with the government's effort to improve and promote connectivity within the country and the region (Damuri, Perkasa, Atje and Hirawan, 2019). After decades of relatively low infrastructure spending from successive Indonesian governments on account of tight budgets, the BRI seemed like a manna from heaven (Hicks, 2019).

President Xi Jinping during his visit to Jakarta in 2013 introduced his signature plan before the Indonesian Parliament. Indonesia which sits between the ancient maritime trade route between East and West is crucial for the BRI. Enhancing inter-island connectivity as well as building and upgrading infrastructure within the country has been the primary concern of the Indonesian government since it is the largest archipelagic country in the world, with 13,466 large and small tropical islands. After taking over office in 2014, President Jokowi announced his Global Maritime Fulcrum (GMF) doctrine at the East Asia Summit on 13 November 2014. The BRI complemented the GMF, which sought towards developing Indonesia's maritime infrastructure. In May 2017, President Joko Widodo attended the first BRI Summit in Beijing. As a part of BRI investment programmes in Indonesia, the government has proposed a number of projects. Among them is MRT East-West Line, a 100 km project rail line that will connect the provinces of Banten, Jakarta, and West Java. Another project is Sulawesi Railway which will connect South Sulawesi and North Sulawesi with 1,513 km long railway. In addition under the BRI there is also tourism project in Manado and North Sulawesi (Damuri, Perkasa, Atje and Hirawan, 2019).

In March 2019, a Senior Minister of Indonesia stated that there is a proposal for 28 projects worth US$ 91.1 billion with Chinese investors as part of its participation in the BRI. Coordinating Maritime Affairs Minister, Luhut Pandjaitan said that the government would offer those projects, which include seaports and industrial estates, power plants, smelters and tourism estates. According to the Indonesia Investment Coordinating Board (BKPM) Chairman, Thomas "Tom" Lembong, these projects would take place in four locations; namely North Sumatra, North Kalimantan, North Sulawesi and Bali. The four locations, he said, were chosen because they all sit on the periphery of the archipelago, coinciding with President Jokowi's ambition to develop the country from the outer areas (Indonesia to propose, 2019).

Malaysia

When the BRI was launched in 2013, Malaysia was one of the most supportive countries as it sees it as providing good opportunities to upgrade and improve its infrastructure. Further, the BRI which expands into digital, green, and public health development is also perceived as an opportunity to help improve its other sectors (Kuo, 2020). The then Barisan Nasional (BN) coalition government of Najib Adbul Razak awarded the Trans Sabah Gas Pipeline (TSGP) and Multi-Product Pipeline (MPP), to China Petroleum Pipeline Bureau (CPPB) in 2016. The work started in 2017 before it came to a halt after the Pakatan Harapan (PH) government came to power in May 2018. The Perikatan Nasional government under Tan Sri Muhyiddin Yassin revived the Sabah portion of the gas pipeline project while the negotiations are still ongoing for the MPP part of the project, which is to deliver gas from Pengerang, Johor, to other parts of Peninsular Malaysia (Frankly Speaking, 2021).

Figure 15.3: Malaysia's East Coast Rail Link

(Malaysia's East Coast, 2020)

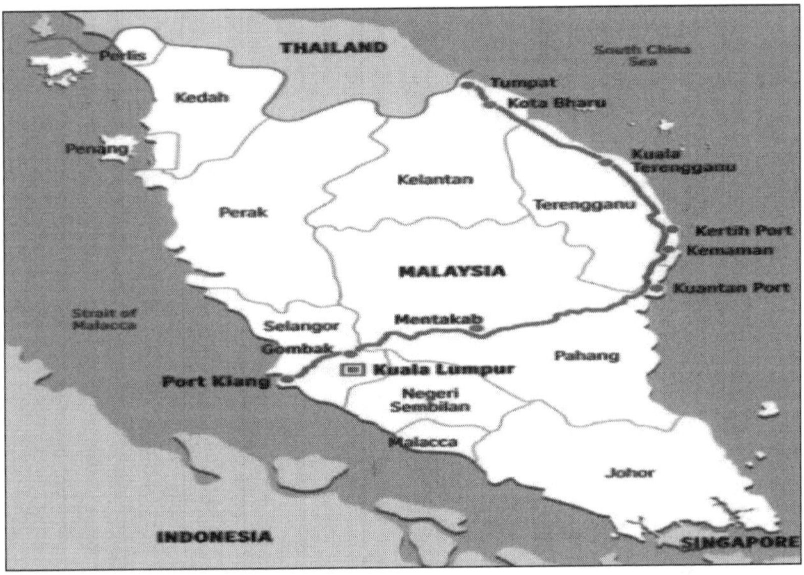

Another mega-infrastructure deal signed with China under the BRI is the East Coast Rail Link (ECRL) as indicated in Figure 15.3. This became the flagship BRI project in Malaysia. As indicated in Figure 15.3, the ECRL project is a 640 km railway link connecting the east coast with the west coast of Malaysia. This is a joint venture between Malaysia Rail Link (MRLSB) and China Communications Construction Company (CCCC). The ECRL will originate at Kota Bharu, the state capital of Kelantan, and terminate at Port Klang in Selangor. It will reduce the travel time from Kota Bharu to WP Putrajaya to approximately four hours (East Coast Rail Link, 2019).

Myanmar

China and Myanmar first signed the China Myanmar Economic Corridor (CMEC) Agreement as part of the BRI in 2017. Under the CMEC 24 projects worth an estimated US$ 2 billion has been signed that encompasses a number of infrastructure projects that strategically connect the oil trade from the Indian Ocean to China's Yunnan province via Myanmar. Key infrastructure investments in the CMEC include a deep-water port, several large-scale energy and transport projects, and the Kyaukphyu Special Economic Zone (SEZ) (Yu, 2021). These projects will form an integral part of the Y-shaped corridor that will connect Kunming to Yangon and Mandalay (Ujvari, 2019).

Figure 15.4: Myanmar-China Oil Pipeline

(Myanmar Pipeline, 2017)

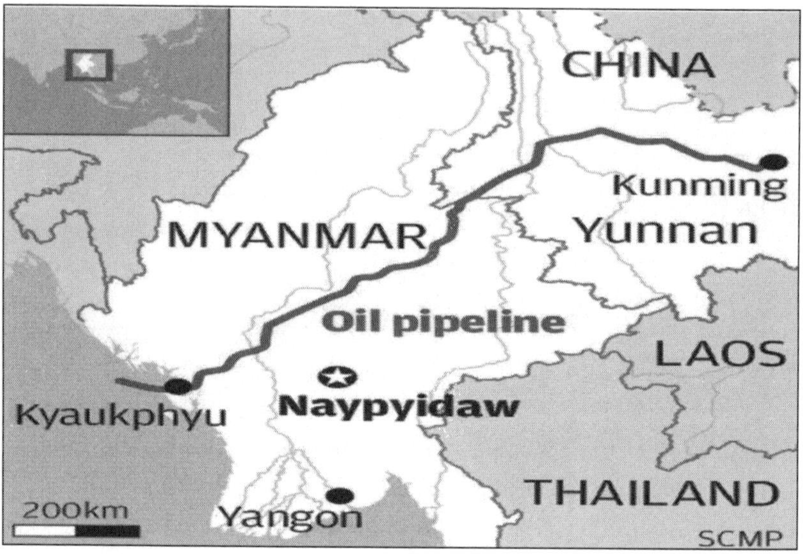

In 2017, the Myanmar-China Crude oil pipeline was also operationalised. The pipeline has enabled China to import crude oil from West Asia and Africa without having to ship through the Strait of Malacca and into the South China Sea. As shown in Figure 15.4, the oil pipeline which is part of the BRI's infrastructure and trade development plan helps the transport of oil to the manufacturing bases in Kunming located in the Yunnan province of China, through the offloading of its tankers in the Western Myanmar town of Kyaukphyu located in the Rakhine State. In Myanmar, this is the most strategic project under the BRI from where twin gas and oil pipelines run across the country to Kunming and thus providing China with an alternative import route to the Malacca Straits. Kyaukphyu has also been designated SEZ, where China's state-owned

CITIC Group has majority stakes in its development (Hallgren and Ghiasy, 2017). During President Xi Jinping's state visit to Myanmar in January 2020, both sides signed another 33 bilateral agreements to facilitate the implementation of the CMEC. In particular, these agreements cover the development of a deep seaport at the Kyaukphyu SEZ, the Muse-Mandalay electric railway and the New Yangon City project (Yu, 2021).

The Philippines

Sino-Philippines relations have been witnessing a dramatic change under the Rodrigo Duterte administration. Both nations have seemed to put into past the July 2016 Permanent Court of Arbitration ruling, moved by the Philippines, which challenged China's historical claims to the South China Sea. The ruling given by the tribunal dismissed China's claim to 80 per cent of the South China Sea, which was based on its nine-dash line and included various reefs and islands. China was also held accountable for disrupting the other Southeast Asian nations' freedom of navigation rights by asserting its territorial claims as well as destroying marine diversity such as corals while building its artificial islands and air strips in the contested sites (United Nations, Division for Ocean Affairs and Law of the Sea, 2013). The group of eminent international lawyers that made up the tribunal for hearing the case stated that, China's historical claims to the South China Sea does not hold valid due to lack of evidence which indicates its historical claims given under its 'nine-dash line' (The South China Sea Arbitration, 2016).

Since the ruling, relations between the Philippines and China have been on a positive trajectory with the Philippines taking part in the first BRI Forum in May 2017. It also became a full member of the Asian Infrastructure Investment Bank (AIIB) in order to attract investment into developing its infrastructure. Under the BRI, the 21st Century Maritime Silk Road that focuses on developing ports is of interest to the Philippines. The sea transit routes through the Maritime Silk Road would be complemented by the series of railway and road networks which would be build through the Silk Road Economic Belt. Thus, together the belt and the road under the BRI would create new links for trade between Eurasia, Africa, and the Americas. Given the geography of the Philippines, the Maritime Silk Road projects under the BRI provide huge opportunities in areas such as port infrastructure development. By 2017, thirteen bilateral cooperation agreements were signed between the China and Philippines, with US$ 24 billion worth of Chinese funding and investment being pledged (Estrada, 2017). During the visit of Chinese President Xi Jinping to the Philippines from 20-21 November 2018, both nations established a Comprehensive Strategic Cooperation. The joint statement after President Xi's meeting with President Duterte saw the conclusion of 29 agreements which also included joint oil and gas exploration and with China being asked to get involved in Duterte's signature US$ 180 billion "Build, Build, Build", infrastructure programme (Harini, 2018).

Thailand

Thailand is located at the centre of Southeast Asia becomes an important link for all means of connectivity. Thailand has potential to become a major logistic hub in which enhancement of its physical infrastructure becomes a pre-requisite (Chirathivat and Cheewatrakoolpong, 2015). Thailand, which is currently pursuing foreign investment for its ambitious US$ 45 billion Eastern Economic Corridor (EEC) development plan, sees the BRI as a great opportunity. In the late 1980s, Thailand's booming economy helped revive the idea of the 'golden peninsula' by Thailand's Prime Minister Chatchai Choonhavan. The intent behind this was to make Thailand function as the economic hub of Southeast Asia. Connectivity in terms of highways, air, and sea transport remains critical as given in Thailand's infrastructure plan (2015-2022) (Department of International Economic Affairs, Ministry of Foreign Affairs, 2017).

The BRI would be one of the major sources of financing Thailand's EEC, which Thai PM Prayuth Chan-o-cha has positioned as the fulcrum of the nation's future economic growth. Speaking to the media on the sidelines of the second Belt and Road Forum in April 2019, PM Prayuth stated that, "Once the BRI is complete, it will allow great connectivity into Thailand, and the EEC, [which] will be a core economic and industrial part of Thailand, so prosperity will spread across the country and across ASEAN" (Green, 2019). The ongoing China-Indochina Peninsula Economic Corridor makes Thailand an important entity under the BRI framework. Thailand is currently part of the High-Speed Railway

(HSR) running across the country and connecting to Laos' Vientiane until it reached China's Kunming in the north. This railway is one of the major connectivity projects between China and Thailand under the BRI framework.

Figure 15.5: China-Thailand High-Speed Railway
(China-Thailand Railway, 2019)

As indicated in Figure 15.5, the railway is divided into two phases: the first is a 250 km long line linking the Thai capital Bangkok and the north-eastern province of Nakhon Ratchasima. The other phase connects Nakhon Ratchasima and the Thai border at Nong Khai Province. Then, a railway bridge linking Nong Khai with the Lao's capital Vientiane will connect the Thai rail with the Laos network (China-Thailand Railway, 2019).

Vietnam

In 2015, Vietnam officially announced its participation in the BRI and expressed its support to the initiative. Vietnam welcomed the BRI and its efforts to promote economic and regional connectivity, which would contribute positively to the common good of the nations. Vietnam stands to benefit from the BRI due to its growing demand for infrastructure investments to fuel the country's growth. BRI brings new opportunities for multinational investing in Vietnam and as a potential catalyst for greater connectivity, it will facilitate manufacturing and cross-border trade in the region (Huy, 2020). Ever since the launch of its economic reform programme—the *Doi Moi* initiative has helped propel Vietnam's economy. From a growth of 2.7 per cent in 1986, Vietnam's economic reform helped push the GDP to an average of 6 per cent growth that continues till today, and despite a slight decline during the Asian financial crisis in 1998, the growth has remained stable. This sustained and high economic growth witnessed in Vietnam has enabled its poverty level to fall from 75 per cent three decades back to roughly 9.8 per cent (Das, Chakraborti and Bhattacharya, 2018).

According to some estimates, Vietnam requires US$ 605 billion from 2016-2040, for its infrastructural development which includes roads, rail, airports, telecoms, electricity, and water. Vietnam, due to the tightening in its financial and legal regulations, is experiencing budgetary constraints. Therefore Vietnam has been seeking the BRI as an alternative source for funding its developmental requirements (Hiep, 2018). During the State visit by President Xi Jinping to Vietnam in November 2015, both sides declared the need towards strengthening the development strategy by promoting the connection between the framework of 'Two Corridors, One Belt' and the BRI. Under this framework, there is the idea of building a common economic development zone between Vietnam and China. On 12 September 2016, Vietnam and China signed a Border Trade Agreement and both sides actively promoting the construction of border economic zones and the improvement of the transportation system (Huy, 2020). Vietnamese President Tran Dai Quang welcomed the BRI when he attended the first Belt and Road Forum in Beijing in May 2017. President Quang emphasised that cooperation under the BRI must ensure "sustainability, effectiveness and inclusiveness, openness, mutual respect and benefits, and compliance with the UN Charter and international law" (Hiep, 2018).

BRI: Challenges and Concerns for Southeast Asia

There have been some resistance to the various BRI projects due to fear of debt servicing, loss of sovereign rights to Chinese companies, unfair financial and contract terms, and lack of local raw materials and workers being hired by Chinese companies for the various projects (Majid, 2018). In Cambodia where the Koh Kong Port, part of the pilot zone projects involves the development of a port followed by the construction of an industrial park. The Chinese company Tianjin Union Development Group has ownership for 99 years with a 100 per cent equity stake. While the ownership was changed from foreign to Cambodian to circumvent domestic laws limiting the size of foreign land concessions; it could lead to the establishment of a proxy Chinese city inside a sovereign state (Mobley, 2019).

Indonesia which has not benefitted from the BRI with its flagship project the Jakarta-Bandung high-speed railway project announced in 2015; being bogged down owing to issues ranging from funding to land acquisition. This has resulted in Indonesia becoming more cautious by favouring a business-to-business structure for its BRI deals, and seeking to avoid government-to-government loans. Jakarta is also keen on ensuring that Chinese-backed projects employ Indonesian workers and relies on the most advanced environmentally friendly technology (Ujvari, 2019).

Under former PM Najib, Malaysia became one of the top investment destinations for projects linked to China's BRI. However, when the new government led by Mahathir Bin Mohamad assumed office following the general election held on 9 May 2018, it began revisiting some of the infrastructure development and connectivity deals singed under the BRI, in order to reduce the national debt. The administration cancelled or deferred some US$ 23 billion worth of projects awarded to Chinese companies by the previous government (Bowie, 2018). In July 2018, Malaysia suspended the construction of the 688 km-long ECRL. This is part of China's BRI that aims to connect the Straits of Malacca to the Northeast peninsular region of Malaysia. The project which cost over US$ 20 billion was suspended by the new Mahathir government which took over Office in May 2019. The new Malaysian government began to re-negotiate the terms of the original agreement with China in order to reduce the cost of the project that was signed under the previous Najib government (Malaysia halts, 2018). Following months of negotiations between Malaysia and China, in April 2019, both sides reached an agreement in order to resume the project whose construction was put on halt. According to a statement from the Malaysian PM's office, the new agreement managed to reduce the cost of the ECRL project to US$ 10.7 billion. Further, the length of the railway line under the project has also been reduced to 648 km from the original 688 km (Malaysia and China, 2019). The Malaysian case is not the only one, since there have also been concerns over the BRI in the other ASEAN states such as Thailand.

Figure 15.6: The Kra Canal Project

(Canal Conundrum, 2019)

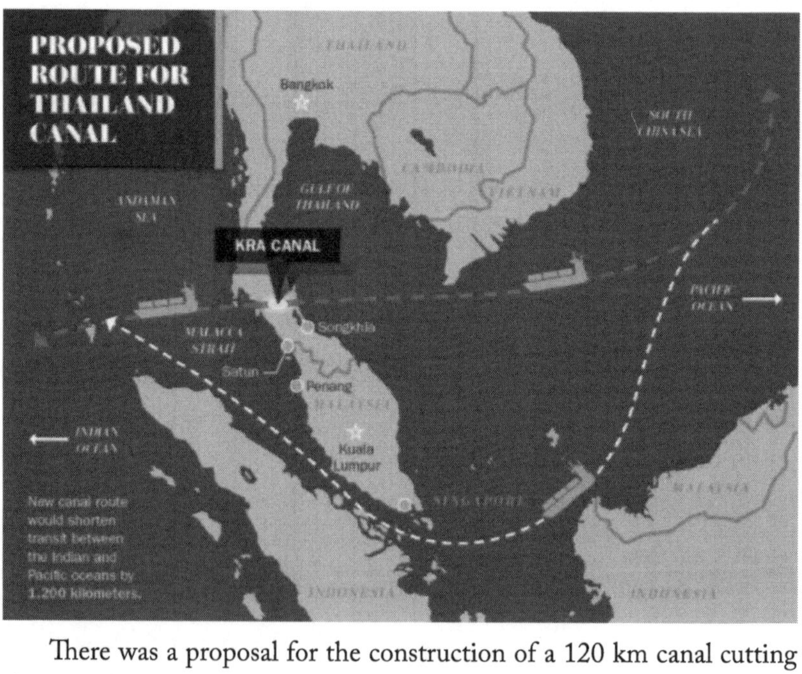

There was a proposal for the construction of a 120 km canal cutting through the Isthmus of Kra in Thailand. As shown in Figure 15.6, this Isthmus is the narrowest part of the Malay Peninsula in southern Thailand which prevents the passage of mid-sized commercial ships along the Mekong River. The construction of a man-made waterway would have cut through Thailand and would establish a bypass to the Strait of Malacca—ending the Malacca dilemma. This would have allowed the Chinese navy to move freely and quickly between its newly constructed bases in the South China Sea and the Indian Ocean. However, in September 2020, Thailand announced that it will scrap the Kra canal project after its government faced intense pressure from the opposition parties and the public. Concerns on the construction of the Kra canal were raised as it could have undermined the independence of other Southeast Asian countries like Myanmar and Cambodia (Big Blow to China, 2020).

Other Southeast Asian countries like Vietnam while having expressed their formal support for the BRI because of the reason mentioned above, it, however, remains cautious about the economic, political, and strategic implications of this initiative. Vietnam is amongst Southeast Asian countries where the implementation of BRI is relatively slow. The biggest challenges facing China's BRI in Vietnam are the concerns of 'debt-trap' and the issue of trust since it passes through the SCS. While the Sino-Vietnamese relations have since early 1990 matured into a normalised relationship with China and Vietnam also establishing a Comprehensive Strategic Partnership in March 2013, the mutual confidence between the two countries has not been fully restored (Chakraborti, 2013).

Tensions between Vietnam and China over the Paracel and Spratly Islands in the South China Sea have intensified in recent years, followed by the 2014 oil rig crisis, which has led to a rising anti-China sentiment in Vietnam. China has been willing to fund projects in Vietnam that includes steel mills, coal-fired power plants, high-speed railways and highways, and so on. Vietnam remains cautious about taking loans from China and has been resorting to securing funding from other sources such as from international financial institutions and Overseas Development Assistance (ODA) partners in Japan. Vietnam prefers Japanese contractors and technologies as they are perceived by the Vietnamese as being more trustworthy in comparison to the ones from China. This cautious approach of Vietnam toward China has been a factor in limiting the implementation of the BRI (Hiep, 2018).

Other major projects under the BRI which include more than two parties such as the China-Thailand-Laos High-Speed Railway railway line is also facing challenges, particularly in the Thailand section of the

HSR. While there have been issues pertaining to land procurement as well as the commercial viability of the project, the delay has also been caused due to disagreements over the terms of the loan set out by the EXIM Bank of China (Green, 2019). In the case of the Philippines where China pledged to invest US$ 24 billion, including US$ 9 billion in loans and US$ 15 billion in direct investments, it has barely materialised (Ujvari, 2019). Further, there has been criticism of the BRI's Maritime Silk Road projects. According to writings from the Philippines' Centre for International Relations and Strategic Studies, the Philippines involvement in the BRI's port infrastructure development would face issues with regard to the implementation given the logistical, political, and financial challenges that prevail within. The Centre has argued that the Philippines need to undertake a comprehensive check before commencing the various port projects under the BRI. This caution has been advised given that a number of port development projects under the BRI in other countries are facing difficulties in terms of implementation as well as inability towards their debt obligations to the Chinese institutions (Estrada, 2017).

In Myanmar where China through the BRI is undertaking investment in securing its energy, there are growing concerns in the long-term uncertainty about the commercial viability and Environmental, Social, and Governance (ESG) risk. Despite Myanmar's openness to loans from China, it has in the past already demonstrated its preparedness to pull the plug on Chinese-backed projects. In 2011, under President Thein Sein the Myitsone dam project estimated to be of US$ 3.6 billion was suspended due to pressure from local and national activists. These were due to the ESG concerns since the dam would have displaced thousands as well as have an impact on the agriculture and fish downstream. Further in August 2018, Myanmar also scaled back on the initial US$ 7.3 billion Kyauk Pyu deepwater port, on the western tip of Myanmar's conflict-torn Rakhine state, due to debt fears (Ujvari, 2019). The February 2021 Myanmar coup has further complicated the business environment in the country, placing Chinese projects directly at risk and threatening its economic interests in the country. Further, the civil unrest, anti-China sentiments and Myanmar's attempt to reduce China's influence have dragged Chinese projects into the centre of the domestic political dispute (Yu, 2021).

Despite these challenges and a sharp drop in total BRI investments since 2019, on account of the COVID-19 pandemic, Southeast Asia remains important. In 2020 Southeast Asia with US$ 16.9 billion surpassed Europe and became the BRI's largest investment destination, accounting for 36 per cent of the total investments. Since the pandemic, Southeast Asia has become more important to BRI investments on account of the COVID-19 disruptions in the West, and growing geopolitical tensions. A large part of BRI investment in Southeast Asia is focused on building supply chain infrastructures, such as Power Construction Corporation's gas-fired power plants in Myanmar and Zhejiang Huayou's nickel and cobalt projects in Indonesia. With these projects, China is looking at exporting excess capacity while importing resources for its manufacturing base (Yu, 2021).

Conclusion

Southeast Asia has long been strategically important for China's interests, with whom the countries of the region have the most diverse cooperation. Through its economic statecraft, China today shares a robust economic relationship with countries in Southeast Asia and has become its major trading partner. This makes the BRI a natural progression in their ongoing partnership. There are also the geostrategic considerations which China continues to downplay by redefining the commercial aspects of the BRI. Challenges exist in the implementation of the various projects under the BRI considering the divergences in terms of the environmental, social, and security risks. This has resulted in regional pushbacks from some of the Southeast Asian countries such as Malaysia suspending the construction of the ECRL and Myanmar downsizing of projects.

There is a dichotomy that despite persisting issues amongst some of the Southeast Asian countries with China, they continue to remain a part of the BRI. This stems out from the fact that the BRI provides opportunities not only for China but for the countries in Southeast Asia. In recent years Vietnam and Thailand have taken a more assertive stance in negotiating the terms of the BRI-related projects; while Malaysia, the Philippines, and Indonesia have been very cautious. In the post-pandemic period, Southeast Asian markets become even more important for China and would thus witness a further increase in terms of BRI investments.

Further, the ongoing challenge to the existing multilateral trading regime and the need for a post-pandemic economic recovery where infrastructure and connectivity would play a major role would push greater dependency between Southeast Asia and China through the BRI.

References

"Big blow to China as Thailand scraps KRA canal project". (2020). *WION*, 4 September, at https://www.wionews.com/world/big-blow-to-china-as-thailand-scraps-kra-canal-project-325142

Bowie, Nile. (2018). "Mahathir puts Uighur rights above China ties", *Asia Times*, at https://www.asiatimes.com/2018/10/article/mahathir-puts-uighur-rights-above-china-ties/

Canal Conundrum. (2019). Indo-Pacific Defence Forum. 28 January, at https://ipdefenseforum.com/2019/01/canal-conundrum/

Chan, Irene. (2017). "Current Trends in Southeast Asian Responses to the Belt and the Road Initiative", *ASEAN and the Indian Ocean: The Key Maritime Links*, at http://www.jstor.com/stable/resrep05888.10

Chakraborti, Tridib. (2013). "Rising India-Vietnam Ties in the Emerging Security Architecture of the Asia-pacific Region", in Rajiv K Bhatia, Vijay Sakhuja, and Vikash Ranjan (eds), *India-Vietnam: Agenda for Strengthening Partnership*. New Delhi: Shipra Publication.

"China-Thailand Railway Project: The Route and Key Events", *CGTN*, 13 August 2019, at https://news.cgtn.com/news/2019-08-01/China-Thailand-Railway-INqEbn7Suc/index.html.

Chirathivat, Juthiphand. And Cheewatrakoolpong, Kornkarun. (2015). "Thailand's Economic Integration with Neighbouring countries and Possible Connectivity with South Asia", Asian Development Bank Institute, Working Paper Series No: 520, April, at https://www.adb.org/sites/default/files/publication/159839/adbi-wp520.pdf.

Damuri, Yose Rizal, Perkasa, Vidhyandika. Atje, Raymond and Hirawan, Fajar. (2019). "The Belt and Road Initiative in Indonesia: Importance, Concerns and Issues on the Implementation", Centre for Strategic and International Studies, at http://www.jstor.org/stable/resrep25409.5

Das, Suranjan, Chakraborti, Tridib and Bhattacharya, Subhadeep. (2018). *Indo-Vietnam Relations in the Emerging Global Order*. New Delhi: KW Publishers Pvt Ltd.

Department of International Economic Affairs, Ministry of Foreign Affairs. (2017). "Thailand's Economic Outlook and Key Economic Politicise", at https://www.thaiindia.net/images/Pages_from_Thailand_Economic_Fact_Sheet_Quarter_1-2560_as_of_July_2017.pdf.

East Coast Rail Link (ECRL) Project, Malaysia. (2019). "Railway Technology", 1 August, at https://www.railway-technology.com/projects/east-coast-rail-link-ecrl-project/.

Estrada, Darlene V. (2017). "The Belt and Road Initiative and Philippine Participation in the Maritime Silk Road", *Centre for International Relations and Strategic Studies*, Foreign Service Institute, Republic of Philippines Vol IV, No 7, April, at http://www.fsi.gov.ph/the-belt-and-road-initiative-and-philippine-participation-in-the-maritime-silk-road/.

Frankly Speaking: China Petroleum gets the best of both worlds. (2021). "The Edge Malaysia", 1 November, at https://www.theedgemarkets.com/article/frankly-speaking-china-petroleum-gets-best-both-worlds.

Ferchen, Matt. (2021). "The Two Faces of China Model The BRI in Southeast Asia", in Florian Schneider (ed). *Global Perspectives on China's Belt and Road Initiative*, Amsterdam University Press.

Green, David. (2019). "Thailand pushes China's Belt and Road despite differing visions", *Nikkei Asian Review*, at https://asia.nikkei.com/Spotlight/Belt-and-Road/Thailand-pushes-China-s-Belt-and-Road-despite-differing-visions.

Hallgren, Henrik and Ghiasy, Richard. (2017). "Security and Economy on The Belt and Road: Three Country Case Studies", SIPRI Insights in Peace and Security, No. 2017/4, December 2017, at http://www.jstor.com/stable/resrep24480.

Hicks, Jacqueline. (2019). "Political sensitivities surround the BRI in Indonesia", *Asia Dialogue*, at https://theasiadialogue.com/2019/01/30/political-sensitivities-surround-the-bri-in-indonesia/.

Hiep, Le Hong. (2018). "The Belt and Road Initiative in Vietnam: challenges and prospects", ISEAS, Newsletter 81, Autumn, at https://iias.asia/the-newsletter/article/belt-road-initiative-vietnam-challenges-prospects.

Hong, Zhao. (2017). "One Belt One Road and China-Southeast Asia Relations", in Lowell Dittmer and Ngeow Chow Bing (eds.), *Southeast Asia and China: A Contest in Mutual Socialization*. Singapore: World Scientific Publishing Co. Pte. Ltd.

Huy, Duong Van. (2020). "A Vietnamese Perspective on China's Belt and Road Initiative in Vietnam", *Contemporary Chinese Political Economy and Strategic Relations: An International Journal*, Vol 6, No. 1, April/May, pp. 145-185.

"Indonesia to propose projects worth US$ 91 billion for China's Belt and Road", *The Straits Times*, 2019, at https://www.straitstimes.com/asia/se-asia/indonesia-to-propose-projects-worth-us91-bilion-for-chinas-belt-and-road.

Karpathiotaki, Pelagia, Tian, Yunhua, Zhou, Yanping and Huang, Xiaohao. "China's Belt and Road Initiative: Contributions to connectivity", in Christopher Findlay and Somkiat Tangkitvanich (eds). *New Dimensions of Connectivity in the Asia-Pacific*. Canberra: ANU Press.

Kambara, Tatsu., and Howe, Christopher. 2007. *China and the Global Energy Crisis: Development and Prospects for China's Oil and Natural Gas*. Cheltenham: Edward Elgar Publishing Limited.

Kha, Sok. (2019). "The Belt and Road in Cambodia: Successes and Challenges", *The Diplomat,* at https://thediplomat.com/2019/04/the-belt-and-road-in-cambodia-successes-and-challenges/.

Kuo, Mercy A. "Malaysia in China's Belt and Road", *The Diplomat,* 23 November 2020, at https://thediplomat.com/2020/11/malaysia-in-chinas-belt-and-road/.

Majid, Tan Sri Munir. (2018). "Conclusion- If Truly Collaborative the BRI can Work for All", China's Belt and Road Initiative (BRI) and Southeast Asia, at http://www.lse.ac.uk/ideas/Assets/Documents/reports/LSE-IDEAS-China-SEA-BRI.pdf.

"Malaysia and China sign deal to resume East Coast Rail Link", (2019). Railway Technology, at https://www.railway-technology.com/news/malaysia-and-china-sign-deal-to-resume-east-coast-rail-link/.

"Malaysia's East Coast Rail Link Back on Track", (2020). Silk Road Briefing, 10 September, at https://www.silkroadbriefing.com/news/2020/09/10/malaysias-east-coast-rail-link-back-on-track/.

"Malaysia halts construction of $20 bn East Coast Railway Link project", (2018). Railway Technology, at https://www.railway-technology.com/news/malaysia-halts-construction-20bn-east-coast-railway-link-project/.

Mattiazzia, Laura. (nd). "One Belt One Road: Its relevance to Australia's Future Prosperity", at https://www.linkedin.com/pulse/one-belt-road-its-relevance-australias-future-laura-mattiazzi.

Mobley, Terry. (2019). "The Belt and Road Initiative", *Strategic Studies,* Vol 13, No. 3 (Fall 2019), pp.52-72.

"Myanmar Pipeline gives China Faster Supply of Oil from Middle East", *South China Morning Post,* 2017, at https://www.scmp.com/new s/china/economy/article/2086837/myanmar-pipeline-gives-china-faster-supply-oil-middle-east.

"Our Bulldozers, Our Rules: China's Foreign Policy could Re-shape a good part of the world Economy," *The Economist,* 2016, at http://www.economist.com/news/china/21701505-chinas-foreign-policy-could-reshape-good-part-world-economy-our-bulldozers-our-rules.

Panwar, Namrata. (2009). "India and China Competing over Myanmar Energy Resources", Working Draft for BISA Conference, at https://www.bisa.ac.uk/index.php%3Foption%3Dcom_bisa%26task%3Ddownload_paper%26no_html%3D1%26passed_paper_id%3D125+&cd=6&hl=en&ct=clnk&gl=in.

Tenth Regional EST Forum in Asia, 14-16 March 2017, Vientiane, Lao. (2017). Intergovernmental Tenth Regional Environmentally Sustainable Transport (EST) Forum in Asia, 2030 Road Map for Sustainable Transport: Aligning with Sustainable Transport Development Goals (SDGs), Country Report Cambodia, at https://www.uncrd.or.jp/content/documents/5132Cambodia_country%20report_EST_VT.pdf.

"The South China Sea Arbitration (The Republic of the Philippine Vs The People's Republic of China)". (2016). *Security-Risks.com.,* at http://www.security-risks.

com/security-trends-south-asia/other-security-trends/south-china-sea-arbitration-summary-of-tribunal-award-6433.html.

Tiezzi, Shannon. "Who Is (and Who Isn't) Attending China's 2nd Belt and Road Forum", *The Diplomat*, 2019. at https://thediplomat.com/2019/04/who-is-and-who-isnt-attending-chinas-2nd-belt-and-road-forum/.

Ujvari, Balazs. (2019). "The Belt and Road Initiative – the ASEAN Perspective", Security Policy Brief, Egmont Royal Institute for International Relations, at http://www.jstor.com/stable/resrep21387.

United Nations Conference on Trade and Development. (2015). World Investment Report 2015: Reforming International Investment Governance, at http://unctad.org/en/PublicationsLibrary/wir2015_en.pdf.

United Nations, Division for Ocean Affairs and Law of the Sea. (2013). Declaration and Statements: Oceans & Law of the Sea, at http://www.un.org/depts/los/convention_agreements/convention_declarations.htm.

V, Harini. (2018). "Xi's visit to the Philippines may be an attempt to 'woo Manila away' from Washington's orbit", CNBC, at https://www.cnbc.com/2018/11/21/china-xis-visit-to-manila-may-be-to-woo-philippines-from-us-expert.html.

Vannarith, Chheang. (2017). "Cambodia Embraces China's Belt and Road Initiative", *Think Asia,* at https://think-asia.org/handle/11540/7213.

Vanyuth, Chea. (2021). "Phnom Penh-Sihanoukville expressway 70 percent completed", *Khmer Times,* 13 December, at https://www.khmertimeskh.com/50987282/phnom-penh-sihanoukville-expressway-70-percent-completed/.

Yan, Jinny. (2018). "The Belt and Road Initiative in Southeast Asia", China's Belt and Road Initiative (BRI) and Southeast Asia, at http://www.lse.ac.uk/ideas/Assets/Documents/reports/LSE-IDEAS-China-SEA-BRI.pdf.

Yu, Kaho. (2021). "The Belt and Road Initiative in Southeast Asia after the COVID-19: China's Energy and Infrastructure investments in Myanmar". ISEAS Perspectives 2021/39, 6 April, at https://www.iseas.edu.sg/articles-commentaries/iseas-perspective/2021-39-the-belt-and-road-initiative-in-southeast-asia-after-covid-19-chinas-energy-and-infrastructure-investments-in-myanmar-by-kaho-yu/.

Part IV
BRI in Arab World

16. BRI and the WANA Region: An Assessment

Fazzur Rahman Siddiqui

Abstract

The Belt and Road Initiative (BRI) is perhaps the most ambitious geo-economics vision in recent history launched by China in 2013. It intends to strengthen hard infrastructure with new roads and railways, soft infrastructure with trade and transportation agreements, and even cultural ties with university scholarships and other people-to-people exchanges.

The West Asia and North Africa (WANA) region occupies a central place in the vision of BRI because of abundance of hydrocarbon resources in the region which would be a catalyst in the success story of the BRI. The WANA has its strategic location between three important seas—the Mediterranean, Red Sea and the Persian Gulf, which are of vital importance for China's trade and oil routes. China's long, traditional cooperation with the WANA region focuses on energy, but is politically based on foreign policies and principles similar to those pertaining to other countries. The BRI provides a new dynamic for deepening cooperation with the Arab world, as the traditional economic relations remain in the energy and daily-necessity goods sectors. Through the BRI, a new framework of cooperation was set up, based on energy cooperation, infrastructure building and trade-investment, and nuclear power industry, space satellites and new types of energy.

In the light of the above, this paper will primarily look into the brief history of the BRI and will also explore how this mega project aims to integrate the major parts of the world in its ambit of trade and commerce. The principle objective of this paper revolves around the critical examination of the engagement of the BRI with the Arab world and how it would benefit the region and in what way China's outreach to the Arab world will equally help China in its pursuit of this mission because of abundance of oil and gas in the region.

Introduction

One of the most significant diplomatic and economic engagements for China in the 21st century has become in the form of launch of the new Silk Road Project, very often dubbed as Belt and Road Initiative (BRI). The 'Belt' (the Silk Road Economic Belt) stretches from western China to Europe via Central Asia. The 'Road' (the 21st Century Maritime Silk Road) links China to Europe via the South China Sea, Indian Ocean and the Red Sea (Sharma, 2019).

The project would connect Europe and Pacific through a series of transcontinental and transoceanic networks that would run across the major Islamic/Arab countries of Africa and Asia. China is using the slogan of BRI to describe the Silk Road Economic Belt (overland route through Central Asia and West Asia) and Maritime Silk Road (the sea land joining the pacific and Indian Ocean with the Mediterranean). The scope of the BRI is broad covering now 149 countries with six economic corridors: The new Eurasia Land Bridge; the China-Central Asia-West Asia Economic Corridor; the China-Pakistan Economic Corridor; the Bangladesh-China-Myanmar Economic Corridor; the China-Magnolia-Russia Economic Corridor and the China-Indochina Peninsula Economic Corridor (Greening the BRI, 2022). Of the six BRI corridors, West Asian corridor is the most critical for Beijing as it acts as a gateway to Chinese connectivity with Europe and the Mediterranean Sea. On the one hand, it means securing much-needed energy security for China and on the other hand, it means expanding economic ties between China and many of the West Asian countries (Manish, 2021).

BRI: A Brief Overview

The plan was first revealed in 2013 during the visit of Chinese President Xi Jinping to Kazakhstan and Indonesia. It was first called Silk Road

Economic Belt and Maritime Silk Road, later One Belt One Road Initiative and finally, it was designated as BRI (Stanley, 2018). It signals a new emerging trend in China's foreign economic policy and has been described by China as the third round of China's opening after development of Special Economic Zone in 1980s and accession to WTO in 2001. The total cost of the BRI is expected to be at the tune of somewhere between US$ 1.2 to 1.3 trillion. The BRI is also an initiative to harness all Chinese opening to the Islamic world in order to promote China as an Islamist-friendly state that stands apart from the US and Europe who have stigmatised Islam and Muslim for centuries (Bianchi, 2019). Given the growing importance of the BRI in global trade and economic sphere, 21 countries of the WANA region have joined the BRI and 18 of them are part of the Arab landscape (Shahwan, 2022).

BRI and Arab World

Over the decades and particularly in the last two decades amidst its economic rise and its subsequent growing reliance on Arab oil and gas, China started seeing the region as a focal point of its strategic outreach. This new Chinese outreach also coincided with Arab's eastward movement in search for new allies after the explicit sign of the US' disengagement from the region after its decades-old economic, strategic and diplomatic presence in the region. The emerging new Arab-China nexus seems to have become essential for the emerging new geopolitical axis in understanding Eurasian International affairs. As an energy-rich zone, Arab oil is likely to play a decisive role in the success story of the BRI and China is hence paying special attention toward the region after the launch of the BRI. Between 2001 and 2016, China's trade exchange with the Arab world rose twelve-fold from US$ 18 billion surpassing that of the US (Noureldin, 2020).

The BRI-inspired neo-globalisation template is the core of China's strategy to expand its reach and influence throughout the structurally attractive Arab market. At the same time, the promise of developing the infrastructure and the reciprocal flow of energy will provide the pivot of neo-globalisation in the Arab world. Definitely, the launching of the BRI and the Middle Eastern Corridor has provided wider scope and greater potential for China but at the same time, the countries in the Arab world have high economic and geopolitical stakes in China's BRI projects. Many countries in this region supply oil and natural gas and also China is the largest trading partner with many countries in the region. For a lot of Arab countries, the promise of an enormous infrastructure and investment programme has become quite attractive. This is due to the fact that most of these countries have slow economic growth as a result of falling oil prices and the existing political instability.

Chinese companies have already been involved in major construction work in the region. For the purpose of steering the BRI further, China created AIIB, where it infused US$ 100 billion in 2016 (Kamel, 2018). The bank has been joined and endorsed by majority of the WANA countries that are the members of the BRI. Similarly, New Silk Road Fund of US$ 40 billion has been created by China to promote private investments along the BRI which has already begun joint endeavours in the region such as power projects in Egypt and UAE. Over the years, the financial relations between China and countries in the region are increasing and more importantly, currency swap agreements have been signed between People's Bank of China and central banks in many countries of the region (Manish, 2021) to facilitate the BRI and it would also help in the internationalisation of Chinese currency Renminbi (RMB). A Chinese bank has signed this agreement for a local currency swap worth US$ 2.6 billion in 2016 (Manish, 2021).

As for energy, China is and will continue to be the world's largest importer of energy, trading with the GCC, Iran, and Iraq that provide 60 per cent of today's imports. During President Xi Jinping's visit to Saudi Arabia, Iran and Egypt in January 2016, he outlined plans to provide US$ 55 billion in loans and investments for infrastructure projects in the Arab world. The AIIB backed by its US$ 100 billion capital, was set to be a main source of funds. Qatar is establishing a US$ 20 billion investment fund for bilateral projects, while the UAE is setting up a US$ 10 billion joint sovereign wealth fund (Manish, 2021).

Apart from the obvious economic importance of China to the region, there are two key reasons why Arab states are showing such interest in the

BRI. Firstly, these countries—most notably the Gulf states—occupy a key strategic position with regard to both the land and maritime routes. This lends their ports an obvious significance which enhance the potentials of their economic prosperity. The second is that with the reduction of fossil fuels now firmly on the agenda, they need to diversify their economies with some alacrity; Saudi Arabia is the most compelling example. The Arab states have propelled the development of other forms of economic investments for infrastructure development to sustain their economies and diversify their trade.

According to China's General Administration of Customs, China in 2018 only imported around 462 million tons of oil, half of which was imported from WANA region, and it was the largest trading partner with eleven WANA countries, including Iran and ten Arab States. In 2019, China had signed agreements with 21 WANA countries including 18 Arab states to join the BRI project. The region's soaring interest in China was also highlighted in China-Arab Policy Paper in 2016 which laid out a detailed plan of strategic cooperation between China and the Arab world. Being an Arab Policy Paper, it ignored the non-Arab states of the region like Iran and Israel. The foremost objective of China in the region has been to dissociate trade and economics from the complexities of regional politics, whereas one of the BRI's defining characteristics has been the deployment of economic tools to serve strategic and political purposes (Manish, 2021).

2016 Visit of President Xi Jinping to the Arab World

The visit of China's President Xi Jinping in 2016 to three major countries (Saudi Arabia, Egypt, and Iran) was primarily to promote the BRI in the region. During this visit, he had announced US$ 55 billion in loans (commercial and preferential) and additional investments in the region (Kamel, 2018). During this visit, China signed a comprehensive strategic partnership with these three countries and later signed MoU with other Arab countries to make them part of the BRI. Under BRI, China has increased its economic ties with the region. According to one report, the Arab world would receive 24 per cent of the total BRI investment (Shrama, 2019) and further the Arab world has been attracted towards the BRI.

Under BRI, China will export labour and technology to the Arab countries and will strengthen education sectors and people-to-people exchanges. Chinese companies like HUAWEI and ZTE have already set up new branches in the region and under the BRI, it is expected to increase investments in future. The 2016 White Paper was different from 2015 Vision and Actions that talked little about the Arab world specifically but announced five cooperation priorities for developing relations with states that are part of the BRI: political coordination, facilities connectivity, unimpeded trade, financial integration, and people-to-people bonds (NDRC PRC, 2015).

The Arab world is situated at the heart of the BRI not only as convergence of three continents but also the Arabian Sea, Mediterranean Sea, Red Sea, Caspian Sea and Black Sea converged in the region. The maritime strategic channels like Hurmuz, Man dab, Bosporus and Dardanelles also fall in the same region. Likewise, Levant as a subset of region is of vital importance to China's BRI project because it is connecting route between Asia, Africa, Europe and the Mediterranean. The Levant region offers an alternative route through the Suez Canal to the Mediterranean Sea through the China-Central Asia-West Asia Economic Corridor (Chaziza, 2020). BRI has further added new impetus to the ties between China and the Gulf region because the latter happens to be rich in natural resources and because of its prosperous economy.

One should also understand that BRI does not stand to benefit all the countries in the region equally given their economic condition, resource endowment and their geographical and strategic locations but some countries are better placed to gain more out of it while others do not enjoy the same benefits. China has invented many small and big tools to promote the BRI in the region which include monitory linkages, deeper investments and enhanced trade relations. China is stepping up its investments, joint ventures, grants and bilateral lending (in the form of commercial and low-interest preferential loans with the long-term payback periods) to the region through Chinese policy banks. Under the BRI, Chinese investment in the fourteen countries of the region reached US$ 136.2 billion in the period until 2016 (Kamel, 2018). It has also signed a local swap currency agreements with Qatar, UAE and Egypt.

It has been done to facilitate the trade between China and the regional countries.

China has already launched many mega projects in the region which converge very well with the Gulf Vision development program launched by Saudi Arabia. The alignment of Saudi Vision 2030 and BRI have a high level of synergy which indicates the growing significance and influence of China in the West Asian region and Vision 2030 of Saudi Arabia has made easy for China to rebrand pre-existing patterns of cooperation in the BRI-Vision project. For sure, oil trade is the pillar of this relationship between the two nations and Kingdom's desire to upgrade its infrastructure has proved to be beneficial for China. Saudi Arabia is the largest trading partner of China in the region with a burgeoning trade volume between the two countries. According to Chinese Foreign Minister Wang Yi, "Saudi Arabia forms an important part of China's BRI and in West Asian region and interconnection between China and the Eurasian hinterland as well as an important hub connecting China with extensive African market" (Manish, 2021).

Many times both sides have claimed that the convergence between BRI and Saudi Vision 2030 will help in enhancing the military ties. In 2017, Saudi Arabian King Salman visited China and extended full support to BRI and in exchange, China too endorsed Saudi Vision 2030 and expressed its willingness to help Saudi Arabia diversify its economy (Manish, 2021). Many Saudi scholars like Samir Ataullah and Amir Tahiri have analysed the convergence between the Vision 2030 and the BRI to highlight the interconnected investment projects as the key feature of both. They are of the view that signing contracts with China will improve Saudi's economic position, thereby contributing to the Kingdom's Vision 2030. The vision offers China various bilateral cooperative opportunities that converge well with the BRI plan from Chinese perspective (Manish, 2021).

Under this vision, there has been a substantial Chinese investment and contracting in Saudi Arabia since the BRI was launched in 2013, valued at US$ 20 billion by the American Enterprise Institute (Fulton, 2022). Similarly, NEOM mega city creates another kind of synergy between Vision 2030 and the Chinese Digital Silk Road (DSR 2015) having many synergies which have paved the way for further Chinese inroads into Saudi Arabia. HUAWEI has been a big part of DSR story in Saudi Arabia which has signed five agreements with Saudi companies focusing on buzz word of the day, "smart" (Fulton, 2022). There are diversification of ties between China and Saudi Arabia despite China and Saudi Arabia being the largest importer and exporter of oil, respectively. Major projects under BRI with Saudi Arabia is an investment in energy sector and trade cooperation and volume trade between the two in 2018 reached US$ 51 billion. In 2019, Saudi oil exports to China surpassed that of Russia and China, over the years, has invested heavily in geological surveys in Saudi Arabia and two major companies Saudi Aramco and Chinese Sinopec signed many agreements in the recent past with a total investment of US$ 8.6 billion. In 2019, Saudi Aramco signed an MoU with the Chinese Zhejiang Free Trade Zone with an emphasis to incentivise Aramco's greater investment in Zhejiang's future downstream growth where Aramco acquired 9 per cent stakes in Zhejiang integrated refinery and petrochemical complex (ARAMCO, 2019).

Infrastructure development is another important sector in which China plans to maximise its investments in Saudi Arabia. China's railway construction cooperation has proved to be beneficial in developing various projects within Saudi Arabia. Part of China's railway diplomacy, Chinese companies have been at the forefront of rail construction in the wider West Asian region as many companies boost their spending on creating or upgrading existing railway infrastructure which also lies at the heart of China's BRI connectivity project. Saudi Railway Company and Chinese technology firm, Huawei signed an MoU for the joint development of smart railway system (Manish, 2021).

The main focus of Vision 2030 is to pivot towards a clean sources of energy—renewable and nuclear—and the Kingdom is looking to invest billion of dollars in wind and solar energy. To make the project successful, Saudi Arabia has begun acquiring a position in Chinese publicly trade wind and solar companies, setting the pace for further partnership in the renewable energy sectors. In 2019 only, two Chinese solar giants unveiled Saudi manufacturing plants in Saudi Arabia (Manish, 2021).

The ports and industrial parks have been central to many of the Chinese projects in the region which would create an economic chain linking China to the Gulf, the Arabian Sea, the Red Sea, and the Mediterranean. In 2018, China had called these industrial parks and port interconnections as two-wheel and two-wing approaches which would be a major feature of Chinese presence in the Arab world (Jonathan Fulton, 2019). The Khalifa port in UAE, Duqm port in Oman, Jizan port in Saudi Arabia, Port Said in Egypt and Ain Sokhna port in Djibouti all form the part of Chinese ongoing projects in the region under BRI. Chinese firms are likely to play role in interconnection projects in Iraq, Syria and Yemen. Under the BRI framework, China has linked trade with development and has emerged as a major provider of economic aid in the region and to ensure the sustainability of the BRI project, it has developed a direct interest in the stability and security of the region.

The BRI has emerged as an important axis of Gulf-China economic partnership as China has adopted an ambitious plan with a total allocation of US$ 1 trillion (Jameel, 2021). China has a strategic partnership with the UAE and this level of relationship might give an additional leverage to the UAE to benefit from the BRI it would be the real beneficiary of the BRI and the project seems to be a catalyst element in its shift towards other partners in the region. The UAE is not only the founding member of AIIB but is very keen to invest in BRI. It is also building a new Arab logistics hub along the BRI route, particularly in Horn of Africa to preserve its economic position as an economic hub in the region. Businesses in the UAE would be the main beneficiary of the progress of the BRI as the major focus of the BRI in the UAE is deepening the financial and commercial engagement. The UAE has been well to the fore in broadening its relationship with China. China is the UAE's second-largest trading partner while the UAE is China's second-largest partner in the Gulf region (Jacques, 2022). A UAE-China investment fund was established in 2015 and the UAE sees itself as becoming a major financial hub. Lying on the key trading routes to Africa, Europe and the Indian subcontinent, the UAE is well-placed to be a major beneficiary of the BRI.

Egypt occupies a central position in the BRI being a gateway to the European markets through its Suez Canal which connects Asia to Europe. Major project under BRI with Egypt involves China-Egypt Suez economic and trade cooperation zone. China has depended on it as its essential shipping mode to Europe, and around 20-25 per cent of the vessels crossing the Suez Canal are Chinese and around 59 per cent of Chinese exchange is through sea transportation (Mohamed, 2022). Many of the Chinese companies have already pledged close to US$ 20 billion in Egyptian infrastructure and obtained contracts for building major portions of the new capital to be established east of Cairo. The Chinese have listed Egypt as one of the top five destinations for mergers and acquisitions activity under the BRI initiative. Chinese direct investments in Egypt leapt to US$ 260 million in 2017 (Sharma, 2019). Egypt is at the centre of the BRI due to the presence of Suez Canal and it is likely to become the capital of new Silk Road and no other country than China has invested in Egyptian Suez Canal Corridor. A Chinese investment company has decided to construct an innovative multi-purpose terminal at Alexandria port. Chinese Railway Construction Company is also constructing a 70-km long railway track in and around the capital town of Cairo (Noureldin, 2020).

China has invested heavily in establishing the China-Egypt Suez Economic and Trade Cooperation Zone, thus China becoming the only country to establish its own state-led economic zone in the Arab world. Apart from providing jobs and offering training to local technicians, the zone plays an important role in enhancing bilateral industrial cooperation and driving cooperation in investments and financing. The China-Africa Development Bank is partially financing the expansion of China-Egypt Suez Economic and Trade Cooperation Zone.

Apart from Egypt, UAE and Saudi Arabia, China has taken the BRI to other regional countries like Iraq, Syria, Kuwait, Oman, Jordan, Lebanon, Bahrain and Qatar. Like with the UAE the major focus of BRI with Qatar is enhancement of financial and commercial engagement. With Iraq, it is about trade and infrastructure and with Oman, it is the development of industrial zone in Duqm. In Jordan, under the BRI, China aims to build a Sino-Jordan university and with Jordan, it also has a strategic partnership while in Kuwait it would establish a Silk city.

BRI: States versus Streets

Notwithstanding the open embrace of the BRI by most of the Arab states because of the huge promises involved in the BRI and rhetoric of the

Chinese authority vis-à-vis the BRI, many of the Arab commentators and political analysts like mentioned above have critical views of BRI as well as have their own suspicion. For them, the BRI is not a rope to connect the whole of the Arab world with the BRI but a shackle to usurp the regional countries of their sovereignty and territorial. They do not see it as an opportunity for their jobless youth as propagated by the Chinese authority because the nature of the project is such where the Chinese companies employ both their own money and labour which leave less scope for the accommodation of indigenous labour forces. Given the growing unemployment and declining economy, the Arab state would always embrace those projects or investments which would ensure jobs for their youth and economic well-being of the country. If many on the Arab streets are happy that BRI would offer jobs to them, there are other conservatives who harbour an apprehension that BRI would come along with an alien culture which has no convergence with local socio-cultural norms that might provoke conflict between the host culture and migrant culture. For many others, it is not about bringing the economic prosperity to the third-world countries like Africa or Asia but its principle objective lies in challenging the US hegemony in the Arab world and project itself as an economic alternative and replace the US, which has been reigning the regional polity for decades.

Given the Chinese side of the version about the BRI, it is explicit to see that lot of promises are involved in it and it is being projected to be an antidote to resolve all the economic plight of the Arab world but it fails to take into account if the Arab polity or the Arab leadership are capable enough to partner the Chinese authority in the successful implementation of the project. What seems to bother many of the policy experts and astute followers of the BRI's origin, evolution and story of its success and failure is the ambiguity involved in the blueprint of the BRI itself which in long term does not seem to have the capability to bring the economic prosperity it is promising to the world.

Conclusion

The BRI today features prominently in China's foreign policy and geo-economics. Under this initiative, the WANA region figures prominently due to its rich hydrocarbon resources along with its need to develop its infrastructure in various Persian Gulf nations. China is trying to present itself as a plausible alternative to the traditional great power politics at play in the region and with fresh tactics. This 'BRI is trying to increase China's economic reach in the WANA region. At the same time, Beijing holds a unique position of being friendly with all the Arab leaders.

The BRI has a huge economic and strategic implication for the region given the declining oil prices, seeping political instability in the region, emergence of complex business environment, weakening central authorities across the territories, lack of economic diversification and all these have curtailed ruling class's ability to tap potential for economic growth. The BRI is likely to fulfil the requirement of high-quality infrastructure to accelerate the investment, provide new jobs, and creates sustainable economic growth. According to the World Bank, the Arab states need around US$ 100 billion investments (Kamel, 2018) to maintain existing infrastructure to serve their burgeoning population and the BRI might be of great assistance to the Arab states. The crisis in the Arab economy, emerging out of decline in oil prices, slower global growth and political instability following 2011 Arab uprising, might be overcome by huge economic assistance under the rubric of the BRI. The BRI, with large-scale transportation and infrastructure networks, has enormous potential to alter regional trade and investment patterns, redefining regional hubs and networks and enhancing the Arab states' contribution to the global value chain. Recent economic development and modernisation process launched by Saudi Arabia, including the privatisation of ARAMCO offers China a good opportunity to further its economic engagement with the Kingdom. Arab countries have found complementarily between their economic and political objectives and BRI and have unanimously endorsed the initiative either by formally signing an MoU with China or by endorsing the initiative.

References

ARMACO, (2019). "Saudi Aramco expands downstream investment in China Zhejiang Free Trade Zone", September 5, 2019, at https://www.aramco.com/en/news-media/news/2019/aramco-expands-downstream-investment-in-china-zhejiang-free-trade-zone#. Accessed on20 July 2022.

Camille Lons, Janathan Fultons, Degang Sun, Nasr Al-Tamimi, "China's Great game in the Middle East", European Council on Foreign Relation, *Policy Brief*, 21 October 2019. https://bit.ly/3GFfEtg. Accessed on March 25, 2022.

Chaziza, Mordechai, (2020). *China's Middle East Diplomacy: The Belt and Road Strategic Partnership*, Sussex Academic Press.

Fulton, Jonathan. (2020). "Strangers to Strategic Partner: Thirty Years of Saudi-Sino Relations", Atlantic Council, 25 August 2020, at https://bit.ly/3vnOeFD. Accessed on 28 March 2022.

——. (2019). "China is Beocmona Major Player in the Middle East", 18 September 2019, at https://bit.ly/3QMeHoU. Accessed on 28 May 2022.

Greening the Belt and Road Initiative. (2022). UN Environment Management Group, May, at https://bit.ly/3sXI7Fv. Accessed on 28 March 2022.

Jameel, Kamil. (2021). "Economic Cooperation among UAE, Iran and Turkey and its relation with the Silk Road", *Khaleej Online, An Arabic Portal*, 27 November 2021, at https://bit.ly/3ogjAdO. Accessed on 26 February 2022.

Kamel, Maha S. (2018). "China's Belt and Toad Initiative: Impositions for the Middle East" , *Cambridge of Review of International Affairs*, University of Waterloo, 2018.

Manish (ed.), (2021). *The Belt and the Road Imitative: Implications for India*, New Delhi: Pentagon Press, p. 191.

Martin Jacques, (2018). "The UAE will have Significance in China's Road Drive", Gulf News, 27 February 2018, https://bit.ly/3OLYhfw. Accessed on 1 January 2022.

Mohamed Noureldin, et al., (2022)."A comprehensive study on strengthening IPR Paradigm affecting regional development based on 'One Belt One Road' collaboration between China and the Middle East", Wiley Academic Paper, School of Public Affairs, University of Science and Technology of China, Hefei, China, 31 August 2020.

NDRC PRC, (2015). "Vision and Action Jointly Building Belt and Road", *Belt and Road Forum for International Cooperation,* March 2015, https://bit.ly/3kmxc4y. Accessed on April 10, 2022.

Sharma, Anu, (2019) ."An Analysis of Belt and Road Imitative and the Middle East", *Asian Journal of Middle Eastern and Islamic Studies,* Volume 13, No. 1, pp. 35-49.

Stanley, M. (2018). "Inside China's Pan to Create a Modern Silk Road, Morgan Stanley", (An English Portal) 14 March 2018, at https://mgstn.ly/33PTBSA. Accessed on January 2, 2022.

17. BRI: An Era of New Arab-China Engagement

Arshad

Abstract

The chapter's primary focus is to examine China's BRI in different regions such as North Africa, the Levant, and the Gulf to provide a holistic picture of China's BRI and its implementation in the Arab World. It also highlights concerns of China and Arab World's regarding the BRI and how the role of the United States in the Arab World as the primary security provider challenges China's aspirations to implement the BRI.

Introduction

Belt and Road Initiative (BRI) is a part of China's 'grand strategy' shaped by Chinese intellectual discourse that structured the nation's foreign policy to protect the state's territorial and political integrity. Diplomacy, military might, and economic power are the core factors of the grand strategy to accomplish its long-term goals. The strategy aimed to strengthen China's relative position by enhancing its capability to gain favourable strategic results, maximise its power and augment its long-term economic prospects (Leverett and Bingbing, 2017, p. 112). BRI desired to accomplish two strategic targets: first, to reduce the dependency on the sea lanes passing through the Malacca and the South China Sea, it was necessary to develop a continental route for energy and trade imports; second, to secure its western province against the threats of instability and violence due to the growing instances of terrorism over the years, China desired to expand its security through a buffer zone between Xinjiang and Central Asia (Indeo, 2018, p. 136).

The combination of domestic and international policy and security factors termed "intermestic" is the core of the BRI initiative (Friedrichs, 2018, p. 163). China's foreign policy seeks to overcome internal security threats to establish and maintain stability and integrity of the country against the rising threats from the terrorists from Xinjiang Uygur Autonomous Region (XUAR) of China, bordering Central Asia (Blank, 2018, p. 181).

The BRI strategy in the Arab World reflects China's domestic drivers and desire to become a global power. In addition, the region's oil resources continue to be significant for China's regional policy. Sun Degang, Deputy Director at Middle East Institute, Shanghai International Studies University, elaborated that Beijing considers the Arab World a "market" of energy, investment, and trade that needs to be protected by its military. China's military relations with Arab countries centred on economic dependencies and short and long-term geopolitical goals. The former was to counter piracy off the coast of Somalia, maintain a logistical base in Djibouti, and protect its UN peacekeeping forces. The latter were its new defence partnerships, security contractors, joint military exercises, arms sales, and active participation in the UN Security missions (Dorsey, 2018, p. 249).

China became the largest foreign investor in the Arab World because the region had approximately 228 million people at the middle-class level with a purchasing power of US$ 1900 annually. China has signed BRI cooperation agreements with 17 Arab countries. It invested in energy, infrastructure development, and real estate in the Gulf region (Yahya, 2019).

China's BRI in the Arab World

Chinese President Xi Jinping's vision of BRI aimed to revive the pre-modern Silk Road. The modern version was to tie the region with China's manufacturing hubs through both land and water infrastructural projects. The "Modern Silk Road" that connected the eastern coastal provinces of China to the Gulf region was revitalising the ancient land and maritime trade and energy relations. Since the new century, oil-rich Gulf countries and fast-growing Asian countries like China have accelerated the exchanges of commodities, people, and capital (Barton, Boer and Wilson,

2006). The connectivity between East Asia (China) and the Arab region in recent years has reached the highest level, shaping the global economy and shifting the World's economic centre of gravity from the US and Europe to the Arab World and East Asia (Glain, 2008).

On 5 June 2014, Beijing held the sixth ministerial meeting of the China-Arab States Cooperation Forum (CASCF). The meeting issued three documents, namely, the "Beijing Declaration", the "Action Plan for 2014-2016," and the "Development Plan for 2014-2024". A comprehensive cooperation strategy was also proposed, known as the "1+2+3 Strategy" (Degang, 2015; BRICS Policy Centre, 2016). One referred to energy cooperation; two referred to improving trade and investment; and three referred to cooperation in new sectors, including nuclear energy, aerospace technology, and new energy. President Xi linked the meeting's objectives with BRI, emphasising infrastructure and trade networks. President Xi also announced the integration of the development of China with Arab states to form a 'community of common interests and a 'community of common identity' (Cheng, 2016, p. 51). The strategy also aimed to bolster the Sino-Arab ties, emphasising the region's geo-economics (Teo, 2019, p. 159).

China's BRI, Maritime Silk Route, and "1+2+3 Strategy" were central to China's 'grand strategy' to grow trade and expand global outreach to access natural resources under the collective strategy. In this way, President Xi altered Deng Xiaoping's foreign policy orthodoxy of "hide your strength, bide your time, never take the lead" (Youvi, 2011). Today's China follows a "more assertive, activist and vigorous international policy to expand Chinese interests in the region and beyond" (Sanger and Wongmay, 2015). China utilised the platforms such as the Forum on China-Africa Cooperation and the Union of the Arab Maghreb to deeper its engagement with the Maghreb countries.

On 14 January 2016, China published *Arab Policy Paper*; it was President Xi's first articulation of a policy toward the Arab World. The paper promoted the "1+2+3" cooperation pattern to upgrade pragmatic cooperation through the principle of broader consultation, joint contribution, and shared benefits. The paper developed a strategic vision that outlined foreign and defence policies to protect its expanding geopolitical, strategic, commercial, and economic interests in the region.

Also, the paper outlined China's role and status as an emerging global power and its relationship with the US in managing and resolving the conflict (Dorsey, 2017, pp. 1-2).

President Xi visited Saudi Arabia, Egypt and Iran in January 2016, to translate the policy paper into reality. Xi signed agreements with three Arab states to co-construct BRI in trade, investment, energy, and communication sectors. They also became the founding members of the Asia Infrastructure Investment Bank (AIIB) (*Beijing Review*, 2016). At the Arab League headquarters, Xi stated that under the framework of the BRI, China "should be builders of peace, promoters of development, boosters of industrialisation, and supporters of stability and partners of people to people exchanges in the Middle East" (*People's Daily*, 2016). China and the Council of Foreign Ministers of the Gulf Cooperation Council (GCC) negotiated to establish a Free Trade Agreement (FTA) and direct currency swaps. While visiting Tehran, President Xi Jinping met Supreme Leader Ali Khamenei of Iran and pointed out that China and Iran are 'natural partners' in implementing the "Belt and Road" initiative.

BRI's Expansion in the Arab World

China expanded its Economic and Technical Cooperation in the Arab Region in infrastructure, transportation, and communications. The AIIB also became a platform for the investment and economic development of the partner countries under the BRI strategy. It prioritised connectivity with the Arab World through maritime routes. From the Arab Region, AIIB was joined by Bahrain, Israel, Iran, Jordan, Oman, Qatar, Saudi Arabia, Turkey, Algeria, Egypt, Sudan, Libya, Morocco and Tunisia (Asia Infrastructure Investment Bank). The regional members have been politically and ideologically in confrontation with each other since 2011 due to the region's changing political dynamics and shifting geopolitical calculus. BRI has expanded into the following geographical sub-regions of the Arab World.

North Africa

On 2 September 2015, President Xi and President Fatah al-Sisi of Egypt signed China-Egypt Production Capacity Cooperation Framework

Agreement. Suez Canal became part of the 'maritime road' of BRI. In terms of energy cooperation, Sinopec International Petroleum Exploration and Production Corporation of China purchased some of the assets owned by Apache Corporation of the US in Egypt. Besides, both the countries made progress in the Suez Economic and Trade Cooperation Zone project (Belt and Road Portal, 2017). A joint project was underway in early 2021 to renovate Cairo's iconic Citystars, carried out by China National Chemical Engineering Company Ltd. The project was seen as the embodiment of BRI and Egypt's Vision 2030 to target common future developments. On 30 November 2021, China and Egypt signed the MoU to establish a Cairo smart agriculture laboratory.

In March 2021, China and Tunisia signed the Economic and Technical Cooperation Agreement. China built the Ben Arous Sports Center and the Tunisian diplomatic academies in Tunisia (Belt and Road Portal, 2021). In November 2021, China and Africa held the Eighth Ministerial Conference Forum on China-Africa Cooperation (FOCAC) to ensure the strengthening of cooperation in the economic, technology and defence sectors. At the 5th China-Arab States Expo, Tunisia announced to host the first Arab-Chinese ministerial meeting in the tourism sector at the end of 2022. Besides, it proposed to create an Arab-Chinese observatory for sustainable tourism and a green economy (Belt and Road Portal, 2021).

In April 2013, the 13th Escort Taskforce of the Chinese Navy visited Algeria. Next year, both countries signed the Comprehensive Strategic Partnership to speed up the implementation of the joint development of the BRI in areas of the economy, trade, investment, energy, mining, and infrastructure. China signed the Economic and Technical Cooperation Agreement with Algeria on 11 October 2020 (Algeria Press Service, 11 October 2020). Besides, China completed many projects in the country, such as the East-West Highway, North-South Highway, the Great Mosque of Algiers, the world-class Centre International de Conferences, and the Opera House in Algiers that became new symbols of Chinese-Algerian friendship (Belt and Road Portal, 2021).

China endorsed the formation of the National Unity Government in Libya and signed a Memorandum of Understanding (MoU) highlighting cooperation in economic, technical, and strategic sectors. In March 2021,

Chinese and Moroccan legislative bodies agreed to enhance the exchanges and cooperation at the political level. China aimed to build a joint China-Africa and China-Arab communities for a shared future in a new era (Belt and Road Portal, 2021). Moroccan Foreign Minister Nasser Bourita said that King Mohammed VI stressed developing relations with China as Morocco's unswerving strategic choice and set up unique working mechanisms to accelerate significant cooperation (Belt and Road Portal, 2020).

Levant Region

China and Israel have established an innovative, comprehensive partnership. Under BRI, Israel intends to connect the Red Sea to the Mediterranean through the Red-Med project. China built landmark projects in Israel, such as the new port of Haifa, the China-Israel Changzhou Innovation Park, and the China-Israel (Shanghai) Innovation Park that took bilateral relations to a higher level. China also invited Israel to participate in the Global Development Initiative. Besides, Haifa in northwestern Israel, the country's principal port, started operations at its newly automated contained port that used the 'smart port' management system and technology of Shanghai International Port Group (Belt and Road Portal, 2021).

In 2018, China and Palestine Authority signed a document to start the Free Trade Agreement. Besides, they also focused on water, agricultural development, power, and industrial projects. China's Foreign Minister Wang Yi issued a four-point proposal to solve the Syrian issue during his visit to Syria. The proposal included respecting Syria's sovereignty and territorial integrity and prioritising the well-being of Syrians. China's Foreign Minister Wang Yi also said that as partners in building the BRI, China and Syria would jointly discuss the ways to push forward mutually beneficial cooperation to rebuild Syria (Belt and Road Portal, 2021). In January 2022, Syria signed the agreement to join BRI formally.

China supported the UNSC channel, the International Syria Support Group, and a Special Envoy in Syrian peace talks. The Uyghur issue became the source of discord between both Turkey and China. China-Jordan promoted Strategic Partnership under the BRI platform to increase investment and business and establish regional peace and stability (Belt and Road Portal, 2020). Turkey and China did not upgrade their relationships to a Strategic Partnership due to their differences over Syria and the failure to reach an agreement on missile sales (Atli, 2018, p. 120). The Turkish government welcomed BRI as an opportunity for greater economic cooperation with China.

Gulf Region

China needed Gulf countries' oil and gas to expand its economy. Therefore, China started upgrading its Strategic Economic Partnership with Gulf Cooperation Council (GCC) countries which later joined BRI. China planned to synergise the BRI with Saudi Arabia's Vision 2030 and deepen bilateral cooperation in energy, infrastructure, investment, and communication technology. China expanded the industrial capacity cooperation with Saudi Arabia. The two countries conducted First Symposium on China and Saudi Arabia relations. China's naval escort fleet used the Port of Jeddah for replenishment. Also, Saudi and Chinese authorities signed an Online Silk Road initiative. In Iraq, China's CITIC, a conglomerate of infrastructure projects, won the bid in November 2021 to construct the Al Khairat Heavy Oil Power Plant Project in Karbala (Kurlantzick, 2020).

In 2013, China played an essential role in the agreement between Iran and the US and European Union (EU) to ensure the exercise of Tehran's rights to use nuclear power with limited capability (Garver, 2016, pp. 123-124). On his visit to Iran, President Xi emphasised bilateral cooperation on four issues: energy cooperation, connectivity cooperation, production capacity, and financial cooperation (*People's Daily*, 2016). China and Iran established the Comprehensive Strategic Partnership in 2016. The two foreign countries held a virtual meeting to reject the US-sponsored Democracy Summit and criticise it for instigating division in the World (Belt and Road Portal, 2021). On 14 January 2022, Iran's Foreign Minister Hussain visited China and announced it was time to implement the 'China-Iran 25 years Cooperation Program.' China is increasing its presence in Iran when Tehran and Washington's relations are going through a tense phase.

Some experts believe that Dubai is emerging as the epicentre of the modern Silk Road under BRI. Around 250,000 Chinese lived in Dubai in 2019 (Zacharias, 2019). Further, China constructed the Dragon Mart in Dubai (Karasik, 2016, p. 2). Qatar is China's leading LNG supplier. China raised the Kuwaiti Sovereign Wealth Fund to US$ 1 billion and constructed Kuwait's Silk City. Also, China established a Sino-Kuwait Refinery Petro-Chemical Integration Project in Guangdong. In Beijing Ninth meeting of the Joint Economic, Trade, and Technical Committee was held with Yemen.

China has supported Bahrain's Economic Vision 2030 and Oman Vision 2040. As a part of Bahrain's Economic Recovery Plan to boost post-pandemic growth, China targeted more than US$ 30 billion in strategic projects in infrastructure construction, big data, e-commerce, and other fields to upgrade Bahrain's economy. China and Oman jointly sought more remarkable development of the China-Oman Strategic Partnership in energy, investment, fisheries, and human resources (*Xinhua Net*, 2021).

In building infrastructure and housing, China invested in projects such as Light Rail Line in Mecca, an oil pipeline in the United Arab Emirates (UAE), and 40,000 housing units in Bahrain (Alterman, 2017, p. 7). China announced a multi-billion-dollar Joint Investment Fund with UAE and Qatar (*People's Daily*, 2016). In monetary cooperation, the People's Bank of China signed Memoranda on Cooperation about Establishing Clearing Arrangements of Renminbi with the central banks of UAE in 2015. Besides, since 2016, Renminbi has been used for trading directly with UAE Dirham and Saudi Rial.

Qatar became the first Arab country in April 2015 to launch a "clearing bank" to manage the transactions in the Chinese Yuan. China announced to expand cooperation with the Arab States in utilising the China-developed BeiDou Navigation Satellite System (BDS) in 2021. It will facilitate the establishment of BDS centres in the Arab states (*China.org*, 2021).

China's Expanding Energy Interests in the Region

China has 70 per cent of its oil dependency on foreign suppliers, and it feared the possibility of disrupting the energy supply chain in the coming times. Arab countries have the World's largest oil reserves. This reality pushed Beijing to establish relations with the littoral states around the Indian Ocean, expand its naval presence, and protect its energy supply chain (*Hindustan Times*, 2021).

The uninterrupted supply of crude oil to China depended upon the absence of any blockade on the Arab Peninsula's chokepoints. Iran controls the Strait of Hormuz, the throat areas of the Gulf, and the Gulf of Oman. It threatened to blockade the Strait of Hormuz when it faced economic sanctions, the strategic channel of world petroleum transport to cut off the energy transport of the Strait (Deghan, 2018). Therefore, China actively engaged with Iran and Gulf monarchies for economic and political benefits. In 2014 alone, China's oil imports from Gulf countries increased to 9 per cent (US Energy Information Administration, 2020). In 2015, China surpassed the US to become the World's biggest oil importer, further increasing its appetite for crude oil from the Gulf countries, Iran and Iraq, which could be ensured by BRI's success in the Region (*The Economist*, 2015). After the withdrawal of US forces in Iraq, China became the largest investor in oil and gas infrastructure. The International Energy Agency claimed that by 2035, China would be able to consume 25 per cent of Iraq's oil production. The relationship between China and Iraq is dubbed "the Beijing-Baghdad Oil Axis" (Blas, 2012). Also, China can increase the access to the oil resources of Iran once the economic sanctions imposed by the US get lifted.

Further, the political situation in Yemen pushed China to cease oil exploration in the Al Hajr field (McAuley, 2015). In 2020, China imported crude oil that totalled roughly US$ 176 billion. Forty-seven per cent of these critical imports came from Arab countries. Saudi Arabia became the largest crude oil supplier as of October 2021 (*Hindustan Times,* 2021). Iran, Iraq, Oman, UAE, and Kuwait were the major oil suppliers to China.

It was likely that through BRI and the "1+2+3 Strategy", China planned to strengthen its economy, and its new trade networks in seas and lands were solidified and protected (Le Miere, 2014, pp. 18-19). In 2015, China launched the "Far Seas" strategy for more proactive naval projection through Blue Water Fleet beyond its near seas, especially in the South China Sea (Himanil, 2015). According to China's *Defense White Paper*, PLAN would alter its focus from "offshore waters defence" to the amalgamation of "offshore waters defence" with "open seas protection" (2015, p. 12). Besides, China's 14th Five Year Plan (FYP 2021-2025) focused on energy economy, green society, ecological civilisation climate, and climate change improvement. It aimed to reduce carbon emissions before 2030 and achieve carbon neutrality by 2060 (Aluf, 2021).

China-US Engagement in the Region

The US is a significant part of the Arab World's security architecture. The US imposed sanctions on Iran, pushing it to find an alternative in China as a counterweight. Egypt and Saudi Arabia shifted their focus to China's growing economic might after sensing the US' reluctance to provide security and economic support (Alterman, 2017, p. 13). The limited capability of China, including the prevailing geopolitical situation in the Gulf and the Indian Ocean, made it difficult for Chinese authorities to challenge the US Navy so far away from their backyards. The option is a sort of 'major powers maritime cooperation" to influence Saudi Arabia, Bahrain, and Iran (Miyake, 2017, p. 6).

The US welcomed Beijing's anti-piracy campaign in the Horn of Africa, including the Peacekeeping Operations mandated by the UN. The US also strengthened its relations with India, Japan, and Australia, and did not include China in Trans-Pacific Partnership largely because of the assertive nature of the Chinese foreign policy (Scobell, 2018, p. 34). An alarmist view, particularly of Professor Noah Feldman, explained that the rivalry between US and China was not on the verge of a 'Cold War' but a 'Cool War'. In this scenario, while, on the one hand, economic cooperation is strengthening, on the other hand, in true classical realism sense, the power struggle was becoming more fundamental. The result was that the emerging 'resource race' might lead to proxy wars in the region between China and US (Feldman, 2015, p. 12).

Many recent analyses, commentaries, and reports shared the perceptions that China and the US are busy in a competition or rivalry in the region. Analysts agreed that the US is losing ground in the region to China because it failed to fulfil its promises to its partners, its strategy of "pivoting" to the Asia-Pacific region, and how it pulled out from Afghanistan and Iraq after failing to handle the terrorism and radicalisation. Besides, the emerging shale gas production reduced US dependency on the region. Experts believe that the BRI is the principal policy tool to expand China's presence in the region (Shichor, 2016, p. 5).

Arab World's Concerns Regarding BRI

The apparent withdrawal of the US from the Arab region seems to engender new sort of cooperation between China and the Arab world. The non-Arab countries, such as Iran and Turkey, have established strong relations with China. Beijing supported Iran's nuclear deal and rejected the sanctions imposed by the US. Turkey struggled to regain its lost streak with Arab countries that it achieved during the Arab Spring. All countries in the Arab World need to protect their relations with the US and other western powers. While opening some opportunities, BRI offered far less than a 'transformative' agenda for China in the region (Small, 2018, p. 189).

West Asian analyst Mehran Kamrava considered the "Beijing Consensus" or "China model" and its appeal to the Arab Region as a political symbol and a practical alternative for economic and governance systems. In a symbolic sense, the "China model" promised rapid economic growth under an authoritarian government. China had no controversial baggage of history in its involvement in the region, and it promised trade and aid to the people and regimes despite their ideological differences (Small 2018, p. 60).

The immediate concerns regarding the BRI projects are the lack of transparency, debt sustainability among the developing countries, and the viability of the success of the BRI model in the Arab World as China attempts to maintain equilibrium within the hostile Saudi Arabia-Iran relations. Newspapers such as *Jordan Times* and Amman-based newspapers have raised concerns about China's 'debt trap' diplomacy. Besides, BRI projects would be seriously affected by the instability generated by Riyadh and Tehran in sectarian and Islamist ideological hotspots such as Yemen, Iraq, Syria, and Qatar (Girard, 2018).

Conclusion

The present situation in the region is fluid. America seems to be reducing its footprints as it shifts focus on the Indo-Pacific region, while China is still playing a significant role in the region. However, China's role in the region will be limited to the economic realm without reaching the political and geostrategic power until the status of the US withdraws from the 'security' provider in the region. BRI is the principal initiative of China to expand its presence in the region. This can be termed an era of new Arab-China engagement. Further, the internal power dynamics of the region have affected the prospects of BRI at a time when concerns regarding the Chinese model of BRI are evident in the region.

References

The China-Arab States Cooperation Forum, *BRICS Policy Center*. (2016). https://bit.ly/3ammvNz. Accessed on 22 November 2022.

Algeria, China ink economic and technical cooperation agreement. *Algeria Press Service*. (2020, October 11). https://bit.ly/3MPKdjq. Accessed on January 19, 2022.

Alterman, J.B. (2017). "The Other side of the World: China, the United States, and the Struggle for Middle East Security", Center for Strategic and International Studies (CSIS), p. 13. http://www.jstor.org/stable/resrep23265.

Aluf. D. (2021). *China's reliance on Middle East oil, gas to rise sharply. Asia Times,* 30 December, at https://bit.ly/3LKeSO2. Accessed on 12 April 2022.

Annual Report on the Development of the Indian Ocean Region (2017): The Belt and Road Initiative and South Asia. (2018). Germany: Springer Singapore.

Asian Infrastructure Investment Bank. *Members and Prospective Members of the Bank*, at https://bit.ly/3sV6zbE. Accessed on 24 January 2022.

Atli, Altay. (2018). "China and Turkey: Sailing through tough waters", in Anderson, J.R. (ed.), *The Red Star and the Crescent: China and the Middle East*. Qatar: Oxford University Press.

Barton, D. Boer, K.D, and Wilson. GP (2006). "The New Silk Road: Opportunities for Asia and the Gulf", *The McKinsey Quarterly*, at https://bit.ly/3GeRiYx

Beijing, New Delhi must shake hands: Chinese Premier Li Keqiang. (2013). *Economic Times*, at https://bit.ly/38kl3dW

Blank, S. (2018). "Silk Roads and Global Strategy: China's Quest", in Anderson, J.R. (ed.), *The Red Star and the Crescent: China and the Middle East*, pp.189-207. Qatar: Oxford University Press.

Blas, J. (2012). "The Beijing-Baghdad Oil Axis", *The Financial Times*, 11 October, at https://on.ft.com/3amo0eF. Accessed on March 19, 2022.

Cheng, J. Y. S. (2016). "China's Relations with the Gulf Cooperation Council States: Multilevel Diplomacy in a Divided Arab World". *China Review, 16* (1), 35-64. http://www.jstor.org/stable/43709960. Accessed on December 12, 2022.

"China attaches importance to Jordan's unique role in international, regional affairs: FM". (2020). *XinhuaNet*, July, at https://bit.ly/3a9XBAv. Accessed on 11 February 2022.

"China, Arab states to expand win-win BDS cooperation". (2021). *China.org*. https://on.china.cn/3NBL3. Accessed on 11 February 2022.

"China, Egypt agrees to boost cooperation under Belt and Road Initiative". (2016). *People's Daily*, at https://bit.ly/38k5seq. Accessed on 18 January 2022.

"China, Morocco agrees to promote mutually beneficial cooperation". (2020). *Belt and Road Portal*, at https://bit.ly/3MNJZcM. Accessed on 11 January 2022

"China, Oman agrees to enhance cooperation, push forward China-GCC free trade talks". (2021). *Xinhua Net,* at https://bit.ly/3GfrKue. Accessed on 11 February 2022.

"China's reliance on Middle East oil increases: Report." (2021). *Hindustan Times,* at https://bit.ly/3lDvNHo. Accessed on 14 March 2022.

China-Algeria cooperation in the post-pandemic era has much potential to unleash. (2021). *Belt and Road Portal.* https://bit.ly/3wMtbNS. Accessed on 23 January 2022.

Chinese FM's visit to Syria to boost bilateral cooperation, says expert. (2021). *Belt and Road Portal.* https://bit.ly/3wLBYzB. Accessed on 16 February 2022.

Chinese, Iranian foreign ministers hold video meeting. (2021). *Belt and Road Portal.* https://bit.ly/38fR46M. Accessed on 11 February 2022.

Degang Sun, D. (2015). "China's Soft Military Presence in the Middle East," *Middle East Institute All About China Series*, https://bit.ly/39XOxikr.

Chinese realiance on Middle East Oil increases: Report, (2021), *Hindutan Times.* https://bit.ly/3AeobUa. Accessed on 22 January 2022.

Deghan, S.K. (2018). Iran threatens to block Strait of Hormuz over US oil sanctions. *The Guardian*, at https://www.theguardian.com/world/2018/jul/05/iran-retaliate-us-oil-threats-eu-visit-hassan-rouhani-trump. Accessed on 19 March 2022.

Dorsey, J.M. (2018). "China's Uyghur: A Potential Time Bomb", in Anderson, J.R. (ed.), *The Red Star and the Crescent: China and the Middle East.* Qatar: Oxford University Press.

Dorsey, M.J. (2017). "China and the Middle East: Venturing into the Maelstrom". *Asian Journal of Middle Eastern and Islamic Studies*, 11(1). https://doi.org/10.1080/25765949.2017.12023322. Accessed on 11 December 2022.

Egypt, Belt and Road Portal, at https://bit.ly/3wKOw9a. Accessed on 12 January 2022.

Feldman, N. (2015). *Cool War: The United States, China, and the Future of Global Competition.* United States: Random House Publishing Group.

Feng, C. (2015). Embracing Interdependence: The Dynamics of China and the Middle East. *General Information.* https://brook.gs/38J9A83. Accessed on 18 March 2022.

Friedrichs, J. (2018). "Intermestic security challenges: Managing transnational bonds". *European Journal of International Security,* 3(2), 162-186.

Garver, W. John, "China and the Iran Nuclear Negotiations: Beijing's Meditation Effort, in Anderson, J.R. (ed.), pp. 123-124, *The Red Star and the Crescent: China and the Middle East.* Qatar: Oxford University Press.

Girard, B. (2018). "China's BRI Bet in the Middle East", *The Diplomat,* https://bit.ly/3Gi3pnE. Accessed on 15 March 2022.

Glain, Stephen S. (2008). "The Modern Silk Road". *Newsweek,* 15 May, at https://bit.ly/3GhhrFX. Accessed on 3 January 2022.

Homi. K. (2017). The Unprecedented Expansion of the Global Middle Class: An Update. *Global Economy & Development,* Working Paper 100. Washington, DC: Brookings Institution.

Indeo, F. (2018). "The Impact of the Belt and Road Initiative on Central Asia: Building New Relations in a Reshaped Geopolitical Scenario", in Zhang, W., Alon, Ilan., and Lattermann, C., (eds.), *China's Belt and Road Initiative: Changing the Rules of Globalization.* Germany: Springer International Publishing.

Karasik, T. (2016). "The GCC's new affair with China. MEI Policy Focus". *Middle East Institute,* 6, at https://bit.ly/3zeAkYX. Accessed on 10 February 2022.

Kurlantzick, J. (2020). "China's Digital Silk Road Initiative: A Boon for developing countries or a danger to freedom?". *The Diplomat,* at https://bit.ly/3MLM5tv. Accessed on 19 February 2022.

Leverett, F., and Bingbing, W. (2017). "The New Silk Road and China's Evolving Grand Strategy", *The China Journal,* p. 77.

McAuley, A. (2015). "Oil's Vulnerable Trade Route". *The National.*

Patey, L. (2016). "China's New Crisis Diplomacy in Africa and the Middle East". *Danish Institute for International Studies,* at http://www.jstor.org/stable/resrep13115. Accessed on 12 December 2022.

President Xi speaks at Arab League headquarters. (2016). *People's Daily,* 22 January, at https://bit.ly/3MQp0WS. Accessed on 19 December 2022.

Sanger, D.E., and Wongmay, E. (2015). "As Obama Plays China Card on Trade, Chinese Pursue Their Own Deals". *New York Times.*

Scobell, A. (2018). "China's Search for Security in the Greater Middle East", in Anderson, J.R. (ed.), *The Red Star and the Crescent: China and the Middle East,* pp. 13-37. Qatar: Oxford University Press.

Shichor, Y. (2016). "Sino-American Crosscurrents in the Middle East: Perceptions and Realities", in Horesh, N. (ed.), *Toward Well-Oiled Relations? China's Presence in the Middle East Following the Arab Spring.* United Kingdom: Palgrave Macmillan UK.

Small, A. (2018). "Choosing not to Choose: The Belt and Road Initiative and the Middle East", in Anderson, J.R. (ed.), *The Red Star and the Crescent: China and the Middle East*. Qatar: Oxford University Press.

Teo, V. (2019). *Japan's Arduous Rejuvenation as a Global Power: Democratic Resilience and the US-China Challenge*. Germany: Springer Singapore.

The State Council Information Office of the People's Republic of China. (2019). "China's National Defense in the New Era", Defense White Paper.

The State Council: The People's Republic of China. (2015). "Chronology of China's Belt and Road Initiative", at https://bit.ly/38Pmgdt. Accessed on 13 January 2022.

The State Council: The People's Republic of China. (2016). Full text of China's Arab Policy Paper, https://bit.ly/3PLkECi

Tunisia, China signs economic, technical cooperation agreement. (2021). Belt and Road Portal, at https://eng.yidaiyilu.gov.cn/qwyw/rdxw/169499.htm. Accessed on 22 January 2022.

Tunisian FM stresses cooperation with China as China-Arab expo starts. (2021). Belt and Road Portal, at https://bit.ly/3wMt98I. Accessed on 14 January 2022.

Xi concludes Middle East trip with promoted ties and cooperation. (2016). *Beijing Review*, at https://bit.ly/3wKcl1P. Accessed on 12 January 2022.

Xi says China to continue promoting relationship with Israel. (2021). *B*elt and Road Portal, at https://bit.ly/3MLM09b. Accessed on 22 November 2022.

Yahya, M. (2019). "How has China's role in the Middle East evolved?", Carnegie Middle East Center, at https://bit.ly/39SHQ0B

Youvi, H. (2011). "Context, not history, matters for Deng's famous phrase". *Global Times*, at https://bit.ly/3NDiRwT. Accesed on 6 December 2022.

Zhang, W. et al. (2018). *China's Belt and Road Initiative: Changing the Rules of Globalization*. Germany: Springer International Publishing.

Part V
BRI in Continental Context: Europe, Africa and Latin America

18. BRI: Narratives and Counter-Narratives from Europe

Ankita Dutta

Abstract

The Belt and Road Initiative, launched in 2013 by China, aims to improve connectivity and cooperation on a transcontinental scale. Since it was launched, BRI has grown into a multifaceted initiative which is aimed at furthering trade, financial integration, enhancing connectivity and development of infrastructure. Through this initiative, Beijing aims to connect the country's hinterland to Europe through Central Asia. The BRI projects in Europe rest on four pillars—rail, road, maritime and digital routes. It tries to fill the gap in infrastructure development in the countries in Central, Eastern and Southern Europe. These countries have emerged as the gateway for the BRI projects in Europe. While the Chinese investments in the infrastructure sector have been welcomed, the BRI has elicited mixed reviews within the continent. On the one hand, the countries of CEE have been the site for Chinese outreach with 17+1 summits, and increased investment in critical areas of infrastructure; the initiative has led to increased concerns in the other European countries, including in relation to transparency of funding, debt-traps. This chapter seeks to analyse the BRI projects in Europe, and looks at the narratives and counter-narratives within the European countries.

Introduction

The Belt and Road Initiative (BRI), launched in 2013, represents President Xi Jinping's most ambitious foreign and economic policies. The initiative aims to improve connectivity and cooperation on a transcontinental scale and is unprecedented in terms of its financial engagement. Through this initiative, Beijing aims to connect the country's hinterland to Europe through Central Asia. This route has been called the Silk Road Economic Belt. The maritime component of the initiative, a 21st Century Maritime Silk Road, is envisaged to connect the fast-growing Southeast Asian region to China's southern provinces through ports and railways. In addition, the initiative also envisages a 'Polar Silk Route' to facilitate connectivity and sustainable economic and social development of the Arctic. The BRI tries to integrate historical symbolism of the ancient Silk Road with the requirements of 21st century. From the time of its inception, the BRI has become global (Sacks, 2021).

The BRI tries to fill in the gap in infrastructure development in the countries in Central, Eastern and Southern Europe. This is primarily because the EU's investment in infrastructure has declined significantly in the past decade, giving space for new players and actors to emerge. This was also highlighted in the European Investment Bank's report of 2019-20 which stated that, "infrastructure investment in Europe stands at a 15-year low of 1.6 per cent of GDP, with the greatest declines seen in regions that are already lagging behind in infrastructure". The report goes on to note that "the comparison with 2008 levels is most striking for the countries of Central and Eastern Europe, where current investment levels are around 35 per cent lower than before the [global financial] crisis" (EIB, 2019). On the other hand, Chinese presence in the continent has expanded exponentially in the past decade. Chinese Foreign Direct Investment (FDI) in Europe has increased to US$ 83 billion in 2020 from US$ 12.52 billion in 2010 (Statista, 2021).

While the Chinese investments in the infrastructure sector have been welcomed, nonetheless, the BRI has received mixed reviews within the continent. While countries in the Central and Eastern Europe (CEE) have been the site for Chinese outreach with 17+1 (former 16+1) summits, and increased investment in critical areas of infrastructure; the initiative has led to increased concerns in the other European countries, especially in relation to transparency of funding, debt-traps, etc. This chapter seeks to analyse the BRI projects in Europe, and looks at the narratives and counter-narratives within the European countries.

BRI in Europe

The BRI projects in Europe rest on four pillars—rail, road, maritime and digital routes. The route from the Arctic can also be added to this dynamics. The continental route is planned through both existing and newly planned railway lines between China and Europe. One of China's biggest infrastructure projects is the *New Eurasian Land Bridge* connecting China to Europe. This land bridge consists of a series of rail corridors running some 7,500 miles (12,000 km) from Yiwu in eastern China to western European destinations such as Madrid and London (Babones, 2017).

As part of the BRI, the initiative aims to improve transportation links between China and the rest of the continent. Once the freight line enters Europe, it connects China to some of the most important capitals and industrial areas on the continent. Railway tracks from China connect Kazakhstan, Russia, Belarus, Poland and Germany (Railfreight.com, 2022). These lines further bifurcate into various directions and connect to the port cities such as Hamburg, Rotterdam, Antwerp, Bilbao, Marseille, Dunkerque, and Vado Ligure. Another branch line that currently ends in Budapest in Hungary is to be further continued to the Balkans through a deal between Hungary, Serbia and China on upgrading the railway link between Budapest and Belgrade in January 2015 (Tonchev, 2017).

The land bridge complements the 21st Century Maritime Silk Road which was announced in October 2013 by President Xi in Indonesia with an idea to accommodate expanding maritime trade traffic. Under this initiative, China planned to invest in port development along the Indian Ocean, from Southeast Asia to East Africa and parts of Europe. This route has also grown to include the Arctic region under the Polar Silk Road initiative. Under its maritime initiative, the Arctic route passes through the North Sea in the Arctic region to connect China to the European ports-hub of Rotterdam in the Netherlands, Antwerp in Belgium and Dunkerque in France. The second maritime route passes through the Indian Ocean to the Mediterranean Sea, where it connects with the Piraeus Port in Greece and further passes through Adriatic Sea towards Venice.

With the advancement of technology, the BRI has grown to include the Digital Silk Road, which focuses on enhancing cooperation in the field of digital and innovation-driven economy. Launched in 2015, the Digital Silk Road has become an intrinsic part of the BRI with its emphasis on the "development and interoperability of critical digital infrastructure such as terrestrial and submarine data cables, 5G cellular networks, data storage centres, and global satellite navigation systems" (Ghiasy and Krishnamurthy, 2021). The presence of Huawei in some countries of Europe, the growing presence of other Chinese technology companies in sensitive sectors and the debates related to security implications of data being collected by Chinese companies are testimony of the ongoing concerns among the EU member states on all aspects of the BRI.

Figure 18.1: BRI in Europe

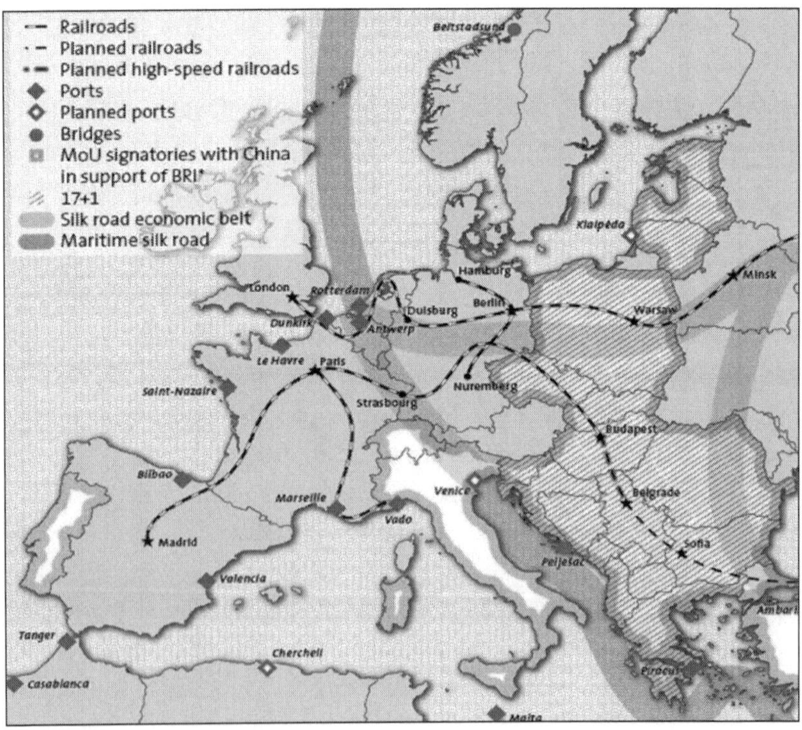

Source: https://isnblog.ethz.ch/economy/the-belt-and-road-initiative-in-europe

Narratives and Counter-Narrative on BRI

Since it was launched in 2013, BRI has grown into a multifaceted global initiative which is aimed at furthering trade, financial integration, enhancing connectivity and developing infrastructure. The Central and Eastern Europe has emerged as the gateway for the BRI projects in Europe. China's intensive outreach to the region can be traced to 2012 with the establishment of the 16+1 initiative (17+1 with the addition of Greece)[1] and increased investments in critical areas. The 16+1 initiative provided a platform for the 12 EU member states and 5 western Balkan states to cooperate with Beijing. As these countries are geographically situated between Western Europe and Asian continent, they are significant for Chinese plans of linking the two regions under the BRI development projects which are envisaged to reduce travel and shipment time between Europe and China.

Moreover, the bilateral relations between these countries and China also need to be factored in while discussing the BRI projects in the region. Since the announcement of the BRI and the regional mechanism of 16+1 platform, these countries have increased their interactions China and have "effectively became part of China's extended neighbourhood as the Western-most tip of the initiative" (Turcsányi, 2020). The importance that China, and the BRI, has gained over the years is visible in both the economic and political interactions. On the economic front, the initiative is aimed at deepening trade and investment cooperation – with China's trade with the CEE countries has increased to US$ 103.45 billion in 2020, and its investments in the region in 2020 were US$ 3.14 billion in sectors such as energy, infrastructure and logistics (*CGTN*, 2021). Infrastructure projects, in particular, have been the most visible investment in the region.

The BRI, while largely associated with CEEC, has also grown in presence in the EU, with many member states signing in as formal partners. The most important and strategic Chinese presence is witnessed in Greece, where the former has refurbished the port of Piraeus; and in Portugal where Beijing has invested in the port of Sines and in Portuguese energy sector. Hungary has emerged as another to be the key destination for Chinese investment in Europe, where they are working on the Budapest-Belgrade railway line and its further extension to Skopje, Macedonia, and further to Athens, Greece. This extension is expected to connect Hungary, which is a landlocked country with the ports in the Mediterranean and Adriatic Seas. There is also the already serviceable China-Europe Land Sea fast intermodal transport route connecting Hungary with the Greek Port of Piraeus, operated by Cosco Shipping, China (*Xinhuanet*, 2017).

The western Balkan States (Serbia, North Macedonia, Bosnia and Herzegovina, Albania and Montenegro) have been in the process of EU accession negotiations for a long time. With the EU's engagement wavering in the region, China has emerged as a critical player, helping these nations to fill the infrastructure development gap. China has not only developed bilateral ties with these countries but also engages with them at the 17+1 level. This has meant that the region has been able to attract Chinese investments, with Beijing becoming a significant economic partner in the region, with investments ranging from the energy sector to infrastructure development.

In terms of investment and BRI projects, Serbia takes the lead in the region. China has invested over €7 billion (Levchenko, 2021) in Serbia, mostly in form of loans to finance the infrastructure and energy projects. An example of this is the Sino-Serbian Friendship Bridge across the Danube in Belgrade. The acquisition of a steel plant in Smederevo by the Chinese Hebei Iron and Steel Company (now the Hesteel Group) for €46 million was the largest foreign investment in Serbia in 2016 (Reuters (b), 2016), and Beijing has also signed an agreement for the construction of a Belgrade-Budapest high-speed railway. In Bosnia and Herzegovina, Exim Bank of China is funding the construction of Preljina-Pozega motorway (*Seenews*, 2018). The Preljina-Pozega motorway is part of Corridor XI—a motorway corridor linking Bari, Italy to Bucharest, Romania via port of Bar, Montenegro and Belgrade, Serbia. Chinese companies are also involved in the development of two thermal power plants—Stanari in the Republic of Srpska and in Tuzla in the Federation of Bosnia and Herzegovina (*The Ecologist*, 2018).

Montenegro and Albania have signed an MoU with China Pacific Construction Group, CPCG, to build a €1.4 billion express highway between Montenegro and Albania—the Adriatic-Ionian motorway (*The Balkan Insight*, 2021). Montenegro has also signed a €689 million loan with the Exim Bank of China for the construction of the Podgorica-Kolasin motorway section which will link the city of Bar on the Adriatic

Sea to the border with Serbia (*France24,* 2021). The China Civil Engineering Construction Corporation is also involved in upgrading a 10km segment of the railway track connecting the port city of Bar with Belgrade. For its part, Macedonia is a crucial land-connect for China as it sits on the commercial route connecting the port facilities in Greece to Budapest, Hungary. It is also an important gateway to central and Western Europe. China is involved in construction of two motorways in the country—Miladinovtzi–Shtip in the east and Kichevo-Ohrid in the west (Shopov, 2022). After the agreement between Hungary, Serbia and China to upgrade the railway link between Budapest and Belgrade in 2015, Macedonia and China also agreed to prepare a feasibility study of the route and cost of modernising the former's railways (Tonchev, 2017).

Albania, given its location on the Adriatic Sea, is central to China's Maritime Silk Road. Moreover, given its energy resources, Shanghai-based Geo-Jade Petroleum Corporation, in 2016, bought the controlling rights of two Albanian oil fields from a Canadian company for US$ 442 million (Reuters, 2016). The Albanian government and the Exim Bank of China agreed to terms on the "construction of the Arbër motorway, a stretch of road running to the Former Yugoslav Republic of Macedonia and on to Bulgaria, thus linking the Ionian Sea and the Bulgarian part of the Black Sea coast. Last but not least, two Chinese companies, China Everbright and Friedmann Pacific Asset Management, have announced the acquisition of Tirana International Airport SHPK, which operates the Albanian capital's airport. The group will run the facility until 2025, with a two-year extension to 2027, subject to approval by the Albanian government" (Tonchev, 2017).

These projects and investments highlight the Chinese idea of closely connecting itself to Europe through a matrix of roads, railways and ports. The appeal of this cooperation lies in the fact that these arrangements are minimally regulated unlike the checks and balances put in place by the EU. Also, with the economic slowdown post-2009 Euro crisis, the region has looked beyond Europe for investments in various sectors. China also finds merit in engaging with the countries of the region. Given their strategic location, these countries have become a major transportation hub connecting the Mediterranean and Central Europe with China through networks of rail and road. Through these projects, the Chinese companies have been able to establish a foothold in the construction and infrastructure development sectors of these countries which has resulted in creating a job market for the large Chinese labour. The economic benefits of the BRI also transcend to the political arena as these infrastructure projects have provided a strong foothold to China in making its presence felt in the region. European nations have taken note of China's growing presence and are working together to highlight the challenges and problems associated with the lack of transparency, differences in rules and regulations and the prospects of debt traps, witnessed in various other BRI projects.

Counter-narratives—Reactions from the EU

While China's expanding footprint in Southeastern, Central, and Eastern Europe has brought socioeconomic opportunities and infrastructure development, it has also led to undermining of political and economic stability and has complicated the EU's ability to reach consensus on key issues. For long, the European policy towards China was driven by the idea of 'reciprocity', where the expectation was that as China would have access to the European market, EU would have the same level of access to the Chinese market. Also, EU expected China to adopt international liberal norms like human rights, rule of law, etc.

The year 2019 marked the beginning of a renewed European approach with the publication of 'EU-China—A Strategic Outlook' which called China "*a strategic competitor for the EU* while failing to reciprocate market access and maintain a level playing field" (emphasis added) (EU-China Strategic Outlook, 2019). It goes on to note that China is "an economic competitor in the pursuit of technological leadership, and systemic rival promoting alternative models of governance" (EU-China Strategic Outlook, 2019). Economically, in 2021, China was the second largest partner for EU exports of goods (10.2 per cent) and the largest partner for EU imports of goods (22.4 per cent). In the past decade (2011-2021), both exports to and imports from China have increased manifold. EU's exports to China were highest in 2021 accounting for €223 billion as compared to €127 billion in 2011. Similarly, EU's imports from China were highest in 2021 accounting for €472 billion and lowest in 2013 with

€239 billion (Eurostat, 2022). While the trade between the two remains high, the Chinese investment has in Europe was down in 2020 from US$ 13.4 billion in 2019 to US$ 7.2 billion (*DW*, 2021). Despite the strong economic ties, there are various underlying issues which have led to increasing problems in the EU-China relations.

BRI has emerged to be one of the stumbling blocks in the EU-China relations. Since its inception, the countries within the EU were split over the benefits of the initiative. The joining of Greece, in 2019, in the 16+1 mechanism was significant as it diluted the regional dimension of the cooperation where the 16 European members were post-Communist States. EU has viewed this mechanism with suspicion and as an attempt by China to undermine the solidarity of the Union. The EU strategy on China emphasised that "all Member States, individually and within sub-regional cooperation format such as the 16+1, have a responsibility to ensure consistency with EU law, rules and policies" (EU-China Strategic Outlook, 2019). It goes on to highlight China's business and investment activity in the Western Balkans acknowledging the contribution of these investments in boosting growth but adds that these investments neglect socio-economic and financial sustainability, which may result in indebtedness and transfer of control of strategic assets from European hands to Chinese.

Stemming from the concerns regarding growing Chinese footprints in the continent and that it is trying to create a wedge in Europe, the EU has remained apprehensive about Beijing's BRI. Member States are divided with countries like Hungary, Italy and Greece which are enthusiastic about the BRI and infrastructural developments, and investments made by China and, countries like France and Germany which are more wary. As mentioned before, China has acquired a majority stake in the Piraeus port for US$ 312.5 million in Greece. The China-Europe Land-Sea Express route connects the port of Piraeus through the railway line from Serbia to Hungary. Similarly, China has heavily invested in Serbia, which is not yet an EU member—therefore the stringent conditionalities imposed by EU rules do not apply. There is a growing debate regarding the BRI as undermining the European interests and flouting the rules regarding environmental standards, non-transparent financial regulations, etc. These were highlighted in the Chinese-built highway project in Montenegro, whose debt climbed to more than 100 per cent of its gross domestic product due to this project. The project—a 25-mile section of a proposed 270-mile highway that would run from Montenegro's Port of Bar on the Adriatic Sea to Belgrade—not only raised questions about decisions made by Montenegro's leadership but it also highlighted the concerns within the EU regarding the unsustainable debts associated with BRI. The development of these projects has raised alarm in the Union where there is a growing realisation that the EU woke up late to the increased Chinese presence in the continent as highlighted by French President Macron's statement that "the period of European naivety is over" (Reuters, 2019).

The division within the EU on its approach toward BRI has made it extremely difficult for the Union to find a comprehensive position towards China. For example, Greece in 2017 blocked an EU statement at the UN which criticised China's human rights record undermining the efforts to confront Chinese crackdown on dissidents and activists. It was observed that it was the first time the EU had failed to make a statement at the UN Human Rights Council. Regarding the Hong Kong national security law, EU's High Representative, Josep Borrell, said on 29 May 2020 that sanctions were not the solution "to our problems with China." On the other hand, the Members of the European Parliament on 20 June 2020 called the law a "comprehensive assault on the territory's freedom" and demanded that the EU adopt sanctions and freeze Chinese assets. The resolution is not binding on the Member States.

Related to this issue, is the idea of protection of strategic assets. Chinese investments in Europe have increased in the past few years resulting in increasing concerns over growing influence of China and how should the EU respond to it. According to a report by *NPR*, various Chinese companies, in the past decade, have acquired critical stakes in almost 13 ports in Europe including in Spain, Italy, Greece, and Belgium. These ports cater to 10 per cent of Europe's shipping container capacity (*NPR*, 2018). The European Commission's report on 'Foreign Direct Investment: Continuous Rise of Foreign Ownership of European Companies in Key Sectors'—released in 2019 states that 9.5 per cent of the companies investing in EU were based out of China, Hong Kong and Macao in 2016, up from 2.5 per cent in 2007 (FDI Report, 2019). In order to protect its strategic assets, the EU in 2019 introduced new mechanisms for screening foreign investments which were aimed at "safeguarding Europe's security and public order in relation to foreign direct investments into the Union" (European Commission Press Release, 2020). The new investment screening mechanism seeks to review investments made in critical sectors such as critical technology, infrastructure as well as transactions done by State-controlled entities or those that are backed by State-led programs such as Made in China 2025.

During the coronavirus pandemic, both the NATO Secretary General and the EU Trade Commissioner warned the Member States to stay vigilant against the buying of strategic assets and sensitive technologies due to the price-fall during the pandemic (*Forbes*, 2020). This led European Commission to adopt a White Paper on Foreign Subsidies in the Single Market on 17 June 2020. With the increasing concerns regarding foreign subsidies facilitating the acquisition of EU companies or market operations, this white paper is perceived to fill in the regulatory gap. Under this, the Commission and Member States will be able to assess the role of the subsidies granted by the non-EU governments and their respective impact on European Economic Area (Baker Mckenzie, 2020). Although the white paper says that the proposed instruments would apply equally to all non-EU countries and would not discriminate against any, there is a clear indication that these regulatory measures are aimed toward the increased investment competition from the State-owned Chinese companies.

Similarly, the growing concerns related to Huawei 5G network have split the opinion within the Union. While consecutive US administrations have pushed for banning of Huawei network, European countries have been debating the security implications of reliance on Chinese technology. The concerns range from privacy issues, economic impact, security, and presence of Chinese suppliers in critical communication networks. Attitude towards Huawei has been ranging from acceptance to increased scepticism-member States like Hungary have welcomed the network in their country saying that it finds no merits in US claims about security breaches (*Budapest Business Journal*, 2019). On the other hand, in Germany, the opinions are split between the lawmakers across the party lines that support US arguments that Huawei network cannot be trusted and the automobile industry which fears that ban on the network could lead to trade retaliation from China—its largest export market (Reuters, 2020). Pressure is also high on the UK to settle its 5G decisions. The UK has broken ranks with the US and has formulated its policy to allow limited role to Huawei in its 5G networks, and has allowed the company to bid for non-core parts of 5G infrastructure (*The Guardian*, 2020).

Despite the divergence of approach between the Member States, the EU has been trying to promote a common European approach to the 5G security risks. In March 2019, European Commission in a report on Cybersecurity of 5G Networks elaborated on three objectives—"risks affecting 5G networks at national level; coordination risk assessment; and to identify common set of measures to mitigate Cybersecurity risks" (European Commission Press Release, 2019). This was followed by a report published by the Member States in October 2019 on coordinated risk assessment of 5G network security. The report identified the main threats, actors, sensitive assets, main vulnerabilities and a number of strategic risks associated with 5G network (European Commission Press Release (b), 2019). This led to the endorsement of a joint toolbox to mitigate the security risks. Under this member states agreed to assess the risk profile of suppliers, strengthen their security requirements, exclusions for key assets considered as critical and sensitive, and to have strategies in place to ensure the diversification of vendors. While these recommendations provide a framework for mitigating the risks of 5G Huawei network, it remains highly unlikely that the Member States would make similar choices and as the issue is of national security, the decision-making lies in the hands of national governments and not with EU.

Towards a European Alternative to BRI

The European Union is not new to the idea of infrastructure development through connectivity. The TEN-T project, initiated by the EU, is a multi-modal project under which a Europe-wide network of "railways lines, roads, inland waterways, maritime shipping routes, ports, airports and railway terminals have been established" (TEN-T, N.A.). This integrated infrastructure would include 217,000 km of railways, 77,000 km of motorways, 42,000 km of inland waterways, 329 key ports and 320 airports. The Core Network is expected to be completed by 2030 and the Comprehensive Network by 2050 (TEN-T, N.A.). The objective of the project is to close gaps, remove bottlenecks and technical barriers, as well as to strengthen social, economic and territorial cohesion in the EU.

In a further push to expand its connectivity initiative, the European Commission and the European External Action Service conducted a Euro-Asian Connectivity Mapping Exercise in 2017 with the objective of defining connectivity to include both "the 'soft' and 'hard' elements, inter and intra-regional connectivity and trade-related policies". It included sectors like Transport (road, rail, air and maritime); Energy (renewable and non-renewable sources); People-to-People Connect (youth and culture, research, innovation, education); and Digital Economy. The Joint Staff Working Document of the mapping exercise stated that, "Economically, socially and environmentally sustainable infrastructure of good quality is paramount for the EU's approach to connectivity. Such infrastructure must be safe and resilient; encompass climate change mitigation and adaptation; adhere to common sets of environmental, social and governance standards to protect investments to yield; and leave no one behind. Fiscal sustainability of connectivity interventions is not only a developmental concern but also has wider political implications" (EEAS, 2016).

This broad definition and characteristics of connectivity formed the basis of EU's strategy on "Connecting Europe and Asia—Building Blocks for an EU Strategy" released in 2018. The strategy highlighted that, "The relationship between the EU and Asia is of global significance and the ties are likely to increase in the coming years. Asia, with roughly 60 per cent of the world population accounts for 35 per cent of the EU's exports (€618 billion) and 45 per cent of the EU's imports (€774 billion)" (Connecting Europe and Asia, 2018). It reiterated that to unlock the economic opportunities and enhance cooperation, Europe and Asia should cooperate to build sustainable and efficient connectivity between the two continents. The strategy document further defines EU's approach towards connectivity as: "Sustainable Connectivity—has to be economically, fiscally, environmentally and socially sustainable in the long term; Comprehensive Connectivity—has to be based on the idea of creating networks which includes transportation, people-to-people, digital, and energy; and the idea of Rules based Connectivity is to promote open and transparent investment processes" (Connecting Europe and Asia, 2018).

These policy approaches highlight the idea of 'European Way of Connectivity' which is characterised to be "economically, fiscally, environmentally and socially sustainable in the long term and international rules-based." Simultaneously, the EU has signed connectivity partnerships with Japan (2019) and India (2021) to support infrastructure development linking the EU and the two countries. It also sought to explore infrastructure projects in their countries and regions including Africa, Indo-Pacific and Central Asia. Its Indo-Pacific guidelines, released in 2021, also put connectivity as one of the key pillars in its outreach to the region. This highlights EU's eagerness to pursue connectivity partnerships with ASEAN, with which it signed a strategic partnership in 2020, and with Australia, Canada, South Korea and the US. The guidelines state that "Full partnership between the EU and its Member States will be crucial in developing this cooperation. The EU will promote investments in digitalisation and better connect Europe to its partners in the Indo-Pacific" (Strategy for Indo-Pacific, 2021).

The Foreign Affairs Council conclusions of July 2021 mandated the High Representative Josep Borrell and the European Commission to draft communication on an EU global connectivity strategy by Spring 2022. The idea was "the need for the EU to pursue a geostrategic and global approach to connectivity. The aim is to advance it's economic, foreign and development policy and security interests and to promote European values" (Council of Europe, 2021). In her September 2021 State of the Union address, European Commission President Ursula von der Leyen announced that the EU will present a new 'template for how Europe can redesign its model to connect the world'. She stated—"We will build Global Gateway partnerships with countries around the world. We want investments in quality infrastructure, connecting goods, people and services around the world. We will take a values-based approach, offering transparency and good governance to our partners. We want to create links and not dependencies.... We want to turn Global Gateway into a trusted brand around the world" (State of Union, 2021).

The EU in December 2021 launched its connectivity initiative called 'The Global Gateway'. The policy provides a consolidated EU's approach toward global connectivity. The key highlight of the policy included the aim to mobilise €300 billion in infrastructure investments between 2021 and 2027. The EU's presented breakdown is as follows (The Global Gateway, 2021):

- Up to €135 billion worth of investments were made possible by the EFSD+, including a new initiative with the EIB that could bring €25 billion of additional investments.
- Grant financing of up to €18 billion under other EU external assistance programmes.
- €145 billion of planned investment volumes by European financial and development of finance institutions.
- The EU aims at coordinating better with its Member States to enhance its strategic role on the boards of the Multilateral Development Banks (MDBs) in support of Global Gateway projects.

The most important part of the initiative is the narrative of the policy. While China is not named in the policy, the references to the Chinese infrastructure plan BRI are quite clear. The narrative is focused on countering Chinese finance, which has been criticised for lack of transparency and burdening governments with unsustainable debt. The policy attempts to differentiate the EU with its ideas of "forging links" instead of "creating dependencies" (The Global Gateway, 2021). The Global Gateway places emphasis on delivering infrastructure which is of highest standards of sustainability, governance, and transparency. The policy initiative aims to present a counter to the Chinese influence by pushing for higher quality, greener, and more transparent infrastructure. It also points out that the EU will explore setting up a "European Export Credit Facility to support European businesses, to help ensure a more level playing field for EU businesses in third country markets, where they are increasingly having to compete with foreign competitors that receive large support from their governments" (The Global Gateway, 2021)—referring to the competition with the firms backed by the Chinese government. The EU's Global Gateway presents a unique opportunity to realise the ambitions of the EU in transforming itself into a geopolitical heavyweight and as an alternative to the Chinese BRI in the global infrastructure landscape.

Conclusion

From the time the BRI was launched in 2013, it has stirred intense debate around the world over its political and economic impact. Europe has not been immune to the initiative and is home to a variety of responses

—from acceptance to scepticism to rejection of the initiatives. Through BRI, China has been able to expand its geo-economic footprint in the continent, particularly in the South and the East. Its involvement in the region has political, economic and security dimensions—taken together with Beijing's activities in Europe has led to the division of opinion on the continent. While the core of the continent, led by France and Germany are pushing for a concerted outlook towards the BRI and the relation with China, the periphery—largely the countries in the Central, Eastern and Southern Europe are pushing for closer economic and political cooperation with Beijing.

Therefore, it is not a surprise that EU has been unable to come to a coherent position in China given the internal divisions. This has made it extremely difficult for the EU to find a comprehensive position toward China. Beijing has used these divisions to its own advantage. China has presented itself as an alternative to the EU's stress on norms, values and regulations. Several member states, such as Hungary and Greece—have signed bilateral memorandums of understanding with China on BRI cooperation. While other EU countries such as France, and Germany, grow more sceptical of the initiative, Italy became the first G7 country to sign an MoU on BRI with China.

In terms of the BRI, China engages with the countries in CEEC through bilateral and sub-regional levels. As these countries share communist past, low-level of economic development as compared to the rest of the continent, and due to their geostrategic locations—they have become a bridge for China to connect with the rest of Europe, by providing a crucial transit corridor. However, the EU has repeatedly highlighted the issues related to norms and procedures, labour standards, debt sustainability, and transparency of the BRI projects. At the June 2017 Belt and Road Forum in Beijing, European Commission Vice President Jyrki Katainen acknowledged the "opportunities presented by growing interconnectivity while stressing that the EU would only endorse the BRI if China adhered to principles such as openness, interoperability, transparency, and sustainability" (Brattberg and Soula, 2018). Other major concerns for the EU remain China gaining control of strategic assets such as ports, airports, etc.; and the risk of weakening environmental, social, or governance standards.

Nonetheless, given the current situation, the initial enthusiasm in these countries for the BRI has given way to lowering of expectations with some heads of governments maintaining distance in the latest edition of the 17+1 summit. The main reason behind this has been many of the promised infrastructure funding has not materialised and that many projects were unable to begin as the funding came in the form of loans or the financing of the project is to be paid back with interest—which had the potential to overwhelm the smaller economies of the region. An example can be taken from Montenegro—the highway from the southern city of Bar was being built by the China Road and Bridge Corporation (CRBC) with an €809 million loan from Exim Bank. The IMF claims that "without construction of the highway, Montenegro's debt would have declined to 59 per cent of GDP, rather than rising to 78 per cent of GDP in 2019. It warns that continued construction of the highway would again endanger debt sustainability" (Eder and Mardell, 2018). Moreover, among the 17+1 members, perceptions of the BRI and China's policy have diversified. Hungary, Croatia and Greece support stronger relations, while Poland and the Baltic states are more cautious because of the possibility of China using its economic clout and the BRI as a political tool.

These developments follow the changing outlook within the EU towards China and its infrastructure development projects. The EU has grown apprehensive about the Chinese intensions, this was visible in a statement signed in April 2018, where all Member States' ambassadors to Beijing (except for Hungary's) emphasised that the BRI "runs counter to the EU agenda for liberalising trade and pushes the balance of power in favour of subsidised Chinese companies" (*DW*, 2018). The question of how China's engagement with the member countries of the EU in a sub-regional format will impact EU-China relations has been present ever since the creation of the 16+1 format in 2012 and the launch of BRI in 2013. It has been argued that the presence of China in these countries runs the risk of diminishing EU's political unity and normative influence on the CEEC's and can reverse the EU's reform agenda in the Western Balkans. However, it needs to be pointed out here that the bulk of Chinese investments in Europe have been to the Big Three—Germany, the UK and France and they continue to remain important.

A long-awaited EU policy on connectivity started to take shape with the launch of EU strategy for connecting Europe and Asia in 2018 and Global Gateway in 2022. The fact that these new strategies received unanimous support from European leadership sends a clear message regarding EU's intentions. These strategies seek to expand and build-on the EU's existing initiatives and aim to leverage the Union's expertise by creating transport links, establishing energy and digital networks, and promoting people-to-people connections. It is aimed at promoting sustainable finance through the use of variety of financial tools. While EU has said that its connectivity policies are not in response to the BRI, they certainly do highlight the growing concerns in the Union. These policies have come along with the push to adopt strict EU investment screening legislation that would impose restrictions on Chinese investments in certain critical sectors.

Whether the EU strategies can help formulate a coherent view among Member States on how to approach the BRI remains uncertain as the implication of these policies and EU's new approach towards China is still a subject of debate. The EU is trying to tread a balanced approach towards China. The issues like apprehensions over BRI, increasing Chinese purchases of strategic infrastructure, etc. are going to dominate the future EU-China debates. However, the EU needs to start planning for a future where China is an economic powerhouse backed by its enormous military might. The EU prefers an issue-based *competition and cooperation* approach whereby they recognise the need to cooperate with China on certain issues like climate change, and agree that Beijing is a systemic rival and economic competitor for the EU. Though there is a realisation in the EU regarding their own dependencies and vulnerabilities that emerged during the pandemic, they have taken tough positions on China recently with the sanctioning of Chinese officials over human rights issues and the European Parliament freezing the ratification of the investment treaty between Brussels and Beijing—the commercial interests of many European countries remain strong. This has also been a primary reason why the EU has also been unable to formulate a coherent China policy.

Note

1. Member States - Albania, Bosnia and Herzegovina, Bulgaria, Croatia, Czechia, Estonia, Greece, Hungary, Latvia, Lithuania, Montenegro, North Macedonia,

Poland, Romania, Serbia, Slovakia and Slovenia. With the addition of Greece, the mechanism became 17+1. However, Lithuania pulled out of the mechanism in May 2021.

References

Babones, Salvatore, "The New Eurasian Land Bridge Linking China and Europe Makes No Economic Sense, So Why Build It?", *Forbes*, 28 December 2017, at https://www.forbes.com/sites/salvatorebabones/2017/12/28/the-new-eurasian-land-bridge-linking-china-and-europe-makes-no-economic-sense-so-why-build-it/?sh=60671ab45c9c, Accessed on 2 April 2022.

Baker Mckenzie, "EU Commission Published White Paper Suggesting New EU Filing Obligations for Companies that have Received non-EU Subsidies", Insights, 19 June 2020, at https://www.bakermckenzie.com/en/insight/publications/2020/06/european-commission-white-paper-non-eu-subsidies, Accessed on 2 April 2022.

Brattberg, Erik and Soula, Etienne, "Europe's Emerging Approach to China's Belt and Road Initiative", Carnegie Endowment, 19 October 2018, at https://carnegieendowment.org/2018/10/19/europe-s-emerging-approach-to-china-s-belt-and-road-initiative-pub-77536, Accessed on 2 April 2022.

Brînză, Andreea, "How China's 17+1 Became a Zombie Mechanism", *The Diplomat*, 10 February 2021, at https://thediplomat.com/2021/02/how-chinas-171-became-a-zombie-mechanism/, Accessed on 2 April 2022.

Budapest Business Journal, 28 April 2019, at https://bbj.hu/special-report/despite-us-concerns-huawei-doing-well-in-hungary_164142, Accessed on 2 April 2022

CGTN, 4 February 2021, at https://news.cgtn.com/news/2021-02-04/China-considers-joining-CPTPP-XBFghDb1nO/index.html, Accessed on 3 April 2022.

"Connecting Europe and Asia - Building blocks for an EU Strategy, European Commission and EEAS", Brussels, September 2018, at https://eeas.europa.eu/sites/eeas/files/joint_communication_-_connecting_europe_and_asia_-_building_blocks_for_an_eu_strategy_2018-09-19.pdf,Accessed on 3 April 2022.

Council of Europe, "A globally connected Europe: Council approves conclusions", 12 July 2021, at https://www.consilium.europa.eu/en/press/press-releases/2021/07/12/a-globally-connected-europe-council-approves-conclusions/, Accessed on 3 April 2022.

DW, 18 April 2018, at https://www.dw.com/en/report-eu-countries-to-be-straitjacketed-by-chinas-new-silk-road/a-43437084, Accessed on 3 April 2022.

DW, 16 August 2021, at https://www.dw.com/en/has-eastern-europe-wised-up-to-chinese-investment/a-58835005#:~:text=The%20value%20of%20Chinese%20direct,%25%20year%2Don%2Dyear, Accessed on 3 April 2022.

Eder, Thomas S. and Mardell, Jacob, "Belt and Road reality check: How to assess China's investment in Eastern Europe", Mercator Institute for China Studies

(MERICS), 10 July 2018, at https://merics.org/en/analysis/belt-and-road-reality-check-how-assess-chinas-investment-eastern-europe, Accessed on 3 April 2022.

EEAS, Shared Vision, "Common Action: A Stronger Europe – A Global Strategy for the European Union's Foreign and Security Policy", June 2016, at http://eeas.europa.eu/archives/docs/top_stories/pdf/eugs_review_web.pdf, Accessed on 3 April 2022.

EIB, "Investment Report 2019/2020: accelerating Europe's transformation - Key findings", 2019, at https://www.eib.org/attachments/efs/economic_investment_report_2019_key_findings_en.pdf, Accessed on 4 April 2022.

"EU-China – A Strategic Outlook", European Commission, March 2019, at https://ec.europa.eu/commission/sites/beta-political/files/communication-eu-china-a-strategic-outlook.pdf, Accessed on 4 April 2022.

Eurostat, "China-EU - international trade in goods statistics", February 2022, at https://ec.europa.eu/eurostat/statistics-explained/index.php?title=China-EU_-_international_trade_in_goods_statistics#EU_and_China_in_world_trade_in_goods, Accessed on 4 April 2022.

European Commission, Press Release, "EU foreign investment screening regulation enters into force", European Commission, 10 June 2020, at https://ec.europa.eu/commission/presscorner/detail/en/IP_19_2088, Accessed on 5 April 2022.

European Commission, Press Release, "Cybersecurity of 5G networks", European Commission, 26 March 2019, at https://ec.europa.eu/digital-single-market/en/news/cybersecurity-5g-networks, Accessed on 5 April 2022.

European Commission, Press Release (b), "Member States publish a report on EU coordinated risk assessment of 5G networks security", European Commission, 9 October 2019, at https://ec.europa.eu/commission/presscorner/detail/en/IP_19_6049, Accessed on 5 April 2022.

France24, 26 November 2021, at https://www.france24.com/en/tv-shows/reporters/20211126-montenegro-s-billion-dollar-road-to-nowhere, Accessed on 4 April 2022.

Forbes, 18 April 2020, at https://www.forbes.com/sites/kenrapoza/2020/04/18/watch-out-for-china-buying-spree-nato-warns/#521a44731758, Accessed on 4 April 2022.

Foreign Direct Investment Report, "Continuous Rise of Foreign Ownership of European Companies in Key Sectors", European Commission, 13 March 2019, at http://trade.ec.europa.eu/doclib/press/index.cfm?id=1993, Accessed on 4 April 2022.

Ghiasy, Richard and Krishnamurthy, Rajeshwari, "China's Digital Silk Road and the Global Digital Order", *The Diplomat*, 13 April 2021, at https://thediplomat.com/2021/04/chinas-digital-silk-road-and-the-global-digital-order/, Accessed on 5 April 2022.

Levchenko, Ihor, "Serbia is under pressure from Chinese investments", Commentaries, New Eastern Europe, 29 November 2021, at https://neweasterneurope.

eu/2021/11/29/serbia-is-under-pressure-from-chinese-investments/, Accessed on 5 April 2022.

NPR, 9 October 2018, at https://www.npr.org/2018/10/09/642587456/chinese-firms-now-hold-stakes-in-over-a-dozen-european-ports, Accessed on 5 April 2022.

Railfreight.com, "Cosco launches new train connection between China and Germany", 22 February 2022, at https://www.railfreight.com/beltandroad/2022/02/22/cosco-launches-new-train-connection-china-germany, Accessed on 5 April 2022.

Reuters, 20 March 2016, at https://www.reuters.com/article/bankers-petrol-ma-geo-jade-idUSL2N16S0B7, Accessed on 5 April 2022.

Reuters (b), 18 April 2016, at https://www.reuters.com/article/us-serbia-privatisation-steel-idUSKCN0XF130, Accessed on 6 April 2022.

Reuters, 22 March 2019, at https://in.reuters.com/article/us-eu-china/eu-leaders-call-for-end-to-naivety-in-relations-with-china-idINKCN1R31H3, Accessed on 6 April 2022.

Reuters, 22 January 2020, at https://www.reuters.com/article/us-europe-usa-huawei-explainer/explainer-as-britain-decides-europe-grapples-with-huawei-conundrum-idUSKBN1ZL1CH, Accessed on 6 April 2022.

Sacks, David, "Countries in China's Belt and Road Initiative: Who's In and Who's Out", Council on Foreign Relations, 24 March 2021, at https://www.cfr.org/blog/countries-chinas-belt-and-road-initiative-whos-and-whos-out, Accessed on 6 April 2022.

Seenews, 25 April 2019, at https://seenews.com/news/serbia-signs-loan-deal-with-chinas-exim-bank-to-build-preljina-pozega-motorway-section-651925, Accessed on 6 April 2022.

Shopov, Vladimir, "Mapping China's Rise in the Western Balkans – Macedonia", ECFR, March 2022, at https://ecfr.eu/special/china-balkans/north-macedonia/, Accessed on 6 April 2022.

State of the Union Address by President von der Leyen, 15 September 2021, European Commission, at https://ec.europa.eu/commission/presscorner/detail/en/SPEECH_21_4701, Accessed on 6 April 2022.

Statista, "Total stock of foreign direct investments from China into EU countries between 2010 and 2020", 2021, at https://www.statista.com/statistics/865563/china-total-outward-fdi-stock-into-european-union-countries/, Accessed on 7 April 2022.

Trans-European Transport Network (TEN-T), European Commission,at https://transport.ec.europa.eu/transport-themes/infrastructure-and-investment/trans-european-transport-network-ten-t_en, Accessed on 7 April 2022

The Balkan Insight, 23 December 2021, at https://balkaninsight.com/2021/12/23/montenegro-close-to-choosing-bechtel-to-build-adriatic-highway/#:~:text=In%20November%202015%2C%20Montenegro%20 and,%E2%80%93%20the%20Adriatic%2DIonian%20motorway, Accessed on 7 April 2022.

The Ecologist, 24 July 2018, at https://theecologist.org/2018/jul/24/china-expands-coal-power-interests-bosnia-and-herzegovina, Accessed on 7 April 2022.

"The EU strategy for cooperation in the Indo-Pacific", European Commission, Brussels, 2021, at https://eeas.europa.eu/sites/default/files/jointcommunication_2021_24_1_en.pdf, Accessed on 7 April 2022.

"The Global Gateway", Joint Communication to the European Parliament, the Council, the European Economic and Social Committee, the Committee of the Regions and the European Investment Bank, European Commission, 1 December 2021, at https://ec.europa.eu/info/sites/default/files/joint_communication_global_gateway.pdf, Accessed on 7 April 2022.

The Guardian, 29 January 2020, at https://www.theguardian.com/technology/2020/jan/29/johnson-faces-tory-rebellion-over-huawei-5g-plans-for-britain, Accessed on 7 April 2022.

Tonchev, Plamen, "China's Road: into the Western Balkans", European Union Institute for Security Studies (EUISS), February 2017, at https://www.iss.europa.eu/sites/default/files/EUISSFiles/Brief%203%20China%27s%20Silk%20Road.pdf, Accessed on 7 April 2022.

Turcsányi, Richard Q., "China and the Frustrated Region: Central and Eastern Europe's Repeating Troubles with Great Powers", *China Report*, 56(1), 2020, pp. 60–77.

Xinhuanet, 8 February 2017, at http://www.xinhuanet.com/english/2017-02/08/c_136039012.htm, Accessed on 7 April 2022.

19. BRI in Africa: From Enthusiasm to Dilemma

Sankalp Gurjar

Abstract

Even before the BRI arrived in Africa, China had established itself as a major economic, investment and infrastructure partner for African countries. The BRI was seen as an attempt to bring the Chinese engagement with Africa in a coherent framework. There are no clear differentiating factors between projects that came up before the unveiling of the BRI and the ones that came up after the launch in 2013. The BRI activity in Africa, just like the rest of the world, has been deliberately kept vague. Therefore, the BRI in Africa has to be understood as part of China's continuing engagement with Africa. Largely, the BRI has neither significantly pushed forward the Chinese engagement with Africa nor has it diverted the Chinese attention away from Africa. In fact, with, without, and despite, the BRI, China's growing presence in, and expanding engagement with, Africa has continued. Keeping this context in mind, the chapter focuses on some of the broad trends and major developments that are clearly discernible in the context of BRI and Africa.

I

The Belt and Road Initiative (BRI) is the signature foreign, strategic, and economic policy project of the current Chinese President Xi Jinping. The BRI was launched in 2013 and since then, has been a key theme in contemporary world politics. The BRI has two components: the land component is known as the Silk Road Economic Belt and then there is a Maritime Silk Route. Through these, the BRI is designed to link up Europe, Asia, and Africa to China via land and maritime connectivity projects, energy pipelines, infrastructure initiatives, and industrial as well as economic corridors. From across the world, 149 countries have signed up cooperation agreements/MoUs for the BRI, of which reportedly 45 are from Africa. Through the BRI, China seeks to expand its global influence and place itself at the centre of international politics and economics in the 21st century.

As it completes a decade, the BRI has generated varied responses. Countries like India and the United States (US) are firmly opposed to the BRI owing to the concerns regarding territorial integrity, sovereignty, financing arrangements, quality of the infrastructure, etc. However, many developing countries in Asia and Africa have become champions of the Chinese initiative. Through the BRI, they seek to draw Chinese financing, technology, and expertise for their own development projects like building of modern railways and developing deep-sea ports. Many of these countries are authoritarian and see the BRI as an alternative that does not put premium on respect for human rights and democracy in exchange for loans. However, the early enthusiasm has waned and a quiet cautiousness, especially on the part of recipient countries, has, nonetheless, seeped in.

For China, investments in dual-use infrastructure projects, through the BRI, in geopolitically important countries serve economic, diplomatic, and most importantly, strategic objectives. The BRI also helps Chinese companies to penetrate new markets, secure access to the strategically important raw materials and minerals, and acquire a stable foothold in regions far away from the Chinese mainland. The Chinese financing and eventual takeover of the port of Hambantota in Sri Lanka in 2017 is a glaring example of the strategic implications of Chinese lending (Gurjar, 2021). Hambantota would be useful in expanding and regularising the Chinese presence in the Indian Ocean. Therefore, while looking at the BRI in Africa, the logic of strategy and geography in the context of China's growing global military footprint, cannot be missed.

The present chapter seeks to analyse the African engagement with the BRI. In the context of China's engagement with Africa through BRI, several pertinent questions could be raised: where does Africa stand in the Chinese strategy of BRI? How is the BRI being received in Africa? What are some of the key BRI projects in Africa? What does Africa gain, if anything, by participating in the BRI? Who gains more by implementing the BRI projects, China or Africa? Does BRI, in any meaningful way, contribute to African development? Will the asymmetric nature of the China-Africa relationship continue and, in many ways, solidify, with the BRI? Will the problem of African indebtedness intensify with the BRI? What are the strategic implications of BRI in Africa? The chapter is anchored in some of these questions.

Before moving forward, it must be noted that there is a vast material available that discusses the various aspects of BRI and its evolving impact on specific sectors, specific countries and/or regions, and on the wider global politics. The scholarly research on the BRI in the form of, but not limited to, newspaper commentaries, actual ground reporting, data-driven reports by international agencies and firms, analysis by the think-tank community, etc. has proliferated in the last decade and is easily available on the internet. The chapter takes on board some of the material related to Africa that is already available in the public domain. However, it does not claim to cover the entire landscape. It is out of the scope of the present inquiry. The BRI is still an evolving reality and is subject to change. Therefore, the analytical portrait of the BRI is neither complete nor comprehensive. Keeping this context in mind, the chapter focuses on some of the broad trends and major developments that are clearly discernible in the context of BRI and Africa.

II

The People's Republic of China (PRC) has been a key partner of Africa since the 1960s. The visit of Chinese Premier Zhou Enlai to ten countries in 1963-64 set the foundations for the China-Africa relationship. During the Cold War, Chinese support for Africa was primarily political and, to an extent, military in nature. Economic ties remained limited. China was a supporter of national liberation struggles on the continent and took anti-imperial, anti-colonial positions. The competition for recognition between PRC and Taiwan was played out in Africa as well. When the PRC was admitted to the United Nations in 1971, 26 countries voted in favour of China while 15 supported Taiwan. China had built a railway line connecting Tanzania with Zambia to reduce Zambia's dependence on the ports of Apartheid South Africa. The railway was the first major

Chinese infrastructure project in Africa and is hailed as one of the best examples of China-Africa cooperation (Oqubay and Lin, 2019).

In the wake of China's brutal suppression of student protests in Tiananmen Square in 1989, African countries continued to engage with isolated China. Since the mid-1990s, China's economic engagement with Africa has gone up significantly. China emerged as a major player in the Sudanese oil industry and also provided diplomatic and military support to the Sudanese regime of Omar-al-Bashir. At the turn of the century, Africa emerged as a key supplier of energy, minerals and raw materials for China's rapid economic growth. In the new millennium, China launched Forum on China-Africa Cooperation (FOCAC) to further deepen the China-Africa ties (Alden and Wu, 2017). Over the last two decades, China has become the largest trading partner of Africa. The bilateral trade stood at US$ 192 billion in 2019. In the two decades, China provided more than 1100 loans to Africa worth US$ 153 billion (SAIS-CARI, 2022). China participates in the UN peacekeeping missions in Africa and has been a key arms supplier and diplomatic partner for many countries. As a result, the relationship has been burgeoning across the sectors. The BRI was introduced in Africa in this context.

The FOCAC summit of 2015 held in the South African city of Johannesburg was the first summit after the launch of the BRI. In the action plan adopted at the summit, China and Africa agreed that "underdeveloped infrastructure is one of the bottlenecks hindering independent and sustainable development of Africa" and therefore, "the two sides will take concrete measures and give priority to encourage Chinese businesses and financial institutions to expand investment" (FOCAC, 2015). Furthermore, the action plan noted that Africa "welcomes the Chinese side's championing "the 21st Century Maritime Silk Road", which includes the African continent, and the two sides will promote mutually beneficial cooperation in the blue economy" (ibid.). The focus on infrastructure and maritime dimensions of the BRI such as the modernisation of ports was clear. China enjoys considerable advantages in infrastructure development and maritime engagement is a priority for expanding Chinese strategic interests.

In 2017, when the first Belt and Road Forum was organised in Beijing, African countries were not absent. The attendees included leaders and government officials from Egypt, Ethiopia, Kenya, and Tunisia. Of these, Ethiopia and Kenya were represented at the level of heads of state (*The Diplomat*, 2017). The second Forum, in 2019, saw the heads of states from five African countries, Djibouti, Egypt, Ethiopia, Kenya, and Mozambique, in attendance. It signalled the growing presence and salience of the BRI in Africa (Tiezzi, 2019). However, the geographic mapping of these five countries also demonstrates the predominance of the countries lying in the Western Indian Ocean (WIO) region that encompasses the African sub-regions like East and Southern Africa and the Horn of Africa (the WIO is defined as the region lying between Egypt in the north, South Africa to the south and Oman in the East).

Meanwhile, at the FOCAC summit of 2018, President Xi Jinping called for the creation of a "China-Africa community with a shared future that pursues win-win cooperation" (*Xinhua*, 2018). He added that "we could both seize the opportunity created by the complementarity between our respective development strategies and the major opportunities presented by the BRI" (ibid.). President Xi wanted to "expand areas of cooperation, unlock new cooperation potential, consolidate our traditional areas of cooperation, and foster new highlights of cooperation in the new economy" (ibid.). China decided to establish a peace and security forum under the rubric of BRI and launched fifty assistance programs to further advance China-Africa cooperation in areas like law and order, UN peacekeeping missions, maritime piracy, and terrorism (ibid.). If there was ever any doubt regarding the strategic intentions behind the BRI, budding China-Africa security cooperation clarified the Chinese stance.

While the Chinese side was keen to engage Africa in the context of BRI, what was the African response? During the visit to Beijing in 2019, the President of Djibouti, Omar Ismail Guelleh had said that the BRI is "unique and will promote international development cooperation, and make significant contributions to creating an interconnected and better world" (Dibie Ike Michae and Reuters, 2019). He thanked "China for the sincere and friendly help which has boosted development and employment of Djibouti and enabled Djibouti to face the future more confidently" (Embassy of the PRC in the USA, 2019). The Chinese base in Djibouti, which came up in 2017, has generated debate in the US,

Europe, and India. In the context of strategic implications of the BRI for smaller countries especially the concerns regarding the debt to China, Guelleh said that "the groundless accusations by some people will not weaken Djibouti's confidence in the BRI and its trust in China" (ibid.).

III

Even before the BRI arrived in Africa, China had established itself as a major economic, investment and infrastructure partner for African countries. The BRI was seen as an attempt to bring the Chinese engagement with Africa in a coherent framework. There are no clear differentiating factors between projects that came up before the unveiling of the BRI and the ones that came up after the launch in 2013. The BRI activity in Africa, just like the rest of the world, has been deliberately kept vague (CMS, 2021). Some analysts call this approach pragmatism on the part of China. It creates confusion and has a potential to selectively brand some projects (perhaps those that are relatively successful) as part of BRI and others (perhaps those which faced hurdles and are stuck) as not falling into the BRI. Therefore, the BRI in Africa has to be understood as part of China's continuing engagement with Africa. Perhaps, projects that were implemented (or even for that matter, inaugurated) after 2013 can be labelled as part of the BRI. Largely, the BRI has neither significantly pushed forward the Chinese engagement with Africa nor has it diverted the Chinese attention away from Africa. In fact, with, without, and despite, the BRI, China's growing presence in, and expanding engagement with, Africa has continued.

While discussing the BRI in Africa, the focus usually turns to the states located in the WIO region. China's growing ties with the Indian Ocean littoral states and rising maritime military presence in the region underpins the engagement with regional states. Countries like Kenya, Tanzania, Djibouti, and Ethiopia are major recipients of Chinese investments. China has engaged with these states for developing modern infrastructure and connectivity projects. Other East and Southern African countries like Uganda and Zambia too figure prominently into the BRI in Africa. However, in the African context, the BRI is not concentrated only in the WIO. West African countries like Nigeria and Cameroon and the resource-rich Democratic Republic of Congo (DRC) located in South-Central Africa are some of the other key participating states in the BRI.

The BRI and Chinese engagement with Africa have primarily focused on the development of infrastructure in Africa. The continent needs modern roads, railways, airports, seaports as well as digital connectivity to drive economic growth. However, for many African countries, getting loans from the traditional Western lending institutions has become a challenge as their record on democracy, human rights and rule of law has left much to be desired. Usually, China steps into this void. The Chinese loans do not come with strings attached for respecting democratic norms or human rights. Engaging with China serves to diversify external partners for African countries. It increases their bargaining power vis-à-vis other major powers. If the visible, hard infrastructure gets developed (with the Chinese financing), it is good politics for ruling African leaders as well. In the bargain, China gets to set the terms of contracts in such a way that eventually, either the loans become too expensive for the recipient countries and/or the country is left with no choice but to repay it by ceding the control of a national asset. It is a trend that is discernible in the case of many projects developed by China across the world including in Africa. Countries like Kenya, Ethiopia, and Uganda are struggling to repay the loans taken from China for developing infrastructure. However, despite the troubles with these and some other countries, the BRI and China's engagement with Africa persists as they need loan for infrastructure desperately.

In the following paragraphs, an attempt is made to provide a macro-view of some of the key projects and engagements.

Ports

An important element of the BRI in Africa is its focus on development of ports in Africa. China has been engaged in developing and operating African ports in a major way. The port development is part of the maritime component of the BRI (Chimbelu, 2019). It has provided China with a solid foothold along the African coastline. The ports are a dual-use infrastructure and hold the potential to provide access as well as logistical support to the Chinese military operating abroad. The ports in Djibouti, Kenya, Tanzania and Mozambique (all of whom are located in the WIO) have generated the maximum attention in the strategic discourse as they are critical in the geopolitics of the Indian Ocean (Léautie, Schaefer, and Shen, 2015).

China has been operating the port of Doraleh in Djibouti since 2016. The port is located near the Chinese base and concerns have been expressed about the possible use of the port by China's People's Liberation Army Navy (PLAN). The PLAN has been active in the waters of the Gulf of Aden since 2008 for anti-piracy patrols. The combination of military base, regular naval presence, ostensibly for counter-piracy operations, and the presence in port, as well as railway projects, provide China with an outsized influence in Djibouti. China had also taken a keen interest in developing the ports of Lamu and Mombasa in Kenya, Bagamoyo in Tanzania and Beira in Mozambique. The Lamu and Bagamoyo were supposed to compete with each other to emerge as the largest ports in Africa. As per reports, "both ports will be larger than any other port in sub-Saharan Africa if completed as planned. They will also be at the centre of much bigger developments, with industrial zones being laid out and intensive farming being proposed" (*BBC News*, 2016). However, as of now, both projects are yet to take off. The shifting winds of domestic politics have been a key contributing factor in these stalled projects (Skidmore, 2022).

All of these projects seemed to have a strategic orientation. The port operations at Djibouti along with a military base have given China a foothold at Djibouti. From the base at Djibouti, it can monitor and influence developments in East Africa, Red Sea, West Asia and WIO. The foothold at Djibouti coupled with the presence at the port of Gwadar in Pakistan and Hambantota in Sri Lanka allows China to project its influence in the region. What's more, it was also in talks with the United Arab Emirates (UAE) for establishing a naval base (Gurjar, 2021). These moves indicate China's growing military presence in the Indian Ocean. Therefore, expanding naval presence and military facilities along the Indian Ocean littoral has been a matter of apprehension for regional states like India.

Recently, as per reports, China was in talks with the Equatorial Guinea for establishing a military base at Bata. The Equatorial Guinea is located along the Gulf of Guinea and a base there would provide China a foothold in West Africa and along the Atlantic. The US considers this as a threat to its national security and had promptly dispatched a senior official to dissuade the government of Equatorial Guinea (Phillips, 2021). However, this incident points toward the expansion of the Chinese military presence in Africa and the BRI is likely to help China to continue to do so.

Airports

China has signed a contract for upgrading and modernising the Entebbe airport of Uganda in 2015. Uganda is a land-locked country and therefore, airport is a strategic asset for the tiny East African country. However, the airport deal has come under scrutiny in the last few months. The Ugandan government has realised that the deal favours China a great deal. As per the reports, "the Ugandan government is required to channel all revenue from the country's only international airport into an account held jointly with the [Chinese] lender" (*AFP*, 2022). Moreover, the government is "required to use part of the revenue to repay the loan each year, before it can invest in public services" (ibid.). It is clear that Uganda is in trouble with these loans. There is a possibility of handing over probably the most important national asset to China over the inability to repay the Chinese loans. It is a repeat of a scenario like that of Hambantota. The deal is so skewed in favour of China that Uganda has recently concluded that there is no way but to go ahead with the contractual obligations as the cost of termination contract is very high. The Ugandan finance minister had apologised to the country over the deal.

Mamamah airport in Sierra Leone was also being developed by China. The estimated cost was US$ 400 million. The project would have been completed in 2022. However, in 2018, after the change of government, the project was cancelled. The aviation minister of the West African state had said that the project was not necessary and that the current international airport would be renovated instead (*BBC News*, 2018). The cancellation of the contract came at a time when the enthusiasm about the BRI seemed to be waning even in Malaysia. The question of African indebtedness and the cost of Chinese financing have been debated in the context of BRI. The case of Uganda and Sierra Leone should warn others of the perils of the Chinese loans and their strategic implications.

Digital Silk Road

If the maritime and land component points towards the development of hard infrastructure, China is keen to establish its influence in the digital domain as well through the Digital Silk Road. Africa is a lucrative market for Chinese telecom and digital companies. As per Chatham House, "the Digital Silk Road, also called the 'Information Silk Road', brings advanced IT infrastructure to BRI countries, such as broadband networks, e-commerce hubs and smart cities" (Kadi, 2019). In fact, "the Digital Silk Road is driven by China's tech giants, most notably Huawei and ZTE, who are able to deliver high-quality fibre optic cables at much lower costs than their European and US competitors" (ibid.).

Unlike the US and Europe, African countries are not interested in banishing the Chinese telecom giant Huawei from the continent. The low cost of Chinese mobiles and digital connectivity are attractive to Africa (Rahn, 2019). Djibouti is connected via the digital Silk Road with the Chinese networks in Pakistan (Chaziza, 2021). Chinese digital footprint is expanding rapidly in countries like Egypt, Tunisia and Morocco as well (Kadi, 2019). Despite the concerns regarding the privacy and security of data, Chinese telecom companies are set to expand in the African market. The control of data and internet in Africa by the Chinese firms has a wide-ranging effect on domestic politics as well as on the flow of information. Authoritarian leaders in Africa seek the Chinese support. Digital tools, built by China, will prove useful in this context.

However, the most visible Chinese engagement in Africa through the BRI is seen in the context of railway development. In the next section, we take a look at some of the key railway projects in Africa.

Railways

Nairobi-Mombasa Standard Gauge Railway (SGR)

The construction for the SGR began in 2013 and was completed in 2017. The 480-km railway line was built at the cost of US$ 3.8 billion (Yusuf, 2020). The SGR connects the port city of Mombasa with the capital Nairobi and has replaced a colonial-era meter gauge railway. The railway was envisioned as a critical first node in the East African transport network with the eventual inland expansion to land-locked South Sudan,

Uganda, and Rwanda (Skidmore, 2022). The SGR seeks to facilitate rapid connectivity for freight transport though it operates passenger trains as well. In 2019, an additional extension to the Naivasha was completed at the cost of US$ 1.5 billion (ibid.).

However, the SGR has been described as the "white elephant" for Kenya. In the wake of Kenya's decision to build the SGR, its debt to China has gone up significantly. Moreover, as of now, the railway is a loss-making unit. Serious questions have been raised about Kenya's ability to repay the loans. Kenya's economic growth has not picked up and therefore, the expected benefits of the SGR are yet to materialise (ibid.). The SGR has been used primarily for transporting goods inland from the port of Mombasa. As a result, the train returns empty on its way back and the expensive route makes it unviable for the businesses to use it (Gorecki, 2020). The expansion to Uganda and Rwanda has not happened as well and in fact, the proposals for loans to extend the railway line further inland to connect these two land-locked countries have been denied by China. Additionally, concerns have been expressed about the environmental impact of the SGR.

Therefore, as a study on the BRI in East Africa noted, "[Kenyan President] Kenyatta's intended legacy project has become a financial morass while Kenya and China struggle to disentangle themselves from one another" (Skidmore, 2022).

Ethiopia-Djibouti Railway Line

Another major railway line constructed by China in East Africa connected the Ethiopian capital Addis Ababa with Djibouti. The modern, 750-km line was built at a cost of US$ 4.5 billion and has been operating since 2017 (Tarrosy & Vörös, 2018). Despite being a standard gauge line and a longer route, the cost of this line stands sharply in contrast with the SGR. Ethiopia-Djibouti railway line has cut the time from three days to 12 hours and has improved the connectivity between land-locked Ethiopia and the ports in Djibouti. However, Ethiopia had struggled to repay the loans for the railway as the line remains underutilised. Besides, the railway line has not been connected with the industrial centres, dry ports, and national depots via the trunk lines (ibid.). Ethiopia also built a light train in the city of Addis Ababa at the cost of US$ 485 million with the

Chinese help. A study has concluded that the "only hope of Ethiopians for profiting from these expensive projects should be the increased trade coming with the freight trains" (Tarrosy and Vörös, 2019).

Interestingly, in 2018, even the Chinese officials had reached a conclusion that "the planning behind many of China's major infrastructure projects abroad has been "downright inadequate", leading to huge financial losses" (Ng, 2018). In the context of Ethiopia's railway project, Wang Wen who works at the China Export and Credit Insurance Corporation, known as Sinosure, noted that "Ethiopia's planning capabilities are lacking, but even with the help of Sinosure and the lending Chinese bank it was still insufficient" (ibid.). With the economic downturn caused by the COVID-19 pandemic and the raging war in the northern province of Tigray, the viability of the operations and the financial sustainability of both railway projects remain in question.

Zambia

In 2021, Zambia a contract with China Civil Engineering Construction Corporation worth US$ 850 million to upgrade the existing railway lines in the country. The project is likely to cover 650-km railway lines and the estimated time for the completion of the project is eight years (*Construction Review Online*, 2021).

Cameroon

In the same year, Cameroon signed a Memorandum of Understanding (MoU) with Chinese companies. The 500-km railway will link up iron ore mining project at Mbalam-Nabeba with the coast of the Gulf of Guinea. As per reports the project "includes the development of iron ore deposits in Cameroon and the Democratic Republic of the Congo" (NS Energy, 2021). However, another railway project connecting the capital Yaounde with Douala, worth US$ 450 million, which began with the Chinese support, has been stalled since 2019 (Miriri, 2021).

Angola

China has rebuilt a 1344-km railway line in Angola that connects the mineral-rich Democratic Republic of Congo to the Atlantic Ocean. Angola is a close partner and a major oil supplier for China and the railway line, known as the Benguela line, was inaugurated in 2015. Plans are afoot to link up copper-rich Zambia with this line (*Euronews*, 2021).

Nigeria

In 2016, the standard gauge railway line between Abuja and Kaduna in Nigeria was inaugurated. The 186-km line has been developed by China. The total project cost was US$ 847 million, of which, US$ 500 million were provided by China's EXIM Bank (Railway Technology, 2020). In 2019, Nigeria signed a contract to build a railway line connecting the capital Abuja with the port city of Warri. The 440-km line would be built at the cost of US$ 3.9 billion. China was to finance 85 per cent of the cost of the project. However, it was reported in November 2021 that Nigeria has turned to the Standard Chartered Bank for loans (Miriri, 2021).

Some Other Infrastructure Projects

As per the Chinese foreign ministry, there are some other infrastructure projects that fall under the BRI. They are "No. 1 National Highway of the Republic of the Congo, the Thies-Touba highway in Senegal, the Port Gentil-Omboue coastal road and the Booué Bridge in Gabon" (Chinese Mission to the African Union, 2021). The Chinese side believes that "these projects have played an important role in boosting regional connectivity and integration" (ibid.). Besides, "projects such as the Doraleh Multi-Purpose Port in Djibouti and the Lome Container Terminal in Togo have been successful in increasing entreport trade" (ibid.). What is more, as per the Chinese foreign ministry "over 1,100 cooperation projects keep running, contributing to the economic recovery of Africa. Moreover, China-Africa cooperation in new areas such as digital economy, aerospace, clean energy and new infrastructure are also scaling up" (ibid.). However, the questions about the sustainability of these projects, the financing arrangements and the problem of debt remain.

IV

The Chinese engagement with Africa has been a matter of intense scholarship and debate. Even before the BRI, China has made deep inroads into the Africa. The BRI has managed to bring the Chinese activities in a coherent framework. China has been active in building railways and developing ports and airports in Africa. The Chinese engagement with Africa helps it to project its growing power, acquire new markets and sources of raw materials. African countries consider China as a key partner in diversifying their external partners. The BRI has seen some successes and some setbacks in Africa. Many countries are engaged with China to bring the investments to fuel their economic growth. However, the vagueness regarding what constitutes the BRI projects and what does not, puts limits on the identifying and analysing the successes/failures of the BRI.

The port projects in East and Southern Africa supported by China are yet to take off. Many are mired in the domestic politics of the host countries. The railway projects implemented by China have reduced the time and improved the connectivity. However, these projects are expensive and with the looming economic crisis in Ethiopia and the inability of Kenyan economy to take off as expected have turned these projects into white elephants. Uganda has realised that the airport modernisation with Chinese financing has been an enormously expensive deal. Many other projects that were in the pipeline are now either renegotiated or are cancelled altogether. Many countries in the continent are rethinking the scale of the proposed investments.

In this context, it remains to be seen whether the BRI will be successful in Africa or not. The attendance of African leaders in the Belt and Road Forum meetings, as well as the FOCAC summits, is not an indication of the success or failure of the BRI. The Chinese presence in Africa is a structural reality. Africa will continue to diversify external partnerships and engage major powers in building infrastructure. Therefore, China and Africa will continue to deepen their relationship with, without or despite the BRI.

References

AFP. (2022). "China puts 'aggressive' terms on Entebbe airport loan: researchers", The East African, 30 March, at https://www.theeastafrican.co.ke/tea/business/china-uganda-entebbe-airport-loan-3733572

Alden, C., and Wu, Y.-S. (2017). "China-Africa Fact Sheet", SAIIA, 30 March, at https://www.saiia.org.za/wp-content/uploads/2015/02/China-Africa-Factsheet.pdf

BBC News. (2018). "Mamamah airport: Sierra Leone cancels China-funded project", 30 March, at https://www.bbc.com/news/world-africa-45809810

BBC News. (2016). "The race to become East Africa's biggest port", 30 March, at https://www.bbc.com/news/world-africa-36458946

Chaziza, M. (2021). "China Consolidates Its Commercial Foothold in Djibouti", *The Diplomat*, 30 March, at https://thediplomat.com/2021/01/china-consolidates-its-commercial-foothold-in-djibouti/

Chimbelu, C. (2019). "Making Chinese investment in African ports work despite risks," *DW*, 30 March, at https://www.dw.com/en/making-chinese-investment-in-african-ports-work-despite-risks/a-49282176

Chinese Mission to the African Union. (2021). "Ambassador Liu Yuxi: Promote China-Africa Belt and Road Cooperation in The New Era", 30 March, at https://www.fmprc.gov.cn/mfa_eng/wjb_663304/zwjg_665342/zwbd_665378/202112/t20211217_10471245.html

CMS. (2021). "Belt and Road Initiative: The View from Africa", 30 March,at https://cms.law/en/media/international/files/publications/publications/bri-view-from-africa?v=1

Construction Review Online. (2021). "Zambia signs US $825m railway lines upgrade contract", 30 March, at https://constructionreviewonline.com/news/zambia-signs-us-825m-railway-lines-upgrade-contract/

Dibie Ike Michae and Reuters. (2019). "Xi calls for advancement of China-Djibouti strategic relationship", *Africa News*, 30 March, at https://www.africanews.com/2019/04/28/xi-calls-for-advancement-of-china-djibouti-strategic-relationship//

Embassy of the PRC in the USA (2019). "Xi Jinping Meets with President Ismail Omar Guelleh of Djibouti", 30 March, at https://www.mfa.gov.cn/ce/ceus//eng/zgyw/t1659802.htm

Euronews. (2021). "Business flourishes as Angola revitalises historic railroad", 30 March, at https://www.euronews.com/2019/05/01/business-flourishes-as-angola-revitalises-historic-railroad

FOCAC. (2015). "The Forum on China-Africa Cooperation Johannesburg Action Plan (2016-2018)", 30 March, at http://www.focac.org/eng/zywx_1/zywj/201512/t20151225_7933575.htm

Gorecki, I. (2020). "Kenya's Standard Gauge Railway: The Promise and Risks of Rail Megaprojects", Afric UpClose, 30 March, at https://africaupclose.wilsoncenter.org/kenyas-standard-gauge-railway-the-promise-and-risks-of-rail-megaprojects/

Gurjar, S. (2021). "China's Growing Global Military Presence: Bases in UAE and Equatorial Guinea?", ICWA, 30 March, at https://www.icwa.in/show_content.php?lang=1&level=3&ls_id=6799&lid=4614&kval=sankalp%20gurjar

Gurjar, S. (2021). "Strategic consequences of Chinese lending", *Deccan Herald*, 17 December.

Kadi, T. H. (2019). "The Promise and Peril of the Digital Silk Road", Chatham House, 30 March, at https://www.chathamhouse.org/2019/06/promise-and-peril-digital-silk-road

Léautie, F. A., Schaefer, M., and Shen, W. (2015). "The Port of Bagamoyo: A Test for China's New Maritime Silk Road in Africa", *The Diplomat*, 30 March.

Miriri, D. (2021). "African nations mend and make do as China tightens Belt and Road", Reuters, 30 March, at https://www.reuters.com/markets/europe/african-nations-mend-make-do-china-tightens-belt-road-2021-11-22/#:~:text=China%20has%20lent%20African%20countries,dried%20up%20in%20recent%20years.

Ng, E. (2018). "Botched Chinese railway project in Africa is a warning to belt and road investors", *South China Morning Post*, 30 March, at https://www.scmp.com/business/banking-finance/article/2170549/botched-chinese-railway-project-africa-warning-belt-and

NS Energy. (2021). "Cameroon partners with China-linked firms to build railway to Mbalam-Nabeba project", 30 March, at https://www.nsenergybusiness.com/news/cameroon-build-railway-mbalam-nabeba-project/

Oqubay, A., and Lin, J. Y. (2019). *China-Africa and an Economic Transformation* (Oxford Scholarship Online ed.). Oxon: Oxford.

Phillips, M. M. (2021). "China Seeks First Military Base on Africa's Atlantic Coast, U.S. Intelligence Finds", *Wall Street Journal*, 30 March, at https://www.wsj.com/articles/china-seeks-first-military-base-on-africas-atlantic-coast-u-s-intelligence-finds-11638726327

Rahn, W. (2019). "Will China's 5G 'digital Silk Road' lead to an authoritarian future for the internet?", *DW*, 30 March, at https://www.dw.com/en/will-chinas-5g-digital-silk-road-lead-to-an-authoritarian-future-for-the-internet/a-48497082

Railway Technology. (2020). "Abuja-Kaduna Rail Line", 30 March, at https://www.railway-technology.com/projects/abuja-kaduna-rail-line/

SAIS-CARI. (2022). "China-Africa Trade Data", 30 March, at http://www.sais-cari.org/data-china-africa-trade

Skidmore, D. (2022). "How China's Ambitious Belt and Road Plans for East Africa Came Apart", *The Diplomat*, 30 March, at https://thediplomat.com/2022/03/how-chinas-ambitious-belt-and-road-plans-for-east-africa-came-apart/?fbclid=IwAR3BUw_ua-VCmvjgf_soGH-T_wjodAMigePYLZtWM_Vh6FSb12teCFtP5Q8

Tarrosy, I., andVörös, Z. (2018). "China and Ethiopia, Part 2: The Addis Ababa–Djibouti Railway", *The Diplomat*, 30 March, at https://thediplomat.com/2018/02/china-and-ethiopia-part-2-the-addis-ababa-djibouti-railway/

Tarrosy, I., andVörös, Z. (2019). "Revisiting Chinese Transportation Projects in Ethiopia", *The Diplomat*, 30 March, at https://thediplomat.com/2019/01/revisiting-chinese-transportation-projects-in-ethiopia/

The Diplomat. (2017). "Belt and Road Attendees List", 30 March, at https://thediplomat.com/2017/05/belt-and-road-attendees-list/

Tiezzi, S. (2019). "Who Is (and Who Isn't) Attending China's 2nd Belt and Road Forum?", *The Diplomat*, 30 March, at https://thediplomat.com/2019/04/who-is-and-who-isnt-attending-chinas-2nd-belt-and-road-forum/

Xinhua. (2018). "Chinese President Xi Jinping's speech at opening ceremony of 2018 FOCAC Beijing Summit", 30 March, at http://www.china.org.cn/world/2018-09/05/content_62273841_2.htm

Yusuf, M. (2020). "Cost of China-built Railway Haunts Kenya", *VoA*, 30 March at https://www.voanews.com/a/africa_cost-china-built-railway-haunts-kenya/6184880.html

20. BRI in Latin America and Caribbean: Expectations and Challenges

Stuti Banerjee

Abstract

Latin America and the Caribbean region do not come into popular imagination when discussing the Belt and Road Initiative (BRI). Nonetheless, today twenty-one nations are part of the BRI with China maintaining close bilateral relations with the other countries that have not yet joined the initiative. China has interests in the region and is pursuing to expand its footprints here but the LAC region also has corresponding interests in deepening its relations with China, including through the BRI. This chapter examines the expectations that the LAC region has from the BRI and the potential challenges the initiative faces here.

The People's Republic of China and Latin America and the Caribbean (LAC) enjoy longstanding relationships that have grown from being distant during the Cold War years to close and/or strategic partnerships in recent years.

In the years after the birth of China, relations were limited and differences abounded the political relations due to the ideological bloc politics of the Cold War. The reforms made to the Chinese economy under Deng Xiaoping, was the beginning of interest in trading commodities from LAC region with China exporting low-added value products to the region. As China's economy started to take off, bilateral economic relations grew with China became the leading importer of minerals and raw materials ensuring that the commodities' trade tied the LAC region to China. Between 2010 and 2013, China extended its presence in Argentina, Brazil, and Peru through investment in infrastructure, energy-related and turnkey projects. Aggregate investment in the region reached US$ 42,716 million between those 3 years, as opposed to US$ 7,342 million during the entire preceding decade (Valderrey, 2020). Apart from trade relations, Chinese foreign direct investments are also growing. In the diplomatic space, Chinese authorities approached the governments in the region through high-level bilateral visits and by engaging with regional organisations to address issues of concern. China is also using non-diplomatic channels such as the presence of overseas Chinese, who play an important role in building a cultural bridge between LAC region and China. This has helped China in expanding its presence in the region while also promoting the Belt and Road Initiative (BRI).

The focus of the chapter is to bring forth the changes, if any, that can be witnessed in the relations between China and Latin America as a result of the introduction of the BRI to the region. It needs to be pointed that China's relations with the countries of the region differs in depth and content. The region is not homogenous but has countries of different geographical size, economic potential, political dispensation, and security challenges. Their relations with China also vary and not all countries of the region share similar relations with China. The paper attempts to understand the LAC region's relations with China, while also highlighting China's interests in expanding the BRI to the region. The paper will also highlight the expectations that the region has from joining the BRI and draws attention to the potential challenges that the BRI faces in the region.

The Belt and Road Initiative in Latin America

The BRI today is known for its geographic expansiveness and overall ambiguity/opaqueness of its projects in part of Asia, Africa and even Europe. One can even find BRI projects as part of the Polar Silk Road in the Arctic. The LAC region does not come into popular imagination when discussing the BRI. One reason is because the region did not feature in the original implementation plans for the New Silk Road concept or subsequent formulations explaining the combination of maritime and land-based corridors. Another reason for the exclusion of the western hemisphere was the overarching presence of the United States, with a third reason being that China perhaps, has taken to expanding its BRI outreach in a phased manner. Nonetheless, the BRI has reached LAC region. Since around 2017, almost 22 countries in LAC region are signatories to BRI memoranda of understanding (MoUs) and/or are actively exploring BRI-branded projects.

This is not to say that the economic relations between the region and China is a result of the BRI. This relationship has its foundations in nearly two decades of diplomatic and economic relations between LAC and China that took off in the period around 2003-2004, based largely on the China-led commodity boom that saw the rapid expansion of Chinese demand for South American raw materials. Under the demand from China, prices of oil, copper, iron ore, soybeans and fish meal soared. The commodities boom along with the reform efforts that had been underway in LAC region since the 1980 and 1990s pushed growth rates and reduced poverty in the LAC countries (Wise, 2021). The contours of the relationship between China and LAC region were established during this period. The BRI has been viewed by many a natural extension of the relations.

Latin America & the Caribbean and China: Relations before the BRI

China and LAC region had political and economic relations before the introduction of the BRI. In the 2000's China started to increasingly look towards the LAC region to gain access to raw material and resources much needed for its economic boom. Even within South America, this trade-based take-off in relations with China was concentrated in a relatively small number of countries and commodity types. Countries rich in minerals such as copper (Chile) and iron ore (Brazil), agricultural resources such as soy (Argentina, Brazil and Uruguay), and fossil fuels such as oil and gas (Argentina, Brazil and Venezuela) all quickly saw China become a number one or number two export partner in the years after 2003 (Ferchen, 2021). China also made a diplomatic push in the region with high-level visits including the visit of then President Hu Jintao to Brazil in 2004.

The increased engagement by China in the region also coincided with the rise of '*the pink tide*'[1] in Latin America. This included, most notably, the coming to power of Luiz Inácio Lula da Silva in Brazil and of Hugo

Chavez in Venezuela. The boom in the economy allowed a number of states of the region to increase social and welfare spending helping reduce poverty. While China's diplomatic outreach was not determined by the political ideologies of the governments in power, it did establish close links with the new left governments of the region and played a part in emerging market solidarity organisations such as with Brazil in the BRICS (Brazil, Russia, India, China and South Africa). In 2015, President Xi Jinping hosted thirty-three member countries of Community of Latin America and Caribbean State (CELAC), and committed to doubling the China-LAC trade to nearly US$ 500 billion by 2025 and investing close to US$ 250 billion in the region over the same period. China's policymakers have made use of its economic heft to fund projects that fulfil the critical infrastructure gaps in many emerging economies including in the LAC region as part of its own internationalised development strategy. According to various scholars, China's investment projects are evaluated more on their impact than on the specific viability of the project in question and most of these infrastructure projects are closely linked to the production of goods and the extraction of resources that are then shipped back to fuel China's own economic development (Wise, 2020).

However, even during this period, the countries that were engaged with China had concerns about that the trade relations looked very much like the dependence that the region had on the United States and Europe in the earlier years. The pattern of Chinese investments during this period to some resource-rich LAC countries led to broader BRI-related concerns about the sustainability of Chinese 'development' projects for the region. The end of the 'commodity-based economic growth from 2013' led to another round of boom-bust trade cycles for the region and despite concerns, most nations have welcomed the offer to join the BRI.

Latin America & the Caribbean and China: Relations after the BRI

In September 2013, Xi Jinping introduced the 'Silk Road Economic Belt' in a speech in Kazakhstan. Shortly after this, he announced China's plans for the '21st-Century Maritime Silk Road' in Indonesia. The two concepts taken together highlight the maritime and continental components of the BRI. In the initial years the BRI's reach was largely to China's neighbourhood in Central Asia and Southeast Asia. In subsequent years it expanded its geographical scope to include Africa and Europe. Official statements highlighted the BRI as a project that "aims to promote the connectivity of Asian, European and African continents and their adjacent seas ... set up all-dimensional, multi-tiered and composite connectivity networks, and realise diversified, independent, balanced and sustainable development" (NDRC, 2015).

China's Policy Paper on Latin America and the Caribbean released in November 2016 highlighted China's commitment to building a new relationship with Latin America and the Caribbean with five salient features, namely, sincerity and mutual trust in the political field, win-win cooperation on the economic front, mutual learning in culture, close coordination in international affairs, as well as mutual reinforcement between China's cooperation with the region as a whole and its bilateral relations with individual countries in the region. The document highlighted, "We (China) aim to bring the comprehensive and cooperative partnership to a new height by bringing the two sides into a community of shared future in which all countries join hands in development" (The State Council, People's Republic of China, 2016). However, it made no mention of the BRI in context of China's relations with the region.

An important precursor to the rollout of the BRI in LAC was the invitation that was sent by China to heads of LAC governments to participate at the inaugural BRI Forum in Beijing in 2017. In his speech President Xi stated that "All countries, from Asia, Europe, Africa or the Americas, can be international cooperation partners of the Belt and Road Initiative" (Belt and Road Forum for International Cooperation, 2017). In his meeting with then Argentine President Mauricio Macri, President Xi described Latin America and Caribbean region as a 'natural extension' of the Maritime Silk Road and the inclusion of LAC into the BRI became more probable. Thereafter, Chinese officials spoke about the LAC region or specific countries being 'important participants' or 'important nodes' in the BRI.

The turning point for LAC incorporation into the BRI occurred during the China-Community of Latin American and Caribbean States (CELAC) Ministerial Forum in Santiago, Chile in January 2018. At the Forum, participants signed a 'Special Declaration on the Belt and Road', in which China extended a broad invitation to LAC countries to join the BRI. The declaration stated that the CELAC welcomes the BRI with interest, for deepening cooperation among Latin American and Caribbean Countries and China in the economic, trade, investment, cultural and tourism sectors, among others (CELAC, 2017). The declaration was the first step, but the real momentum has been generated at the bilateral level with the signing of BRI-related MoUs with China.

For China, the BRI in Latin America has allowed it to strengthen its presence in the region that has been dominated by the United States. LAC's wealth of natural resources is another important aspect of this relationship with Chinese companies involved in extraction projects across the continent. The BRI has also helped China strengthen its relations with Central America and the Caribbean which was limited in the pre-BRI years. The first country to join the BRI was the Central American nation of Panama in 2017 a few months after it switched diplomatic recognition from Taiwan to China. In the initial stages, the majority of those signing MoUs were smaller countries in Central America and the Caribbean, or South American members of the so-called New Left such as Venezuela, Ecuador and Bolivia. In 2018, a number of countries in the region signed MoUs (Antigua and Barbuda, Barbados, Bolivia, Chile, Costa Rica, Cuba, Dominica, Dominican Republic, Ecuador, El Salvador, Grenada, Guyana, Surinam, Trinidad and Tobago, Uruguay, and Venezuela), and a further three joined in 2019 (Barbados, Jamaica and Peru). Argentina, one of the larger economies of the region joined the BRI in 2022 along with Nicaragua making a total of 22 countries in the region that have signed BRI agreements with China.

Other larger economies of the region such as Brazil, Colombia and Mexico are yet to sign similar agreements but they are strengthening their relations with China. China's pragmatic approach is highlighted by the fact that even nations that have not officially joined the BRI, for political or other reasons, can still benefit from China's approach to outward investment, thus blurring the differences between BRI and non-BRI projects. For example, Brazil though not formally part of the BRI is one of the largest recipients of Chinese infrastructure funding in South America and the relations between the two nations continue to grow stronger. Similar evidence of increased China-

Colombia convergence can be found in almost all spheres, especially in the healthcare sector where Colombia accepted Chinese aid. During President Duque's visit to China in 2019, the Colombian government launched a Colombia-China Initiative, a mechanism meant to promote the BRI's objectives of connectivity without formally joining the initiative. Chinese state-owned companies have been entrusted with two of the country's most important infrastructure projects: the Bogotá Metro line construction and the RegioTram project. Mexico, again, is not a member of China's BRI, but it is involved with Chinese investors and State-owned enterprises for financing a variety of projects. One of these is Veracruz Port, officially known as Heroica Veracruz, a major port city and municipality on the Gulf of Mexico. China is an important source of inbound Foreign Direct Investment (FDI) in Mexico. Mexico is China's main largest commercial partner in Latin America and is strengthening its ties with the latter; nonetheless, it has to balance its ties with the United States which makes it difficult for Mexico to become a part of the BRI, for the moment.

Chinese Interests in LAC Region: The Push for BRI

China's rise as a principal global power has considerably altered the global political landscape as well as the country's vision of global governance. Consequently, there has been a shift in the strategic narrative by Beijing on international politics. The BRI demonstrates China's ascendance in the global arena strategically, politically and economically (Das, 2017). Under President Xi 'going out' foreign policy, China has become more proactive in its outreach and it is within this framework that China has engaged more with the LAC region.

China's interest remains to secure access to commodities and foodstuffs, markets for its goods and services, and strategic technologies through collaborations under the BRI or other bilateral agreements. China's economically focused strategy is strongly influenced by its perceived interdependence between building and controlling infrastructure, achieving reliable access to much-needed factor inputs (raw materials) and markets, and ultimately realising for itself the greatest portion of value added for the associated transactions (Ellis, N.A.).

It has been largely assumed that the LAC region does not find much importance within Chinese foreign policy with the BRI arriving in LAC in 2017, five years after its launch. It has also been thought that since LAC region has been traditionally viewed to be within the United States' sphere of influence, China has not engaged with the countries here. However, as has been pointed out, even before the BRI, China and the region had robust economic relations. In fact, China has diaspora linkages with the Caribbean through the Chinese indentured labour that were brought to work on the sugar plantations. The second wave of free voluntary migrants also arrived from China to the Caribbean in later years. The diaspora has helped foster closer links between the island nations and China.

China has expanded and diversified its relationships with the countries of the region over the past two decades. Although economics remains the central axes of the relations, China is increasing its focus on pursuing political and to some degree, security objectives through defence sales and joint exercises. The strategic location of some LAC countries as land bridges between the Pacific and the Atlantic Oceans and close proximity to the United States have perhaps also increased China's need to expand its footprint in the region.

Within the economic sphere, the availability of resources is an advantage for LAC countries. The LAC region is rich in minerals and other resources that are much needed by China as it strives to become a technology hub. Apart from raw materials LAC exports to China also include food grains and other agricultural resources that help allay China's domestic food security concerns. Approximately half of China's demands for agricultural products from the region have been concentrated in Brazilian soyabeans (US-China Economic and Security Review Commission, NA)

Another need for Beijing is to mitigate mounting economic challenges and slowing growth in China through overseas investment and the creation of markets abroad for Chinese goods and materials. As part of its broader economic development strategy, Beijing is using BRI to export massive quantities of steel and aluminium, find new markets for Chinese products, and help its public, as well as private sector enterprises, earn profits.

Figure 20.1: Chinese Investment in Latin America and the Caribbean (LAC) in US$ billion

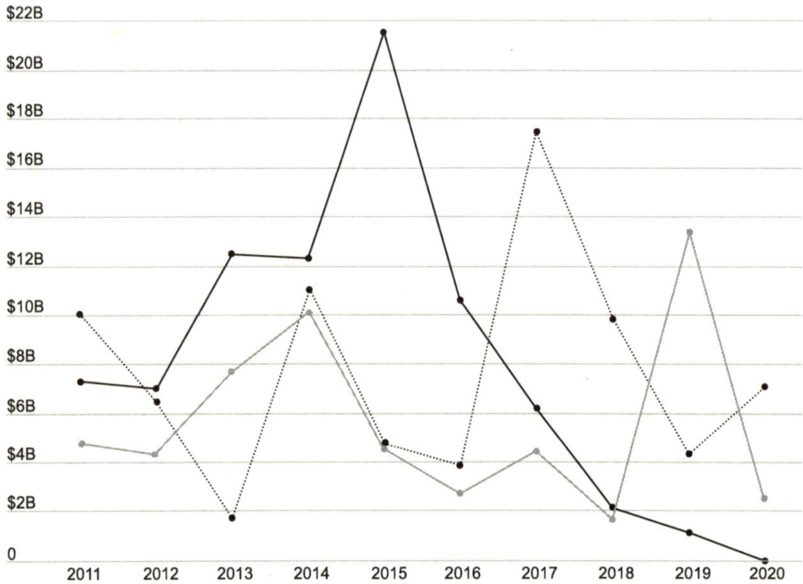

Legends

—— (Black)-Loans from Chinese Development Banks and Export-Import Bank of China to LAC government and State-Owned Enterprises

—— (Grey)-Announcements of LAC Greenfield foreign direct investments where Chinese firms carry out their own regional projects

.... (Dotted)-Chinese mergers and acquisitions in LAC, including public and private Chinese firms.

Source: https://foreignpolicy.com/2021/10/01/china-belt-road-initiative-latin-america-united-states-g-7-build-back-better-world-investment/

China also seeks to influence Latin American policies in favour of its interests at local, state, and national levels. BRI-linked economic initiatives, and China's narrative and diplomatic push tied to the promise of BRI infrastructure funding and investments, translate into significant Chinese influence in developing countries. Engagement represents a prime opportunity for officials to combat anti-China narratives and shape the perceptions of leaders. This has translated in China being able to convert a number of countries of the LAC region to switch recognition from Taiwan to China, reducing the diplomatic space available to the island nation.

China is also investing in Latin America to secure access to energy resources. This includes multi-billion dollar investments by Chinese state-owned oil companies in Brazil's pre-salt formation, along with oil and gas pipeline and other infrastructure, and investments in oil and gas blocks offshore Guyana. China is also increasingly using LAC region as a platform to explore new areas of cooperation within the ambit of the BRI. This includes renewable and clean energy and the region as China faces common challenges related to climate change to their geographical, economic and social conditions. Thus, while it is a 'taker' of traditional energy resources, it is helping the energy transition in the region.

Deconstructing the BRI in LAC: Expectations and Potential Challenges

Presently the BRI project has no match in geographical reach, size of projects, scope, and resources involved. The inclusion of LAC as part of the BRI raised considerable expectations in the region. These not only included a significant expansion of economic relations but also led to strengthening of political relations. Many LAC governments and companies consider BRI an opportunity for furthering their international engagement while helping the region address developmental challenges. As in other regions of the world, a main allure of BRI is expanded access to China, a growing export destination and source of external financing (Zhang, 2019). Nevertheless, critics of the initiative point to the insurmountable debt, the lack of transparency in deal-making and the possibility of unrestrained leadership of China.

Expectations from BRI by LAC

There is a conscious effort in the LAC region to overcome the economic dependency on the United States. Rifts in the relations widened under President Donald Trump. The Trump Administration was not viewed favourably by the region and as the United States moved its attention from its relations with LAC to focus on the Indo-Pacific, the region focused away from the United States to China. With the BRI there is an expectation in the region that it will aid and increase bilateral trade and investment from China to LAC. Based on the current trajectory of China-LAC trade, it is expected to exceed US$ 700 billion by 2035, more than twice as much as in 2020. In 2000, Chinese participation accounted for less than 2 per cent of LAC's total trade. In 2035, it could reach 25 per cent (Serebrisky, 2020).

Expectations are that the BRI would also lead to a diversification within the trade from the current concentration on primary products to more high-end manufactured goods. The LAC region would like to move away from the emphasis on extractive industries and export of raw materials to manufacturing and services sectors. Similarly, it is hoped that the BRI would lead to an increase in the amount of Chinese outward FDI in the region which would further help build this new industrial base.

LAC countries have a large, and increasing, infrastructure quantitative, qualitative and efficiency gap. Traditionally LAC has a bias against investment in infrastructure assets with a focus on current expenditure with limited focus on long-term investments. From 2008 to 2018, the countries of the region invested an average of 2.8 per cent of GDP in infrastructure, significantly below that in other emerging regions (Serebrisky, 2020). The lack of quality assets, inadequate maintenance and poor service provisions has negatively impacted the quality of life of its population and the competitiveness of its economies. The evidence available for the region demonstrates needs not yet covered in terms of the provision of basic services. There were 18.5 million people in Latin America without access to electricity in 2014; in 2015 there were 24 million without access to improved sources of drinking water and 90 million without improved sanitation facilities. In addition, there are currently a large number of infrastructure services that does not work properly and that creates bottlenecks to sustainable growth (Chauvet, 2020). The COVID-19 pandemic has further laid bare some of the challenges that the region faces in this regard.

According to the Inter-American Development Bank (IADB), guaranteeing access to quality infrastructure would help in delivering sustainable and quality services to the region's households and firms. This is needed for building a dynamic and digitalised economy which, in turn, can create opportunities for innovation and growth, especially for small and medium industries, while encouraging job creation. In addition, high-quality infrastructure permits the region's integration in continental and global value chains. The Bank, in its report titled, 'The infrastructure gaps in Latin America and the Caribbean' highlighted that the region needs to invest US$ 2,220.7 billion in water and sanitation, energy, transportation, and telecommunications infrastructure. Of that total, new infrastructure requires allocations of 59 per cent, while 41 per cent should go to maintaining existing assets and replacing assets that are obsolescent. Infrastructure will require at least 3.12 per cent of the region's GDP every year until 2030 (IADB, 2021). Given the BRI's emphasis on infrastructure connectivity and the global expansion of Chinese firms in the sector, particularly in Africa and Asia, LAC region hopes to see more involvement of China in such projects (Jenkins, 2021).

While traditional infrastructure continues to be central to the BRI, digital technology and renewable energy is increasingly gaining prominence. In addition to transport infrastructure like roads, railways, and ports, as well as energy infrastructures like dams, coal-fired power plants, and energy grids, Chinese officials have been keen to include digital infrastructure and digital connectivity as part of the BRI. With the 'Digital Silk Road' (DSR) there is a strategic push by China to embed its technological standards internationally. Some DSR projects are traditional BRI-style infrastructures, such as submarine communication cables and mobile phone networks. Nonetheless, China has made it clear that DSR encompasses all types of digital development along the Belt and Road, including fintech, Internet of Things, smart cities and digital healthcare. According to the IADB, close to 60 per cent of the population of the region does not have access to quality digital infrastructure. The need for enhanced access to digital infrastructure, especially to overcome the economic damage of the pandemic, for the LAC countries is clear. The countries of the region are keen to join the DSR but are wary of evolving technological standards, costs and local sentiments on cyber security (CMS Chile, 2021). This has been compounded by the geopolitical tensions with the United States pushing back against DSR project by discouraging LAC nations from joining 5G networks of Chinese companies such as Huawei and instead pushing its own Clean Network Program, which intends to restrict or eliminate Chinese involvement in telecom networks that connect to US networks, cloud systems and applications that handle US data. Nonetheless, with many countries of the region in need of new technology with the Chinese option available at competitive prices, there is potential for LAC countries to join the DSR.

Another emerging area of collaboration within the BRI is renewable energy and green technology. Over the past few years, Chinese investments in LAC have grown in renewable as the region makes a conscious shift to renewable energy. Currently close to 24 per cent of the region's energy is estimated to come from non-fossil sources (CMS Chile, 2021). This is advantageous for China, which is the world leader in building renewable energy equipment making it well placed to provide support, expertise, equipment and investment to governments of the region. China is also investing in power distribution and building grids that is required for the distribution of renewable energy. With western investments limited and provided with a number of considerations, LAC nations have focused on China's strengthen in this sector and the commercial viability of the projects. For China, the advantage of such projects has been that they are easier and cheaper than traditional infrastructure projects and often easier to monetise.

The pandemic has brought the need to focus on robust healthcare infrastructure. Income disparity is one of the highest in LAC region with a large number of people employed in the unorganised sector. The forced shut down of economic activities by governments as a measure to prevent the spread of the virus has further highlighted the income disparity in the region. It has also brought to the forefront the need to build robust public healthcare systems for the people. The Health Silk Road predates the pandemic, but the current health crisis has brought a renewed focus on it. First proposed in 2015, China's National Health and Family Planning Commission formulated a plan to build health cooperation including 'infectious disease prevention and control', into the overall BRI framework. With the pandemic, China is promoting the HSR more than ever; especially in LAC countries where the deficiencies in public healthcare have become visible. During the pandemic, China's 'health diplomacy' strategy has been well received in most of the region. It is estimated that China donated US$ 215 million of medical aid to LAC countries during the first year of the pandemic. Much of this aid has come from Chinese businesses rather than directly from the Chinese government once again blurring the lines between BRI and non-BRI projects. A number of countries of the region are also inoculating their citizens against COVID-19 with Chinese vaccines (CMS Chile, 2021).

There is little doubt that China's medical outreach has created a generally positive impression in the region. Across the region, there is considerable scope for investment in 'next generation' medical infrastructure, telemedicine and other means of digital healthcare that bring a synergy between DSR and HSR. China and the countries of the region hope that cooperation in such projects would help build the strong foundations for similar cooperation in other aspects of BRI (CMS Chile, 2021).

The expectation of the countries of the region is that benefits of the BRI would help them address the developmental challenges they face. The hopes are that China would become a stable, long-term development partner for the region have also received a boost from the BRI's arrival However, the risk of overestimating benefits from BRI projects affects the successful implementation of the project. Overestimating the positive impacts or benefits of infrastructural projects can result in high exploitation or inadequate use of the infrastructure developed.

Potential Challenges for BRI in LAC

Domestically within the LAC, there are limited concerns with Chinese investments in projects. The region is in dire need of infrastructure and other development projects. As has been pointed, the LAC governments have historically underinvested in infrastructure projects. With limited financial capacity to invest in domestic projects, economies which remain under stress due to mismanagement and corruption, the assistance provided by China, within the ambit of BRI or outside it, is most welcome. The region is aware of the debt trap aspect of the BRI or projects funded by China, however, since most countries of the region are or have been in debts it is not a major concern for them. The countries of the region have in the past taken assistance from the International Monetary Fund (IMF) and faced debts. The stringent conditions applied by the IMF have made the organisation unpopular in the region.

The governments and businesses in the region are also aware that they are a mineral-rich region with limited capacity to extract the minerals or develop required infrastructure, they also feel that China has the expertise in this field and are open to Chinese enterprises-State owned or private to come to LAC. The region has for long been trying to build a centralised infrastructure platform however, it has not materialised due to many reasons such as differences within the nations and differing priorities. China's BRI allows them to be part of a development platform without taking on the responsibilities of the projects.

For the region becoming part of the BRI is an extension of their two-decade deep relations with China and is viewed as an added advantage to attract Chinese investments and companies while ensuring a ready market for LAC exports. In view of the above, the two potential challenges that the BRI faces in the region are the United States and the concerns that the public have with respect to projects in environmentally sensitive areas.

The countries of the region have a hurdle in balancing their relations with China and the United States. As the largest power in the region, which has close political, economic and security relations with nearly all countries, the growing presence of China is not a welcome sign for the United States.

In the past few years, United States lending to and investments in the LAC region has decreased. Despite leading the World Bank and regional development banks, the United States has not encouraged them to invest in infrastructure development projects allowing China to fill the gaps in financing and investments. Relations between the United States and the LAC region further deteriorated under President Donald Trump. The comments by President Trump on illegal migrants from the region, the lack of attention to the region by officials and the perception that the United States did not consider LAC heads of government as equals formed a negative view of the United States in the region. Further, the extension of the BRI in LAC corresponded with the increasing critical view of the United States administration towards China and its influence in LAC. It has also coincided with a growing rift in United States-China relations, with the United States warning countries against letting Chinese companies, especially technology firms from gaining access to core industries such as telecommunication, development of ports and railways, mines etc.

Although the United States has monitored this burgeoning relationship with wariness for years, its efforts to dissuade Latin American governments from deepening ties with China have been limited to warnings. Overall, Washington has failed to offer the region economic alternatives to Chinese funding for infrastructure projects. Nonetheless, the Biden Administration, along with the G-7 countries, announced the Build Back Better World (B3W) initiative. It has been projected as an alternative to the BRI and LAC is the first region being looked at under the initiative. To this end, officials from various U.S. departments visited Colombia, Ecuador and Panama to discuss projects that could be financed under the initiative.

While the countries of the region are open to investments from the United States, the investments from the northern neighbour have been relatively small when compared to Chinese investments. The United States would have to increase its contributions significantly. The other issue is that B3W projects are likely to be high-value projects in four identified sectors of climate, health and health security, digital technology, and gender equity and equality. The BRI policy on the other hand engages in projects based on five priority areas of infrastructure connectivity; unimpeded trade; financial integration; and connecting people ensuring that it has a wider reach.

Other concerns have been about commodity dependence and the unsustainable environmental and social impacts of ties between China and LAC, all of which were already clear well before the rollout of the BRI, but have been accentuated by the extension of the BRI to the region (Ferchen, 2021).

Within the Caribbean, Chinese investments have also been the subject of critique. Scholars, the media, opposition politicians and a number of civil society actors have raised questions about the low levels of transparency in Chinese negotiations and the mounting debts that the Caribbean economies now face after taking numerous Chinese loans. They have also raised concerns about poor labour standards, incomplete or low-quality projects, environmental impacts, and the prospects for broad socio-economic development on the back of an infrastructure-focused blueprint (Gonzalez-Vicente, 2021). With growing awareness of the environment, and the perception that Chinese projects and investments sidestep environmental protection norms, the governments of the LAC region have to balance environmental needs alongside economic development. Despite China's growing domestic affinity for renewable energy, some observers fear that China will use BRI to export its fossil fuel-based economy to the developing world. As China tries to reposition itself in the global economic order by focusing on higher-value goods and services, high-emission manufacturing industries may migrate to developing BRI host nations. In an ecologically rich region such as the LAC, such disruptions would influence the livelihoods of the people who are dependent on local environmental resources. The Twin Ocean Railroad or the Amazonian railways is a US$ 10 billion project links Brazil's Atlantic coast to Peru's Pacific coast and the Nicaragua Inter-Oceanic Grand Canal project have been eclipsed by the certainty of its environmental impact and also the viability of the project. Projects such as Peru's Amazon Waterway - the dredging of Peruvian tributaries of the basin's lifeblood in order to facilitate the transit of goods- are controversial. Indigenous communities' worry that dredging will impact piscine populations, disrupt fish migration impacting food security and cause harm to the rainforest region. China, on its part, is trying to address the concerns not just in Peru but in other projects around the world. It is using its expertise to deliver low carbon technologies to emerging economies through the BRI. The Green Investment Principles (GIP) for the BRI was launched in 2018 to accelerate green investments in the BRI, including through greater use of project finance, risk mitigation tools, and green finance.

Conclusion

China's close economic relations with the LAC region has grown in the past two decades with China having replaced the United States as the most important economic partner for most countries of the region. With the countries of the region joining BRI and/or contemplating joining the BRI, and China blurring the lines between BRI and non-BRI initiatives this relationship will continue to grow.

As this chapter has underlined, the expectation from joining the BRI outweighs the challenges. The region continues to grapple with developmental challenges and has limited financial capacity to address them. China is increasingly being seen as a partner that can help them overcomes these challenges. While cooperation with China is not without its risks, the governments and businesses in the region believe the benefits outweigh the risks.

The BRI has not changed the nature of the dynamics of the relations between the LAC countries and China, but it has allowed China to strengthen its relations with Central America and Caribbean nations. With some of the larger economies of the region such as Argentina now part of the BRI and Brazil, Colombia and Mexico supportive of strong bilateral ties, China has replaced the United States as the preferred trading partner in the region. For the region, membership of the BRI is viewed as an added advantage in gaining access to Chinese investments as it is a priority policy of President Xi. While there have not been much investments from China within the ambit of the BRI in LAC when compared to other regions such as Africa and Asia, the situation may change as LAC looks for a post-pandemic economic future. The trend since 2019 shows that China has been conservative in its investments in large infrastructure and energy projects in LAC. However, the COVID-19 crisis has opened new areas of cooperation in the form of the Health Silk Road (HSR) and the Digital Silk Road (DSR), which are becoming new areas of cooperation. The pandemic has contracted the economies of most nations of the region. China is one of the few countries which have reported quick recovery and the region hopes that this would translate to increased exports from the region to China.

The BRI has led to an economic activity in the LAC region, which has experienced an arduous cycle of debt and sluggish growth in the decades building up to its engagement with China. Both through the BRI and its bilateral agreements, China has invested into the region's infrastructural sectors and Chinese finance has allowed regional economies to seek sources of financing that do not impose the type of conditionality promoted by institutions such as the IMF or the World Bank. While the BRI has faced criticism from some countries for entrapping emerging economies into debts, for LAC countries, already used to debt crisis situations, it provides them with an alternative source of developmental capital.

The BRI and ties with China are likely to grow irrespective of the pressures from the United States to reverse this trend and is unlikely to be in a position to invest on the scale that China is willing and able to in the region. The region is also looking to diversify its political and diplomatic relations which are heavily tilted towards the United States. The BRI continues to be a win-win for both the LAC countries and for China.

Note

1. The pink tide was period in 2000s when a number of countries in the LAC region elected left oriented governments to power.

References

Carol Wise, (2020), *Dragonomics: How Latin America is Maximising (or Missiing out on) China's International Development Strategy*, New Haven, Yale University Press.

CELAC-China Forum (2017), Special Declaration Of Santiago Of The II Ministerial Meeting Of The CELAC-China Forum On The Belt And Road Initiative, at https://celac.rree.gob.sv/wp-content/uploads/2018/04/Special-Declaration-II-CELAC-CHINA-Forum-22.1.18.pdf

CMS Chile, (2021), "Belt and Road Initiative The view from Latin America", at https://cms.law/en/media/international/files/publications/publications/bri_the-view-from-latin-america?v=2

Francisco Javier Valderrey, Miguel A. Montoya and Adriana Sa´nchez (2020), "Latin America: The East, Wing of the New Silk Road", *Competition and Regulation in Network Industries*, 2020, Vol. 21(1) 34–62, at https://journals.sagepub.com/doi/pdf/10.1177/1783591719853537

Inter-American Development Bank (2021), Infrastructure Gaps in Latin America and Caribbean, IADB, at https://publications.iadb.org/publications/english/document/The-Infrastructure-Gap-in-Latin-America-and-the-Caribbean-Investment-Needed-Through-2030-to-Meet-the-Sustainable-Development-Goals.pdf

Matt Ferchen, (2021), "The BRI in Latin America: New Wine in Old Bottle?", in Florian Schneider (ed.), *Global Perspectives on China's Belt and Road Initiative*, Amsterdam, Amsterdam University Press. "Belt and Road Forum for International Cooperation", (2017), Full text of President Xi's speech at opening of Belt and Road forum, http://2017.beltandroadforum.org/english/n100/2018/0306/c25-1038.html

National Development and Reform Commission, Ministry of Foreign Affairs, and Ministry of Commerce of the People's Republic of China (2015), Vision and Actions on Jointly Building Silk Road Economic Belt and 21st Century Maritime Silk Road, https://www.mfa.gov.cn/ce/ceuk//eng/zywl/t1251719.htm

Pablo Chauvet, Taotao Chen, AzharJaimurzina, Run Xu, Ying Jin, (2020), "China: current and potential role in infrastructure investment in Latin America", International Trade, 144, United Nations ECLAC, at https://repositorio.cepal.org/bitstream/handle/11362/45205/1/S1900859_en.pdf

Pepe Zhang (2019), "Belt and Road in Latin America: A regional game changer?", Atlantic Council, at https://www.atlanticcouncil.org/in-depth-research-reports/issue-brief/belt-and-road-in-latin-america-a-regional-game-changer/

R. Evan Ellis, NA, "Deconstructing the Belt and Road Initiative: China's Use of

Connectivity to Advance Its Strategic Economic Position in Latin America". Ruben Gonzalez-Vicente (2021), "Over Hills and Valleys Too China's Belt and Road Initiative in the Caribbean", in Florian Schneider (ed.), *Global Perspectives on China's Belt and Road Initiative*, Amsterdam, Amsterdam University Press, at https://www.jstor.org/stable/j.ctv1dc9k7j.10.

Rhys Jenkins (2021), "China's Belt and Road Initiative in Latin America: What has Changed?", *Journal of Current Chinese Affairs*. December 2021. doi:10.1177/18681026211047871

Shalei Das (2017), "Extending to South America", in Srikant Kondapalli and Hu Xiaowen (eds), *One Belt One Road: China's Global Outreach*, Delhi, Pentagon Press.

The State Council, People's Republic of China, (2016), Full text of China's Policy Paper on Latin America and the Caribbean, at http://english.www.gov.cn/archive/white_paper/2016/11/24/content_281475499069158.htm

Tomás Serebrisky, Juan Pablo Brichetti, Allen Blackman, Mauricio Mesquita Moreira (2020), "Sustainable and digital infrastructure for the post-COVID-19 economic recovery of Latin America and the Caribbean: A Roadmap To More Jobs, Integration And Growth", IADB, at https://publications.iadb.org/publications/english/document/Sustainable-and-Digital-Infrastructure-for-the-Post-COVID-19-Economic-Recovery-of-Latin-America-and-the-Caribbean-A-Roadmap-to-More-Jobs-Integration-and-Growth.pdf

U.S.-China Economic And Security Review Commission, (NA), China's Influence In Latin America And The Caribbean, at https://www.uscc.gov/sites/default/files/2021-11/Chapter_1_Section_2--Chinas_Influence_in_Latin_America_and_the_Caribbean.pdf

Part VI
BRI and Two Challenges of Recent Times

21. BRI: Challenges of Pandemic and Conflict

Athar Zafar

Abstract

BRI is a multi-billion dollar project involving 149 countries across continents. Nevertheless, despite the fact that the initiative involves governments of many countries seeking investments from China, the projects under the initiative are now increasingly attracting critical observations from intellectuals, policy planners and even protests by common people in recipient countries.

The general lack of transparency has been a major concern and a drawback. The initiative also has the perils of over-dependency on a single source for supplies and the unidirectional mode of logistics planning.

BRI has been facing multiple challenges, including of not respecting territorial integrity of affected countries in formulation and execution of projects. In recent years, the COVID-19 pandemic and the Russian military operation in Ukraine have created dilemmas over projects' continued implementation and sustainability.

The pandemic and the environment of trans-regional insecurity have the potential to severely affect the project's feasibility. It is to be seen how the initiative overcomes the two challenges.

Introduction

The Belt and Road Initiative (BRI) launched by China in 2013 is completing a decade of its announcement. The initiative has a major thrust from the Chinese government. The BRI aims to achieve policy coordination, improve infrastructure connectivity, strengthening of trade and investment cooperation. It also seeks financial integration and supports people-to-people collaboration. So far, economic cooperation and strategic calculations seem to drive the agenda of BRI. Despite inherent risks and challenges, the initiative was welcomed by various participating countries, many of whom also attended the BRI Forums hosted by Beijing. Over the years, BRI has emerged as a factor affecting the global economy, direction of flow of capital, trade patterns, and influencing the geo-strategic orientations of nations and economies.

Economic planning and continued high growth rate for an extended period in China had created excess industrial capacity and financial resources enabling it to formulate big investment plans in the country and abroad. By the turn of the century, China had emerged as a new big player in the international investment and infrastructure development sectors. Around the same timeframe, the world was trying to recover from the 2007-08 global economic meltdown. There was also a significant drop in international investments by advanced economies in many developing countries and regions. According to World Investment Report 2010, there was a 'drastic decline' in foreign direct investment flows worldwide in 2009 (UNCTAD, 2009). China, on the other hand, remained focused throughout this period on its economic development and securing resources through diplomacy. Gradually, it had accumulated sufficient extra capacity and funds for making investments abroad. It was ready to launch a major programme on a global scale.

In such a backdrop, the stage was ready for investments by major economic player and China was able to fulfil the requirement of improving connectivity through both the land and maritime routes by creating necessary infrastructure. Interestingly, the BRI announcements were not made in China or from the podium of any major global economic platform. The multi-billion dollar BRI was announced by President Xi Jinping at a university gathering in neighbouring Kazakhstan in September 2013 among intellectuals, teachers and students in Astana (now Nursultan), and the maritime component was announced to the Indonesian Parliament in November 2013. It is also to be noted that President Xi had assumed the office of presidency only a few months back when the projects were officially launched. Subsequently, certain projects that were already completed or announced earlier were included in the BRI's project list (CSIS, 2018).

Many countries in different regions of the world welcomed the initiative initially despite reservations expressed by major global and regional players. Chinese initiative was received positively by different countries as they needed the investments for their infrastructure development. Further, China had no overt strings attached with regard to the domestic politics of the recipient countries, such as human rights and democracy, as generally highlighted by the West and institutions led by it while making investments in non-Western countries. It is an ambitious project of China and though estimates vary on total investments in BRI, Morgan Stanley predicted in 2018 that the overall expenditure could reach US$ 1.2-1.3 trillion by 2027 (Chatzky and McBride, 2020).

Nevertheless, after the initial fervour, reality started to set in and one after the other countries started facing the economic and political challenges with regard to the Chinese BRI investments. The contracts' details generally remain out of the public purview making it to be looked at with suspicion. The approved projects are usually awarded to Chinese companies or China's state-owned enterprises, which bring their own men and machine that impacted employment generation and skill transfer to the target countries. In this way, China maintained its control on aspects of implementation and the investment capital mostly remained within the country. On the other hand, recipient countries were also wary of becoming China's export market. Such an approach caused concerns and criticism.

The BRI is formulated and implemented through the top-down approach and it is among the lacunae of the project. It is largely driven and controlled by the financing side—China. Generally, the projects lack international transparency standards and the recipient countries have little say in formulation and implementation. The clauses of the deal are not made available to the people, thereby, generating anxiety and concerns. In the post-COVID situation, there is a re-thinking over various projects. Secondly, taking cues from the COVID-induced logistics and supply challenges, many countries of the world are pursuing to have a resilient supply chain mechanism and reducing their dependencies on a single-source supply. The US and Western countries have started the decoupling drive aimed at making Western economies less dependent on a single or very limited production and transportation system.

Gradually, certain BRI projects started getting negative coverage, protests were held by the people in affected areas. Following the passage of time and the consequences of over investments becoming more visible, the projects increasingly started facing challenges, especially in Sri Lanka, Pakistan and African countries. Questions were raised over the stated objectives of China's investment in different parts of the world that whether they would serve the interest of the local people. The initiative now started facing negative publicity.

These are not the only challenges to the BRI projects. In recent past, COVID-19 and the Russian military operation in neighbouring Ukraine have dealt blows to the initiative. It seems that in the short term and long term, both the human security challenge (COVID) and state security threats (Russia-Ukraine conflict) are set to affect on the BRI in more than one way. It is to be observed whether the projects will be able to overcome the challenges and fulfil the aspirations of recipient countries.

Impact of COVID-19 on BRI's Health

The pandemic-led restrictions imposed a high cost on the BRI and the countries dependent on the supply chain network. There were delays and disruptions due to the measures taken by affected countries with regard to quarantine and containment (Passi, 2020). Borders were closed and in many areas, cross-border transportation came to a halt. So far, the problems with the BRI were either due to China's domestic economic issues or the protests against it, which in a sense were specific to a particular country or region. The most daunting challenge to the BRI in last couple of years has come from unexpected quarters of global health and international military operations in the critical Eurasian region. They have been quite severe in their magnitude and impact. The COVID-19 pandemic, which incidentally was first reported in China in late 2019, brought the global health infrastructure to its knees. There were hundreds of thousands of casualties, it impacted millions of individuals and exposed the neglect of the healthcare system across the globe.

The BRI is vast in scale and was hit by the COVID-19 pandemic, which was similarly widespread in its reach across the world but quite devastating in impact. The magnitude of the coronavirus pandemic was incomprehensible as the globalised world was for the first time probably

facing the consequences of a globalised health scare impacting every way of life of the people in all parts of the world.

Political Impact

As the virus spread, China was criticised for its handling of the COVID infections in the country in initial days, especially not warning the world in time of the impending crisis. Gradually, the infection spread and so the uncertainty about the continuation of BRI projects grew. Beijing had to issue statements of assurances that the projects face no economic dilemma and it is going to continue. A Chinese official said 'As the situation improves we have confidence that the projects will come back and the execution of them will speed up' (Reuters, 2020).

Nevertheless, the reality is that the pandemic impacted the BRI. China had to scale down some projects after several countries expressed concerns and wanted to review and downsize the commitments. They cited high costs, corruption and sovereignty issues. The so-called flagship project of the BRI, the China-Pakistan-Economic Corridor (CPEC), also started getting negative attention as reports indicate that projects face delays due to the pandemic (ANI, 2021). Rail projects in Indonesia and Nigeria, and development of special economic zone in Cambodia were reportedly halted (Mouritz, 2020). Disclosures of various clauses and publication of conditions associated with the Chinese investments, especially in Sri Lanka, and Pakistan led to protests and questions were raised over the primary objectives of China's investment in different parts of the world whether it was in the economic interests of recipient country or had strategic objectives of the financing country. It is said that countries, such as Kyrgyzstan, Cambodia, Djibouti, and Montenegro would seemingly require relief in debt to sustain the BRI (Mouritz, 2020). Some projects had to be renegotiated, downsized, cancelled, deferred or put on hold (Passi, 2020).

In recent decades, tens of millions of people had come out of poverty in many countries of Asia and Africa. COVID-19 is pushing them back into poverty. As per UN development report estimates, COVID-19 could push over 200 million into extreme poverty (UN, 2020). The movement of people and goods were halted resulting into massive economic hardships. Loss of employment in large numbers, shortfall in remittances,

restriction on the movement of labour and higher travel costs, were among the consequences of the pandemic, which were felt more severely in developing countries.

Economic Impact

Since the BRI was run by a single country, any trouble in its economy was bound to impact economic activities in parts of the world where BRI projects were underway. A similar thing happened when China was reeling with the pandemic, continuation of projects became uncertain. The economic impact on various projects of BRI has been severe as the pandemic countered what the BRI claimed to promote. Though no major projects already announced were cancelled, in 2020 Chinese officials informed that about 20 per cent of BRI projects have been 'seriously affected' by the pandemic (Reuters, 2020). It was reported that about 40 per cent of projects are affected with little adversity while another 40 per cent are partially affected.

Intermittent recurrence of the mutated virus infection in China has also become a cause of concern in some quarters. It not only raises questions over the efficacy of the Chinese vaccines but also led to slowing down the global economic recovery. In March-April 2022 strict measures of total lockdown were taken by Beijing, which led to restrictions on movement of people and goods in many Chinese cities and halt in operations at ports in China causing cascading impact on international trade and transport. The continued economic difficulty can potentially cast doubt on projects that are being formulated or their cost could be scrutinised more rigorously (Mouritz, 2020).

It has been observed in recent years that China is facing structural economic problems. Pandemic is not the only reason for slower economic growth. Many in China have emphasised that besides pandemic, the country faces various other risks, including the global supply chain disorder, the rising costs of raw materials and weaker consumer demand (Kumar, 2022). These factors have negative impact on China's economic growth, which has slowed down in the past decade. Therefore, it remains to be seen whether the country is willing to fund the project as before. It may be reported that Chinese investments into the BRI countries declined by 54 per cent in 2020 as compared to 2019 (Wang, 2021).

China has emerged in recent years not only as a production hub for the global supply chain, it is also a supplier of raw materials for production in different parts of the world. Trade flow was disrupted across the supply chains as goods supplied from China to the world market were disrupted. In 2020, China alone accounted for about 16 per cent of the world's output (Bhowmick, 2021). No country wants to be dependent on one particular country or region for its supplies. Following the consequences of the coronavirus, the economies, which are particularly reliant on supply chains, realised the shortcomings of single-source supply dependency. The restrictions imposed on the movement of raw material had a subsequent impact on the availability of finished goods, including medical supplies and electronic chips for the auto industry.

The disruption is causing many producers to look for dispersed production facilities in different geographies so that the operations are least impacted due to uncertain developments in a particular area. The pandemic has sped up the process to diversify the supply and markets in economic engagement. To avoid such a scenario in future, countries will objectively re-think their terms of engagement with the BRI or at least diversify the market sources. Already there are reports suggesting many corporations shifting or diversifying their manufacturing centres from China.

Sensing the criticism and backlash over the origin of the coronavirus and aimed at reducing the negativity associated with the BRI, China made an effort to link the BRI with the health diplomacy for recipient countries. The country started 'medical diplomacy' in order to reach out to the pandemic-stricken country with necessary supplies of medicine, vaccines, other items, and visits by medical professions. It is also observed that in the face of criticism China has shown some flexibility in re-negotiating the terms of investment, which are favourable to the recipient countries. There is also pressure on China and the recipient countries to disclose the terms of investment to make a better sense of the intended investments by the stakeholders. In short, the BRI has also been a learning curve for China.

Shadow of Russia-Ukraine conflict on BRI

After a stretched post-COVID period of great trouble and when the global economy was slowly moving towards recovery, it was again hit by an unexpected

Russian military operation against its western neighbour Ukraine. Incidentally, both Russia and Ukraine are parties to the BRI projects. Seemingly, geopolitical factors are the primary reasons behind this conflict between the two neighbouring countries. However, it has given BRI the second shock in recent years after being hit by the COVID-19 pandemic.

Russia has been an important link between China's connectivity corridors with European markets. Many of the BRI routes passed through the vast and secured territory of Russia taking goods from China to Europe. In recent years, the surface connectivity between East and West has been gaining renewed traction. Instead of long caravan of animals, now the trade is primarily through long-distance goods trains. Boosting rail freight from China to Europe through multiple routes passing Kazakhstan, Russia and Belarus have been a key element of the BRI (Nathan, 2022). Rail connectivity has grown substantially over the years. The China Railway Express (CRE) or China-Europe Railway Express is a 'key logistical cog' in China's BRI (Ji, 2022). As per China's state railway operator, while only 17 train trips were made along the Eurasian route, a decade ago, in 2021 a record of 15,183 train trips transported 1.46 million 20-foot equivalent unit (TEU) containers (Ji, 2022).

In the case of Russian operations against Ukraine, the impact on BRI will not only be due to fighting between the two BRI countries but also on account of the western sanctions against Russian economy. The decoupling of Russian economy from the western financial and economic systems will be profound for the Chinese initiative. This move of the West is negatively affecting even other economies who are not involved in the conflict.

In the long run, each connectivity drive will try to hedge itself from any inter-state conflict among the stakeholders. Chinese exporters will try to avoid sending goods passing through the territories targeted by the Western sanctions. It is also likely that in the near future the trend toward development of road and rail routes will be readjusted between China and Europe. A growing number of Western companies have already stopped taking bookings for transit through Russia (Majorie, 2022). According to reports, the conflict has resulted into non-availability of shipping routes, services are being suspended by logistics firms and freight rates are on steep rise (Weizhen, 2022).

Another impact could be the emergence of alternative routes bypassing Russia. Alternatively, the current routes, which are not affected by the sanctions, will become more prominent. Recently, countries in the region have announced to provide for a corridor through the Caspian Sea. Georgia, Azerbaijan, Turkey and Kazakhstan have signed a quadrilateral declaration on the Trans-Caspian East-West Corridor. At the same time, the declaration highlighted the significance of the Baku-Tbilisi-Kars (BTK) railway line in promoting competitive transportation between Asia and Europe (Maryana, 2022).

China and Europe are working in tandem to connect each other smoothly without passing through the territory of Russia. Earlier, in November 2021, the Asian Infrastructure Investment Bank (AIIB) and the European Bank for Reconstruction and Development (EBRD) had announced to co-finance a rail link project in Turkey to improve linkages between Asia and Europe (AIIB, 2021). The project finances construction of 67 kilometres of new double-track, electrified, high-speed railway from Istanbul to Bulgarian border (Chris, 2021).

In the aftermath of insecurity and crisis due to the conflict between Russia and Ukraine, it seems that new routes and ports are likely to get more prominence in the East-West linkages. For example, the Poti Port in Georgia off the eastern Black Sea coast, having a new multifunctional terminal, can see increased Chinese and Central Asian cargo that was so far transported via Russian ports (Chris, 2021).

In case the conflict prolongs, it can lead the attention of the West remain focussed on Europe. Sustained military assistance and financial packages, including for refugees, can have an impact on European economies. Similarly, there is a possibility that the conflict may result into reduced purchasing power capacity of the people in these areas resulting into a decline in demand of goods, including those imported from China thereby impacting the BRI.

Conclusion

The BRI has been a major economic and now 'increasingly strategic project of China'. It has the potential to redefine international trade and communication. Massive liquidity has been injected into the project. The BRI has the distinction of being the first such international infrastructure and industrial development plan that involves 149 countries across the world but mainly bilaterally. The shortcomings of such a unilateral project is that its sustainability gets intrinsically linked to the health of the investor economy. The pandemic and the subsequent military operations in Ukraine by Russia have impacted the economic conditions, including of the financer and the recipients. China as well as the countries that have signed up to the BRI have been facing serious economic challenges in recent times. Many BRI investment recipient countries are in dire economic conditions, but not necessarily only due to the projects. The pandemic has also exposed the condition of the health infrastructure across the developed and developing countries. Consequently, the primary focus of these countries would be boosting up their health infrastructure. Connectivity projects may be accorded a secondary importance.

The BRI projects have come under increased scrutiny in the recipient countries due to perceptions of unequal benefits. In coming days BRI is to compete with many other projects launched by nations and multilateral groups. The International North-South Transport Corridor (INSTC), Japan's Quality Infrastructure Investment (QII), the Eurasian Economic Union (EAEU) by some CIS countries, including Russia, the Global Gateway of the European Union, the Blue Dot Network (BDN) announced by the US, and latest Build Back Better World (B3W), which has been proposed by the G-7. It seems that the world is likely to be more connected in the near future and it is readying itself to have smooth transport and connectivity in case of any eventuality.

The two shocks of COVID-19 pandemic and the Russian-Ukrainian military conflict have impacted the perception of secured supply chains and highlighted the significance of resilient connectivity linkages. These two consecutive heavy bumps in the journey of the implementation of BRI may make the implementation of the projects challenging. Even when normalisation of supply chains and international travel is fully restored, it seems unlikely that the BRI can continue as planned. In order to prepare for any future eventuality, the recipient countries will be taking appropriate measures. They will pursue diversification and inclusion of local human and material resources in implementing the projects.

Despite the challenges, China is likely to continue making investments through the BRI. Given the country's excess capacity, strong economic and financial conditions, no conditions attached to the loans and investment directly impacting the domestic politics of a recipient country and lack of availability or difficult conditions for alternative funding from Western countries and institutions, are among reasons that will likely help sail the BRI projects in troubled waters. However, the scale of investment may not be as before.

It is also certain that to make the projects more acceptable the level of transparency has to increase; it has to become inclusive and participatory. The BRI parties must respect territorial integrity of other stakeholders and benefits should reach to common people and all involved.

In the near future, the BRI project is likely to continue as a significant factor in international economic and infrastructure development. However, the mid and long-term prospects of the initiative remain exposed to the evolving political strands within the ruling party of China and the country's economic performance amid growing international calls for production and supply chain realignments. China's conduct on its land and maritime borders with several neighbouring countries is being watched with concern regionally and internationally and it is likely to impact the perception of China's motives behind international project partnerships. Further, many nations and institutions are gearing up to provide finances for mega infrastructure initiatives. Some of them have already been announced, thereby making the alternative financing available. All these developments are likely to weigh in when a country takes up any initiative from any side.

References

Asian Infrastructure Investment Bank (AIIB), (2021). "AIIB Approves EUR300 million for Ispartakule-Cerkezkoy Railway Project," 14 December, at https://www.aiib.org/en/news-events/news/2021/AIIB-Approves-EUR300-million-for-Ispartakule-Cerkezkoy-Railway-Project.html, Accessed on 9 May 2022.

Bhowmick, Soumya (2021). "The changing face of globalization," *Asia Times*, 26 March, at https://asiatimes.com/2021/03/the-changing-face-of-globalization/, Accessed on 30 March 2022.

Chatzky, Andrew and McBride, James (2020). "China's Massive Belt and Road Initiative," *Council on Foreign Relations*, 28 January, at https://www.cfr.org/backgrounder/chinas-massive-belt-and-road-initiative, Accessed on 20 March 2022.

Center for Strategic and International Studies, (2018). "China's Belt and Road Initiative: Five Years Later," 25 January, Report, at https://www.csis.org/analysis/chinas-belt-and-road-initiative-five-years-later-0, Accessed on 5 April 2022.

Chris, Devonshire-Ellis, (2022). "How Damaging Are Russian Sanctions On China-EU Rail Trade And The Belt & Road Initiative?," *Silk Road Briefing*, 7 March, at https://www.silkroadbriefing.com/news/2022/03/07/how-damaging-are-russian-sanctions-on-china-eu-rail-trade-and-the-belt-road-initiative/#:~:text=But%20on%20the%20other%20hand%2C%20the%20EU%20has,the%20European%20Bank%20for%20Reconstruction%20and%20Development%20%28EBRD%29. Accessed on 21 March 2022.

Wang, Christoph N. (2021). "China Belt and Road Initiative (BRI) Investment Report 2020," *Green Finance & Development Center*, 21 January, at https://greenfdc.org/china-belt-and-road-initiative-bri-investment-report-2020/, Accessed on 5 April 2022.

Ji Siqi,(2022). "What is the China-Europe Railway Express, and how much pressure is it under from the Ukraine crisis?," *South China Morning Post*, 6 March, at https://www.scmp.com/economy/global-economy/article/3169239/what-china-europe-railway-express-and-how-much-pressure-it, Accessed on 15 March 2022.

Kumar, Sanjeev (2022). "China's Economic Challenges and Priorities for 2022," ICWA, 22 January, at https://www.icwa.in/show_content.php?lang=1&level=3&ls_id=6957&lid=4730, Accessed on 12 May 2022.

Majorie van Leijen, "Sanctions or not: these companies stop transit through Russia," *railfreight.com*, 3 March, at https://www.railfreight.com/railfreight/2022/03/03/sanctions-or-not-these-companies-stop-transit-through-russia/?gdpr=accept, Accessed on 21 March 2022.

Maryana Akhmedova, (2022). "Georgia, Azerbaijan, Turkey, Kazakhstan sign declaration on Trans-Caspian East-West Corridor," *Trend News Agency*, 31 March, at https://en.trend.az/business/transport/3575705.html, Accessed on 29 April 2022.

Mouritz, F. (2020). Implications of the COVID-19 Pandemic on China's Belt and Road Initiative. *Connections, 19*(2), 115-124, at https://www.jstor.org/stable/26937614.

Nathan, Hutson, (2022). "Russian invasion dealing China a Silk Road economic setback," *Eurasianet,* 21 March, at https://eurasianet.org/perspectives-russian-invasion-dealing-china-a-silk-road-economic-setback, Accessed on 20 April 2022.

Reuters, (2022)"China says one-fifth of Belt and Road projects 'seriously affected' by pandemic," 19 June, at https://www.reuters.com/article/us-health-coronavirus-china-silkroad-idUSKBN23Q0I1, Accessed on 14 April 2022.

Passi, Ritika (2020). "The BRI and Covid-19: A tale of two crises," 28 May, at https://www.orfonline.org/expert-speak/bri-covid-19-tale-two-crises-66929/, Accessed on 18 April 2022.

UNCTAD "World Investment Report 2010," at https://worldinvestmentreport.unctad.org/wir2010/chapter-1-fdi-trends-and-prospects/, Accessed on 4 April 2022; Vol. 19, No. 2, "The Security Impacts of the COVID-19 Pandemic", (Spring 2020), pp. 115-124.

Weizhen Tan, (2022). "How the Russia-Ukraine war is worsening shipping snarls and pushing up freight rates," CNBC, 11 March, at https://www.cnbc.com/2022/03/11/russia-ukraine-war-impact-on-shipping-ports-air-freight.html, Accessed on 30 March 2022.

22. Epilogue: Regions and Reflections

Sanjeev Kumar

The academic exposition on Belt and Road Initiative (BRI) in different regions of the world has identified and highlighted a number of broad trends. First, the scope of BRI has been widening from economic and energy to include political, socio-cultural, digital, health, education, and security dimensions. The blurring of lines between China's economic and strategic ambitions is much evident following the implementation of BRI. There is an attempt by China to forge bilateral cooperation agreements with various countries in different sectors under the rubric of BRI. Two sovereign states can sign such agreements in normal circumstances without referring them as BRI. However, since the BRI is President Xi Jinping's signature project, the state has consistently attached importance to the initiative and urged countries to join it. While cooperation with participating countries is the main official agenda, the experiences of the BRI in various regions suggest that the project exhibits inherent contradictions at conceptual as well as execution level and the participating countries have raised many concerns. Some have been listed below.

In recent past, China's leadership has highlighted that world is undergoing 'once in a century transformation' and 'the period of strategic opportunity' no longer exists for China. In this context BRI has been implemented as China's 'top-level cooperation initiative'. BRI primarily referred to new Silk Road Economic Belt and 21st Century Maritime Silk Road (MSR). However, China has expanded its ambitions with the introduction of Digital Silk Road, Polar Silk Road, Health Silk Road, Green Silk Road, Innovation Silk Road and Air Silk Road. Now, BRI is increasingly considered as a strategic project of China. It has been cited by Chinese experts as a 'critical instrument' to realise the Community of

Common Destiny and has been directly linked to the Chinese Dream–political and strategic concepts proposed by China in the third era. Experts have also considered BRI as 'the first step towards the creation of China's system of alliances' to protect Chinese interest abroad.

Second, China has prepared a dedicated website on the BRI (yidaiyilu.gov.cn) in order to disseminate official information and data in six different languages regarding the initiative, including in Chinese, Arabic, English and Russian. However, there is hardly any official definition of what constitute a BRI project. This creates anomaly and confusion in some participating countries as discussed in chapters of this book. Further, some projects that were already completed or announced prior to September 2013, were highlighted as BRI project. Recently, Bangladesh had to refute the statement of Bangladesh-based Beijing sponsored-organizations that the Padma Bridge has been constructed as a part of BRI (ANI, 2022). Fact remains that there are Chinese funded projects in non-participating countries having same features of BRI projects. The research paper on Latin America and the Caribbean in this book notes that differences between BRI and non-BRI projects in the region are blurred. China's bilateral trade with BRI participating countries has also been highlighted by Chinese officials as a benchmark to judge the success of BRI. However, there is hardly any difference between China's bilateral trade with BRI participating and non-participating countries. For example, the volume of India's trade with China has been rising even though India is not a BRI party.

Third, there are variations in estimates about China's direct investment in BRI participating countries. Significantly, recent data released by Ministry of Commerce of the PRC (May 2022) suggest that during the period from 2013 to 2021, China's direct investment in countries along the Belt and Road totalled US$ 161.3 billion. Further, Chinese enterprises have invested US$ 43.08 billion in overseas economic and trade cooperation zones established in countries along the Belt and Road. The trade volume between China and BRI countries accounted for 29.7 per cent of China's total foreign trade in 2021, from 25 per cent in 2013 (Ministry of Commerce, PRC, 2022). These figures released by the Chinese government indicate that the achievements of BRI are not something extraordinary as far as China's direct investment and percentage increase in trade with countries along the Belt and Road is concerned. On the other hand, the BRI participating countries have also made substantial investment in China. The Ministry informs that the BRI participating countries have invested US$ 71.2 billion in China. China signed new contracts of about US$ 1.08 trillion (from 2013 to 2021), with countries along the Belt and Road for engineering projects in transportation, electricity and other areas, with a US$ 728.6 billion 'business volume' completed (ibid.). The volume of business completed is far bigger than the China's direct investment with countries along the Belt and Road. This requires further in-depth study, mainly from the perspective of recipient countries.

Fourth, China had announced six international economic corridors under its BRI. Despite controversies, CPEC is a work in progress and it establishes that strategic considerations are more important for China in the region. However, there is very little progress as far as five other international economic corridors are concerned. Further, it may be noted that the BCIM Economic Corridor has a different history and it predates China's BRI. Significantly, the annexure along with Joint Communiqué issued during the Second Belt and Road Forum (2019) under the heading "Economic corridors and other projects catalysed and supported by connectivity" also included multilateral projects such as International North-South Transport Corridor (INSTC). Inclusion of INSTC in such a document released by China opens a new debate about the role of BRI.

Fifth, China is aggressively pursuing its maritime strategy across the Indo-Pacific region, which has caused contestations with countries having stakes in the region. The Indo-Pacific has increasingly become a focus area of strategic and economic importance in regional and global discourse. Some experts in China see the concept of FOIP as a challenge to the MSR. However, there is a need to stress that a free, open and inclusive order in the Indo-Pacific, based upon respect for sovereignty and territorial integrity of all nations and the right to freedom of navigation and over-flight for all in the international water is essential for peace, development and security of the entire region. The publication examines broader economic, political and security implications of large-scale Chinese investments under MSR. Further, it includes a host of alternative connectivity initiatives by the US and the EU and indicates their impact on the BRI.

Sixth, the financial sustainability of BRI is primarily dependent on the health of Chinese economy. In recent past, Chinese experts have noted that apart from COVID-19 pandemic, the country faces multiple risks, including the global supply chain disruption, the rising costs of raw materials and weak consumer demand (Yang, 2021). These factors have affected China's economic growth. Consequently, investments from China have reduced in last couple of years. Further, in the era of economic slowdown and 'new normal' in China, BRI creates a definitive perception that the initiative has been launched to create new markets and derive economic benefits by building infrastructure and industrial corridors as well as creating transportation and communication networks in the region and beyond. Chinese producers of steel, concrete, cement and other construction materials as well as Chinese engineering and construction firms stand to benefit from these projects. A number of papers in the volume explain that the primary motive behind China's BRI is to address domestic vulnerabilities, including closing the developmental gap between coastal and non-coastal regions within the country.

Seventh, state-owned enterprises (SOEs) are perhaps the biggest interest group in China. Some studies suggest that Chinese projects are less open to international participation. Out of all contractors participating in Chinese-funded projects within the Reconnecting Asia database (2018), an overwhelming 89 percent were Chinese companies. The fact remains that the BRI projects have provided a new market for Chinese SOEs. For a large number of workers of big SOEs, BRI projects have ensured employment and livelihood in the period of slowdown in the Chinese economy.

Eighth, the energy component/dimension of BRI vis a vis various regions, exhibit China's attempt to secure energy for sustained domestic economic development while overcoming 'Malacca dilemma'. It intends to establish efficient energy corridors from its sources in Eurasia and Southeast Asia to its manufacturing/industry hubs in China. The implementation of BRI projects has enabled further acquisition of overseas energy resources, energy supply to China and bilateral energy cooperation in the regions in a more coordinated manner. Further, China has highlighted energy cooperation as a top priority with Arab world under the framework of BRI.

Ninth, Digital Silk Road (DSR) is becoming an increasingly important component of the BRI, aimed to construct a "community of common destiny in cyberspace". This has also been seen as a strategic push by China to embed its technological standard globally. The deepening of the technology related tensions between China and the US is part of strategic rivalry between the two countries. Further, DSR has received mixed response from different regions. The control and security of data and internet security implications of reliance on Chinese technology is an issue of intense debate in Europe. Despite data privacy concerns, China's technology giants are welcomed in regions, such as Africa while in regions like South Asia, Southeast Asia, Latin America and the Caribbean it has become a debatable issue.

Tenth, the initial enthusiasm about the BRI in many countries seems to dissipating now. Countries of various regions welcomed BRI and signed cooperation agreement hoping that it would bring sufficient financing/ investment for their infrastructure development requirements. However, the Chinese model of investment has proved to be problematic for many recipient countries. Generally, Chinese companies import Chinese material and equipment as well as labour in the recipient country, which create tension for local population. This was evident in local protests held in various regions, including South and Central Asia. This has created a negative perception about China. In some regions like West Asia, the cultural differences between host and migrant labours have been seen as a potential concern.

Eleventh, connectivity projects must be pursued in a manner that respects sovereignty and territorial integrity of other countries. CPEC is an example, which directly impinges on India's sovereignty and such core concerns of India remains unaddressed by China. Such an approach by China also impacts regional and global order and geopolitical dimension in different regions as China aims to acquire a dominant position in Asia and the world.

Twelfth, BRI projects in different regions have common and some unique dimensions concerning domestic dynamics of recipient countries as evident in various chapters. The issue of transparency is increasingly emerging as a critical subject in the domestic politics of many recipient countries across various regions. Some countries have acknowledged that their infrastructure modernisation with investments from China has been an enormously expensive deal and they are struggling to repay loans taken from China. The issue of 'debt trap' or 'debt fear' has emerged as a major concern in many countries along the BRI network. This is primarily because responsible debt financing practices have not been followed to avoid unsustainable debt burden on recipient countries. A recent study has identified 53 fragile emerging economies facing debt troubles and it notes that "more than a third of the world's most debt-distressed countries also number among those most indebted to Chinese lenders" (*Economist*, 2022).

Thirteenth, it seems that South Asia has become the most contested region as almost all participating countries of the region have witnessed large or small protests against BRI projects. The countries are fearful about 'debt trap' as the case of Sri Lanka is evident for everybody to study. The Hambantota example served as a warning for countries in South Asia and other regions who were looking for similar economic deals with China. Further, China's geopolitical ambitions and the objective to change the equation of power in South Asia is still the core of its foreign policy objective, therefore, it sees major stakeholder of the region, i.e., India with an element of mistrust. In an interview to Bloomberg on 8 June 2022, the then Sri Lankan President Gotabaya Rajapaksa remarked that now China has less interest in South Asia and it has shifted its strategic focus from South Asia to Southeast Asia. This certainly indicates that China is facing a huge challenge in South Asian region.

Fourteenth, India was perhaps the first country to raise concerns on BRI related to international norms, practice of good governance, rule of law, transparency, equality as well as its core concerns on sovereignty and territorial integrity. The implications for India are at least at three different levels: first, at the international structural level, there is competition for models of development. The 19th National Congress of the CPC suggested that China model will be exported and the SOEs will be supported in their drive to go across the globe (Kondapalli, 2021). India's model of development follows a demand-driven consultative process and values international norms and principles. India's model of assistance is more favourable to the interests of the recipient countries. Second, as discussed in various chapters of the book, BRI projects in different regions have invited common and different reactions. The issue of transparency of projects have become a major concern now. Expansion and strengthening of connectivity is an integral part of India's economic and diplomatic initiatives in different regions which are undertaken through a consultative and consensus building approach. Under the 'Act East' policy, India is pursuing the Trilateral Highway project; under its 'Neighbourhood First' policy it is developing multimodal linkages with Myanmar and Bangladesh; under its 'Go West' strategy, it is engaged with Iran on Chabahar Port, and with Russia, Iran and other partners in Central Asia on the INSTC. Third, at the neighbourhood level in South Asia, India is involved in a number of initiatives, including at sub-regional level. The BBIN initiative is aimed at enhancing logistics efficiencies in South Asian region. Several bilateral projects in the region, including those focusing on capacity building have received appreciation from the host country. Experts from China, such as Qian Xuemei, appreciate Indian model to deliver major projects in Afghanistan, he notes: "In terms of concrete projects, India's aid is more comprehensive and covers more widely than that of China" (Qian, 2018).

Fifteenth, President Xi Jinping announced BRI first time in Central Asia and the region is extremely important from the perspective of China's national security interests, resource security and economic development. Evidence suggests that BRI has not radically changed Chinese investment prolife in Central Asia. According to the Chinese Government data, trade between China and Central Asian countries has grown by more than 100 times in the past 30 years. However, China's relationship with Central Asian countries is not trouble free. The region's trade is balanced in favour of China. Negative perception of BRI and China, especially in Kazakhstan and Kyrgyzstan is much evident. Experts also believe that China may act 'more boldly' in post Ukraine conflict period in Central Asia.

Sixteenth, the current phase of BRI is characterised by rethinking, renegotiation, downsizing and even cancellation of projects by recipient countries in some regions/continents especially South Asia, Southeast Asia and Africa. By and large, participating countries are now adopting a more 'cautious' approach towards BRI related projects. Evidence suggests that each BRI project is now negotiated more rigorously between China and the participating countries. The study also indicates that some countries have taken more assertive stance in negotiating the terms and conditions of the BRI projects. Further, it has been established that BRI projects have been significantly affected by the COVID-19. The pandemic and Russian military operations in Ukraine have created dilemmas over projects' implementation and sustainability in some areas.

Seventeenth, the cost of renegotiated and cancelled projects is considerable for China. Infrastructure can also be understood as a double edged sword. On the one hand if the project is planned professionally and executed properly, it can add to the overall development of the recipient country and may provide employment and other opportunities for its citizens. On the other, if the project is planned poorly and executed in a way which creates suspicion about China's intentions among stakeholders and masses of the recipient country, it may lead to renegotiation or cancellation of the project. The second scenario is now becoming evident in many countries as the projects are bound by confidentiality clause. BRI projects have been stalled, deferred, renegotiated and cancelled due to high costs/ overpricing, corruption, and inability to sustain Chinese loans with high interest rate. A substantial portion of Chinese financing under the CPEC consists of loans that are at commercial rate. Evidence also suggests that the first phase of the Hambantota Port project in Sri Lanka was a US$ 307 million loan at 6.3 per cent interest (Hillman, 2020). This is very high interest rate as compared to the interest rates of multilateral developments banks. In Africa, the contract for upgrading and modernising the Entebbe airport of Uganda has come under scrutiny in recent past. The Ugandan government has realised that the deal greatly favours China. However, they need to go ahead with the contractual obligations as the cost of termination of contract is very high. Consequently, these developments have damaged the reputation of China among the masses of recipient countries.

Eighteenth, the responses of countries from East Asia such as, Japan and South Korea to China's BRI bring a different flavour. Even though Japan and South Korea are outside the projected route of BRI, the initiative has emerged as an important issue of foreign and security policies for both the countries in their domestic debate. The approach that Japan has adopted towards BRI evolved from an initial balancing approach to complex engagement featuring conditional cooperation and outright competition driven by a complex mix of strategic, economic and even normative considerations. South Korea has taken a very cautious approach towards BRI as the US-China strategic competition is intensifying in the region and Korean perception with regard to BRI has been influenced by various concerns related the BRI projects in different regions of the world.

Nineteenth, the evolving relations between China and the US have its implications for current global and regional order. It has been argued that the geo-political goals associated with the BRI have significant economic and strategic consequences for the US. The study has highlighted the US administrations' response to China and various policy framework adopted to safeguard American interests.

Twentieth, there have been varied responses to the BRI from countries and regions besides the emergence of alternative initiatives and narratives. The internal power dynamics of different regions have also affected prospects of the BRI in different way. The future of BRI has been an issue of debate among experts. The focus of study on country-specific and regional aspects of BRI brings experiences and response from China's neighbouring and distant regions. Given the current global economic and geopolitical circumstances, competition with alternative initiatives may intensify in future. Consequently, China's 'major country diplomacy' is poised to get more priority in future.

Finally, the current debate in China favours 'true multilateralism' in international affairs. However, the contradiction is that a major initiative, like BRI, does not follow the principles and norms of multilateralism. Therefore, it is logical to highlight the importance of AIIB model of 'consensual initiative' over the BRI's 'unilateral initiative'.

President Xi Jinping proposed a Global Development Initiative (GDI) in September 2021, which has been described as another 'global public product' following the BRI. In April 2022, he announced the Global Security Initiative (GSI) at the Boao Forum for Asia. The GDI and GSI are seen as new international initiatives by China to confront and overcome the challenges that the country is facing in current regional and international environment. It makes the debate interesting as China's model of 'major country relationship' is facing challenges and some experts see GDI as an 'expansion' of BRI. This subject needs further in-depth study.

References

ANI (2022). "Padma Bridge in Bangladesh: Chinese design to influence Dhaka failed@, 22 June 2022, at https://theprint.in/world/padma-bridge-in-bangladesh-chinese-design-to-influence-dhaka-failed/1007406/

Economist (2022). "The 53 fragile emerging economies", at https://www.economist.com/finance-and-economics/2022/07/20/the-53-fragile-emerging-economies

Hillman, Jonathan E. (2021). *The Emperor's New Road: China and the project of the Century,* Washington DC, CSIS.

Kondapalli, Srikanth (2021). "China's Belt and Road Initiative and Implications for India" in Manish ed. *The Belt and Road Initiative: Implications for India,* Pantagon, New Delhi.

Ministry of Commerce, PRC (2022). "Press conference on integrating domestic and foreign trade and fostering dual circulation development", 25 May 2022, at http://english.scio.gov.cn/pressroom/2022-05/25/content_78236271.htm

Qian Xuemei (2018). "Comparing China's and India's Aid to Afghanistan", *China International Strategy Review 2017,* Special Issue (Beijing: Foreign language Press 2018).

Yang Shanshan (2021). "Three Takeaways from China's Key Conference for 2022 Economic Plan", 13 December 2021, Beijing, at https://news.cgtn.com/news/

Index